Zvikomborero Kuwana

AWAKENING
THE TRIBES OF AFRICA

'Come out of her and return to the covenant with the God of Abraham, Isaac and Jacob'

Published by Zvikomborero Kuwana

Awakening the tribes of Africa: Come out of her and return to the covenant with the God of Abraham, Isaac and Jacob

Published by Zvikomborero Kuwana

Copyright © 2025 by Zvikomborero Kuwana

First edition 2025

ISBN 978-1-83492-209-6

ISBN 978-1-83492-210-2 (e-book)

All rights reserved

No part of this work may be reproduced or transmitted in any form or by any means, electronic, photographic or mechanical, including photocopying and recording on record, tape or laser disk, on microfilm, via the Internet, by e-mail, or by any other information storage or retrieval system, without prior written permission from the copyright owner.

Scripture quotations marked KJV are taken from the King James Version. Public domain. Scripture quotations marked NKJV are taken from the New King James Version®. Copyright © 1982 by Thomas Nelson. Used by permission. All rights reserved. Scripture quotations marked ESV are taken from the ESV® Bible (The Holy Bible, English Standard Version®). Copyright © 2001 by Crossway, a publishing ministry of Good News Publishers. Used by permission. All rights reserved. Scripture quotations taken from the Amplified® Bible (AMPC), Copyright © 1954, 1958, 1962, 1964, 1965, 1987 by The Lockman Foundation. Used by permission. lockman.org". "TS2009 scripture taken from The Scriptures, Copyright by Institute for Scripture Research. Used by permission".

Emphasis in bold, use of capital letters and the usage of Paleo Hebrew names and words within Scriptures quoted are the author's own.

While the author has made every effort to provide accurate, up-to-date source information at the time of publication, statistics and other data are constantly updated. The author does not assume responsibility for errors or for the changes that occur after publication. Further, the author does not have any control over and does not assume any responsibility for third-party websites or their content.

The author has made every effort to obtain permission for and acknowledge the use of copyrighted material. Refer all enquiries to the author at zvi@awakeningthetribes.africa

Views reflected in this publication are not necessarily those of the publisher, nor the printer.
Cover design and typesetting by Arkhive Africa

Produced / Printed and bound in South Africa by
Print on Demand PTY (Ltd)
5 Koets str, Parow Industria, 7493

Then Moses said to God, "Indeed, when I come to the children of YASHARA'AL (ISRAEL) and say to them, 'The God of your fathers has sent me to you,' and they say to me, 'What is His name?' what shall I say to them?" And God said to Moses, "I AM WHO I AM. (AHAYAH)" And He said, "Thus you shall say to the children of YASHARA'AL, 'I AM has sent me to you.'" Moreover, God said to Moses, "Thus you shall say to the children of YASHARA'AL: 𐤉𐤄𐤅𐤄 **YAHUAH** *God of your* ***fathers***, *the God of Abaraham (Abraham), the God of Yatsakhaq (Isaac), and the God of Yaaqab (Jacob), has sent me to you. This is My name forever, and this is My memorial to all generations.'*
Exodus 3:13-15 NKJV

And I heard another voice from heaven saying, **"Come out of her, my people,** *lest you share in her sins, and lest you receive of her plagues.*
Revelation 18:4 NKJV

And I will establish My covenant between Me and you and your descendants after you in their generations, for an everlasting covenant, *to be God to you and your descendants after you.*
Genesis 17:7 NKJV

Dedication and thanks

Firstly, I give thanks to the GOD (ALAHYM) of Abraham, Isaac, and Jacob for guiding me through this most exhilarating journey and for granting me the privilege of experiencing all that I did while writing this book. It is in no way my own writing, as He is the one who commissioned the book, provided the topics, and supplied the content. I can claim no credit.

After Abba YAHUAH (as is the name that the ALAHYM (GOD) of Abraham, Isaac and Jacob gave to His people), I give very special thanks to my wife and our two boys, who have endured many hardships on the journey we have travelled over the past 14 years. Through periods of homelessness, not being able to pay school fees and much financial turmoil, they have been resolute and never once lost hope or gave up on me. I am overwhelmed by your love, patience and determination. I love you more than you will ever know.

The journey of 'coming out of her' and pursuing the truth that leads back to the covenant with Abba YAHUAH can be brutal and extremely lonely, with long periods in the desert wilderness, but it is worth every moment. Looking back, I would not change it for anything.

Sometimes one must walk away from what is comfortable and lose friends to uncover 'The Truth'. Often, one faces ridicule and rejection in the pursuit of 'The Truth'. It is because of the discoveries made that I reference GOD here with the ancient Paleo Hebrew word ALAHYM and alter some of the standard biblical names and terminology I have used all my life, which I know most readers still use. More on this will come later. My heartfelt gratitude goes to our wider family, whose steadfast support has carried us through.

To the many friends we have met along life's path, thank you for standing beside us with unwavering encouragement.

To the dedicated team who so generously gave their time and skills to bring this book to life, I extend my sincere appreciation.

And finally, to you, the reader — thank you for investing your valuable time and resources in choosing to read *Awakening the Tribes of Africa*. My prayer is that these pages will inspire profound moments of dialogue between you and the ALAHYM of Abraham, Isaac, and Jacob, leading you to the discovery of the truth — His truth.

Back to family: Tinotenda and Tadiwanashe, my deepest prayer is that you will embrace 'what is written', and teach it to your children; and your children to their children so that our family bloodline will never depart again from the covenant of the ALAHYM of Abraham, Isaac and Jacob, Abba YAHUAH.

I pray the same for every other family.

Pamhidzai, ndinokuda nemoyo wese .

"For there is nothing hidden that shall not be disclosed, nor anything secret that shall not be known and come out into the open." (Luke 8:17 AMPC)

Zvikomborero

CONTENTS

Endorsement	xii
Foreword	xiv
Preface	xxii

SECTION 1: "A BLESSED PEOPLE WHO ARE CURSED"

Chapter 1. Introduction: my journey leading to this book	1
Chapter 2. The rewriting of history	14
Chapter 3. The incredible blessing that is in our hands	35

SECTION 2: "WE ARE CERTAINLY 'A CONQUERED' PEOPLE"

Chapter 4. The 12 'domains of control' used to conquer Africa	41
Chapter 5. Reflecting the 12 'domains of control' biblically through Deuteronomy chapter 28	51
Chapter 6. Linking the Deuteronomy 28 curses to the reality of Africa's lived and living experience	67
Chapter 7: The biblical answer to why this has happened	88

SECTION 3: "LAYING THE FOUNDATION TO UNDERSTAND THE CREATOR'S DESIGN"

Chapter 8. Who is our God, what is His name, and who is He?   98
- His Name
- The confrontation and battle of the Gods
- Who is 𐤉𐤄𐤅𐤄 YAHUAH?
- Whose name are we calling upon?

Chapter 9. Biblical definitions and equations   133
- 𐤉𐤄𐤅𐤄 YAHUAH's Commandments
- 𐤉𐤄𐤅𐤄 YAHUAH's Law
- The foundation of the Law – the 10 Commandments

- The Greatest Commandment
- Linking the 10 Commandments to the Greatest Commandment
- Sin according to 𐤉𐤄𐤅𐤄 YAHUAH
- Establishing what Truth is
- Definition of 'what is good' to 𐤉𐤄𐤅𐤄 YAHUAH
- How Abba 𐤉𐤄𐤅𐤄 YAHUAH wants to be loved
- The obedience (love) of 𐤉𐤄𐤅𐤔𐤏 YAHUSHA
- Defining 'the Word of 𐤉𐤄𐤅𐤄 YAHUAH' & the overcoming saints and remnant

SECTION 4: "BUILDING ON THE FOUNDATION TO UNDERSTAND HOW YAHUAH'S DESIGN WORKS"

Chapter 10. The consequences of idol worship and removing His name	192
Chapter 11. The law of 𐤉𐤄𐤅𐤄 YAHUAH and the law of sacrifice to attain righteousness	202
Chapter 12. The power of repentance and forgiveness	232
Chapter 13. Understanding what the Kingdom of 𐤉𐤄𐤅𐤄 YAHUAH is	240
Chapter 14. The Ark of the Covenant	272

SECTION 5: "NAVIGATING THROUGH EXISTING NARRATIVES IN SEARCH OF TRUTH"

Chapter 15. Searching for the truth of biblical identities	291
Chapter 16. The path to 'heaven' or the New Jerusalem	358
Chapter 17. A call to Holiness	385
Chapter 18. The big elephant in the room named Jew(ish) Israel	394

SECTION 6: "THE BATTLE FOR SPIRITUAL FREEDOM"

Chapter 19. Confronting and overcoming the primary enemy	422

Chapter 20. The uncleanness in the religion of Christianity and
    the church   444
Chapter 21. Fighting against 𐤉𐤄𐤅𐤄 YAHUAH   486
Chapter 22. Confronting and resisting the white horse
    that came conquering and to conquer Africa   498
Chapter 23. The call to come out of her   534

SECTION 7: "THE SOLUTIONS"

Chapter 24. The biblical antidote for the curse of Africa   549
Chapter 25. Back to the 12 domains of control   567

SECTION 8: "TRIBES OF AFRICA AWAKEN TO YOUR GOD"

Chapter 26. What does 𐤉𐤄𐤅𐤄 YAHUAH Require of Africa?   583
Chapter 27. African Leaders arise and shine   588
Chapter 28. Personal parting words   604

Endorsement

I first met Zvikomborero Kuwana eight years ago during my tenure as CEO of the Durban Chamber of Commerce and Industry. From the beginning, I admired his unique gift for translating God's Kingdom principles into practical, values-driven strategies for the marketplace. Over the years, he has become a trusted advisor and a household name among Christian businesspeople seeking to build enterprises rooted in Kingdom purpose.

Yet this book places Zvikomborero in a league of his own. It is, without question, one of the most compelling and thought-provoking works I have ever read — boldly decoding God's original intent for Africans and their wealth.

In these pages, Zvikomborero elevates the conversation about Kingdom governance to a new level. He has always asked probing questions about Africa's role in the global economy and why our continent so often finds itself at the bottom of the economic food chain. The questions he raises here echo the silent cries many Africans have carried deep within for generations. He gives voice to a deep-seated longing — the sorrow we have borne for decades — echoing the haunting words of the late African American singer Brook Benton: "Why Lord, the color of my skin is said to be an awful sin." This book courageously addresses that cry and points to the God-shaped answer at the heart of Africa's destiny.

At a time when Africans everywhere are wrestling with their identity and purpose, this book arrives as a practical manual and prophetic blueprint. The depth of research woven into these pages makes it an invaluable encyclopedia for African people and tribes, both on the continent and in the diaspora. Zvikomborero's insights will ignite further study and inspire a fresh pursuit of truth about who we are, who we were meant to be, and how we must return to our God to live lives of higher value and purpose. This work is for everyone who longs to see Africa rise to become all that God created her to be. As we know, where the original intent of a thing is unknown, misuse is inevitable. This book restores that understanding. I believe all Africans — and indeed all who care about Africa's flourishing — will gain immeasurably from every page.

My prayer is that every reader approaches these pages not merely with curiosity but with an open heart. Let this work challenge you to see yourself, your family, your community, and your nation through new eyes — Kingdom eyes. May it spark fresh conversations in our homes, our boardrooms, our churches, and our schools. May it encourage us to raise children who know who they are and whose they are. May it push us to build enterprises and institutions that honor God and uplift communities, so that we may truly see Africa rise into the fullness of her calling.

It is my deep honor to commend this work to you. I trust it will touch and transform you as profoundly as it has me.

Dumile Cele
Former CEO of the Durban Chamber of Commerce & Industry

Foreword

For many years, I have wrestled with the same questions my brother Kuwana has asked in his book: *Why is Africa the way it is?* Why is Africa so rich and blessed with natural resources, yet its people live like beggars? Why do the resources of Africa enrich other parts of the world, while Africans themselves remain impoverished? It has never made sense to me.

Yet, one thing is clear: the Most High has a definite plan and purpose for Africa. The abundance and blessings scattered across this continent are no accident—they are proof of divine intent. *To whom much is given, much is also required.*

I have also often pondered why Revelation chapter 11 would allude to Jesus being crucified in Egypt—that is, in Africa—and not in Jerusalem. Could it be pointing back to the slaughter of the Passover Lamb in Egypt on the night of Israel's deliverance? Or does it point to a deeper mystery?

If it truly points to Jesus being killed in Africa, then what does that mean? It means that the place of His death is also the place of His resurrection reality. And where the reality of His resurrection is manifested, the power of His resurrection is revealed. This means that the harvest resulting from His death will find expression in Africa. This is why Nigeria stands as a "trigger nation" for this harvest, Kenya as the "land of manifestation" of the harvest, and South Africa as the place from which the "sound of the harvest" will go out to the nations of the world. This is a prophetic reality where the map of Africa is the shape of a Shofar in the hand of God, with the South serving as the mouth into which the breath is blown. And while, on the surface, it may not look like any of this is happening in these nations, the spiritual reality is already brewing and will manifest in God's time.

And how profound is it that, by divine providence, the man who carried Jesus' cross—Simon of Cyrene—was an African? Could this act have served as a prophetic sign of the suffering Africans would face in fulfilling God's purpose in the current season on earth? I believe it did.

The fact that the one who carried Christ's cross was from Africa is itself a prophetic sign of the struggles Africans have borne, the journey they must walk through, and the blessing attached to that mandate.

Now, let me take you back to the beginning. The subtitle of this book is: *"Come out of her and return to the covenant with the God of Abraham, Isaac, and Jacob."* There is a reason for this. While many scholars and African philosophers may reject the idea that Africa must return to the God of the Biblical patriarchs—and may even ask what connection Africa has with Abraham—I will share a few things. These come both from the Scriptures and personal stories. I do not present them as a source of debate or to force an opinion, but rather to reveal a biblical pattern: the blessings of Africa are tied to Abraham, through the covenant God made with him, a covenant that includes Africa. For it is written: *"Out of Egypt, I called My Son."* And Egypt is in Africa.

How It Began

When it comes to Biblical prophecies or declarations from God, they are often multi-dimensional and multi-layered in their expression. This means that while God may make a prophetic declaration concerning one particular people or nation—as recorded in Scripture—He often ties other peoples and nations into that same declaration.

This is because, while we humans mostly see only what is in front of us or what lies just behind us in our immediate history, God sees from the very beginning of time to the very end. He is the Author of the story of His dealings with all races and peoples of the earth. To truly grasp this story—and how it is woven in layers that require divine wisdom to unpack—we must clothe ourselves in humility.

Here is where I am going with this.

Genesis 15:13–14
"Then the Lord said to Abram: Know certainly that your descendants will be strangers in a land that is not theirs and will serve them, and they will afflict them four hundred years. And also, the nation whom they serve I will judge; afterward they shall come out with great possessions."

This passage opens a scene within God's story concerning Abram: that his descendants would be taken as slaves into a foreign land for four hundred years.

Fast forward to Genesis 42: famine strikes Canaan, and Jacob—the grandson of Abraham—sends his sons to Egypt to buy grain. By then, Joseph (Jacob's son) had already been taken to Egypt. After enduring his own process within God's unfolding story, Joseph had risen to become prime minister of Egypt.

In Genesis 46, Jacob and his entire family relocated to Egypt. There, the prophecy given to Abraham began to unfold: his descendants dwelt in Egypt, eventually as slaves, for four hundred years (technically four hundred and thirty years—the additional thirty being the period God used to prepare Moses for the mandate of deliverance).

But here is the key: when most people hear of Egypt, they think of the physical nation in North Africa. Biblically, however, Egypt is not merely a geographical nation but also a **spiritual system**—a power with vast influence over humanity.

This perspective leads to a pressing question: *which people in known world history were taken from their land in ships, carried into foreign nations, and served as slaves for four hundred years?* The answer is Africans.

Egypt Is a System, Not Just a Nation

Egypt, biblically, represents more than a nation—it symbolises a **spiritual system of oppression** over the sons of men.

This is why Revelation 11 speaks of Jesus being "crucified in Egypt," even though Scripture tells us He was crucified on a hill in Jerusalem. Egypt, in this sense, is not geographical but spiritual.

The same is true of **Babylon**. Historically, Babylon was an ancient kingdom in the region now called Iran. Yet Babylon also represents a spiritual system that has influenced the world since the days of the Tower of Babel, where its foundations were laid. "Babel" itself means confusion. Its root was in the land of Shinar, and Shinar was birthed by the spirit of wickedness (see Zechariah 5). From that foundation came the spiritual system of Babylon.

But what is wickedness? Wickedness is **any system that subverts the authority of God and robs His people of their liberty.**

The Return

It is important that I share this part of my story in the Foreword, not only to bring clarity to what I have already written, but also to connect it to the central call of this book: *"Come out of her and return to the covenant with the God of Abraham, Isaac, and Jacob."*

There is much that Africans must come out from: the spiritual systems of Egypt and Babylon, the system of greed born from the rebellion of Cain, and every other structure that has used the very hands and resources of Africans to keep Africans in servitude. The season we are in now is about **"The Return."** But a return cannot happen without separation—hence the command: *"Come out from among them." (2 Corinthians 6:17)*

Let me share a few encounters that shaped my understanding of this return.

Badagry – 2014

In September 2014, while still living in Lagos, Nigeria, the Lord instructed me to travel to Badagry, a coastal town near the border of Nigeria and the Benin Republic. I was told to stay there for seven days. Before leaving, He asked me to take with me a stone He had shown me a week prior.
So, I called my friend whose family has a home in Badagry. I had called him to help me find a place where I can stay for seven days. He went ahead and told his parents, and I was invited to stay with them in their home.

Badagry, as history records, was one of the infamous slave ports where Africans were forced onto ships bound for the Americas. One of its sites is called *The Point of No Return*, a grim reminder of those who passed through its arch, never to return home.

Two days after arriving at Badagry, I was accompanied by two guys whom my friend had told to take me around. We went to the site called The Point of No Return. As we got there, the Lord told me to pass through the arch (The Point of No Return), walk into the ocean, bring out the stone from my pocket, and throw it as far as I could into the ocean. He also asked me to declare that everything stolen from Africa through that gateway—people, resources, knowledge, history—must be restored to the continent.

Then came another instruction: to rename the site. I declared that it would no longer be The Point of No Return, but rather **"The Point of the Return."**

Only later did I realise that this declaration happened on Rosh Hashanah, the Jewish New Year of 2014. Rosh Hashanah marks the beginning of the civil year, according to the teachings of Judaism, and is the traditional anniversary of the creation of Adam and Eve, the first man and woman according to the Hebrew Bible, as well as the initiation of humanity's role in God's world. The timing was no coincidence.

Mombasa – 2017

In January 2017, shortly after my wedding in Nairobi, which took place on the 1st of that same month, my wife and I travelled to Mombasa for our honeymoon. Yet even this journey carried divine instructions. Mombasa, like Badagry, is a coastal town with a slave port still standing as a witness to history.

There, we were told to set up an altar of thirteen stones, pour clean water over them, and remove one stone to be used later. At the slave port, we carried out a prophetic act, using the thirteenth stone, similar to what I had done in Badagry.

Ghana – 2019

Two years later, in 2019, the Ghanaian government declared "The Year of Return", marking 400 years since the first enslaved Africans were taken to the Americas. Millions of people of African descent have since been making their way back to the continent, some even reclaiming citizenship.

I do not claim credit for these movements, but I cannot ignore the prophetic link between those symbolic acts in Badagry and Mombasa and what began unfolding in Ghana and beyond. Just as God told Abraham that his descendants would return after 400 years, so too does Africa stand at a prophetic threshold.

The Purpose of the Return

The return is not merely about the restoration of stolen people, resources, and history. More importantly, it is about a **return to the covenant**—to the God of Abraham, Isaac, and Jacob.

Some may ask: What does the slavery of Africans have to do with the slavery of Abraham's descendants? While they may not be the same according to human timelines, they are the same according to God's prophetic timelines. According to Deuteronomy 28:68, which nation of people in the history of the world was taken into strange nations in ships? Remember, Egypt and Babylon mean both a place and a system.

Here lies a sober warning: Africans in the diaspora must begin to return to the continent. The global system is closer to collapse than many realise, and nuclear conflict is no longer unthinkable. When the great powers of the earth collide in a nuclear war, where will safety be found? **Africa will be the refuge**. In fact, there is an old prophecy that speaks of this reality.

You can search online for it. It is wisdom to begin returning now, to rebuild and prepare.

But let the return not be with the spirit of conquest, as if to replace the Europeans and continue their exploitative legacy. Return as brothers and sisters, as sons and daughters of the soil, joining hands with those on the continent to restore and build the Motherland.

Imagine, for a moment, an Africa where her scattered children return—not only with wealth and knowledge, but with humility and a heart to build. Imagine an Africa where this return is aligned with the covenant blessings of Deuteronomy 28. That Africa will not just be restored—it will be reborn.

Samuel Irewolede Phillips
Creative Director, Msingi Afrika Magazine, Kenya.

Preface

The purpose of this book is to take you on a journey to invoke critical thinking, ask questions, seek truth, and knock on the door that opens the pathway to the truth that leads to a new reality of the blessing that has been divinely scripted for Africa. It is a divinely ordained reality that awaits us as Africans if we follow the instructions given in the divine script and come into alignment with how things have been designed to work in the Creator's instruction book.

It is a new reality of blessing that is waiting for us on the other side of the door if we choose to pursue it. It is a new reality that fulfils the Creator's plan for Africa to be His source and symbol of blessing upon the earth, as its people fulfil their calling to be a light to the world by living in covenantal agreement and relationship with Him.

As a fellow African, a son of the soil of Africa, I will share snippets of the journey that I have walked, which has taken me from trying to find meaning by conforming to the status quo, to coming out and pursuing what lies beyond the often rigid walls of mainstream narratives that we have been indoctrinated into, particularly in the sphere of religion. On this journey, I have made many discoveries, and it is these discoveries that I will be sharing.

The intention behind this book is not to impose my discoveries or even teach them, but rather to ignite a desire within Africans to go on their own journeys of discovery in search of truth. What you will find in this book are clues that stir up a deeper need for the reader to go 'treasure hunting' to find the truth themselves and not rely on what another man or institution of religion says. One of the key precepts of wisdom from the Creator's instruction book is 'you shall know the truth and the truth shall set you free.'

If indeed knowing the truth is a foundational key to freedom, would Satan, the devil, the one known as the father of lies, and the one who deceives the whole world, not use lies as his primary strategy to ensure that we are bound in captivity? Lies are the ropes that tie us down to the status quo, whereas the truth is the sword that cuts through the ropes, releasing us to step into a magnitude of freedom we did not even realise existed.

"Is what I believe to be true based on what someone else has told me, or is it based on what I have confirmed through my own research and study"? This is one of the most important questions I have learnt to constantly ask myself. The more I realised that most of what I believed to be true was based on what I had been told, the more I understood that I was a prime candidate for deception, and, therefore, I needed to start my own process of asking, seeking, and knocking for truth. This became my treasure hunt for truth, but not just for truth, but 'The Truth'.

Reaching a point in your 40s and 50s where you realise that most of what you have believed to be true all your life might be a lie is an uncomfortable place to be in, especially when it touches on the spiritual foundation that one is standing and has stood upon with such confidence.

That is the place I got to.

It is a place where I pondered the possibility that what I had built my own life upon and taught my family was flawed. Many times, my thoughts were 'let sleeping dogs lie,' but at the same time, I was so aware that the eternal ramifications of ignoring what I was going through were too high. So, it started the most humbling process of admitting that I was deceived and that I, therefore, needed to deconstruct the foundation and pillars that formed the frame upon which my life was built, trusting that on the other side, I would be able to reconstruct a foundation and pillars from scratch.

The deconstruction of a foundation comes with the collapse of everything that was built on top of it, and that is exactly what happened. However, at the same time came the exhilaration and joy at the prospect of rebuilding on a new foundation.

"You have turned for me my mourning into dancing; You have put off my sackcloth and clothed me with gladness." (Psalm 30:11)

The dictionary defines revelation as follows: (1) a surprising and previously unknown fact that has been disclosed, (2) the making known of something that was previously secret or unknown, and (3) the divine or supernatural disclosure to humans of something relating to human existence.
Revelation can render what we know today irrelevant. My hope is that everything that will be presented in the pages of this book will serve as stepping stones for you to inquire for yourself and find the conclusions the Most High Alahym wants you to.

As one who lived in so much pride and who continues to be intentionally aware of that pride lurking in me, I have come to realise that pride is the enemy of revelation. It is the pride of man that often stands in the way of truth, and pride can lead to destruction when we hold on to a conditioned conclusion that is false.

The levels of cognitive dissonance I experienced while writing this book were off the charts, and I expect the same will be the case for most as you read this book, but I urge you to push through, notwithstanding.
May this book inspire you to seek, and if you end up retaining the beliefs

you already hold, there is no loss, but if you discover something, then it is a gain for you.

I believe the primary war that we as Africans need to fight is one between truth and lies.

I hope that this book will become 'a sword of truth' that will help many Africans to cut away the ropes that tie them down so that Africa can finally "arise and shine" to fulfil her destiny.

For this to happen, I believe there is a Master Key that we need to understand and get access to.

Searching for the Master Key

Is there a Master Key that has been designed to unlock the door to Africa's divine destiny?

Over several decades, the potential of Africa to arise as a leading beacon of light to the rest of the world has been debated and discussed with great excitement. Many prophecies of the glory arising upon Africa have been proclaimed and sung by the people of the many tongues, tribes, and nations across the continent. The sons and daughters of Africa, young and old, and from peasant farmers to kings and presidents, have discussed the problems Africa faces, and many have also come up with solutions.

But is it possible that there is a Master Key to Africa's deliverance and redemption that, when used, will open the door for all that has been prophesied and spoken concerning Africa to be brought to fulfilment? A Master Key that is hidden in our identity as Africans and is directly linked to an everlasting agreement (a covenant) with the Alahym of Abraham,

Isaac, and Jacob.

A Master Key of such great value that it can only be found by following strict divine instructions that will open the locks of the doors and pathways that lead to it. A Master Key that can only be used when all the unchangeable preconditions that govern its usage are met.

This book is about finding keys that will unlock the multiple doors that will lead us to the Master Key. Each chapter in the book presents the reader with keys to interconnected doors that provide access to the next stage of the journey towards accessing the Master Key. As all the keys are collected and applied, they merge to become the Master Key, which is in the hands of The Master Himself, who is the One who has the authority to open doors that no man can shut and, likewise, close doors that no man can open.

The real treasure is the Master Himself, who holds the Master Key.

The key of the house of David I will lay on his shoulder; **So he shall open, and no one shall shut; and he shall shut, and no one shall open.** *(Isaiah 22:22 NKJV)*

'These things says He who is holy, He who is true, "He who has the key of David, **He who opens and no one shuts, and shuts and no one opens***" (Revelation 3:7b NKJV)*

"A blessed people who are cursed"

Section 1

Contents

Chapter 1. Introduction: My journey leading to this book
Chapter 2. The rewriting of history
Chapter 3. The incredible blessing that is in our hands

CHAPTER ONE

Introduction: My Journey Leading To This Book

I was born into a family that had followed the Christian faith for two generations before me. Both my paternal and maternal grandparents were ardent Christians, having been 'reached' by missionaries in the late 1800s to early 1900s. This zeal for the faith spread through the family line and became a foundational cornerstone for us. Such is probably a similar story amongst many African families.

In 2010, a journey began for me that was triggered by four needling questions that settled in my heart and would not leave until I found answers to them.

Here are the questions:

1. **"Why do I live in a country where people who supposedly profess Christianity are the majority, and yet there is very little evidence of the culture that the Bible speaks of prevailing in the society?"**

    In fact, the reverse appeared to be true. Many African nations claiming the highest percentages of Christian populations often proved to be among the most corrupt, the most materialistic, marked by a fixation on wealth, and displaying behaviour contrary to the teachings of the Bible.

2. **"How is it possible that Africa is now considered to be the most Christian evangelised continent (with 'crusades' where millions of people seemingly pledge allegiance to Christianity daily) and yet there is no manifestation of 'the blessing' that the Bible speaks of that should flow upon a people who are walking in agreement with God?"**

    Again, the opposite seemed to be the case with the equation almost always reading as follows, 'more Christianity in Africa equals more poverty' and likewise 'more churches in Africa equals more poverty'.

3. **"Why has God blessed us with such abundance in the riches and wealth of natural resources, far more than any other people on earth, and yet we continue to be the begging bowl of the world?" "Why does everyone else in the world prosper from what we as Africans have been given, and yet we are the poorest people on earth, failing to convert our God given wealth from the land into prosperity for all on the continent?"**

    Again, the contradiction of seeing the nations of Africa with churches on every street corner, having all-night prayer vigils, declaring words of faith, national prayer breakfasts, and yet the reality was and remains that the fountain of poverty continues to flow steadily upon the people despite their supposed commitment to Christianity.

4. The first three questions lead to the fourth, which will form a big part of what follows in this book.

"Are we, as dark-skinned people, cursed by God, and does He really love us in the same way as He loves Caucasians (white skinned people)? Because when I look at systemic poverty, depravity, the scourge of sickness and disease, it always seems to be the dark-skinned people in the world who are affected the most."

Once again, the contradiction is evident. How can this be when we have churches on every street corner, when we are celebrating that we are now the most Christian evangelised continent, when we are so spiritual, praying, fasting, and engaging in spiritual warfare like no other continent, and yet the reality is that things are getting worse?

What I had embraced as true and as the foundational principles for my life simply stopped making sense, and I could no longer keep up the pretence that all was well.

In my mind, the difficult, nagging questions I had to face became: "Is Christianity real?" "Is the Bible true?" "Who exactly is God, and how do I get to know Him?"

The dots were not connecting – there was too much contradiction between what the Bible says and the reality I was experiencing all around me. I was not seeing the evidence of what the Bible says should be happening, and so either the Bible was false, or perhaps what Christianity had taught me about the Bible was false, or maybe my concept of God and who He is was false.

It is these four questions that launched my journey of seeking truth and answers. This is what this book is all about – sharing my journey so far of seeking truth in a world that is largely built on lies.

History is filled with many stories of wars and conquests where one people group, tribe, or nation defeats another and then controls them. Most, if not all, these conquests are linked to the insatiable desire for the acquisition of resources (in the form of both labour and natural wealth) for economic gain and power.

In this book, the terms 'the conqueror' and 'the conquered' will be used quite a lot.

The term 'the conqueror' refers to those who have left their own lands of abode in quest of the acquisition of what belongs to another. Likewise, the term 'the conquered' refers mainly to indigenous/native peoples whose lands have been invaded so that what belongs to them is brought under subjugation to 'the conqueror'.

I spent most of 2024 studying history from the perspective and narrative of 'the conquered'. Mainstream narratives of history are primarily driven by the victorious ("the conquerors") to justify their 'victories' over the defeated ("the conquered") and the reasons and means they used to conquer them. This is done to create a foundation of generational self-righteousness to secure their position in the future. The main narratives of history in the world today are based on Greco-Roman, Ottoman, Germanic, and Anglo-Saxon 'victories'.

Sadly, the African narrative and likewise that of most 'dark-skinned people' and indigenous/native people in most lands across the earth is largely 'lost' in mainstream history because they constitute the majority of 'the conquered'.

This same trend permeates deeply into narratives of religion, and especially Christianity, through the images used in depictions of biblical characters and assumptions made about biblical identities, definitions of words, locations where events took place, and many more issues that will be raised in this book.

Greco-Roman power captured the original ancient Hebrew text of the Bible and influenced the decisions on which scriptural texts made it into the recognised canon of the 66 books of the Bible and which ones did not. Scripts of the biblical books such as Enoch, Jasher, Jubilees, Esdras, Maccabees, etc., to name a few, which are referred to as the apocrypha today, have been retained in the Ethiopian Bible and provide fascinating insights that have been 'hidden' because they did not fit the narrative that "the conqueror" wanted in the scriptures. Such evidence of this capture and manipulation is seen in how certain Holy scriptures were translated or left out to suit 'the conquerors' narrative, as was seen in the example of the 'Negro Slave Bible' which was first published in 1807 and used as a mechanism through which to conquer and oppress the Negroes. The same applies to other versions of the Bible that have been released, even up to today, and used as weapons of suppression of either people or truth. It seems that identities and certain sections of 'the Truth of the Word/the Holy Scriptures' have been captured by 'the conquerors' at the expense of 'the conquered', but even more critically at the expense of life-giving truth that The Most High GOD of Abraham, Isaac, and Jacob made available for all mankind.

One of the big questions that I was seeking answers to in my search was "What is the historical narrative of the native tribes in the USA and Canada, the native Aborigines in Australia, the Māori in New Zealand, and of course, us here in Africa?" "What about the descendants of those who ended up being taken from the continent in slave ships to the various lands in the Americas?"

I remember, as a child, watching 'Cowboy and Indian' movies on a black and white television or going to the bioscope (as cinemas were called then), in which the narrative would always be that of the 'savage, uncivilized, ungodly, hostile native Indians' attacking without provocation the 'heroic and virtuous Bible carrying settler Cowboys' who had discovered the Americas and were bringing civilization. The same 'uncivilised native villain' script was used in almost all African, slavery, and Aboriginal documentaries that I watched as a child. Deep in my heart, I carried the painful emotions and confusion of why we, as Africans, were created inferior based on the colour of our skin. Little did I know at the time that the basis of this 'conquering spirit' is found in the Doctrine of Discovery that came from the Catholic Church.

The Doctrine of Discovery

The Doctrine of Discovery is a policy enacted initially by the 15th-century Catholic Church proclaiming the right of Christian nations to take possession of the lands of non-Christians in the interest of saving their souls. Non-Christians were not recognised as legitimate landowners, and any lands 'discovered' by Christian explorers were claimed as the property of the so-called discoverers' nation. The Doctrine of Discovery (also known as the Discovery Doctrine) is articulated, first, by a papal bull issued in 1452, another in 1455, and the best-known in 1493, shortly after the 1492 expedition of Christopher Columbus and his 'discovery' of the so-called New World. The 1493 papal bull made clear the duty of Christian explorers to seize the lands of non-Christians to Christianise the inhabitants and bring them within the folds of European Christian civilisation.

Shortly after the European colonizers first encountered the indigenous population of the Americas in 1492, they returned armed with the policy issued by Pope Alexander VI in 1493, which claimed that any land, anywhere, not under the flag of a sovereign Christian nation, could be taken by whoever 'discovered' it, and whatever indigenous people found there converted to Christianity.

Native Americans and, in fact, most indigenous tribes across the earth did not believe one could own land because, unbeknown to them, they followed the biblical principle as is written in Leviticus 25:23 where the GOD of Abraham, Isaac and Jacob had given an instruction that, 'the land must not be sold permanently because the land is Mine, for you are strangers and sojourners with Me.' And so in obedience to this principle, most indigenous tribes believed that they were to be stewards of the land and not title deed owners, while, to the European colonisers, owning land was their God-given right.

The Doctrine of Discovery had major implications for Africa as it formed the foundation of the strategy to conquer the continent as a precursor to the 1884-1885 Berlin Congo West Africa Conference, where the formal partitioning of Africa took place, and the land of Africa and its people became the fiefdom of European nations.

Capturing 'The Way'

The pressing question that weighed heavily on my mind and demanded an answer was, "Is it possible that the religion of Christianity was used as a great weapon in 'the conqueror's' arsenal to conquer 'the conquered'? It seemed to be a sacred cow that should not be challenged, but I soon found myself asking, "What is the religion of Christianity anyway? Is it not what was created when the Greco-Romans (mainly through the emperor Constantine) captured 'The Way' (as the ancient followers of the Messiah called their faith) and added their own culture (doctrines of demons and traditions of man adopted from the pagan worship of the Romans and the philosophy of Greek men) which promoted the worship of Greek gods, and yet who claimed to be the 'church fathers' of Christianity holding the right to determine biblical doctrine? Did they not capture the pure word of the Bible to defile it and make it conform to their agenda of domination?

As a clarifying note, "The Way" is the true doctrine of the Good News, as the true and original followers of the Holy Scriptures were named as a group. More on this will be addressed further in the book, but for scriptural references' sake, the term 'people of The Way' can be found in these verses: Acts 9:2, Acts 19:23, Acts 24:14 and Acts 24:22, amongst others.

One of the paths I have and continue to relentlessly pursue is "What was 'The Way' before the rulers, principalities and powers of Greece and Rome captured it and tampered with it? Is this not what we all need to get back to?

Is the key that we are looking for linked directly to returning to the original of what was given in the full scriptures of the Bible, and not what "the conqueror" has established as doctrine?

This journey is, has been and will continue to be very controversial and provocative. I suppose this is the sort of questioning of the 'status quo' that would have resulted in being declared a Christian heretic, excommunicated, and burnt at the stake in past times.

Getting in touch with my position as 'the conquered'

A big part of my journey was connecting with my position as "the conquered".

On the 23rd of September 2023, I climbed Mt Nyangani, which is the highest mountain in my birth country of Zimbabwe. The climb was a sort of reclamation of my lost heritage, if you will. My great-grandfather and the Kuwana clan used to call the foothills of that mountain home until they were removed when Cecil John Rhodes decided he needed a 97,000-acre estate around the mountain, and hundreds of families in that area were dispossessed of their land in the 1890s, becoming nomads as a consequence. (It was quite sobering for me to think that this happened as recently as 80 years before I was born). The entire countries of Zimbabwe and Zambia then became known as Rhodesia (Southern and Northern). We became "conquered" as an entire people group and given the name/identity of one man, Rhodes, as we would be born in Rhodesia and carry a national identity as Rhodesians.

I later undertook two more significant trips to Germany/Europe in November 2023 and February 2024 to coincide with the 140th anniversaries of the 15th of November start and 26th of February end (1884 to 1885) of the Berlin Congo West Africa conference where Africa was truly 'conquered' as 14 Western nations decided how they would colonise and divide Africa as spoil among themselves (with no representation from Africa allowed at the meeting). The fate of the land and resources of Africa (and the inheritance of its people) was, therefore, decided without an African even being present. The final Berlin Act of 1885 to plunder Africa was signed 'in the name of the Lord' as the signed agreement shows. Interestingly, Christianity was a part of the strategy, since the Catholic Church's 1452, 1455 and 1493 Doctrine of Discovery Papal Bulls had given license for indigenous lands to be freely taken if the natives were not deemed to be Christian.

Explorers and Christian missionaries played a vital role in setting the stage for the Berlin conference. They mapped territories, negotiated treaties with local populations, and promoted narratives justifying European expansion into the continent. Figures such as Henry Morton Stanley conducted expeditions into the Congo Basin on behalf of King Leopold II of Belgium. He established treaties with local leaders that later led to Belgium's sovereignty over the region. Missionaries carried out similar tasks, seeking

INTRODUCTION: MY JOURNEY LEADING TO THIS BOOK

to spread Christianity and Western values across the continent. These missionaries often aligned their goals with those of colonial expansion. Missions established in these regions were used as early posts of European values, blending their religious objectives with political ones. Reports by explorers and missionaries painted Africa as a land of opportunity and a perfect target for the 'civilising mission', and so Christianity became the primary tool used to conquer us.

 GOD, who are You, and do You truly love us?

During these two trips to Germany, I was able to stand on the actual street (Wilhelmstraße) and location where the Berlin Congo West Africa Conference took place and was presided over by the German Chancellor Otto Von Bismarck, who was under the King of Prussia, Kaiser Wilhelm I, of the royal house of Hohenzollern at the time. I also then had the opportunity to meet the great-grandson of Kaiser Wilhelm I, and engage with that bloodline family (Hohenzollern) over the events that took place before and after 1884-1885. It was a surreal time of much reflection as I continued to ask The Most High, "But why did this happen to us and why did You allow it if You truly love us?"

 GOD, who are You, and do You truly love us?

It is undeniable that some of the greatest mass killings/genocides of a people group have occurred against indigenous native peoples. It is estimated that Africa lost 10 to 20 million people during the Transatlantic slave trade. It is estimated that Africa lost 10 to 20 million people just in the Congo between 1885 and 1908 due to the mass murders sanctioned by King Leopold of Belgium. It is estimated that about 100,000 Herero and Namaqua people in Namibia died in 1904 - 1907 at the hands of Germany. It is estimated that 10 to 30 million Native Americans were lost during the 15th to 19th centuries. Similarly, the Khoi San population was decimated in South Africa by the Dutch settlers. These will not find much mention in mainstream narratives of history, let alone the fact that the main perpetrators carried the 'badge' of Christianity. I will never forget being at Elmina Slave castle in 2016 (which back in the day was the largest slave shipping point on the Gold Coast of Ghana) and seeing how upstairs they had a chapel with Bible verses written all over the wall and yet one floor below there were slaves tied up and kept in the most inhumane conditions before being led through the 'door of no return' into ships. Upstairs, men were 'worshipping the Lord' and downstairs, men, women and children were being loaded into slave ships. Christianity and slavery were separated by the mere distance of a floor and a staircase. I wept bitterly!!!!!!

 GOD, who are You, and do You truly love us?

Could the people who carried the 'conquering spirit' and became the major authorities of this crusading and conquering form of Christianity have been led by the same Holy Spirit of the Bible, and carried the love of the GOD of Abraham, Isaac and Jacob and of His Son YAHUSHA* in them as they 'conquered' through slavery, colonisation and apartheid? (*The explanation of the name YAHUSHA will be made in Chapter 8).

 GOD, who are You, and do You truly love us?

Could "the conqueror" have been driven by the greatest two commandments, to love the Most High GOD and to love their neighbours? I don't know. I am not the one to judge. Maybe God was using them as instruments to exert His righteous judgement to fulfil His word, that captivity and oppression would come upon those (we and our forefathers) who turned away from Him and

INTRODUCTION: MY JOURNEY LEADING TO THIS BOOK

broke the covenant (agreement) they had with Him.

 GOD, who are You, and do You truly love us?

But what I do know is that the Holy scriptures tell us that the Holy Spirit will lead us into all truth and that the truth shall set us free. It is a truth that, if embraced, shall set both the 'conquered' and 'conqueror' into the path that leads to freedom. The GOD of Abraham, Isaac and Jacob will use the good and the bad of what happened in the past, and likewise He will use both the 'conquered' and the 'conqueror' for His good and the fulfilment of His plan according to His script and unchangeable design, which He reveals in the Bible. This is one of the topics which will be addressed.

As already mentioned, since 2010, I had often pondered if 'Africa and indigenous people, the darker-skinned people' are and were 'chosen' to be cursed. I also greatly pondered about Africa and where and how it fits into the biblical script so that we can use that as a mechanism to understand our history and our future.

I had wondered what our Father, the GOD of Abraham, Isaac and Jacob's view was of Elmina Castle or of the signing of the Berlin Congo Act of 1885, amongst many other things that have been done in the name of 'the Lord'. This made me think, but "Who is 'the Lord'? Does he/He have a name? When we use the title 'the Lord,' are we all referencing the same person or deity?

Could such momentous events as slavery, colonialism, and the oppression of an entire people not be matters the Bible addresses?? How do we investigate the script and design of what is revealed through the Holy scriptures, and establish our identity and hence our story within it, so that we can make sense of what has happened to us and what we need to do to come into what the script says our end will be?

At the end of every question in my mind was another question.

 GOD, who are You, and do You truly love us?

The counterfeit Jesus and Gospel

Which Jesus do I follow, and which gospel do I believe?

We must carefully analyse whether or not we have been indoctrinated to accept another 'Jesus' (Messiah) and a different 'gospel' as the scriptures warn us against. Another 'Jesus' or 'gospel' implies a counterfeit, one that looks very similar to the truth but is a lie. Is it possible that we have accepted the one that comes in his own name?

*For **if someone comes and proclaims another Jesus** than the one we proclaimed, or if you receive a different spirit from the one you received, or **if you accept a different gospel** from the one you accepted, you put up with it readily enough. (2 Corinthians 11:4 ESV)*

*As we said before, so say I now again, **if any man preach any other gospel** unto you than that ye have received, let him be accursed. (Galatians 1:9 KJV)*

*I am come in my Father's name, and ye receive me not: **if another shall come in his own name, him ye will receive**. (John 5:43 KJV)*

What Messiah has been presented to Africa and what gospel has been preached?

These are some of the questions that will be answered as we journey together through the chapters that lie ahead.

CHAPTER TWO

The Rewriting of History
"History Through the Eyes of the Conqueror and the Silencing of Indigenous Narratives"

History, as it is widely recorded and taught, is often shaped by the perspectives of those in power, particularly the conquerors, colonisers, and ruling elites. This phenomenon caan be summarised by the phrase *"history is written by the victors."* Throughout time, dominant civilisations have documented events to justify their expansion, glorify their achievements, and suppress the voices and experiences of those they have subdued.

This often takes place through several intentionally orchestrated ways, including:

1. Control of Records and Language

Conquering powers typically impose their language, education systems, and cultural frameworks. By doing so, they marginalise or completely erase the oral traditions, spiritual beliefs, and written accounts of indigenous populations. Over generations, this leads to the loss or distortion of native perspectives, values, and historical memory.

2. Destruction and Replacement of Indigenous Knowledge

Conquests often involved the destruction of sacred texts, monuments, and institutions of the conquered peoples. Examples include:

- The burning of the Library of Alexandria and the destruction of Mesoamerican codices by Spanish conquistadors.
- British colonial suppression of African and Indian historical records and oral histories.

3. Mythmaking and Justification

Colonial powers crafted historical narratives that portrayed themselves as civilisers or liberators, while painting indigenous peoples as primitive, violent, or backward. This justified colonisation, slavery, and exploitation, while obscuring the true human cost and resilience of native communities.

4. Lost Oral Traditions and Cultural Erasure

Many indigenous histories were passed down orally, through stories, songs, and rituals. When these cultures were disrupted or decimated, their historical memory was often lost with them. The lack of written records, from a Western scholarly perspective, was used to invalidate their history.

The historical narrative we inherit is often incomplete or biased because it reflects the viewpoint of the conquerors. As a result, the rich and complex histories of indigenous peoples have been silenced, distorted, or lost. Understanding this dynamic is essential for decolonising history and honouring the diverse human experiences that shaped our world.

How does this translate into Africa?

Rewriting History: "Changed narrative concerning Africa"

Examining how Africa's history has been manipulated is a topic deserving of its own book, but for now, a few examples will do to illustrate the point. Here are some clear instances of how African history has been portrayed through the lens of conquest, leading to the erasure or distortion of indigenous narratives.

1. Colonial Education Systems Rewrote African History

Example: British and French colonial rule (19th–20th centuries)

- European colonisers imposed Western curricula across Africa, which taught African children that their history began with colonisation.

- Pre-colonial African civilisations, like Great Zimbabwe, Mali, Songhai, and Nubia, were ignored or downplayed.

- African contributions to science, architecture, governance, and culture were omitted, while Europe's role was glorified.

African children were taught to see their own people as inferior and their past as primitive, creating generational identity crises.

2. The Destruction of African Historical Records

Example: Timbuktu manuscripts (Mali)

- Timbuktu was once a global centre of education and trade. It housed tens of thousands of manuscripts on science, law, medicine, and philosophy.

- During French colonisation, many manuscripts were taken, destroyed, or disregarded as irrelevant because they didn't align with Western narratives.

The intellectual legacy of Africa was hidden, giving the false impression that Africa had no written history or academic tradition.

3. The "Discovery" Myth of African Lands

Example: European explorers like David Livingstone and Henry Morton Stanley

- European narratives described African regions as "discovered" by white explorers, even though Africans had lived, traded, and governed there for millennia.

- Rivers, lakes, and towns were renamed after European figures (e.g., Victoria Falls, Lake Victoria).

Indigenous knowledge of geography and society was dismissed, while European names and maps were imposed as the "official history" a legacy that endures to this day.

4. Denial of Advanced African Civilisations

Example: Great Zimbabwe (11th–15th century)

- When Europeans encountered the stone city of Great Zimbabwe, they refused to believe black Africans built it. Some even went so far as to claim it was built by the Phoenicians or Arabs.

- Archaeological evidence clearly proves it was an indigenous African achievement.

African achievements were stripped of authorship to fit the colonial belief that Africans were incapable of complex civilisation.

5. Oral Histories Silenced or Dismissed

Example: Zulu, Akan, and Igbo oral traditions

- African societies preserved history orally through griots, elders, and storytellers.
- Colonial anthropologists and historians dismissed oral history as "unreliable," elevating only European written sources.

Rich and nuanced African historical accounts were ignored, weakening cultural continuity and historical pride.

6. The Role of Slavery and Christianity in Historical Narrative

Example: Transatlantic Slave Trade and Missionary Accounts

- Slave traders and missionaries wrote about Africa in ways that justified exploitation, describing Africans as heathens needing salvation or labour.
- Christian missionary schools rarely acknowledged the trauma of slavery or the resistance of African communities.

History was framed to vindicate colonisers and suppress African resistance, agency, and humanity.

Across Africa, colonisation not only conquered land and people, but it also conquered memory and history. The narratives of African greatness, spirituality, knowledge, and resilience were systematically overwritten. Today, reclaiming and recentring African voices is essential to telling the true and complete history of the continent.

This same 'erasure' of historical truth also occurred with the Bible.

Rewriting History: "Changed narrative with respect to the Bible"

Biblical history has been significantly shaped and, in many ways, distorted by the dominance of Greco-Roman narratives over the original Semitic (Israelite/Hebrew) context, especially after the destruction of Yarushalayim (Jerusalem) and during the rise of Christianity as a Roman state religion. Here's a breakdown of how the ancient Israelite narrative was suppressed or reshaped to fit Greco-Roman frameworks.

1. Hellenisation of Scripture and Theology

Example: After Alexander the Great's conquests (4th century BCE), Greek culture and language were imposed across the Near East, including Israel (Judea).

- The Septuagint (Greek translation of the Hebrew Scriptures) shifted key Hebrew concepts into Greek philosophical terms.

- Hebrew terms like *Torah* (instruction) became *nomos* (law), altering their meaning from covenantal guidance to rigid legalism.

- Greek dualism (spirit vs. flesh) began to influence interpretations of sin, salvation, and the human condition, which is very different from the Hebrew worldview, which saw body and spirit as unified.

Impact: Greek philosophy became the lens for interpreting the Bible, marginalising the Hebraic worldview of the original authors.

2. Roman Suppression and Destruction of Israelite Centres

Example: The destruction of Yarushalayim (Jerusalem) in 70 CE and the Bar Kokhba revolt in 135 CE led to:

- The diaspora (scattering) of Israelites and the loss of their political-religious centre.

- The renaming of Judea to Palestina by Emperor Hadrian to erase Israelite identity.

- The banning of the Hebrew language and Israelite customs in Roman territories.

Impact: The physical and cultural destruction of Israel led to the dominance of Roman Christianity, which began to define biblical history without the Israelite roots.

3. Replacement Theology (Supersessionism)

- Early Church fathers (e.g., Justin Martyr, Augustine) taught that the Church had replaced Israel as God's chosen people.

- Biblical promises made to Israel were 'spiritually' reassigned to the Gentile Church.

- The Old Testament was seen as outdated, legalistic, and merely a precursor to the "spiritual" truths of the New Testament.

Impact: The historical and prophetic identity of Israel in scripture was spiritualized or dismissed, severing the Church from its Hebraic foundation.

4. Latinisation and Europeanisation of Scripture

- The Bible was later translated into Latin (Vulgate), then into European languages, reinforcing Western cultural values and perspectives.

- Artistic depictions of biblical figures (e.g., Jesus, Moses, apostles) were Europeanised—light-skinned, Hellenistic in appearance and clothing.

Impact: This created a cultural disconnect, presenting biblical characters as Europeans rather than Middle Eastern, Semitic people.

5. Suppression of Non-Greek/Hebrew Texts

- Texts like the Book of Enoch, Jubilees, and other Hebrew writings that were valued in early Jewish-Christian communities were excluded from the canon by later Greco-Roman Church councils.

- These writings often carried strong Israelite identity and prophetic messages connected to covenant, judgment, and end-times hope.

Impact: The exclusion of these texts helped remove the deeper Israelite eschatological narrative from mainstream Christian theology.

6. Political Control of Biblical Interpretation

- Under Constantine and later Roman emperors, Christianity was institutionalised, and scripture was interpreted to support imperial authority.

- Messianic Jewish believers (those who accepted Jesus but still followed the Torah) were marginalised or persecuted.

- The Sabbath was changed from the 7th day (Saturday) to Sunday to distance the Church from Judaism.

- Biblical feasts such as Passover were replaced by Easter, and the other feasts were removed from Christian doctrine.

Impact: The biblical faith of YAHUSHA and the apostles, rooted in the Israelite covenant, was rebranded into a Greco-Roman religion, which led to the changing of YAHUSHA's name to Jesus. This is a subject which will be covered in greater detail further in the book.

The suppression of the Israelite narrative by Greco-Roman powers fundamentally altered how biblical history has been understood. What began as a Semitic, covenant-based movement rooted in a real people and land was transformed into a universalised religion shaped by Greek philosophy and Roman imperial goals. Recovering the Hebraic context of Scripture is essential to restoring its true historical and spiritual meaning.

Another perspective on the rewriting of history lies in the many connections between the manipulation of Africa's history and its relationship to the Bible and vice versa — a key reason for writing *Awakening the Tribes of Africa*.

Rewriting History: "Linking the Changed Narrative of the Bible and Africa together"

Throughout history, those who conquer have not only taken land and resources, but they have also taken control of the narrative. Nowhere is this more evident than in the rewriting of African history and the reinterpretation of biblical history. By examining both cases, we find a powerful, interlinked example of how historical memory has been altered to support systems of domination, colonisation, and religious imperialism.

1. Erasure of Indigenous Identity

- **Africa:** Advanced civilisations, such as Great Zimbabwe, Nubia, and Timbuktu, were denied or reattributed to outsiders. Africans were described as primitive, without culture or history.

- **Bible:** Ancient Israelites, who are Afro-Asiatic Semitic people, were later portrayed in Western Greco-Roman art, theology, doctrine and literature as white, European-looking figures. This shifted the identity of biblical characters, making it easier to align the Bible with European dominance.

  Link: In both contexts, original identities were stripped to support the myth of European superiority.

2. Religion as a Tool of Empire

- **Africa:** Christianity was introduced by European colonisers who used it to pacify populations and promote obedience to colonial authority. Indigenous spirituality was demonised or outlawed.

- **Bible:** The Hebrew scriptures, originally written in the context of a covenantal relationship with the GOD of Abraham, Isaac and Jacob for Israel initially and extended to all nations thereafter, were reinterpreted through Greco-Roman philosophical and imperial lenses, turning the faith into an institution of empire.

  Link: The covenantal nature and transformative essence of both African spirituality and the original biblical message were hijacked to support foreign rule.

3. Suppression of Historical Memory

- **Africa:** Oral histories and cultural heritage were dismissed, with colonial education teaching that Africa had no history before the arrival of the Europeans. Oral traditions, native governance systems, and intellectual achievements were erased or belittled.

- **Bible:** Hebrew scriptures were reinterpreted through Greek and Roman philosophy, silencing the original Israelite voice and context. Greek philosophy replaced Hebrew thought, and Hebrew texts that were deemed 'undesirable to the empire' were excluded from the canon. The Hebraic worldview, which emphasised unity between physical and spiritual realities, was replaced with Greek dualism.

  Link: Both Africa and ancient Israel were disconnected from their historical memory, making colonised people more vulnerable to manipulation.

4. Displacement and Loss of Heritage

- **Africa:** Africans were uprooted through the transatlantic slave trade, colonisation, and land dispossession. Their languages, customs, and histories were violently disrupted. The 'scramble for Africa', which was legalised through the Berlin Congo West Africa Conference of 1884-1885, subjugated an entire continent to the control of Western powers.

- **Bible:** After the Roman destruction of Yarushalayim (Jerusalem) in 70 CE and the suppression of the Bar Kokhba revolt in 135 CE, Israelites were scattered and lost their identity and heritage (the lost tribes of Israel). Greco-Roman Christianity redefined the Church as the "New Israel," displacing the original covenant people and establishing a new theology based on this replacement.

  Link: In both instances, the rightful inheritors of identity and heritage were physically and spiritually displaced.

5. Renaming and Reframing of the Narrative

- **Africa:** Geographical borders on the continent were drawn based on the Berlin Congo West Africa Conference, with tribes and families being split by Western-drawn borders to create countries that did not exist before. The indigenous names of places and peoples were replaced with colonial names. The entire continent was renamed, eradicating its ancient names and disconnecting people from their ancestral legacy.

- **Bible:** Hebrew festivals were replaced with Greco-Roman holidays (e.g., Sabbath replaced by Sunday, Passover by Easter). Hebrew names were Latinised or Hellenised (e.g., YAHUSHA to Jesus) whilst the cultural context of the Hebrew-derived Bible was changed into a Greco-Roman narrative.

    Link: Renaming was a form of domination and a mechanism to achieve cultural erasure and rebranding to reflect the 'conqueror's' values.

The 'conquerors' of both Africa and biblical history didn't just reshape borders or laws; they reshaped memory. By distorting identities, suppressing native voices, and recasting historical and spiritual truths through their lenses, they created a false narrative that has lasted for centuries. The journey to healing and restoration must include the reclamation of both African history and the original Hebraic roots of the Bible. Only then can we begin to uncover the truth buried beneath centuries of conquest.

Tribes of Africa, our history must not only be remembered, but it must also be reclaimed.

It is worthwhile to take a step further and lay the platform to link Africa and ancient biblical history by outlining and comparing two culturally-based paradigms of thought.

The first comparison is between Hebraic and Greco-Roman cultural thinking, and the second comparison is between Hebraic and typical African cultural thinking.

How we think: Hebraic versus Greek thinking

The primary culture and mindset of thought that the Bible and all that took place within it come from an ancient Hebrew culture and way of thinking. For example, the stories told, their cultural context, and the meaning of the parables and visions can only be fully interpreted when filtered through the cultural thinking of the day. As an example, in ancient Hebrew, the word that is translated in Greek and then into English as 'virgin' has two meanings in ancient Hebrew. It could mean 'a young lady of marriage age, ready to be married', or it could mean 'a woman who has not yet had a sexual relationship', or it could mean both. Something seemingly insignificant as this can change the whole doctrine that has been established based on the interpretation of the word 'virgin'.

The majority of the doctrine that has been followed in Christianity to date was established by the so-called 'church fathers' who were primarily Greek-influenced philosophers and theologians. Likewise, most of the translations from the original ancient Hebrew texts into Greek and Latin were done by Greco-Roman thinkers and translators.

Here's a summary of some of the key differences between Hebraic and Greek thinking, which helps explain how biblical interpretation was changed when filtered through Greek and later

Roman philosophical frameworks. These differences will be useful to remember as one reads the rest of the book's content.

1. Concrete vs. Abstract Thinking

- **Hebraic Thinking:**
    - *Concrete and action-oriented.*
    - Truth is experienced through relationships (with the primary relationship being with God), obedience, and observable outcomes.
    - Example: "Love" is shown through action (obedience).
    - "I love God because I obey Him".

- **Greek Thinking:**
    - *Abstract and theoretical.*
    - Truth is defined by ideas, logic, and intellectual understanding.
    - Example: "Love" is an intellectual construct, defined and discussed philosophically, often disconnected from practice.
    - "I love God because I know I love Him".

2. Holistic vs. Dualistic View of Reality

- **Hebraic Thinking:**
    - Sees body, soul, and spirit as *integrated and unified.*
    - Life is a whole; there is no division between the sacred and secular.

- **Greek Thinking:**
  - Introduced *dualism*: spirit is good, matter is corrupt.
  - Created a split between the spiritual (holy) and the physical (profane).

3. Function vs. Form

- **Hebraic Thinking:**
  - Focuses on *function and purpose*. Something is "good" if it fulfils its purpose (e.g., a good tree produces good fruit).

- **Greek Thinking:**
  - Focuses on *form, structure, and appearance*. Something is "good" based on ideals or theoretical models (e.g., Plato's ideal forms).

4. Relationship vs. System

- **Hebraic Thinking:**
  - Emphasises *covenant relationship* with God and others.
  - Laws are about relational faithfulness and community order.
  - Relational-based (relationship first, then the transactions).

- **Greek Thinking:**
  - Emphasises *systems of logic and philosophy*.
  - Religion becomes a structured belief system with

- doctrines and creeds.
   - Transactional-based (transaction first, then the relationship).

5. Narrative vs. Propositional Truth

- **Hebraic Thinking:**
  - Truth is communicated through *story, history, and parable*.
  - The Bible reveals truth through lived experience and God's interaction with people.

- **Greek Thinking:**
  - Truth is communicated through *statements, definitions, and logical propositions*.
  - Theology becomes a set of abstract principles or philosophical arguments.

6. Community vs. Individualism

- **Hebraic Thinking:**
  - Oriented around *community, family, and nation*.
  - Identity is collective and covenantal.

- **Greek Thinking:**
  - Leans toward *individual autonomy and self-realisation*.
  - Focus on personal virtue and self-improvement.
  - "Self-made millionaire, Self-help programs, Religion/

God is to serve me"

Category	Hebraic Thinking	Greek Thinking
Nature of Truth	Lived, relational, action-based	Abstract, intellectual, theoretical
View of Reality	Holistic (spiritual + physical unified)	Dualistic (spirit vs. matter)
Key Expression	Story, symbol, obedience	Logic, reason, definition
Goal of Life	Faithfulness to covenant and community	Attaining personal knowledge or virtue
Knowledge of God	Through experience and relationship	Through philosophy and debate
Ethics	Based on obedience and love	Based on abstract principles

When Christianity shifted from its Hebraic roots to a Greco-Roman worldview (especially after the 4th century CE), it became less about living in covenant with God and others and more about believing the right doctrines and abstract truths. This shift dramatically changed how the Bible is interpreted, how God is perceived, and how faith is practised.

How we think: Hebraic versus 'traditional African' thinking

Hebraic and traditional African thinking and worldviews align closely in values, structure, and spiritual understanding. Both are relational, communal, oral, holistic, and covenantal. This explains why Africans historically connected more deeply with the Bible when it was taught in its Hebraic roots, before being filtered through Greco-Roman abstractions and Western cultural frameworks.

Here's a brief, summarised comparison between Hebraic and African worldviews:

1. **Holistic Worldview**

    - **Hebraic Thinking:**

        o Life is a unified whole, and there is no division between sacred and secular.

        o God is involved in all aspects of life: family, work, justice, agriculture, etc.

    - **African Thinking:**

        o Strongly holistic as spirituality is woven into all aspects of daily life.

        o Ancestral traditions, community rituals, and daily labour are all spiritual acts.

Both reject compartmentalised religion and embrace a life where spirituality is integrated into every domain of life.

2. **Community Centred Identity**

    - **Hebraic Thinking:**

        o Identity is rooted in the *nation*, family, and tribe.

        o The covenant with God is collective and not just individual.

    - **African Thinking:**

        o Personhood is defined through *Ubuntu* ("I am because we are").

        o The community comes before the individual.

Both systems prioritise communal harmony, shared responsibility, and generational continuity.

3. Oral Tradition and Storytelling

- **Hebraic Thinking:**
  - Oral transmission was key (e.g., parables, psalms, genealogies).
  - History and theology were passed through storytelling.

- **African Thinking:**
  - Griots, elders, and storytellers preserved and transmitted knowledge.
  - Proverbs and oral narratives carry wisdom.

Both emphasise the power of the spoken word and storytelling as tools for the dissemination of knowledge, wisdom and culture, and as legitimate sources of truth.

4. Covenant and Communal Obligation

- **Hebraic Thinking:**
  - Covenant with God required justice, hospitality, and care for the poor, widows, and orphans.
  - Blessings and curses were tied to obedience as a nation.

- **African Thinking:**
  - Community rules and taboos are what maintain order and harmony.
  - Reciprocity and moral obligation were expected in extended families and clans.

Common ground: Both operate based on relational accountability, not just legal obligation.

5. Respect for Elders and Generational Wisdom

- **Hebraic Thinking:**
    - Elders are seen as wise leaders and gatekeepers of tradition.
    - Lineage and genealogy were central to identity and communal purpose.

- **African Thinking:**
    - Elders are spiritual and cultural authorities.
    - Ancestral/Forefather wisdom guides moral and social behaviour.

Both hold elders and ancestors/forefathers in high regard, preserving continuity across generations as seen when The Most High gives His name as the GOD of Abraham, Isaac and Jacob.

6. Spiritual View of Nature and Time

- **Hebraic Thinking:**
    - Nature is a creation of God with spiritual meaning (e.g., rain as a blessing, drought as judgment).
    - Time is cyclical and event-oriented (feasts, seasons, jubilees).

- **African Thinking:**
    - Nature is spiritual, with all things having sacred meaning.

- Time is circular, marked by agricultural seasons, festivals, and ancestral memory.

Both see time and nature as sacred cycles, not just linear progressions.

The African way of thinking is similar to the Hebraic in nature, and it is the very form of thinking that the religion of Western Christianity sought to remove from Africa and other indigenous people groups, as they deemed it 'uncivilised and backward'.

The Greco-Roman-based form of Christianity is foreign to the 'thinking DNA' of Africa because our DNA is ancient Hebraic in nature. Greco-Roman Christianity has placed a 'blanket of captivity' over the true nature and identity of who the African has been created to be. Through that, we have lived a 'fake' spiritual existence for generations.

CHAPTER THREE

The Incredible Blessing That Is In Our Hands

As we embark on the journey, it is important to set a baseline by briefly recognising the amazing blessing that we as Africans have been given and hence the potential of what can be ours in the future, depending on what we do with what has been placed in our hands.

What follows is common knowledge to most people, but it is good to be reminded of how blessed we are.

Africa is widely regarded as the most resource-rich continent on earth, possessing a vast array of natural resources that are critical to the global economy. These include:

- **Minerals and Metals**: Africa holds over 30% of the world's mineral reserves, including:
    - 90% of global platinum reserves
    - 70% of tantalum
    - 60% of cobalt

- o 40% of gold
- o Significant deposits of diamonds, manganese, uranium, and chromium

- **Oil and Natural Gas**: Countries like Nigeria, Angola, Libya, and Algeria are major oil producers. Africa accounts for about 12% of the world's oil production.

- **Agricultural Land and Water**: With around 60% of the world's uncultivated arable land, Africa has immense potential to become a global agricultural powerhouse. Its major river systems and lakes also provide abundant freshwater resources.

- **Forests and Biodiversity**: The Congo Basin is the world's second-largest tropical rainforest and is crucial for global carbon sequestration and biodiversity.

- **Renewable Energy Potential**: The continent is rich in solar and wind energy resources, especially in the Sahara and Sahel regions, offering vast opportunities for clean energy development.

Africa's natural resources, coupled with its rapidly growing and youthful population, position the continent for significant economic transformation:

1. Resource-Driven Industrialisation

- Properly managed, Africa's natural resources can drive industrialisation by creating value-added industries such as mineral processing, oil refining, and manufacturing.

- This can reduce dependency on raw exports and boost intra-

African trade, especially through the African Continental Free Trade Area (AfCFTA).

- The African Continental Free Trade Area (AfCFTA) is the largest free trade area in the world by number of countries, aiming to:
    o Connect 1.4 billion people
    o Create a $3.4 trillion economic bloc
    o Boost intra-African trade by over 50%

AfCFTA can break down economic silos, encourage regional manufacturing, and position Africa as a unified market for global investors and supply chains.

2. Agricultural Expansion

- With its vast arable land and favourable climate, Africa can lead a green revolution, becoming a global leader in food production.

- Investment in Agro-processing and sustainable farming could reduce food imports and increase exports.

3. Youth Demographic Dividend

- Over 60% of Africa's 1.4 billion population is under 25 years old. By 2050, Africa will be home to one-third of the world's youth and 25% of the global population (based on the projected growth to 2.5 billion).

- This young labour force can drive innovation, productivity, and entrepreneurship, and this youth bulge presents a massive labour force and a growing consumer base. With proper investments in education, skills, and healthcare, Africa can turn this into a global advantage similar to what East Asia achieved in past decades.

4. Renewable Energy Development

- Africa's solar and wind potential can address energy deficits and industrial power growth, especially in rural and off-grid areas.

- Renewable energy development could also attract climate-conscious investment and create green jobs.

- With global demand rising for clean energy and critical minerals, Africa's resource wealth positions it as a crucial player in the energy transition and global supply chains.

Africa's unparalleled wealth of natural resources and dynamic, youthful population offer a unique economic opportunity. The continent is poised to leapfrog legacy infrastructure, going straight to mobile banking, e-commerce, and digital health, and thereby build a strong, high-value services economy with the natural resource strength. This technological leap can fuel inclusive growth and innovation, especially when it comes to establishing new value chains and ecosystems that will see more of the value-added wealth coming to Africa. If well harnessed through sustainable governance, infrastructure investment, education, and industrial policy, Africa can transition from a resource-exporting continent to a diversified and innovation-driven economy. This transformation holds promise not just for Africa, but for global development, stability, and environmental sustainability.

We, as Africans, have the potential to become the next global economic power, contributing to global innovation, sustainable growth, and economic rebalancing in the 21st century.

This is what we have in our hands. This is what the Creator has given us to steward.

The first mandate the Creator gave our ancestor Adam in the Garden of Eden was to 'tend and keep it', as it is written in Genesis 2:15. *"Then the Most High Alahym took the man and put him in the garden of Eden to tend and keep it."* To 'tend and keep' is stewardship. Interestingly, the meaning of Adam in Hebrew is tied to the word "adamah", which means ground, earth, soil and hence reflects the biblical idea that Adam was formed from the dust of the ground (Genesis 2:7). It can also be linked to the Hebrew word "dam", which means blood.

The issue between people and the land which they were divinely given to steward is of extreme importance because of the link between man and the land. Africa is the garden that we have been given to 'tend and keep,' and our ability to do so is directly linked to our relationship and agreement with the One who gave us this instruction.

"We are certainly 'a conquered' people"

Section 2

Contents

Chapter 4. The 12 'domains of control' used to conquer Africa

Chapter 5. Reflecting the 12 'domains of control' biblically through Deuteronomy chapter 28

Chapter 6. Linking the Deuteronomy 28 curses to the reality of Africa's lived and living experience

Chapter 7: The biblical answer to why this has happened

CHAPTER FOUR

The 12 'domains of control' used to conquer Africa

One of the most fascinating explorations along this journey for me was researching the 12 'domains of control' that have been used historically and even today, to take control of a nation or people group. These are the main 'domains of control' that are used in empire building. One can see how each was used in the establishment of the Greco-Roman empire, the Ottoman empire, the British empire (even as most in Africa have grown up under the British Commonwealth) and even what the Bible refers to as the 'Babylonian empire' today (which will be one of the major points addressed further in the book).

I will highlight these 'domains of control' and briefly discuss them in terms of how they have been applied to Africa and how they, sadly, still apply today.

Below are the core areas most often targeted by regimes, empires, or groups attempting to dominate a state:

1. **Spirituality/Religion**
2. **Culture**

3. **Economy**
4. Rulership (Political & Government Institutions)
5. Military/Security
6. Media/Information
7. Education
8. Legal System
9. Technology/Infrastructure
10. Healthcare/Social Services
11. Natural Resources
12. Finance/Banking

The first three domains of spirituality, culture, and economy are highlighted as those that directly determine the worldview and affect the mindset of the population and drive different levels of human experience within a society: the moral, the symbolic, the material, and also the practical capacities. To fully control a population or nation, influence over all three is a core strategy. Historical and modern empires and regimes that achieved long-lasting control often understood this and sought to dominate these domains of control, either directly or through proxies.

Here's how and why:

1. **Spirituality/Religion:**

The primary aim of the domain of spirituality is to control the belief systems of a population and is a strategy that has been successfully executed through the spread of the institutionalised religions of Catholicism, Christianity (Greco-Roman and Anglo-Saxon empires) and Islam (Ottoman empire). These are the 3 main proxies through which Africa's spirituality has been dominated to ensure:

- **Legitimacy & Obedience**: Religion often underpins moral authority and can be used to legitimise rulers (e.g., the "divine right of kings," or theocratic regimes), or conformance to set doctrines that can be determined by institutionalised religion (Catholicism, Christianity, Islam).

- **Control of Values**: Religious institutions influence people's sense of right and wrong, acceptable behaviour, and identity.
- **Mobilisation & Suppression**: Religion can be used to inspire collective action or, conversely, to encourage obedience, submission, or passivity (e.g., "render unto Caesar, render unto the church, or render unto Allah").

The introduction briefly addressed the Doctrine of Discovery, a decree of the Catholic Church that gave European powers license to seize and dominate lands inhabited by non-Christians. Through this doctrine, much of the world was forcefully brought under European rule, enabling centuries of colonisation, dispossession, and the silencing of Indigenous sovereignties. It is worthwhile, however, to expand on it here, as this will help bring many other ideas covered in this section and book into context regarding why the spiritual/religious 'domain of control' is so foundationally important to everything else.

The Doctrine of Discovery is a historical concept that has had a profound impact on the relationship between European colonisers ('the conqueror') and indigenous peoples ('the conquered') around the world.

The Doctrine of Discovery is a principle of international law that was developed in the 15th century, primarily by European powers such as Spain, Portugal, and England. The doctrine held that European explorers and colonisers ('the conqueror') had the right to claim ownership of lands they "discovered," regardless of the presence of indigenous peoples (who became 'the conquered').

- Key elements of the Doctrine of Discovery:
  - **First discovery**: European explorers who arrived first in a 'new land' had the right to claim it for their country.
  - **Right of conquest**: European powers believed they had the right to conquer and subjugate indigenous peoples.
  - **Terra nullius**: Lands were considered "empty" or "unoccupied" if they were not inhabited by Christians or Europeans, disregarding Indigenous peoples' existing ownership, laws, and cultural ties to the land.
  - **Papal authority**: The Catholic Church played a significant role in legitimising the Doctrine of Discovery, with several popes issuing bulls and decrees that supported European colonisation.

The Doctrine of Discovery has had far-reaching consequences for indigenous peoples ('the conquered') worldwide:

- **Land expropriation**: European colonisers used the doctrine to justify the taking of land from indigenous peoples.
- **Cultural destruction**: Indigenous cultures, languages, and traditions were suppressed or destroyed.
- **Violence and genocide**: The doctrine was used to justify violence and genocide against indigenous peoples.
- **Ongoing marginalisation**: The legacy of the Doctrine of Discovery continues to affect indigenous communities today, with ongoing struggles for land rights, self-determination, and cultural preservation.

2. **Culture:**

The primary aim of the domain of culture is to control 'meaning and identity' within the population. It is a strategy that has the ultimate objective of replacing the indigenous culture with that of the 'conqueror', which in the past has been labelled as 'bringing civilisation to natives' and typically has been enforced in Africa through -

- **Narrative Framing**: Control of cultural narratives (history, language, education, media) that influence national identity and group cohesion.
- **Soft Power**: The use of music, literature, entertainment, and tradition to shape cultural perceptions and hence subtly align populations with the empire or regime's goals.
- **Legislated Compliance**: Establishing a societal class hierarchy based on cultural compliance, which determines levels of access to resources.

3. **Economy:**

The primary aim of the domain of economy is to ensure the control of the nations or continents' resources (as in the case of Africa) and control the terms of access to economic participation for the indigenous population. This is typically achieved through systems and structures that ensure:

- **Material Dependence**: Economic systems determine people's access to food, shelter, and jobs, and this is used as a mechanism to give 'the conquerors' enormous leverage and power over the people.
- **Class Control**: Economic stratification allows elites (either foreign or local) to maintain power structures and control capital and finances as a means of controlling rulership (political and government) outcomes.
- **Tools of Reward/Punishment**: The ability to offer or withhold economic benefits helps enforce loyalty as this is implemented through channels like welfare, employment

and taxation, to name a few.
- **Extraction and Exploitation**: The exploitation of local resources and people for the benefit of an elite and, in Africa's case, a foreign elite in the Western world. Discussion will be made further in the book, highlighting the impact on Africa of the 1884-1885 Berlin Congo West Africa Conference through which the Western world took control of all of Africa's economic assets, and has continued to enjoy this unholy privilege ever since.

These 3 domains of control (Spiritual/religious, Cultural and Economic) are foundational, with the other 9 domains of control typically acting as supporting 'structures' that are uniquely designed to determine how the nation/continent ('the conquered') will be governed and systems put in place to ensure that the control becomes systemic and perpetual. To truly control a nation, a regime doesn't need total dominance in all areas, but the more domains it controls, the more resilient, persuasive, and coercive its power becomes. Most regimes, empires, colonisers, or groups attempting to dominate a state will seek to blend soft and hard control mechanisms across these fields to suppress dissent and ensure compliance.

4. **Rulership (Political & Government Institutions)**

- **Why It Matters**: Control over the state apparatus (legislature, judiciary, executive) allows one to write, enforce, and interpret laws to benefit and serve the interests of the controlling group.
- **This is often done by:**
    - Installing loyalists in key offices and, in the case of Africa, colonial powers would have their own governors.
    - Manipulating elections or suspending democratic

processes and denying voting rights to certain parts of the population.
- Restructuring government systems to ensure they serve the interests of the controlling power.

5. **Military and Security Forces**

- **Why It Matters**: The monopoly on violence is essential to suppress resistance, enforce laws, and defend power.
- **This is often done by:**
    - Control over the military chain of command.
    - Cultivating paramilitary or secret police forces.
    - Surveillance systems and repression of dissent.

6. **Media and Information**

- **Why It Matters**: Control of information flow is crucial for managing public opinion, spreading propaganda, and silencing opposition.
- **This is often done by:**
    - Owning or regulating media outlets.
    - Censorship of news, the internet, books, and social media.
    - Spreading disinformation or controlling the narrative.

7. **Education System**

- **Why It Matters**: Education shapes future citizens' worldview, knowledge base, pride and dignity in their identity and heritage and hence loyalty to their collective as a people, making them easier to manage/govern.

- **This is often done by:**
  - Revising history and curricula.
  - Banning independent or critical thought.
  - Promoting cultural ideology in schools.
  - Removing indigenous languages as a medium of learning and replacing them with 'the conquerors' language.

8. **Legal System / Judiciary**

- **Why It Matters**: The judiciary enforces rules and can be weaponised to legitimise authoritarian actions.
- **This is often done by:**
  - Ensuring the law is determined by design to serve the interests of the controlling group.
  - Appointing partisan judges.
  - Criminalising dissent.
  - Using legalism to target enemies (lawfare).

9. **Technology and Infrastructure**

- **Why It Matters**: Infrastructure (digital and physical) gives logistical control over population movement, communication, and economy.
- **This is often done by:**
  - Surveillance systems (e.g., facial recognition, internet monitoring, tracking devices).
  - Control over telecoms, transportation, and utilities.
  - Cybersecurity and data monopolies.

10. Healthcare and Social Services

- **Why It Matters:** Health and welfare systems can be used to earn legitimacy, exert control, or punish dissent through selective access.
- **How It's Done:**
    - Withholding services from "undesirables".
    - Creating dependency on state benefits.
    - Leveraging public health crises (e.g., pandemic policy, International Health Regulations granting the WHO unprecedented control over global populations).

11. Natural Resources and Environment

- **Why It Matters:** Control of water, land, minerals, and food supplies allows domination of rural populations and economic leverage.
- **This is often done by:**
    - Expropriating land or resource-rich regions.
    - Weaponising scarcity or environmental policy.
    - Granting resource control to loyal elites.

12. Finance and Banking

- **Why It Matters:** Control over capital flows, currency, and credit gives deep control over businesses, NGOs, and even individuals.
- **This is often done by:**
    - Controlling central banks and financial regulations.
    - Freezing assets of enemies or dissidents.
    - Forcing financial dependence on the state.

THE 12 "DOMAINS OF CONTROL" USED TO CONQUER AFRICA

Here is a table with a quick overview of how the domains of control are weaponised:

'DOMAIN OF CONTROL'	PURPOSE
Spirituality/Religion	Morality authority, obidience
Culture	Identity, narrative control
Economy	Resource control, reward/punishment
Rulership (Political & Government) Institutions	Lawmaking, system control
Military/Security	Physical power, repression
Media/Information	Mind control, propaganda
Education	Indoctrination, generational control
Legal System	Legitimation, repression
Technology/Infrastructure	Surveillance, logistics
Healthcare/Social Services	Dependence, public legitimacy
Natural Resources	Strategic leverage
Finance/Banking	Economic coercion

It is worthwhile for the reader to review their nation and the continent of Africa through this lens and to reflect on how each of these 'domains of control' has been active from the colonial era and through the current governments in power (which could be proxies for preserving the interests of the colonial empire).

Where were your nation and the continent of Africa in relation to these 12 'domains of control' before the Berlin Congo West Africa Conference of 1884, in the early 1900s, during the winds of change of independence from the 1960s up to South Africa's independence in 1994, and now in 2025 and beyond?

How have these 12 'domains of control' changed over that period?

 Tribes of Africa, who is really in control?

CHAPTER FIVE

Reflecting On The 'Domains Of Control' Biblically Through The Book Of Deuteronomy, Chapter 28

In the next two chapters, I will take you through two other investigative reflections I pursued.

The first, taking the 12 'domains of control' and comparing them to the curses that are mentioned in the scriptures with specific reference to Deuteronomy 28:15-68.

The second, taking the curses listed in Deuteronomy 28:15-68 and comparing them with the reality of what Africa and people of African descent across the world have experienced and endured in the past and continue to experience and endure today.

Deuteronomy 28 is a chapter that outlines the blessings that are given to the people (or nation) who meet the terms of the agreement (covenant) they have with the GOD of Abraham, Isaac and Jacob; and likewise, it also outlines the exact curses that come upon people (or nation) who violate the agreement that they have with the GOD of Abraham, Isaac and Jacob. It is, therefore, a good place to baseline the difficulties that

Africa has gone through and is still going through today.

Deuteronomy 28:1-68 NKJV

Verses 1 to 14 speak of the blessings

- "Now it shall come to pass, if you diligently obey the voice of the Lord* your God, to observe carefully all His commandments which I command you today, that the Lord* your God will set you high above all nations of the earth. [2] And all these blessings shall come upon you and overtake you, because you obey the voice of the Lord* your God: [3] "Blessed shall you be in the city, and blessed shall you be in the country. [4] "Blessed shall be the fruit of your body, the produce of your ground and the increase of your herds, the increase of your cattle and the offspring of your flocks. [5] "Blessed shall be your basket and your kneading bowl. [6] "Blessed shall you be when you come in, and blessed shall you be when you go out. [7] "The Lord* will cause your enemies who rise against you to be defeated before your face; they shall come out against you one way and flee before you seven ways. [8] "The Lord* will command the blessing on you in your storehouses and in all to which you set your hand, and He will bless you in the land which the Lord* your God is giving you. [9] "The Lord* will establish you as a holy people to Himself, just as He has sworn to you, if you keep the commandments of the Lord* your God and walk in His ways. [10] Then all peoples of the earth shall see that you are called by the name of the Lord*, and they shall be afraid of you. [11] And the Lord* will grant you plenty of goods, in the fruit of your body, in the increase of your livestock, and in the produce of your ground, in the land of which the Lord* swore to your fathers to give you. [12] The Lord* will open to you His good treasure, the heavens, to give the rain to your land in its season, and to bless all the work of your hand. You shall lend to many nations, but you shall not borrow. [13] And the Lord* will make you the head *and not the tail; you shall be above only, and not be beneath, if you heed the commandments of the Lord* your God, which I command you today, and are careful to observe them. [14] So you shall not turn aside from any of the words which I command you this day, to the right or the left, to go after other gods to serve them.*

Verses 15 to 68 speak of the curses

- *[15] "But it shall come to pass, if you do not obey the voice of the Lord* your God, to observe carefully all His commandments and His statutes which I command you today, that all these curses will come upon you and overtake you: [16] "Cursed shall you be in the city, and cursed shall you be in the country. [17] "Cursed shall be your basket and your kneading bowl. [18] "Cursed shall be the fruit of your body and the produce of your land, the increase of your cattle and the offspring of your flocks. [19] "Cursed shall you be when you come in, and cursed shall you be when you go out. [20] "The Lord* will send on you cursing, confusion, and rebuke in all that you set your hand to do, until you are destroyed and until you perish quickly, because of the wickedness of your doings in which you have forsaken Me. [21] The Lord* will make the plague cling to you until He has consumed you from the land which you are going to possess. [22] The Lord* will strike you with consumption, with fever, with inflammation, with severe burning fever, with the sword, with scorching, and with mildew; they shall pursue you until you perish. [23] And your heavens which are over your head shall be bronze, and the earth which is under you shall be iron. [24] The Lord* will change the rain of your land to powder and dust; from the heaven it shall come down on you until you are destroyed. [25] "The Lord* will cause you to be defeated before your enemies; you shall go out one way against them and flee seven ways before them; and you shall become troublesome to all the kingdoms of the earth. [26] Your carcasses shall be food for all the* birds of the air and the beasts of the earth, and no one shall frighten them away. [27] The Lord* will strike you with the boils of Egypt, with tumors, with the scab, and with the itch, from which you cannot be healed. [28] The Lord* will strike you with madness and blindness and confusion of heart. [29] And you shall grope at noonday, as a blind man gropes in darkness; you shall not prosper in your ways; you shall be only oppressed and plundered continually, and no one shall save you. [30] "You shall betroth a wife, but another man shall lie with her; you shall build a house, but you shall not dwell in it; you shall plant a vineyard, but shall not gather its grapes. [31] Your ox shall be slaughtered before your eyes, but you shall not eat of it; your donkey shall be violently taken away from before you, and shall not be restored to you; your sheep shall be given to your enemies, and you shall have no one to rescue them. [32] Your sons and your daughters shall be given to another people, and your eyes shall look and fail with longing for them all day long; and there shall be no strength in your hand. [33] A nation whom you have not known shall eat the fruit of your land and the produce of your labor, and you shall be only oppressed and crushed continually. [34] So you shall be driven mad because of the sight which your eyes see. [35] The Lord* will strike you in the knees and on the legs with severe boils which cannot be healed, and from the sole of your foot to the top of your head. [36] "The Lord* will bring you and the king whom you set over you to a nation which neither you nor your fathers have known, and there you shall serve other gods—wood and stone. [37] And you shall become an astonishment, a proverb, and a byword among all nations where the Lord* will drive you. [38] "You shall carry much seed out to the field but gather little in, for the locust shall consume it. [39] You shall plant vineyards and tend them, but you shall neither drink of the wine nor gather the grapes; for the worms shall eat them. [40] You shall have olive trees throughout all your territory, but you shall *not anoint yourself with the oil; for your olives shall drop off. [41] You shall beget sons and daughters, but they shall not be yours; for they shall go into captivity. [42] Locusts shall consume all your trees and the produce of your land. [43] "The alien who is among you shall rise higher and higher above you, and you shall come down lower and lower. [44] He shall lend to you, but you shall not lend to him; he shall be the head, and you shall be the tail. [45] "Moreover all these curses shall come upon you and pursue and overtake you, until you are destroyed, because you did not obey the voice of the Lord* your God, to keep His commandments and His statutes which He commanded you. [46] And they shall be upon you for a sign and a wonder, and on your descendants forever. [47] "Because you did not serve the Lord* your God with joy and gladness of heart, for the abundance of everything, [48] therefore you shall serve your enemies, whom the Lord* will send against you, in hunger, in thirst, in nakedness, and in need of everything; and He will put a yoke of iron on your neck until He has destroyed you. [49] The Lord* will bring a nation against you from afar, from the end of the earth, as swift as the eagle flies, a nation whose language you will not understand, [50] a nation of fierce countenance, which does not respect the elderly nor show favor to the young. [51] And they shall eat the increase of your livestock and the produce of your land, until you are destroyed; they shall not leave you grain or new wine or oil, or the increase of your cattle or the offspring of your flocks, until they have destroyed you. [52] "They shall besiege you at all your gates until your high and fortified walls, in which you trust, come down throughout all your land; and they shall besiege you at all your gates throughout all your land which the Lord* your God has given you. [53] You shall eat the fruit of your own body, the flesh of your sons and your daughters whom the Lord* your God has given you, in the siege and desperate straits in which your enemy shall distress you. [54] The sensitive and* *very refined man among you will be hostile toward his brother, toward the wife of his bosom, and toward the rest of his children whom he leaves behind, [55] so that he will not give any of them the flesh of his children whom he will eat, because he has nothing left in the siege and desperate straits in which your enemy shall distress you at all your gates. [56] The tender and delicate woman among you, who would not venture to set the sole of her foot on the ground because of her delicateness and sensitivity, will refuse to the husband of her bosom, and to her son and her daughter, [57] her placenta which comes out from between her feet and her children whom she bears; for she will eat them secretly for lack of everything in the siege and desperate straits in which your enemy shall distress you at all your gates. [58] "If you do not carefully observe all the words of this law that are written in this book, that you may fear this glorious and awesome name, THE Lord* YOUR GOD, [59] then the Lord* will bring upon you and your descendants extraordinary plagues—great and prolonged plagues—and serious and prolonged sicknesses. [60] Moreover He will bring back on you all the diseases of Egypt, of which you were afraid, and they shall cling to you. [61] Also every sickness and every plague, which is not written in this Book of the Law, will the Lord* bring upon you until you are destroyed. [62] You shall be left few in number, whereas you were as the stars of heaven in multitude, because you would not obey the voice of the Lord* your God. [63] And it shall be, that just as the Lord* rejoiced over you to do you good and multiply you, so the Lord* will rejoice over you to destroy you and bring you to nothing; and you shall be plucked from off the land which you go to possess. [64] "Then the Lord* will scatter you among all peoples, from one end of the earth to the other, and there you shall serve other gods, which neither you nor your fathers have known—wood and stone. [65] And among those nations you shall find no rest, nor shall the sole of your foot have a resting place;*

but there the Lord* will give you a trembling heart, failing eyes, and anguish of soul. [66] Your life shall hang in doubt before you; you shall fear day and night, and have no assurance of life. [67] In the morning you shall say, 'Oh, that it were evening!' And at evening you shall say, 'Oh, that it were morning!' because of the fear which terrifies your heart, and because of the sight which your eyes see. [68] "And the Lord* will take you back to Egypt in ships, by the way of which I said to you, 'You shall never see it again.' And there you shall be offered for sale to your enemies as male and female slaves, but no one will buy you."

Please note: * The title 'the Lord' is used here and will be discussed further in chapter 8.

Linking the 12 domains of control to the Deuteronomy 28 curses

Whether viewed as divine warning, sociopolitical allegory, or historical pattern, Deuteronomy 28 describes the total unravelling of a nation (or people) when key domains of life, those we now recognise as 'domains of control', are lost or subverted and captured. The linking of the two serves both as spiritual insight and political diagnosis, bridging biblical truth with power structures.

The curses described in Deuteronomy 28:15-68 which outline the consequences of biblical Israel's (the bloodline descendants of Jacob) disobedience to their covenant with the ALAHYM of Abraham, Isaac and Jacob, remarkably align with the major domains of societal control and national collapse we've been discussing. Whether one interprets this chapter in Deuteronomy theologically, historically, or politically, the curses relate to breakdowns (or takeovers) in the same critical areas of national life (domains of control) that must be dominated to either preserve or subjugate a nation.

Here is how they align, domain by domain:

1. **Spirituality / Religion**

    - **Deuteronomy Parallel:**
        - "You will serve other gods... gods of wood and stone" (v.36)
        - "You shall serve gods which neither you nor your fathers have known – wood and stone". (v64)
    - **Meaning:** The people will lose their spiritual autonomy and be forced into foreign religious systems, symbolising loss of identity and divine protection.
    - **Connection:** Loss of spiritual control often accompanies cultural and political subjugation. Conquerors historically replace or co-opt native spirituality to erase resistance. Such replacement in some instances would entail replacing the gods of wood and stone that the indigenous people served with those of the conquerors, such as the wooden cross in Christianity or the stone Kabbalah in Islam. This is a topic that will be discussed in greater detail further in the book.

2. **Culture**

    - **Deuteronomy Parallel:**
        - "Cursed shall you be when you come in and cursed shall you be when you go out" (v19)
        - "Your sons and your daughters shall be given to another people" (v32)
        - "You shall become an object of horror, scorn and ridicule among all the nations" (v.37)
        - "You shall beget sons and daughters, but they shall not be yours, for they shall go into captivity" (v41)

- "The sensitive and very refined man among you will be hostile toward his brother, toward the wife of his bosom and towards the rest of his children" (v54)

- "Likewise, the tender and delicate woman will refuse the husband of her bosom and reject and kill her children" (v56-57)

- **Meaning:** Cultural degradation and humiliation before others, including developing systems of superiority that establish perpetual inferiority within 'the conquered'.

- **Connection:** Dominated cultures are often mocked, suppressed, or assimilated, and cultural pride is replaced with shame and loss of historical identity.

3. **Economy**

    - **Deuteronomy Parallel:**
        - "Cursed shall you be in the city, and cursed shall you be in the country" (v16)
        - "Cursed shall be your basket and your kneading bowl" (v17)
        - "Cursed shall be the fruit of your body and the produce of your land" (v18)
        - "You shall not prosper in your ways, you shall only be oppressed and plundered continually, and no one shall save you" (v29)
        - "You shall build a house, and you shall not stay in it, you shall plant a vineyard but shall not gather its grapes" (v30)
        - "Your ox will be slaughtered before your eyes, your donkey shall be violently taken away from you, your sheep shall be

given to your enemies" (v.31)

- "A nation you do not know shall eat the fruit of your land and the produce of your labor and you shall be oppressed and crushed continually" (v.33)
- "You will sow much seed in the field but harvest little" (v.38)
- "You shall plant vineyards and tend them, but you shall neither drink of the wine nor gather the grapes" (v.39)
- "You shall have olive trees throughout your territory, but you shall not anoint yourself with the oil" (v.40)
- "Locusts shall consume all your trees and the produce of your land" (v.42)
- "You shall be plucked off the land" (v.63)

- **Meaning:** Economic exploitation and poverty.
- **Connection:** Foreign domination of economic systems leads to the extraction of wealth, debt slavery, and economic collapse, which is the hallmark of imperial control.

4. **Rulership (Political/Government) Institutions**
   - **Deuteronomy Parallel:**
     - "You shall serve your enemies" (v.47)
     - "The Lord will bring a nation against you... they will reign over you, and eat the increase of your livestock and the produce of your land, they shall not leave you grain or new wine or oil, or the increase of your cattle and the offspring of your flocks" (v.49-51)
     - "They shall besiege you at all your gates until your high and

fortified walls come down throughout your land" (v.52)

- **Meaning:** Political sovereignty is lost to foreign rule.
- **Connection:** This speaks directly to political takeover—a nation loses autonomy and becomes a puppet or colony of a stronger power.

5. **Military and Security**
   - **Deuteronomy Parallel:**
     - *"Your enemies will oppress you at all your gates" (v.52)*
     - *"The Lord will cause you to be defeated before your enemies" (v.25)*
   - **Meaning:** Loss of military strength and inability to defend the homeland.
   - **Connection:** Control over armed forces is essential to national survival; without it, a nation becomes vulnerable to internal collapse and external conquest.

6. **Media / Information (Symbolic in Ancient Context)**
   - **Deuteronomy Parallel:**
     - *"The Lord will send on you cursing confusion" (v.20)*
     - *"You will grope about at noon as the blind grope in the dark" (v.29)*
   - **Meaning:** Confusion, lack of clarity, absence of truth.
   - **Connection:** In modern terms, this reflects loss of **information clarity**, leading to societal disorientation—key for propaganda and control in contemporary times.

7. **Education / Generational Control**

    - **Deuteronomy Parallel:**

        o *"Your sons and daughters will be given to another people" (v.32)*

    - **Meaning:** The next generation will be **raised under foreign influence**.

    - **Connection:** This reflects educational and cultural indoctrination—future generations lose the values and history of their ancestors, becoming loyal to foreign powers.

8. **Legal System / Justice**

    - **Deuteronomy Parallel:**

        o *"You will be oppressed and robbed continually, and no one will save you" (v.29)*

    - **Meaning:** Legal protection disappears.

    - **Connection:** The rule of law is corrupted or turned against the people; this is characteristic of authoritarian regimes or colonial systems.

9. **Technology / Infrastructure (Analogous in Ancient Terms)**

    - **Deuteronomy Parallel:**

        o *"Your high fortified walls, in which you trusted, will fall" (v.52)*

    - **Meaning:** Destruction of national defences and infrastructure.

    - **Connection:** Modern equivalent could be loss of control over digital infrastructure, surveillance, or critical national systems.

10. **Healthcare / Well-being**

    - **Deuteronomy Parallel:**
        - "Cursed shall be the fruit of your body" (v18)
        - "The Lord will make a plague cling to you" (v21)
        - "The Lord will strike you with wasting disease, with fever and inflammation" (v.22)
        - "The Lord will strike you with the boils of Egypt, with tumors, with the scab and with the itch, from which you cannot be healed." (v27)
        - "The Lord will strike you with madness and blindness and confusion of heart" (v28)
        - "The soles of your feet to the top of your head will be covered with painful boils" (v.35)
        - "Then the Lord will bring upon you and your descendants extraordinary plagues, great the prolonged plagues and serious and prolonged diseases" (v59)
        - "Moreover, the diseases of Egypt") v60-61
        - "The Lord will give you a trembling heart" (v67)
    - **Meaning:** Health collapse—both personal and societal.
    - **Connection:** Public health is often a casualty of national decline, exacerbated by mismanagement or war. Health crises can weaken resistance and morale.

11. **Natural Resources**

    - **Deuteronomy Parallel:**

- - *"The fruit of your womb, the crops of your land and the calves of your herds will be cursed" (v.18)*
  - *"Your heavens which are over your head shall be bronze, and the earth which is under you shall be iron" (v.23)*
- **Meaning:** Environmental and agricultural failure.
- **Connection:** Environmental degradation or external resource control strips a nation of its capacity to sustain itself independently.

12. **Finance and Debt**

    - **Deuteronomy Parallel:**
      - *"The foreigner among you will rise higher and higher... you will borrow from them, but they will not borrow from you, he shall be the head and you shall be the tail" (v.43-44)*
    - **Meaning:** Debt dependency and financial servitude.
    - **Connection:** This is a direct reference to the shift in **economic sovereignty**, where financial control lies with foreign lenders or colonial powers—a precursor to loss of all other forms of independence.

Here is a quick view table:

Deuteronomy 28:15-68 reads like a prophetic blueprint of national breakdown via external and internal domination, covering:

CURSE CATEGORY	MODERN CONTROL DOMAIN
Loss of God's protection / spiritual confusion	Spirituality / Religion
Cultural shame and mockery	Culture
Crop failure, economic servitude	Economy
Foreign rulers	Rulership (Political & Government Institutions)
Military defeat	Security / Military
Blindness, confusion	Media / Information
Children taken	Education / Indoctrination
Legal helplessness	Legal System
Walls fall	Infrastructure
Diseases	Healthcare
Environmental and agricultural collapse	Natural Resources
Borrowing from others	Finance / Banking

From a biblical perspective, it is interesting to consider the prophetic words in the book of Revelation, chapter 13, where it speaks of a time soon coming when **people will not be able to buy and sell unless they have the 'mark of the beast'**. I often wonder if this 'mark of the beast' will effectively comprise a technology/infrastructure-based system that will connect the other 11 'domains of control' together to enforce population control, suppress dissent and ensure global compliance to a long-planned 'empire building' agenda? Perhaps achieving a New World Order.

> o *Then I saw another beast coming up out of the earth, and he had two horns like a lamb and spoke like a dragon. [12] And he exercises all the authority of the first beast in his presence, and causes the earth and those who dwell in it to worship the first beast, whose deadly wound was healed. [13] He performs great signs, so that he even makes fire come down from heaven on the earth in the sight of men. [14] And he deceives those who dwell on the earth by those signs which he was*

granted to do in the sight of the beast, telling those who dwell on the earth to make an image to the beast who was wounded by the sword and lived. [15] He was granted power to give breath to the image of the beast, that the image of the beast should both speak and cause as many as would not worship the image of the beast to be killed. [16] He causes all, both small and great, rich and poor, free and slave, to receive a mark on their right hand or on their foreheads, [17] **and that no one may buy or sell except one who has the mark or the name of the beast, or the number of his name.** *[18] Here is wisdom. Let him who has understanding calculate the number of the beast, for it is the number of a man: His number is 666. (Revelation 13:11-18 NKJV)*

CHAPTER SIX

Linking The Deuteronomy 28 Curses To The Reality Of Africa's Lived And Living Experience

Applying Deuteronomy 28 and the framework of national control domains to Africa reveals a powerful lens through which the continent's historical and contemporary struggles can be understood. Whether approached from a spiritual, political, or socioeconomic standpoint, many of the curses and patterns described in that biblical chapter align closely with Africa's experience of:

- Slavery
- Colonization
- Post-colonial dependency
- Resource exploitation
- Cultural erosion
- Foreign spiritual and institutional domination

Interestingly, no collective group of people in the world and no continent on earth maps as perfectly onto the Deuteronomy 28 framework as Africa does in both historical and structural terms, both historically and presently. This is something that should cause Africa and people of African descent (or connection) to want to explore biblical identities. Is this correlation merely coincidental or a sign to point to a truth that 'the empires' that have conquered Africa have tried to keep concealed?

Here's how each 'domain of control' and the link to Deuteronomy 28:15-68 connect to Africa and the African diaspora's reality:

1. Spirituality / Religion

- **Deuteronomy Link:**
    - *"You will serve other gods... gods of wood and stone" (v.36)*
    - *"You shall serve gods which neither you nor your fathers have known – wood and stone". (v64)*

- **African Reality:**
    - **Indigenous spirituality** was often demonised, suppressed, or replaced by foreign religions during colonisation.
    - Today, many African nations are deeply spiritual, but the dominant religious structures of Catholicism, Christianity and Islam are rooted in **Western or Arab influence,** creating **external spiritual dependencies.**
    - Religious leaders sometimes promote passivity instead of transformation, echoing colonial teachings of "suffer now, be rewarded in heaven.", and likewise spread doctrines that have been established that are contrary to the truth of ancient scriptures.

The majority of the further writings in this book will address this area as it is the most important 'domain of control' that Africa needs to break out of if Africa is to reestablish its position of control in the other 11 domains.

2. **Culture**

- **Deuteronomy Link:**
    - *"Cursed shall you be when you come in and cursed shall you be when you go out" (v19)*
    - *"Your sons and your daughters shall be given to another people" (v32)*
    - *"You shall become an object of horror, scorn and ridicule among all the nations (racial slur)" (v.37)*
    - *"You shall beget sons and daughters, but they shall not be yours, for they shall go into captivity" (v41)*
    - *"The sensitive and very refined man among you will be hostile toward his brother, toward the wife of his bosom and towards the rest of his children" (v54)*
    - *"Likewise, the tender and delicate woman will refuse the husband of her bosom and reject and kill her children" (v56-57)*

- **African Reality:**
    - Colonial education and media taught Africans to see their own cultures as **primitive or backward.**
    - African languages, clothing, and traditions were replaced with European standards.
    - Today, most African youth see Western culture as superior, which is a direct outcome of cultural subjugation.

3. Economy

- **Deuteronomy Link:**
    - *"Cursed shall you be in the city, and cursed shall you be in the country"* (v16)
    - *"Cursed shall be your basket and your kneading bowl"* (v17)
    - *"Cursed shall be the fruit of your body and the produce of your land"* (v18)
    - *"You shall not prosper in your ways, you shall only be oppressed and plundered continually, and no one shall save you"* (v29)
    - *"You shall build a house, and you shall not stay in it, you shall plant a vineyard but shall not gather its grapes"* (v30)
    - *"Your ox will be slaughtered before your eyes, your donkey shall be violently taken away from you, your sheep shall be given to your enemies"* (v31)
    - *"A nation you do not know shall eat the fruit of your land and the produce of your labor and you shall be oppressed and crushed continually"* (v33)
    - *"You will sow much seed in the field but harvest little"* (v.38)
    - *"You shall plant vineyards and tend them, but you shall neither drink of the wine nor gather the grapes"* (v39)
    - *"You shall have olive trees throughout your territory, but you shall not anoint yourself with the oil"* (v40)
    - *"Locusts shall consume all your trees and the produce of your land"* (v42)

- o   *"You shall be plucked off the land" (v63)*
- **African Reality:**
  - o   Africa is rich in **natural resources,** yet many countries remain poor because the value is extracted by **foreign corporations.**
  - o   Systems of **neo-colonialism** keep African economies dependent on Western powers, China, or global institutions like the IMF and World Bank, which establish sole control on the terms of the engagements.
  - o   Widespread unemployment and poverty persist despite massive resource wealth.

4. Rulership (Political & Government Institutions)

- **Deuteronomy Link:**
  - o   *"You shall serve your enemies" (v47)*
  - o   *"The Lord will bring a nation against you... they will reign over you, and eat the increase of your livestock and the produce of your land, they shall not leave you grain or new wine or oil, or the increase of your cattle and the offspring of your flocks" (v.49–51)*
  - o   *"They shall besiege you at all your gates until your high and fortified walls come down throughout your land" (v52)*
- **African Reality:**
  - o   Colonisers dismantled traditional governance systems and replaced them with **European-style bureaucracies.**
  - o   After independence, many leaders were **installed or supported by foreign power**s (e.g., France, UK, Belgium,

USA, etc) to protect external interests.

- Corruption often persists due to **institutional designs** that reward previous colonial interests and proxy local elites.

5. Military / Security

- **Deuteronomy Link:**
    - *"Your enemies will oppress you at all your gates" (v.52)*
    - *"The Lord will cause you to be defeated before your enemies" (v.25)*

- **African Reality:**
    - Post-independence Africa saw **foreign-trained militaries** used to enforce internal repression or foreign interests.
    - Many coups were either backed or tolerated by global powers.
    - Ongoing insecurity (e.g., terrorism, civil wars) is often worsened by foreign arms sales and geopolitical meddling.
    - Foreign military bases and operations on the continent.
    - Sponsored wars and conflicts.

6. Media / Information

- **Deuteronomy Link:**
    - *"The Lord will send on you cursing confusion" (v.20)*
    - *"You will grope about at noon as the blind grope in the dark" (v.29)*

- **African Reality:**
  - African media have long been dominated by **foreign news outlets** (e.g., BBC, CNN, Al Jazeera), which frame narratives about the continent.
  - Western portrayals of Africa as poor, chaotic, or dangerous shape both **external policies and internal identity.**
  - Independent journalism is often stifled by political elites or foreign influence.

7. Education

- **Deuteronomy Link:**
  - *"Your children will be given to another people..." (v.32)*
- **African Reality:**
  - Colonial education trained Africans to serve colonial administrations and not to govern or innovate independently.
  - Curriculum in many African countries still emphasises **European history and literature** over local knowledge.
  - The **"brain drain"** continues, as the most educated Africans often leave for better opportunities abroad.

8. Legal System / Justice

- **Deuteronomy Link:**
  - *"No one will save you" (v.29)*
- **African Reality:**

- Legal systems in Africa are often colonial holdovers using **Roman, British, or French codes**, which are not suitable or applicable to local contexts.
- Justice is often inaccessible or biased, especially for the poor or marginalised.
- Elites often avoid accountability through manipulated legal systems.

9. Technology / Infrastructure

- **Deuteronomy Link:**
  - *"Your fortified walls... will come down" (v.52)*
- **African Reality:**
  - Infrastructure in many regions is **underdeveloped or externally financed**, giving others control over its construction and operation.
  - Digital dependence on Western or Chinese tech firms raises issues of surveillance and data sovereignty.

10. Healthcare

- **Deuteronomy Link:**
  - *"Cursed shall be the fruit of your body" (v.18)*
  - *'The Lord will make a plague cling to you" (v.21)*
  - *"The Lord will strike you with wasting disease, with fever and inflammation" (v.22)*
  - *"The Lord will strike you with the boils of Egypt, with tumors, with the scab and with the itch, from which you cannot be healed." (v.27)*

- "The Lord will strike you with madness and blindness and confusion of heart" (v.28)
- "The soles of your feet to the top of your head will be covered with painful boils" (v.35)
- "Then the Lord will bring upon you and your descendants extraordinary plagues, great the prolonged plagues and serious and prolonged diseases" (v.59)
- "Moreover, the diseases of Egypt") v.60-61
- "The Lord will give you a trembling heart" (v.67)

- **African Reality:**
  - Public health systems are often **under-resourced and externally funded.**
  - Disease outbreaks (e.g., HIV/AIDS, Ebola) have been **exacerbated by weak systems** and foreign experimental interventions.
  - Dependency on NGOs and global health institutions limits **national sovereignty in health policy** and exposes Africa's people to sinister agendas.

11. Natural Resources

- **Deuteronomy Link:**
  - "The fruit of your womb, the crops of your land and the calves of your herds will be cursed" (v.18)
  - "Your heavens which are over your head shall be bronze, and the earth which is under you shall be iron" (v.23)
  - "The produce of your land will be consumed by others" (v.33)

- **African Reality:**
  - Africa supplies **critical minerals, oil, and agricultural goods,** yet profits are exported.
  - Land grabs and foreign agribusiness deals reduce local control.
  - Resource wealth often fuels **conflict** and elite enrichment, not national development.

12. Finance and Debt

- **Deuteronomy Link:**
  - *"You will borrow and not lend" (v.44)*
  - *"The foreigner among you will rise higher and higher... you will borrow from them, but they will not borrow from you, he shall be the head and you shall be the tail" (v.43-44)*

- **African Reality:**
  - Most African countries carry **massive external debt,** often to the IMF, World Bank, or China.
  - These debts come with policy conditions that restrict autonomy (e.g., cuts to education, health).
  - Financial systems remain largely **foreign-dominated,** including banking, insurance, and fintech sectors, which enables the free outflow of illicit profiteering and laundering from Africa.

The list of curses listed in Deuteronomy finishes off with the Most High taking the people (whom He established a covenant but they broke it) back to Egypt in ships, being offered for sale to the enemy, with no one to redeem them (buy them out of slavery) (v68).

> ○ *"And the Lord will take you back to Egypt in ships, by the way of which I said to you, 'You shall never see it again.' And there you shall be offered for sale to your enemies as male and female slaves, but no one will buy you."* (Deuteronomy 28:68 NKJV)

This final verse paints the picture of the literal forms of chattel slavery that Africa has experienced.

Africa has experienced various forms of slavery throughout its history. Here are some of the different types of slavery that took place in Africa:

- **Trans-Saharan Slave Trade (7th-19th centuries):** This trade involved the enslavement of Africans by Arab and Berber traders, who transported them across the Sahara Desert to the Mediterranean region.
- **Transatlantic Slave Trade (15th-19th centuries):** This infamous trade saw millions of Africans forcibly enslaved and transported to the Americas, primarily by European colonisers.
- **Indian Ocean Slave Trade (14th-20th centuries):** This trade involved the enslavement of Africans and Asians, who were transported to the Middle East, India, and other parts of Asia.
- **Domestic Slavery (pre-colonial and colonial periods):** Many African societies practised domestic slavery, where enslaved people were integrated into households and communities.
- **Debt Bondage (pre-colonial and colonial periods):** This form of slavery involved nations being forced into servitude to pay off debts or fines.
- **Child Slavery (pre-colonial and colonial periods):** Children were often enslaved in Africa, particularly in the context of

domestic slavery or as soldiers.
- **Sex Trafficking and Forced Marriage (ongoing):** Unfortunately, sex trafficking and forced marriage continue to be significant problems in many African countries today.
- **Modern-Day Slavery (ongoing):** Many forms of modern-day slavery persist in Africa, including forced labour, child labour, and human trafficking.

It is a fact of truth that most of the Western world's base economies were built by the free labour of African slaves and the free resources obtained from the mineral riches of Africa through colonisation.

Below is the answer I got from ChatGPT when I put in the following request: "give me a summary on the topic on the foundation of the USA and European economies being built on free slave labour from Africa and access to Africa's resources through colonization".

ChatGPT said:

Summary: The Foundation of the USA and European Economies on African Slave Labor and Colonization

The economic rise of both the United States and European powers was significantly fueled by the exploitation of Africa, first through the transatlantic slave trade and later via colonization and resource extraction.

Slave Labor as Economic Engine:

Between the 16th and 19th centuries, over 12 million Africans were forcibly taken from the continent and enslaved, primarily in the Americas. In the U.S., the labor of African slaves was central to the growth of key industries such as cotton, tobacco, sugar, and rice, especially in the Southern states. This unpaid labor produced enormous profits for plantation owners, banks, insurance companies, and trading firms, many of which became the backbone of the U.S. economy.

In Europe, nations like Britain, France, Portugal, and the Netherlands accumulated massive wealth through their involvement in the slave trade, slave-run plantations in the Caribbean and the Americas, and the shipping industries that supported them.

Colonization and Resource Extraction:

From the late 19th century during the "Scramble for Africa," European powers divided and colonized nearly the entire African continent. This allowed direct control over Africa's vast natural resources, including gold, diamonds, rubber, oil, copper, and agricultural products. Colonial powers structured African economies to serve European interests, extracting raw materials for European industries while stifling local development.

Economic Legacy:

The profits from slavery and colonialism helped finance the Industrial Revolution in Europe and the economic expansion of the United States. These systems created structural advantages that positioned Western nations as global economic powers, while leaving African nations underdeveloped, exploited, and politically unstable even after gaining independence.

This history underscores how Western economic dominance was deeply tied to systems of oppression and exploitation, the consequences of which continue to shape global inequalities today. (Source ChatGPT)

ChatGPT interestingly gives a very clear answer that supports everything that has already been covered above regarding how the

Western world has applied and continues to apply the 'domains of control' for the purpose of plundering Africa and growing their economies.

As I once said to a friend, "If Africa had access to 400 years of free labour and free resources from other people, Africa would be an economic superpower. The notion that America and the Western world are economically prosperous because of Judeo-Christian principles is the biggest fallacy – they are economically powerful because they used the 'domains of control' to plunder others for their benefit."

What Africa has had to endure is part of the curse described in Deuteronomy 28.

It is worthwhile noting that the Bible speaks of the **trading of human bodies and souls** as one of the main commodities that scripture refers to as Babylon, an 'empire' whose collapse is spoken of in Revelation 18:9-18

As it is written:

- *"The kings of the earth who committed fornication and lived luxuriously with her will weep and lament for her, when they see the smoke of her burning, [10] standing at a distance for fear of her torment, saying, 'Alas, alas, that great city Babylon, that mighty city! For in one hour your judgment has come.' [11] "And the merchants of the earth will weep and mourn over her, for no one buys their merchandise anymore: [12] merchandise of gold and silver, precious stones and pearls, fine linen and purple, silk and scarlet, every kind of citron wood, every kind of object of ivory, every kind of object of most precious wood, bronze, iron, and marble; [13] and cinnamon and incense, fragrant oil and frankincense, wine and oil, fine flour and wheat, cattle and* sheep, horses and chariots, and **bodies and souls of men.** *[14] The fruit that your soul longed for has gone from you, and all the things which are rich and splendid have gone from you, and you shall find them no more at all. [15] The merchants of these things, who became rich by her, will stand at a distance for fear of her torment, weeping and wailing, [16] and saying, 'Alas, alas, that great city that was clothed in fine linen, purple, and scarlet, and adorned with gold and precious stones and pearls! [17] For in one hour such great riches came to nothing.' Every shipmaster, all who travel by ship, sailors, and as many as trade on the sea, stood at a distance [18] and cried out when they saw the smoke of her burning, saying, 'What is like this great city?'* (Revelation 18:9-18 NKJV)

Here is a summarised table of Deuteronomy 28 vs. Africa with a domain-by-domain comparison.

DOMAIN OF CONTROL	THE DEUTERONOMY 28 CURSE	AFRICAN REALITY
Spirituality / Religion	"You will serve other gods..." (v.36)	Indigenous religions replaced or suppressed by foreign systems; spiritual dependency on outside teachings
Culture	"You will become a byword..." (v.37)	Cultural self-rejection, preference for Western norms, loss of native languages and traditions
Economy	"Foreigners will eat the fruit of your labor..." (v.33)	Resource-rich continent with wealth extracted by foreign corporations; high poverty and unemployment
Rulership (Political & Government Institutions)	"A nation you do not know will rule over you..." (v.36)	Colonial rule was replaced with foreign-backed regimes and ongoing political interference

DOMAIN OF CONTROL	THE DEUTERONOMY 28 CURSE	AFRICAN REALITY
Military / Security	"You will be defeated before your enemies..." (v.25)	Internal insecurity, foreign military bases, reliance on external aid and training
Media / Information	"You will grope at noon..." (v.29)	Foreign control of narratives, limited indigenous media power, and misinformation shaping perceptions
Education	"Your children will be given to other people..." (v.32)	Eurocentric curricula: brain drain of skilled youth; low investment in education rooted in local realities
Legal System / Justice	"You will be oppressed and robbed, and none will save you..." (v.29)	Inaccessible or corrupt justice systems; legal structures are often still colonial in design
Technology / Infrastructure	"Your fortified walls will fall..." (v.52)	Infrastructure underdeveloped or foreign-controlled; digital sovereignty issues
Healthcare / Social Services	"The Lord will strike you with disease..." (v.22, 27)	Underfunded health systems; dependence on foreign aid, vaccines, and programs
Natural Resources	"Your land's produce will be consumed by others..." (v.33)	Minerals, oil, and farmland are exploited by external interests; local communities see little benefit
Finance / Banking	"You will borrow and not lend..." (v.44)	Massive external debt burdens; IMF, World Bank, and China influence policy; financial dependence

In conclusion, the Deuteronomy 28 pattern of curses in Africa can be seen both as a spiritual and geopolitical diagnosis of Africa's long struggle with:

- Spiritual confusion

- Foreign domination
- Internal corruption
- Identity and Cultural erosion
- Economic and institutional dependency

To conclude this section, it is important to include a summary of what has happened to the rest of the African family, the family in the Americas and other parts of the world, the descendants of those taken during the Transatlantic Slave Trade.

- **Spirituality:** Stripped of ancestral faith, given distorted theology to reinforce slavery.
- **Culture:** True identity deliberately erased (names, language, history)
- **Economy:** Generations of forced labour, exclusion from wealth-building systems
- **Justice:** Structural racism in policing and the legal system.
- **Education:** Segregated, underfunded schools; curriculum omits African roots.
- **Media/Perception:** Portrayed as criminal or inferior in mainstream culture.

Now that we have spoken about the problem, we need solutions.

The big question for every African who has this knowledge and understanding should be, 'What is the solution, and what do we need to do to redeem this 'cursed' position we find ourselves in?'

This critical query will be addressed further.

But, before we move on, it is important to emphatically reiterate the reasons for the blessings (Deuteronomy 28:1-2) and the curses

(Deuteronomy 28:15). By accurately diagnosing the root issues, we can be directed to find effective solutions.

- *"Now it shall come to pass,* **if you diligently obey the voice of the Lord your God, to observe carefully all His commandments which I command you today,** *that the Lord your God will set you high above all nations of the earth. [2] And all these blessings shall come upon you and overtake you, because you obey the voice of the Lord your God: (Deuteronomy 28:1-2 NKJV)*
- *"But it shall come to pass,* **if you do not obey the voice of the Lord your God, to observe carefully all His commandments and His statutes which I command you today,** *that all these curses will come upon you and overtake you: (Deuteronomy 28:15 NKJV)*

As I believe has been clearly shown, Africa is currently in 'the curse' and we need to find the antidote that will shift us into 'the blessing'.

Other indigenous people ('the conquered') across the world

Since this book is mainly targeted towards an African audience, it does not go into detail concerning other indigenous peoples across the world who have faced similar conquest and control. Such is a similar story for the Indigenous Peoples of the Americas (especially Native Americans) and other Aboriginal groups (Australia, New Zealand, Pacific Islands, etc.). These are people who carry the same story of:

- **Spirituality:** Indigenous religions were outlawed or demonised by missionaries.
- **Culture:** Erasure of languages, traditions, and names; use of boarding school systems.
- **Economy:** Land dispossession; poverty on reservations;

- systemic exclusion.
- **Military/Security:** Massacres, forced removals (e.g. Trail of Tears in the USA).
- **Education:** Generational indoctrination through colonial schools.
- **Health:** Widespread disease, trauma, poor healthcare infrastructure, and alcoholism/drug abuse.

The Holy scriptures give us insight into the fall of empires that have already been predetermined in the 'divine script' that The Most High GOD of Abraham, Isaac and Jacob has established. The empires and kingdoms of 'man' shall be broken into pieces and destroyed as the empire/Kingdom of the GOD of Abraham, Isaac and Jacob is established as the everlasting empire/Kingdom.

The biblical book of Daniel gives some insight into this.

- *"This is the dream. Now we will tell the interpretation of it before the king. [37] You, O king, are a king of kings. For the God of heaven has given you a kingdom, power, strength, and glory; [38] and wherever the children of men dwell, or the beasts of the field and the birds of the heaven, He has given them into your hand, and has made you ruler over them all—you are this head of gold. [39] But after you shall arise another kingdom inferior to yours; then another, a third kingdom of bronze, which shall rule over all the earth. [40] And the fourth kingdom shall be as strong as iron, inasmuch as iron breaks in pieces and shatters everything; and like iron that crushes, that kingdom will break in pieces and crush all the others. [41] Whereas you saw the feet and toes, partly of potter's clay and partly of iron, the kingdom shall be divided; yet the strength of the iron shall be in it, just as you saw the iron mixed with ceramic clay. [42] And as the toes of the feet were partly of iron and partly of clay, so the kingdom shall be partly strong and partly fragile. [43] As you saw iron mixed with ceramic clay, they will mingle with the seed of men; but they will not adhere to one another, just as iron does not mix with clay.* [44] **And in the days of these kings the God of heaven will set up a kingdom which shall never be destroyed; and the kingdom shall not be left to other people; it shall break in pieces and consume all these kingdoms, and it shall stand forever.** *[45] Inasmuch as you saw that the stone was cut out of the mountain without hands, and that it broke in pieces the iron, the bronze, the clay, the silver, and the gold—the great God has made known to the king what will come to pass after this. The dream is certain, and its interpretation is sure." (Daniel 2:36-45 NKJV)*

Likewise, the book of Revelation Chapter 11:15-18 gives us the conclusion for the conquering empires of man, as all the so-called world superpowers (kingdoms of this world), are subdued. Britannica insightfully defines a superpower as "a state that cannot be ignored on the world stage and without whose cooperation no world problem can be solved."

The following quote is from the https://worldpopulationreview.com/country-rankings/world-superpowers website. "As of now, only the United States meets the standards to be classified as a superpower. However, this classification has faced scrutiny in recent times. Presently, academic discussions have identified China, the European Union, India, and Russia as potential contenders for achieving superpower status." There might be great prophetic insight in the statement that 'only the United States meets the standards to be classified as a superpower'.

YAHUAH has no regard for the kingdoms of this world, as those that tried to rule and destroy the earth shall themselves be destroyed.

- *And the seventh angel sounded; and there were great voices in heaven, saying,* **The kingdoms of this world are become the kingdoms of our ALAHYM, and of His MASHYACH; and He shall reign for ever and ever.** *[16] And the four and twenty elders, which sat before YAHUAH on their seats, fell upon their faces, and worshipped YAHUAH, [17] saying, We give thee thanks, O YAHUAH ALAHYM Almighty, which art, and wast, and art to come;* **because thou hast taken to thee thy great power, and hast reigned.** *[18] And the nations were angry, and thy wrath is come, and the time of the dead, that they should be judged, and that thou shouldest give reward unto thy servants the prophets, and to the saints, and them that fear thy name, small and great;* **and shouldest destroy them which destroy the earth.** *(Revelation 11:15-18 KJV)*

CHAPTER SEVEN

The Biblical Answer To Why This Has Happened

From the two scriptures already given several times from Deuteronomy, we can deduce that the reason the curse came is due to disobedience.

- o *"Now it shall come to pass,* **if you diligently obey the voice of the Lord* your God,** *to observe carefully all His commandments which I command you today, that the Lord* your God will set you high above all nations of the earth. [2] And all these blessings shall come upon you and overtake you, because you obey the voice of the Lord* your God: (Deuteronomy 28:1-2 NKJV)*
- o *"But it shall come to pass,* **if you do not obey the voice of the Lord* your God,** *to observe carefully all His commandments and His statutes which I command you today, that all these curses will come upon you and overtake you: (Deuteronomy 28:15 NKJV)*

The GOD of Abraham, Isaac, and Jacob entrusted His word to a chosen people, making them custodians of His covenant

— an agreement intended, through them, to be extended to all humanity. Other nations did not receive this covenant directly, for it was God's purpose that, through the seed of Jacob, it would be made known to every tongue, tribe, and nation. Yet because the seed of Jacob entered into and accepted its terms, they bear the highest level of accountability and responsibility for it — far more than those nations who neither knew of the covenant nor entered into it.

- *He declares His word to Jacob, His statutes and His judgments to Israel. He has not dealt thus with any nation; And as for His judgments, they have not known them. Praise the Lord*! (Psalms 147:19-20 NKJV)*
- *For He established a testimony in Jacob, and appointed a law in Israel, Which He commanded our fathers, that they should make them known to their children; (Psalms 78:5 NKJV)*

There was and is an agreement (Covenant) between the GOD of Abraham, Isaac and Jacob with His people (the seed of Jacob), and what happened (and still happens) to them would always be based on the terms of that agreement which states that if they obey the terms of the agreement, they will be blessed, but if they disobey or break the terms of the agreement they will be cursed.

And so, the position that they (the seed of Jacob) find themselves in will always be determined by the choices they make. Even though there might be an oppressor ('the conqueror') who would conquer them, the reason for the GOD of Abraham, Isaac and Jacob allowing it to happen would be because of their own choice of disobedience.

THE BIBLICAL ANSWER TO WHY THIS HAS HAPPENED

This means what happened to them (the seed of Jacob) was neither the fault of the GOD of Abraham, Isaac, and Jacob, nor was it the fault of the oppressor ('the conqueror') who conquers them. It would be their own fault for the choice they made to disobey and for breaking the terms of the agreement they had with the GOD of Abraham, Isaac, and Jacob.

The people in covenant (agreement) with the GOD of Abraham, Isaac and Jacob would need to take responsibility and accountability for their own actions as per their agreement with their GOD.

If we conclude that there is a link between the curse of Africa and that which the ALAHYM of Abraham, Isaac and Jacob said in Deuteronomy 28, and also conclude that Africans are the people on this earth who most fit the identity to which the curses apply, we would need to find out what the solution is to overcome them biblically.

Why did the GOD of Abraham, Isaac and Jacob not prevent it?

Why did the GOD of Abraham, Isaac and Jacob allow it?

Is it possible that the Most High GOD, the GOD of Abraham, Isaac and Jacob, our Father and Creator allowed Africa to be cursed and in fact orchestrated our conquest because our biblical identity as the people He made the covenant (agreement) with and so He ensures that the terms of that agreement are adhered to without compromise (otherwise He would be a GOD who lies and breaks agreement). He allowed it to happen as fulfilment of what He foretold (as prophesied through the Holy prophets) would happen to us in accordance with the choices we make based on the terms of the agreement (covenant) - receiving blessings for obedience and receiving curses for disobedience.

The answer is quite simply YES; The GOD of Abraham, Isaac and Jacob allowed it and, in fact orchestrated it because He said so when He gave us the terms of the agreement (the covenant) and told us that everything would be determined (good or bad) based on the choices we make. Obedience according to the terms of the agreement would allow us to walk on a path of 'the blessing and life'. Disobedience to the terms of the agreement would set us on the path of 'the curse and death'. As it is written in Deuteronomy 30:1-20 (NKJV).

- *"Now it shall come to pass, when all these things come upon you, the blessing and the curse which I have set before you,* and you call them to mind among all the nations where the Lord* your God drives you, [2] *and you return to the Lord* your God and obey His voice, according to all that I command you today, you and your children, with all your heart and with all your soul, [3] that the Lord* your God will bring you back from captivity, and have compassion on you, and gather you again from all the nations where the Lord* your God has scattered you.* [4] If any of you are driven out to the farthest parts under heaven, from there the Lord* your God will gather you, and from there He will bring you. [5] Then the Lord* your God will bring you to the land which your fathers possessed, and you shall possess it. **He will prosper you and multiply you more than your fathers.** [6] And the Lord* your God will circumcise your heart and the heart of your descendants, *to love the Lord* your God with all your heart and with all your soul, that you may live. [7] "Also the Lord* your God will put all these curses on your enemies and on those who hate you, who persecuted you. [8] And you will again obey the voice of the Lord* and do all His commandments which I command you today.* **[9] The Lord* your God will make you abound in all the work of your hand, in the fruit of your body, in the increase of your livestock, and in the produce of your land for good. For the *Lord will again rejoice over you for good as He rejoiced over your fathers, [10] if you obey the voice of the Lord* your God, to keep His commandments and His statutes which are written in this Book of the Law, and if you turn to the Lord* your God with all your heart and with all your soul.** *[11] "For this commandment which I command you today is not too mysterious for you, nor is it far off. [12] It is not in heaven, that you should say, 'Who will ascend into heaven for us and bring it to us, that we may hear it and do it?' [13] Nor is it beyond the sea, that you should say, 'Who will go over the sea for us and bring it to us, that we may hear it and do it?' [14] But the word is very near you, in your mouth and in your heart, that you may do it. [15] "See, I have set before you today life and good, death and evil, [16] in that I command you today to love the Lord* your God, to walk in His ways, and to keep His commandments, His statutes, and His judgments, that you may live and multiply; and the Lord* your God will bless you in the land which you go to possess. [17] But if your heart turns away so that*

> *you do not hear, and are drawn away, and worship other gods and serve them, [18] I announce to you today that you shall surely perish; you shall not prolong your days in the land which you cross over the Jordan to go in and possess.* **[19] *I call heaven and earth as witnesses today against you, that I have set before you life and death, blessing and cursing; therefore choose life, that both you and your descendants may live;*** *[20] that you may love the Lord* your God, that you may obey His voice, and that you may cling to Him, for He is your life and the length of your days; and that you may dwell in the land which the Lord* swore to your fathers, to Abraham, Isaac, and Jacob, to give them." (Deuteronomy 30:1-20 NKJV)*

I must share a comment the editor of the book wrote to me when she reached this point.

"I would just like to clarify whether you are saying that Africans are the covenant people, thereby replacing Israel… or whether, through some other means, Africans came into contact with the Sovereign God who then placed the same demand on them as He had on Israel. Whether it is either of the two or a third option, I recommend fleshing out this biblical identity more strongly to support the position you have laid out."

I, therefore, felt that it would be a question every person reading will also be asking at this point and is worthy of addressing with the following response below.

The unravelling of true biblical identities is made in Chapters 15 and 18 to substantiate the claim I am making that the covenant was established with people of African descent.

THE BIBLICAL ANSWER TO WHY THIS HAPPENED

- Tribes of Africa, we cannot point our finger to blame and hate 'the oppressor' ("the conqueror") or even seek revenge. What has happened to us is because of the choices we and our forefathers made, which violated the agreement we have with the GOD of Abraham, Isaac and Jacob.

- Tribes of Africa, the extremely good news is that the GOD of Abraham, Isaac and Jacob, the one who established the covenant (the agreement) with our forefathers, has given His solution to take us from the curse to the blessing.

This is what the next few sections of this book will now explore so that we can reach a solution that will invoke the GOD of Abraham, Isaac and Jacob to fight for our freedom and restoration according to what He said in the agreement (covenant) He made with our ancestors/forefathers.

"Laying the foundation to understand the Creator's design"

Section 3

Contents

Chapter 8. Who is our God, what is His name, and who is He?

- His Name
- The confrontation and battle of the Gods
- Who is YAHUAH?
- Whose name are we calling upon?
- YAHUAH is love, love is YAHUAH

Chapter 9. Biblical definitions and equations

- YAHUAH's Commandments
- YAHUAH's Law
- The foundation of the Law – the 10 Commandments
- The Greatest Commandment
- Linking the 10 Commandments to the Greatest Commandment
- Sin according to YAHUAH
- Establishing what Truth is
- Definition of 'what is good' to YAHUAH
- How Abba YAHUAH wants to be loved
- The obedience (love) of YAHUSHA
- Defining 'the Word of YAHUAH' & the overcoming saints and remnant

This marks the point in the book where we now turn to depend upon the testimony of the Holy Scriptures.

From this point onwards, each chapter will be extensively driven by scripture references, because the Holy scriptures must speak for themselves. It is also through the scriptures that the Spirit of the (ALAHYM) GOD of Abraham, Isaac and Jacob will confirm truth, or likewise reprove where there has been error in the presentation of the points being made.

I, therefore, ask that you do not take the words or opinions of a man (mine) that can and are often flawed as the truth, but that you allow the Spirit of the (ALAHYM) GOD of Abraham, Isaac and Jacob to teach, guide and lead you into all truth on each matter that is presented.

The scripture reference passages will carry highlights so that the volume of **'The Voice'** in those scriptures is increased to help discern the content that is shared together with them.

The key is for **'The Voice'** to speak above the content shared.

Give unto YAHUAH, O you mighty ones, Give unto YAHUAH glory and strength. [2] Give unto YAHUAH the glory due to His name; Worship YAHUAH in the beauty of holiness. [3] **The voice of YAHUAH is over the waters;** *The God of glory thunders; YAHUAH is over many waters. [4]* **The voice of YAHUAH is powerful; The voice of YAHUAH** *is full of majesty. [5]* **The voice of YAHUAH** *breaks the cedars, Yes, YAHUAH splinters the cedars of Lebanon. [6] He makes them also skip like a calf, Lebanon and Sirion like a young wild ox. [7]* **The voice of YAHUAH** *divides the flames of fire. [8]* **The voice of YAHUAH** *shakes the wilderness; YAHUAH shakes the*

Wilderness of Kadesh. *[9]* **The voice of YAHUAH** *makes the deer give birth and strips the forests bare; And in His temple everyone says, "Glory!" [10] YAHUAH sat enthroned at the Flood, and YAHUAH sits as King forever. [11] YAHUAH will give strength to His people; YAHUAH will bless His people with peace. (Psalm 29:1-11 NKJV)*

CHAPTER EIGHT

Who Is God, What is His Name, and Who is He?

There are many gods and many lords that are worshipped and served throughout the world. It was like that in ancient times, and it is still applicable today.

In Old Testament times, we see Pharaoh saying to Moses that he (Pharaoh) does not know the GOD of the Hebrews that Moses was presenting to him, because He only knew his Egyptian gods. Names like Ra or perhaps 'the holy trinity' of Egypt, Osiris, Isis and Horus come to mind as some of the hundreds of gods Egypt knew and worshipped.

'As it is written' -

And afterward Moses and Aaron went in, and told Pharaoh, thus saith the LORD* God of Israel, Let my people go, that they may hold a feast unto me in the wilderness. **And Pharaoh said, Who is the LORD*, that I should obey his voice to let Israel go? I know not the LORD*, neither will I let Israel go.** *And they said, The God of the Hebrews hath met with us: let us go, we pray thee, three days' journey into the desert, and sacrifice unto the LORD* our God; lest he* *fall upon us with pestilence, or with the sword. (Exodus 5:1-3 KJV)*

Just like in New Testament times, when Paul was ministering in the Greco-Roman territories, he encountered the many gods that they worshipped. Probably gods like Zeus, Poseidon, Hades, Apollo, Saturn, the queen of heaven, Diana, Sol Invictus (who Emperor Constantine worshipped), Jupiter, Juno, Minerva, Mercury, to name a few.

'As it is written':

- *Now while Paul waited for them at Athens, his spirit was stirred in him, when he saw the city wholly given to idolatry. Therefore disputed he in the synagogue with the Jews, and with the devout persons, and in the market daily with them that met with him. Then certain philosophers of the Epicureans, and of the Stoicks, encountered him. And some said, what will this babbler say? other some,* **He seemeth to be a setter forth of strange gods:** *because he preached unto them Jesus, and the resurrection. (Acts 17:16-18 KJV)*
- *Then Paul stood in the midst of Mars' hill, and said, Ye men of Athens, I perceive that in all things ye are too superstitious. For as I passed by, and beheld your devotions,* **I found an altar with this inscription, TO THE UNKNOWN GOD.** *Whom therefore ye ignorantly worship, him declare I unto you. God that made the world and all things therein, seeing that he is Lord of heaven and earth, dwelleth not in temples made with hands; neither is worshipped with men's hands, as though he needed anything, seeing he giveth to all life, and breath, and all things; and hath made of one blood all nations of men for to dwell on all the face of the earth, and hath determined the times before appointed, and the bounds of their habitation; that they should seek the Lord, if haply*

> *they might feel after him, and find him, though he be not far from every one of us: for in him we live, and move, and have our being; as certain also of your own poets have said, For we are also his offspring. (Acts 22-28 KJV)*

- After these things were ended, Paul purposed in the spirit, when he had passed through Macedonia and Achaia, to go to Yarushalayim (Jerusalem), saying, After I have been there, I must also see Rome. So he sent into Macedonia two of them that ministered unto him, Timotheus and Erastus; but he himself stayed in Asia for a season. And the same time there arose no small stir about that way. For a certain man named Demetrius, a silversmith, **which made silver shrines for Diana**, brought no small gain unto the craftsmen; whom he called together with the workmen of like occupation, and said, Sirs, ye know that by this craft we have our wealth. Moreover ye see and hear, that not alone at Ephesus, but almost throughout all Asia, this Paul hath persuaded and turned away much people, **saying that they be no gods, which are made with hands:** so that not only this our craft is in danger to be set at nought; **but also that the temple of the great goddess Diana should be despised, and her magnificence should be destroyed, whom all Asia and the world worshippeth.** And when they heard these sayings, they were full of wrath, and cried out, saying, Great is Diana of the Ephesians. (Acts 19:21-28 KJV)

Back in Old Testament times, we see that the various nations that Israel encountered had their respective gods whom they worshipped and served. Scriptures mention various pagan gods such as Dagon,

Baal, and Molech, to name a few, as it is written.

- *And you shall not let any of your descendants pass through the fire to **Molech,** nor shall you profane the name of your God: I am the Lord. (Leviticus 18:21 NKJV)*
- *You also took up the **tabernacle of Molech, And the star of your god Remphan, Images which you made to worship;** And I will carry you away beyond Babylon.' (Acts 7:43 NKJV)*
- *Then the Philistines took the ark of God and brought it from Ebenezer to Ashdod. When the Philistines took the ark of God, they brought it into the **house of Dagon and set it by Dagon.** And when the people of Ashdod arose early in the morning, there was Dagon, fallen on its face to the earth before the ark of the Lord*. So they took Dagon and set it in its place again. And when they arose early the next morning, there was Dagon, fallen on its face to the ground before the ark of the Lord*. The head of Dagon and both the palms of its hands were broken off on the threshold; only Dagon's torso was left of it. Therefore neither **the priests of Dagon** nor any who come into Dagon's house tread on the threshold of Dagon in Ashdod to this day. But the hand of the Lord* was heavy on the people of Ashdod, and He ravaged them and struck them with tumors, both Ashdod and its territory. And when the men of Ashdod saw how it was, they said, **"The ark of the God of Israel must not remain with us, for His hand is harsh toward us and Dagon our god."** (I Samuel 5:1-7 NKJV)*
- *As they called them, So they went from them; They sacrificed to the **Baals,** and burned incense to carved images. (Hosea 11:2 NKJV)*

- *God has not cast away His people whom He foreknew. Or do you not know what the Scripture says of Elijah, how he pleads with God against Israel, saying, "Lord, they have killed Your prophets and torn down Your altars, and I alone am left, and they seek my life"? But what does the divine response say to him? "I have reserved for Myself seven thousand men who have not bowed the knee to **Baal**." (Romans 11:2-4 NKJV)*
- *But then, indeed, when you did not know God, **you served those which by nature are not gods**. (Galatians 4:8 NKJV)*

In New Testament times, we see reference being made to 'Satan as being the god of this world' multiple times.

- *But if our gospel be hid, it is hid to them that are lost: in whom **the god of this world** hath blinded the minds of them which believe not, lest the light of the glorious gospel of Christ, who is the image of God, should shine unto them. (2 Corinthians 4:3-4 KJV)*
- *Now is the judgment of this world: now shall **the prince of this world** be cast out. (John 12:31 KJV)*
- *But I say, that the things which the Gentiles sacrifice, **they sacrifice to devils**, and not to God: and I would not that ye should have **fellowship with devils**. (1 Corinthians 10:20 KJV)*
- *Again, **the devil** taketh him up into an exceeding high mountain, and sheweth him all the kingdoms of the world, and the glory of them; (Matthew 4:8 KJV)*

Today we know that the different religions have their respective gods whom they worship and serve, from the God of the religion of Christianity, to the god of the religion of Judaism, to the god of the religion of Islam, to the god of the religion of Buddhism, all the way to those who worship the god of Self. Various movements like New Age have a design of who their god is, and likewise secret societies like the Freemasons, Illuminati and others too numerous to mention here.

Because of the plethora of gods, THE SOVEREIGN GOD, THE MOST HIGH, THE ANCIENT OF DAYS, THE EVERLASTING ONE, the Creator of the Heavens and the earth gave His people His Name so that it would be His identifier for them and for all the other nations they would encounter as His name is proclaimed throughout the nations.

Looking at the Strong's Concordance definition of God helps put into better context why the term or title God, without reference to a name, can be very meaningless.

Strong's Number H430 references the word, God

Original Word: אלהים

Transliterated Word: 'elôhîym in modern Hebrew (or Alahym (collective), Aluah (singular, possessive) in ancient Hebrew)

Strong's Definition says that it is the plural of H433; gods in the ordinary sense; but specifically used (in the plural {thus} especially with the article) of the supreme God; occasionally applied by way of deference to magistrates; and sometimes as a superlative: - {angels} X {exceeding} God (gods) ({-dess} {-ly}) X (very) {great} {judges} X mighty.

Brown-Driver-Briggs' defines God as: (a) rulers, judges, (b) divine ones, (c) gods, god, goddess, (e) godlike.

In the Bible, the original word translated as God is used in the following ways:

god (2074), gods (190), god's (7), judges (3), mighty (2), great (2), goddess (2), judge (1), godward (1), godly (1), exceeding (1), angels (1)

So, the word and title God/god could refer to different spiritual entities that are not the ALAHYM (GOD) of Abraham, Isaac, and Jacob.

I will be constantly referring to the Most High, Almighty, using the Paleo Hebrew word ALAHYM (collective instance) and ALUAH (singular possessive instance). I purposely do this to immerse the reader in the Paleo Hebrew language, which I further explain chapters to come.

Before Moses was sent on His assignment to be the deliverer of the children of Israel from bondage in Egypt, Moses knew he could not go and just say God has sent me, he needed to know the name he should use to identify the God who was sending him, because he knew that the Israelites had been exposed to many gods in Egypt. Likewise, THE SOVEREIGN ALUAH, THE MOST HIGH, THE ANCIENT OF DAYS, THE EVERLASTING ONE, the Creator of the heavens and the earth, the ALAHYM of the Hebrews, knew that it was time that the Israelites knew Him by name so that they would never be confused or unsure which Alahym would deliver them from bondage.

'As it is written':

> o *And Moses said unto ALUAH, Behold, when I come unto the children of Israel, and shall say unto them, The ALAHYM of your fathers hath sent me unto you; and they shall say to me, what is his name? what shall I say*

> unto them? And ALUAH said to Moses, "I AM WHO I AM. (AHAYAH)" And He said, "Thus you shall say to the children of Israel, 'I AM has sent me to you.' " ¹⁵ Moreover ALUAH said to Moses, "Thus you shall say to the children of Israel: 𐤉𐤄𐤅𐤄 YAHUAH (YHUH) ALAHYM of your fathers, the ALAHYM of Abraham, the ALAHYM of Isaac, and the ALAHYM of Jacob, has sent me to you. This is My name forever, and this is My memorial to all generations.' (Exodus 3:13-15 KJV)

- Aluah spoke further to Moses and said to him, "I am 𐤉𐤄𐤅𐤄 YAHUAH. ³ I appeared to Abraham, to Isaac and to Jacob, as El Shaddai. Yet by My Name, 𐤉𐤄𐤅𐤄 YAHUAH, did I not make Myself known to them. (Exodus 6:3 KJV)

- And she will bring forth a Son, and you shall call His name 𐤉𐤄𐤅𐤔𐤏 YAHUSHA (YAHUAH saves/YAHUAH my salvation), for He will save His people from their sins." (Matthew 1:21 KJV)

- ⁵ For even if there are so-called gods, whether in heaven or on earth (as there are many gods and many lords), ⁶ yet for us there is one 𐤉𐤄𐤅𐤄 YAHUAH, the Father, of whom are all things, and we for Him; and one Master YAHUSHA Mashiach, through whom are all things, and through whom we live. (1 Corinthians 8:5-6 KJV)

𐤉𐤄𐤅𐤄 are the Paleo (ancient) Hebrew pictograph and letter-based name which The Most High gave to Moses, and is in the original texts that were written using the Paleo Hebrew alphabet.

The name is made up of the Paleo Hebrew letters **YAD HAY UA HAY**; which is pronounced phonetically as **YAH-U--AH (YAHUAH)**, which means **'He who gave breath/gives life'**. This is the name the Most High identified Himself as to Moses and the name He has chosen mankind to call Him by as is written in the Dead Sea scrolls and other ancient Hebrew scrolls. It is the name that Greco-Roman power removed from the bible and replaced it with God or Lord.

YAHUAH is He who gives 'the breath' or **RUACH** in Hebrew. RUACH HA QADASH, which means the Holy Spirit, 'The =HA, and Holy =QADASH, and Spirit = RUACH'.

Sadly, His given name ✡YY✡⌐ ⌐Y⌐≠ YAHUAH (He who gave breath/gives life) as the God of Abraham, Isaac and Jacob was removed approximately 6,828 times from the Bible and replaced by 'The LORD' or 'God'. It seems that was an intentional move by the so-called 'church fathers' of the religion of Christianity to erase His Holy name in direct violation of the 3rd commandment, as it is written –

> o *Thou shalt not take the name of YAHUAH thy Aluah in vain; for YAHUAH will not hold him guiltless that taketh his name in vain. (Exodus 20:7 KJV)*

Similarly, the name of the SON OW✡⌐Y YAHUSHA (which is derived from the name of the Father and means 'YAHUAH IS SALVATION') was also removed and replaced by the Greek name Iesous, and then Iesus in Roman Latin and then Jesus when the letter J was introduced into the English alphabet in 1524. In some instances, He is referred to as 'the Lord'.

The name Jesus did not appear anywhere until the year 1628 in the 5th edition of the King James Version of the Bible.

It is estimated that the name YAHUSHA was replaced approximately 971 times in the King James Version Bible and around 1,046 times in the New International Version. Again, an intentional move by the so-called 'church fathers' of the religion of Christianity to remove from the Bible the name that people are to call upon to be saved. The name that we are to use when praying to the Father. The name that causes demons to tremble and flee in fear.

A name is critical, as scripture shows us.

- *There is a given name to call on to be saved. It is YAHUAH.*
  - *For whosoever shall **call upon the name** of YAHUAH shall be saved. (Romans 10:13 KJV)*
- *There is a given name to pray to the FATHER and to ask of Him. It is YAHUSHA.*
  - *And whatsoever ye shall **ask in my name**, that will I do, that the Father may be glorified in the Son. If ye shall **ask anything in my name**, I will do it. (John 14:13-14 KJV)*
  - *Ye have not chosen me, but I have chosen you, and ordained you, that ye should go and bring forth fruit, and that your fruit should remain: that whatsoever ye shall **ask of the Father in my name**, he may give it you. (John 15:16 KJV)*
  - *And in that day ye shall ask me nothing. Verily, verily, I say unto you, Whatsoever ye shall ask the Father in my name, he will give it you. Hitherto have **ye asked nothing in my name**: ask, and ye shall receive, that your joy may be full. These things have I spoken unto you in proverbs: but the time cometh, when I shall no more speak unto you in proverbs, but I shall shew you plainly of the Father. At that day **ye shall ask in my name**: and I say not unto you, that I will pray the Father for you: (John 16:23-26 KJV)*
- *There is a given name that carries the authority to cause demons to submit.*
  - *And the seventy returned again with joy, saying, Master,*

> even the devils are subject unto us **through thy name.** (Luke 10:17 KJV)

- There is a given name that every tongue will confess and every knee bow to. It is YAHUSHA.
  - *Wherefore God also hath highly exalted him, and **given him a name which is above every name:** that at the name of YAHUSHA every knee should bow, of things in heaven, and things in earth, and things under the earth; and that every tongue should confess that YAHUSHA is Master, to the glory of YAHUAH the Father. (Philippians 2:9-11 KJV)*

I have often wondered what the cause and effect is of having used (and continuing to use) the name Jesus, a man-made name that was created to replace the name YAHUSHA (or Yeshua in modern Hebrew) that the Father gave His SON.

I liken it to the following, "Imagine you are the owner of a business and you name your first born son John and place your authority in that name and instruct your workers that if they use the name of John as they run errands for you, they will immediately have access to what they need and all of what you have provided for them to do their job. But someone else comes along and gives the workers a different name to use, let's say George (because they claim that George is a translated or transliterated version of the name John), and so the workers now go about doing their errands in the name of George and completely discard the name (John) that you have given them and the name which carries your authority. I think this would cause some major problems!"

I wonder what the cause and effect of this has been, is today and will be in the future.

Could this be a major constraint that we are dealing with today in the spiritual realm because we have not been praying to the FATHER in the name that He gave His SON, but rather we have been praying to Him using a name that man has given?

I, however, do not doubt that the FATHER has a level of grace, as He knows how we have been deceived, and has hence responded to our calls to Him despite our error.

Proverbs 30:4 asks one of the most critical questions I believe the FATHER is asking all of us, as it is written:

> o *Who has ascended into heaven, or descended? Who has gathered the wind in His fists? Who has bound the waters in a garment? Who has established all the ends of the earth?* **What is His name, and what is His Son's name, if you know?** *(Proverbs 30:4 NKJV)*

Every created thing knows there is a name to praise, and it is not the title God or Lord. Creation knows the name of YAD HAY UA HAY; phonetically, YAH-U-AH (YAHUAH). Creation knows the name of 'HE WHO GIVES BREATH/GIVES LIFE'.

> o *Praise ye YAH-U-AH. Praise ye YAH-U-AH from the heavens: Praise him in the heights. [2] Praise ye Him, all his angels: Praise ye Him, all His hosts. [3] Praise ye Him, sun and moon: Praise Him, all ye stars of light. [4] Praise Him, ye heavens of heavens, and ye waters that be above the heavens. [5] Let them praise the name of YAH-U-AH: For He commanded, and they were created. [6] He hath also stablished them for ever and ever: He hath made a decree which shall not pass. [7] Praise YAH-U-AH from the earth, Ye dragons, and all deeps: [8] Fire,*

> *and hail; snow, and vapours; Stormy wind fulfilling his word: [9] Mountains, and all hills; Fruitful trees, and all cedars: [10] Beasts, and all cattle; Creeping things, and flying fowl: [11] Kings of the earth, and all people; Princes, and all judges of the earth: [12] Both young men, and maidens; Old men, and children: [13] Let them praise the name of YAH-U-AH: For His name alone is excellent; His glory is above the earth and heaven. [14] He also exalteth the horn of His people, The praise of all His saints; Even of the children of YASHARA'AL, a people near unto him. Praise ye YAH-U-AH.*
> *(Psalm 148:1-14 KJV)*

Perhaps we, as His people, are the ones who have forgotten His name and no longer praise His name and why creation is groaning for the revealing of the true sons of YAHUAH.

- **For the creation waits with eager longing for the revealing of the sons of YAHUAH.** (Romans 8:19 ESV)

One of the things that has become very clear to me during this journey is that not everyone who mentions the title 'God' or 'Lord' is referencing YAHUAH, the ALAHYM of Abraham, Isaac and Jacob. Likewise, not everyone who says 'Lord Jesus' is referencing YAHUSHA, the SON of YAHUAH, the ALAHYM of Abraham, Isaac and Jacob. In the same vein, not everyone who speaks of the spirit is referencing the Set Apart/Holy Spirit who comes of YAHUAH, the ALAHYM of Abraham, Isaac and Jacob.

It is important to recognise that 'God' and 'Lord' are titles and not names. Baal in Hebrew means Master or Lord or Possessor of Husband. Baal ('Lord') is also the name of the pagan god associated with the Canaanites and Phoenicians. This is one of the reasons

I am intentionally using the ancient Hebrew terms ALAHYM (collective) and ALUAH (singular)

The titles God and the Lord, and the very name Jesus (in replacement of YAHUSHA), have been stripped of their sacred weight, too often uttered with lips untouched by reverence and hearts void of holy fear. I guess the Bible does tell us that there is a 'god of this world' and a 'lord/ruler of this world' who is Satan, and so many use the term God and Lord to refer to him. In the past I would get excited whenever I heard someone say God or Lord, but no longer, because I have come to realise that their God and Lord could be very different to YAHUAH, the ALAHYM of Abraham, Isaac and Jacob, likewise their Jesus could be very different to YAHUSHA the SON of YAHUAH, the ALAHYM of Abraham, Isaac and Jacob and likewise the spirit they refer to could be very different to the Holy Spirit, the RUACH HA QADASH of YAHUAH, the ALAHYM of Abraham, Isaac and Jacob.

- *"Not everyone who says to me, 'Lord, Lord,' will enter the kingdom of heaven, but only the one who does the will of my Father who is in heaven. Many will say to me on that day, 'Lord, Lord, did we not prophecy in your name and in your name drive out demons and, in your name, perform many miracles?' Then I will tell them plainly, 'I never knew you. Away from me, you evildoers! (Matthew 7:21-23 KJV)*
- *"In that day" declares YAHUAH, "you will call me 'my husband'* **you will no longer call me 'my Baali'**. *(Hosea 2:16 KJV)*

The Confrontation and Battle of Gods

The confrontation of Gods played a primary role for the nation of YASHARA'AL (the bloodline descendants of Jacob, the 12 tribes) as they battled with other nations.

This is seen very clearly when YASHARA'AL was being challenged by the Philistines through Goliath. The dialogue between David and Goliath illustrates this, and importantly, David knew that as one who was in covenant with YAHUAH, the ALAHYM of Abraham, Isaac and Jacob, the battle would be settled based on His and YASHARA'AL's agreement (covenant) with their GOD (ALAHYM).

Below are excerpts from David's dialogue with Saul and his exchange with Goliath., 'as it is written':

- *Then David spoke to the men who stood by him, saying, "What shall be done for the man who kills this Philistine and takes away the reproach from YASHARA'AL?* **For who is this uncircumcised Philistine, that he should defy the armies of the living God?"**

- *But David said to Saul, "Your servant used to keep his father's sheep, and when a lion or a bear came and took a lamb out of the flock, [35] I went out after it and struck it, and delivered the lamb from its mouth; and when it arose against me, I caught it by its beard, and struck and killed it. [36] Your servant has killed both lion and bear; and this* **uncircumcised Philistine** *will be like one of them,* **seeing he has defied the armies of the living God."** *[37] Moreover David said, "YAHUAH, who delivered me from the paw of the lion and from the paw of the bear, He will deliver me from the hand of this Philistine." And Saul said to David, "Go, and YAHUAH be with you!"*

- *[43] So the Philistine said to David, "Am I a dog, that you come to me with sticks?"* **And the Philistine cursed David**

by his gods

- *[45] Then David said to the Philistine, "You come to me with a sword, with a spear, and with a javelin.* **But I come to you in the name of YAHUAH of hosts, the God of the armies of YASHARA'AL,** *whom you have defied. [46] This day YAHUAH will deliver you into my hand, and I will strike you and take your head from you. And this day I will give the carcasses of the camp of the Philistines to the birds of the air and the wild beasts of the earth,* **that all the earth may know that there is a God in YASHARA'AL.** *[47] Then all this assembly shall know that YAHUAH does not save with sword and spear;* **for the battle is YAHUAH's,** *and He will give you into our hands." (1 Samuel 17:26, 34-37, 43, 45-47 NKJV)*

We see a similar battle situation when King Jehoshaphat went to fight the joint armies of Ammon, Moab and Mount Seir, as it is written in 2 Chronicles, chapter 20. It is worthwhile reading about this encounter.

A final example in the 'confrontation and battle of Gods' is when the prophet Elijah challenged the prophets of the god Baal, as it is written:

- *[20] So Ahab sent for all the children of YASHARA'AL, and gathered the prophets together on Mount Carmel. [21] And Elijah came to all the people, and said,* **"How long will you falter between two opinions? If YAHUAH is God, follow Him; but if Baal, follow him."** *But the people answered him not a word. [22] Then Elijah said to the people, "I alone am left a prophet of YAHUAH; but* **Baal's prophets** *are four hundred and fifty men. [23] Therefore let them give us* two bulls; and let them choose one bull for themselves, cut it in pieces, and lay it on the wood, but put no fire under it; and I will prepare the other bull, and lay it on the wood, but put no fire under it. **[24] Then you call on the name of your gods, and I will call on the name of YAHUAH; and the God who answers by fire, He is God.**" So all the people answered and said, "It is well spoken." [25] Now Elijah said to the prophets of Baal, "Choose one bull for yourselves and prepare it first, for you are many; and call on the name of your god, but put no fire under it." [26] So they took the bull which was given them, and they prepared it, and **called on the name of Baal** from morning even till noon, saying, "O Baal, hear us!" But there was no voice; no one answered. Then they leaped about the altar which they had made. [27] And so it was, at noon, that Elijah mocked them and said, "Cry aloud, for he is a god; either he is meditating, or he is busy, or he is on a journey, or perhaps he is sleeping and must be awakened." [28] So they cried aloud, and cut themselves, as was their custom, with knives and lances, until the blood gushed out on them. [29] And when midday was past, they prophesied until the time of the offering of the evening sacrifice. But there was no voice; no one answered, no one paid attention. [30] Then Elijah said to all the people, "Come near to me." So all the people came near to him. And he repaired the altar of YAHUAH that was broken down. [31] And Elijah took twelve stones, according to the number of the tribes of the sons of Jacob, to whom the word of YAHUAH had come, saying, "YASHARA'AL shall be your name." [32] Then with the stones **he built an altar in the name of YAHUAH;** and he made a trench around the altar large enough to hold two seahs of seed.

[33] And he put the wood in order, cut the bull in pieces, and laid it on the wood, and said, "Fill four waterpots with water, and pour it on the burnt sacrifice and on the wood." [34] Then he said, "Do it a second time," and they did it a second time; and he said, "Do it a third time," and they did it a third time. [35] So the water ran all around the altar; and he also filled the trench with water. [36] And it came to pass, at the time of the offering of the evening sacrifice, that Elijah the prophet came near and said, **"YAHUAH God of Abraham, Isaac, and YASHARA'AL, let it be known this day that You are God in YASHARA'AL** *and I am Your servant, and that I have done all these things at Your word. [37]* **Hear me, O YAHUAH, hear me, that this people may know that You are YAHUAH God, and that You have turned their hearts back to You again."** *[38] Then the fire of YAHUAH fell and consumed the burnt sacrifice, and the wood and the stones and the dust, and it licked up the water that was in the trench. [39] Now when all the people saw it, they fell on their faces; and they said,* **"YAHUAH, He is God! YAHUAH, He is God!"** *[40] And Elijah said to them, "Seize the prophets of Baal! Do not let one of them escape!" So they seized them; and Elijah brought them down to the Brook Kishon and executed them there. (I Kings 18:20-40 NKJV)*

These ancient battles were not won or lost based on natural strength. What determined victory was which God fought for his people. When the Israelites kept the covenant (the terms of agreement) with YAHUAH, the ALAHYM of Abraham, Isaac and Jacob, He would fight for them, and they would win. And if they were not keeping the covenant (the terms of agreement) with YAHUAH, the

ALAHYM of Abraham, Isaac, and Jacob, the Israelites would lose the battle because YAHUAH would not fight for them. This is a part of how YAHUAH has designed things to work.

🔥 **Tribes of Africa,** it is critical for us to understand that the confrontations between tribes or nations are always a confrontation of the gods of those tribes or nations. It is foremost a spiritual issue before it is an issue of the battle of men (flesh and blood).

YAHUAH judged and destroyed all the gods of Egypt as He delivered His people and brought them to the point where He established His everlasting covenant (terms of agreement) with the 12 tribes of YASHARA'AL through His servant Moses. As He speaks to them, He declares His name 'I AM YAHUAH' so that there would never be any confusion about which God (Alahym) was delivering them out of bondage.

> o *'For I will pass through the land of Egypt on that night, and will strike all the firstborn in the land of Egypt, both man and beast;* **and against all the gods of Egypt I will execute judgment: I am YAHUAH.** *[13] Now the blood shall be a sign for you on the houses where you are. And when I see the blood, I will pass over you; and the plague shall not be on you to destroy you when I strike the land of Egypt. [14]'So this day shall be to you a memorial; and you shall keep it as a feast to YAHUAH throughout your generations. You shall keep it as a feast by an everlasting ordinance. [15] Seven days you shall eat unleavened bread. On the first day you shall remove leaven from your houses. For whoever eats leavened bread from the first day until the seventh day, that person shall be cut off from YASHRAEL. [16] On the first day there shall be a holy convocation, and on the seventh day there shall be a holy convocation for you.*

No manner of work shall be done on them; but that which everyone must eat—that only may be prepared by you. [17] So you shall observe the Feast of Unleavened Bread, for on this same day I will have brought your armies out of the land of Egypt. Therefore you shall observe this day throughout your generations as an everlasting ordinance. [18] In the first month, on the fourteenth day of the month at evening, you shall eat unleavened bread, until the twenty-first day of the month at evening. [19] For seven days no leaven shall be found in your houses, since whoever eats what is leavened, that same person shall be cut off from the congregation of YASHRAEL, whether he is a stranger or a native of the land. (Exodus 12:12-19 NKJV)

- *In the third month after the children of YASHARA'AL had gone out of the land of Egypt, on the same day, they came to the Wilderness of Sinai. [2] For they had departed from Rephidim, had come to the Wilderness of Sinai, and camped in the wilderness. So, YASHARA'AL camped there before the mountain. [3] And Moses went up to YAHUAH, and YAHUAH called to him from the mountain, saying, "Thus you shall say to the house of Jacob, and tell the children of YASHARA'AL: [4] 'You have seen what I did to the Egyptians, and how I bore you on eagles' wings and brought you to Myself. [5] Now therefore,* **if you will indeed obey My voice and keep My covenant, then you shall be a special treasure to Me above all people; for all the earth is Mine. [6] And you shall be to Me a kingdom of priests and a holy nation.'** *These are the words which you shall speak to the children of YASHARA'AL. (Exodus 19:1-6 NKJV)*

Who is ⹏⸺ 𐤄𐤅𐤄𐤉 YAHUAH?

YAHUAH is our Judge.

YAHUAH is our Lawgiver.

YAHUAH is our King.

YAHUAH is the one who saves us.

As it is written:

- *For **YAHUAH is our judge, YAHUAH is our lawgiver, YAHUAH is our King;** he will save us. (Isaiah 33:22 KJV)*
- *Gather my saints together unto me; Those that have made a covenant with me by sacrifice. And the heavens shall declare his righteousness: **For YAHUAH is judge himself.** Selah. (Psalm 50:5-6 KJV)*
- *But **YAHUAH is the judge:** He putteth down one, and setteth up another. (Psalm 75:7 KJV)*
- *Before YAHUAH; For he cometh to judge the earth: With righteousness shall he judge the world, And the people with equity. (Psalm 98:9 KJV)*
- *For we must all appear before the judgment seat of MASHYACH (Christ); that every one may receive the things done in his body, according to that he hath done, whether it be good or bad. (2 Corinthians 5:10 KJV)*
- *Do not speak evil of one another, brethren. He who speaks evil of a brother and judges his brother, speaks evil of the law and judges the law. But if you judge the law, you are not a doer of the law but a judge. **There is one Lawgiver, who is able to save and to destroy.** Who are you to judge another? (James 4:11-12 NKJV)*

YAHUAH is our Father.

YAHUAH is our Creator.

YAHUAH is our Husband.

As it is written:

- And because you are sons, YAHUAH has sent forth the Spirit of His Son into your hearts, crying out, **"Abba, Father!"** Therefore you are no longer a slave but a son, and if a son, then an heir of YAHUAH through MASHYACH (Christ). (Galatians 4:6-7 NKJV)
- **For your Maker is your husband, YAHUAH of hosts is His name;** And your Redeemer is the Holy One of YASHARA'AL; He is called the God of the whole earth. (Isaiah 54:5 NKJV)

Did the so-called 'church fathers' of the religion of Christianity intentionally remove the names of YAHUAH and His SON YAHUSHA as a strategy to try to remove THEM from the battlefield of the spiritual war that is being waged, so that we would not call on their names? SELAH!!!

It might be a total coincidence and irrelevant that the Greek name (I)esous and later changed to the Roman Latin name Iesus and then to (J)esus seems very similar to the name of the Greek god (Z)eus; perhaps it's not, and I am being a conspiracy theorist!!!

Whose name are we calling upon?

- *"If you do not carefully observe all the words of this law that are written in this book, that you may fear **this glorious and awesome name, YAHUAH YOUR ALUAH,*** (Deuteronomy 28:58 NKJV)

- ***If My people who are called by My name*** *will humble themselves, and pray and seek My face, and turn from their wicked ways, then I will hear from heaven, and will forgive their sin and heal their land. (II Chronicles 7:14 NKJV)*

Tribes of Africa, His Name is Holy, Set Apart and special unto those who are in covenant with Him. Let us rejoice as we call unto Him by His Name YAHUAH

- ***I am YAHUAH, and there is no other;*** *There is no Alahym besides Me. I will gird you, though you have not known Me, that they may know from the rising of the sun to its setting That there is none besides Me.* ***I am YAHUAH, and there is no other;*** *I form the light and create darkness, I make peace and create calamity; I, YAHUAH, do all these things.' (Isaiah 45:5-7 NKJV)*
- ***I, even I, am YAHUAH, and besides Me there is no savior.*** *I have declared and saved, I have proclaimed, and there was no foreign god among you; Therefore you are My witnesses," Says YAHUAH, "that I am Alahym. Indeed before the day was, I am He; And there is no one who can deliver out of My hand; I work, and who will reverse it?" Thus says YAHUAH, your Redeemer, The Holy One of YASHARA'AL: "For your sake I will send to Babylon, and bring them all down as fugitives— The Chaldeans, who rejoice in their ships. (Isaiah 43:11-14 NKJV)*
- *Sing to YAHUAH,* ***sing praises to His name;*** *Extol Him who rides on the clouds, By His name YAHUAH, and rejoice before Him. (Psalms 68:4 NKJV)*
- *But now,* ***O YAHUAH, You are our Father;*** *We are the clay, and You our potter; And all we are the work of Your hand. (Isaiah 64:8 NKJV)*

Today, people know who you are based on your name and surname, not on your title of Mr. or Mrs., or Dr or Advocate. After the title, there is a name. Similarly, there must be a name after the title, Lord.

If someone comes in the name of 'the Lord' or the name of 'God', I have no idea who they are representing until they tell me which Lord or God they are referring to. It could be the 'god of this world' or it could be a Lord from the UK House of Lords. In whose name are they coming in? Who has sent them? This is important to know.

- "*I have manifested **Your name** to the men whom You have given Me out of the world. They were Yours, You gave them to Me, and they have kept Your word. (John 17:6 NKJV)*
- *I have come in **My Father's name,** and you do not receive Me; **if another comes in his own name,** him you will receive. (John 5:43 NKJV)*

Hebraic names have profound meaning, and removing the original name strips away the meaning. If YAHUAH gave His SON the name with the meaning 'YAHUAH SAVES' (YAHUSHA), changing it to anything else including Jesus removes the meaning. This is part of the difference between the Hebraic and Greek mindsets. Hebraic names speak of the purpose for which they have been given, Greco-Roman names do not. Most Bantu language names carry purpose and meaning.

A name is an identifier, an indicator of purpose, a mark of authority, honour, revealed character, reputation and power.

There is power and authority in a name.

In ancient Hebrew, names have meaning and are central to identity and culture.

For example, looking at the original names of some of the prophets and servants of YAHUAH:

- Jeremiah is YARAMAYAH, which means 'exalted by YAHUAH' or 'appointed by YAHUAH.'
- Isaiah is YASHAYAHU, which means 'salvation of YAHUAH.'
- Ezekiel is YACHAZQEL, which means 'YAHUAH strengthens.'
- Zechariah is ZAKARYAHU, which means 'remembered by YAHUAH.'
- Joel is YAUL, which means 'YAHUAH is Alahym.'
- Josiah is YOSHIYAHU, which means 'YAHUAH supports or YAHUAH will save.'
- Joseph is YOSAF, which means 'YAH will increase or to add'
- Elijah is ELIYAHU, which means 'My Alahym (God) is YAH'
- John is YOCHANON, which means 'YAHUAH is gracious/has shown favour'.
- Matthew is MATTIYAHU, which means 'gift of YAHUAH'
- Mary is MIRYAM, which means 'beloved of YAHUAH'
- Paul is SHA'UL, which means 'ask for/requested from YAH'

HALLELUYAH, Praise YAH (YAHUAH) for how He reveals purpose and calling in the names He has given us.

Their names reflect the direct purpose and calling that YAHUAH gave them, and their lives fulfilled that purpose. This is something that is completely lost when original names are translated or transliterated to Greco-Roman (Hellenised) names.

In Hebraic and African culture and language, a person's name speaks of their identity and purpose as a verb, as it is a proclamation of the assignment they carry.

This Greco-Roman transliteration of names was perhaps one of the strategies used to try to erase truth.

I recall very distinctly how our parents, in colonial times, were encouraged to give us what were termed 'Christian' names (essentially requiring us to have a Greco-Roman/Anglo-Saxon name) instead of a name in our indigenous language. HalleluYah (praise Yah) that some of our grandparents and parents still bestowed upon us names from our mother tongues that reflect purpose, meaning and calling.

In the same way YAHUAH placed His name in His SON YAHUSHA, He did the same in the city that is called by His name, YARUSHALAYIM.

> o *Since the day that I brought forth my people out of the land of Egypt I chose no city among all the tribes of YASHARA'AL to build an house in, that my name might be there; neither chose I any man to be a ruler over my people YASHARA'AL:* **[6] but I have chosen YARUSHALAYIM (Jerusalem), that my name might be there;** *and have chosen David to be over my people YASHARA'AL. (2 Chronicles 6:5-6 KJV)*

When we remove the original name of YAHUAH many things in the Bible lose their real meaning and purpose, stripping us of foundational understanding of what is being said and how it intertwines into the tapestry of His revealed plan for us.

Dry bones arise and live, tribes of Africa arise and live.

Dry bones arise and live, as it is written:

> o *The hand of YAHUAH came upon me and brought me out in the Spirit of YAHUAH, and set me down in the midst of the valley; and it was full of bones. [2] Then He caused me to pass by them all around, and behold, there were very many in the open valley; and indeed they were very dry. [3] And He said to me, "Son of man, can these bones live?" So*

I answered, "O YAHUAH Aluah, You know." [4] Again He said to me, "Prophesy to these bones, and say to them, 'O dry bones, hear the word of YAHUAH! [5] Thus says YAHUAH Aluah to these bones: "Surely I will cause breath to enter into you, and you shall live. [6] I will put sinews on you and bring flesh upon you, cover you with skin and put breath in you; and you shall live. Then you shall know that I am YAHUAH." [7] So I prophesied as I was commanded; and as I prophesied, there was a noise, and suddenly a rattling; and the bones came together, bone to bone. [8]Indeed, as I looked, the sinews and the flesh came upon them, and the skin covered them over; but there was no breath in them. [9] Also He said to me, "Prophesy to the breath, prophesy, son of man, and say to the breath, 'Thus says YAHUAH Aluah: "Come from the four winds, O breath, and breathe on these slain, that they may live." [10] So I prophesied as He commanded me, and breath came into them, and they lived, and stood upon their feet, an exceedingly great army. [11] Then He said to me, "Son of man, these bones are the whole house of YASHARA'AL. They indeed say, 'Our bones are dry, our hope is lost, and we ourselves are cut off!' [12] Therefore prophesy and say to them, 'Thus says YAHUAH Aluah: "Behold, O My people, I will open your graves and cause you to come up from your graves, and bring you into the land of YASHARA'AL. [13] Then you shall know that I am YAHUAH, when I have opened your graves, O My people, and brought you up from your graves. [14] I will put My Spirit in you, and you shall live, and I will place you in your own land. Then you shall know that I, YAHUAH, have spoken it and performed it," says YAHUAH.' [15] Again the word of YAHUAH came to me, saying, [16] "As for you, son of man, take a stick for yourself and write on it: 'For Judah and for the children of YASHARA'AL, his companions.' Then take another stick and write on it, 'For Joseph, the stick of Ephraim, and for all the house of YASHARA'AL, his companions.' [17] Then join them one to another for yourself into one stick, and they will become one in your hand. [18] "And when the children of your people speak to you, saying, 'Will you not show us what you mean by these?'— [19] say to them, 'Thus says YAHUAH Aluah: "Surely I will take the stick of Joseph, which is in the hand of Ephraim, and the tribes of YASHARA'AL, his companions; and I will join them with it, with the stick of Judah, and make them one stick, and they will be one in My hand." ' [20] And the sticks on which you write will be in your hand before their eyes. [21] "Then say to them, 'Thus says YAHUAH Aluah: "Surely I will take the children of YASHARA'AL from among the nations, wherever they have gone, and will gather them from every side and bring them into their own land; [22] and I will make them one nation in the land, on the mountains of YASHARA'AL; and one king shall be king over them all; they shall no longer be two nations, nor shall they ever be divided into two kingdoms again. [23] They shall not defile themselves anymore with their idols, nor with their detestable things, nor with any of their transgressions; but I will deliver them from all their dwelling places in which they have sinned, and will cleanse them. Then they shall be My people, and I will be their Aluah. [24] "David My servant shall be king over them, and they shall all have one shepherd; they shall also walk in My judgments and observe My statutes and do them. [25] Then they shall dwell in the land that I have given to Jacob My

> *servant, where your fathers dwelt; and they shall dwell there, they, their children, and their children's children, forever; and My servant David shall be their prince forever. [26] Moreover I will make a covenant of peace with them, and it shall be an everlasting covenant with them; I will establish them and multiply them, and I will set My sanctuary in their midst forevermore. [27] My tabernacle also shall be with them; indeed I will be their Aluah, and they shall be My people. [28] The nations also will know that I, YAHUAH, sanctify YASHARA'AL, when My sanctuary is in their midst forevermore." (Ezekiel 37:1-28 NKJV)*

The reason Ezekiel chapter 37 is so critical for Africa will be expounded upon in Section 5.

🌿 Awaken tribes of Africa!!!!!!

🌿 Having addressed the matter of names, please note that for the remainder of this book, the original names *YAHUAH* and *YAHUSHA* will be used consistently in place of "The LORD," "The Lord," "Jesus," and instances where "God" has been used in substitution for the true Hebraic names.

YAHUAH not only placed His name in the name of His SON YAHUSHA, He also did so with the people/nation (Jacob and his descendants) that He established the covenant (agreement) with as His firstborn. He gave them His name as He named them **YASHARA'AL**. And so, the name **YASHARA'AL** will be used to replace the modern name Israel and serve as a way to distinguish the fact that reference is not being made to the political state of Israel nor the people who call themselves Jews today. (More details of this will be covered in Section 5)

As it is written, *'Then you shall say to Pharaoh, 'Thus says YAHUAH:*

"YASHARA'AL is My son, My firstborn.' (Exodus 4:22 KJV)

- **YASHARA'AL** means 'YAHUAH will prevail' or 'He who struggles with YAHUAH' or 'Prince of YAHUAH'

Other names and terms that will occasionally appear in the book in their original form, so that we learn them in their original ancient Hebrew format, are:

- Abraham is **ABARAHAM**
- Isaac is **YATSAKHAQ**
- Jacob is **YAAQAB**
- Jerusalem is **YARUSHALAYIM,** which means 'to find peace or to establish wholeness' or 'city where YAHUAH establishes peace and wholeness'.
- Judah is **YAHUDA,** derived from Yadah 'to praise or to give thanks', and so YAHUDA means 'praised one or one who is praised'.
- Jews are **YAHUDYM**, meaning 'people of YAHUDA (Judah)
- Lord (as used in the bible in lower case) is **ADUN,** which means 'master'.
- In ancient Hebrew, the word translated as GOD in singular, possessive English is **ALUAH**, which means 'our power, the mighty one'. Likewise, the word translated as God in the collective is ALAHYM (as already given previously)
- In ancient Hebrew, the word translated 'the Christ' is **HA MASHYACH**, which means 'the anointed one of YAHUAH'.
- In ancient Hebrew, the word translated 'Holy Spirit' is **RUACH HA QADASH**, which means 'the breath, the wind, spirit of Holiness'.

Why is this even relevant?

There is a promise that YAHUAH has given to restore to His people a pure language, and through that they will serve Him with one accord. As it is written:

> o *"Therefore wait for Me," says YAHUAH, "Until the day I rise up for plunder; My determination is to gather the nations To My assembly of kingdoms, to pour on them My indignation, All My fierce anger; All the earth shall be devoured with the fire of My jealousy. [9]* **"For then I will restore to the peoples a pure language,** *that they all may call on the name of YAHUAH, to serve Him with one accord. (Zephaniah 3:8-9 NKJV)*

Tribes of Africa, I believe that the restored language will be the Ancient Hebrew that He initially used to communicate with His people, and so it is worthwhile to get a glimpse of it today as we anticipate the day/time He leads us back into it, so that we can serve Him with one accord.

The nations might have their gods, but blessed is the nation whose Alahym is YAHUAH.

> o ***Blessed is the nation whose Alahym is YAHUAH,*** *the people He has chosen as His own inheritance. (Psalms 33:12 NKJV)*

Let us not be fooled; just because we hear a famous music artist thank God when they receive a Grammy award or a Prime Minister say, 'God bless Israel', or a President say, 'God bless America', or we see 'in God we trust' on the American one dollar note, it is not necessarily referring to the ALAHYM of Abraham, Isaac and Jacob, YAHUAH. In most cases, it is not, for there are many gods.

Let us not follow just because we have heard someone say God.

As we conclude this chapter, let us answer the question, who is

YAHUAH?

YAHUAH 𐤉𐤄𐤅𐤄 is LOVE and LOVE is YAHUAH 𐤉𐤄𐤅𐤄

We have spoken of YAHUAH by His position within His Kingdom as our Judge, Lawgiver and King. We have also spoken about Him as our Father, Creator and Husband. In each of these positions, He fulfils a role, but His overarching nature is love, because YAHUAH is love.

> o *Beloved, let us love one another: for love is of YAHUAH; and everyone that loveth is born of YAHUAH, and knoweth YAHUAH. [8] He that loveth not knoweth not YAHUAH;* **for YAHUAH is love.** *(1 John 4:7-8 KJV)*

As much as YAHUAH is our Judge, He judges because He loves righteousness and justice. It is because of His great love that He has compelled Himself to judge injustice and unrighteousness. It is because of His great love that He has compelled Himself to judge when there is sin, because He hates sin.

Because YAHUAH is love, He desires that every sinner repent and find the way back to right standing (righteousness) with Him, but He will always hate sin.

> o *YAHUAH is not slack concerning His promise, as some men count slackness; but is longsuffering to us-ward,* **not willing that any should perish, but that all should come to repentance.** *(2 Peter 3:9 KJV)*

Because YAHUAH is love, He desires that all be saved and come to know the truth.

> o *For this is good and acceptable in the sight of YAHUAH our Saviour; [4]* **who will have all men to be saved, and to**

come unto the knowledge of the truth.
(1 Timothy 2:3-4 KJV)

YAHUAH loves us so much that He revealed and made plain the way He has designed things to work in His creation and Kingdom. He designed a system which will always work in our favour if we follow the rules and instructions He gives. He did not hide His design; He made it plain because it is His greatest desire that we make the right choices and live in the blessings He has already placed for us when we choose to walk on the path of obedience. It is because of His love that He revealed how the Kingdom works, so we would never be left wondering and confused why things happen in the way they do. In His love, He has made things very predictable because they are all based on the rules He has established and revealed to us throughout His Word.

Since YAHUAH is love, I will quote 1 Corinthians 13:1-13, exchanging love with YAHUAH

- *Though I speak with the tongues of men and of angels, but have not YAHUAH (love), I have become sounding brass or a clanging cymbal. [2] And though I have the gift of prophecy, and understand all mysteries and all knowledge, and though I have all faith, so that I could remove mountains, but have not YAHUAH (love), I am nothing. [3] And though I bestow all my goods to feed the poor, and though I give my body to be burned, but have not YAHUAH (love), it profits me nothing. [4] YAHUAH (love) suffers long and is kind; YAHUAH (love) does not envy; YAHUAH (love) does not parade itself, is not puffed up; [5] does not behave rudely, does not seek its own, is not provoked, thinks no evil; [6] does not rejoice in iniquity, but rejoices in the truth; [7] bears all things, believes all things, hopes all things, endures all things. [8] YAHUAH (love) never fails. But whether there are prophecies, they will fail; whether there are tongues, they will cease; whether there is knowledge, it will vanish away. [9] For we know in part and we prophesy in part. [10] But when that which is perfect has come, then that which is in part will be done away. [11] When I was a child, I spoke as a child, I understood as a child, I thought as a child; but when I became a man, I put away childish things. [12] For now we see in a mirror, dimly, but then face to face. Now I know in part, but then I shall know just as I also am known. [13]* **And now abide faith, hope, YAHUAH (love), these three; but the greatest of these is YAHUAH (love).** *(I Corinthians 13:1-13 NKJV)*

Tribes of Africa, because YAHUAH is love, He exhorts us to love. The task that lies ahead cannot be accomplished without YAHUAH, and therefore, it cannot be accomplished without love.

- **Beloved, let us love one another, for love is of YAHUAH; and everyone who loves is born of YAHUAH and knows YAHUAH. [8] He who does not love does not know YAHUAH, for YAHUAH is love.** [9] In this the love of YAHUAH was manifested toward us, that YAHUAH has sent His only begotten Son into the world, that we might live through Him. [10] In this is love, not that we loved YAHUAH, but that He loved us and sent His Son to be the propitiation for our sins. [11] Beloved, if YAHUAH so loved us, we also ought to love one another. [12] No one has seen YAHUAH at any time. If we love one another, YAHUAH abides in us, and His love has been perfected in us. [13] By this we know that we abide in Him, and He in us, because He has given us of His Spirit. [14] And we have seen and *testify that the Father has sent the Son as Savior of the world. [15] Whoever confesses that YAHUSHA is the Son of YAHUAH, YAHUAH abides in him, and he in YAHUAH. [16]* **And we have known and believed the love that YAHUAH has for us. YAHUAH is love, and he who abides in love abides in YAHUAH, and YAHUAH in him.** *(I John 4:7-16 NKJV)*

The very nature of the design of the Kingdom of YAHUAH is love, and that is why He established commandments and laws to govern the realm of His rule and reign, as we will explore in the next few chapters.

CHAPTER NINE

Biblical Definitions and Equations

Reading the word of YAHUAH and interpreting it using a Greek (Greco-Roman) mindset can cause a lot of distortion, which, unfortunately, has happened extensively and, therefore, conceals the truth of many things that can only be made clear when studied through an ancient Hebraic mindset.

YAHUAH always speaks through an ancient Hebraic mindset, whereas the 'so-called' Greco-Roman church fathers developed the doctrine and theology that has formed the foundation of the religion of Christianity through the lens of a Greek mindset.

YAHUAH speaks about everything from a starting point of covenant, whereas a Greek mindset starts with systems of logic and philosophy. This is why we must consider going on journeys to completely relearn what the scriptures are actually saying through the lens of the correct cultural mindset.

This is one of the reasons YAHUSHA used parables and said these words,

> o *And the disciples came and said to Him, "Why do You*

> speak to them in parables?" [11] He answered and said to them, **"Because it has been given to you to know the mysteries of the kingdom of heaven, but to them it has not been given.** [12] For whoever has, to him more will be given, and he will have abundance; but whoever does not have, even what he has will be taken away from him. [13] **Therefore I speak to them in parables, because seeing they do not see, and hearing they do not hear, nor do they understand. [14] And in them the prophecy of Isaiah is fulfilled, which says: 'Hearing you will hear and shall not understand and seeing you will see and not perceive; [15] For the hearts of this people have grown dull. Their ears are hard of hearing, and their eyes they have closed, lest they should see with their eyes and hear with their ears, lest they should understand with their hearts and turn, so that I should heal them.'** [16] But blessed are your eyes for they see, and your ears for they hear; [17] for assuredly, I say to you that many prophets and righteous men desired to see what you see, and did not see it, and to hear what you hear, and did not hear it. (Matthew 13:10-17 NKJV)

YAHUSHA was literally saying that many would hear what was being spoken, but would not be able to understand and comprehend because their mindsets are not aligned with YAHUAH.

It is worthwhile to look at the differences in thinking mentioned in chapter 2 on the topic, 'How we think: Hebraic versus Greek thinking'.

Now that we have established who our ALAHYM is and know His name, we can go forward to understand the divine design of how He has designed things to work according to the covenant

(His agreement with us) and how we can align with that covenant (agreement). This is a prerequisite to understanding what the Kingdom of YAHUAH is and how we participate in it.

If we don't have the right definitions and standards that YAHUAH sets, we will be led astray and end up being the ones who YAHUSHA spoke about as those *who 'hear but shall not understand and seeing will see and not perceive'*.

Words can have multiple definitions and meanings (especially when reflected through the differences of the Greek and Hebraic mindsets), so we must get this absolutely right by understanding how the Bible defines words. This is such an essential point, therefore, that this section is one of the most intensive and extensive in the book, as it is where the root of deception often emanates from.

One of the most humbling parts of the journey for me was realising how illiterate I was concerning the Word of YAHUAH (The Bible), and how ignorant I was on how to read it and use it as the full instruction manual of how the ALAHYM of Abraham, Isaac and Jacob has designed things to work in all of creation. The more I learnt about Biblical definitions (the meaning of words used in the Bible), the more I saw how scriptures from the beginning to the end are interwoven together to reveal a 'well-designed system' that works meticulously and can never be corrupted and circumvented. Instead of taking individual verses and trying to make them say what I want, as I had done all my life, the Bible became alive as it began to speak, revealing that YAHUAH's design of how things work is not haphazard or a mystery, but is laid out in plain sight if we choose to search for it as a great treasure. It is a great treasure that can only be found by connecting the entire Bible verse by verse, line by line and precept by precept, here a little, there a little, until we suddenly grasp that what seemed hidden to man has in fact been always freely available to us.

- *Again, **the kingdom of heaven is like unto treasure hid in a field;** the which when a man hath found, he hideth, and for joy thereof goeth and selleth all that he hath, and buyeth that field. [45] Again, the kingdom of heaven is like unto a merchant man, seeking goodly pearls: [46] who, when he had found one pearl of great price, went and sold all that he had, and bought it. (Matthew 13:44-46 KJV)*
- *It is the glory of YAHUAH to conceal a thing: **But the honour of kings is to search out a matter.** (Proverbs 25:2 KJV)*
- *Whom shall he teach knowledge? and whom shall he make to understand doctrine? them that are weaned from the milk, and drawn from the breasts. [10] **For precept must be upon precept, precept upon precept; line upon line, line upon line; here a little, and there a little:** (Isaiah 28:9-10 KJV)*
- *Study to shew thyself approved unto YAHUAH, a workman that needeth not to be ashamed, **rightly dividing the word of truth**. (2 Timothy 2:15 KJV)*

Based on the instruction to read and search the Bible, verse by verse, precept by precept, line by line, here a little and there a little, I would like to share some key Biblical word definitions and how they link together and form equations that show how the Most High YAHUAH has designed things to work. It is these equations that show us the preconditions and the dependent events that always accompany what YAHUAH as 'the Creator' promises and how they relate to the two paths that are fixed within the design, the path of 'the blessing and life' and the path of 'the curse and death'. Paths that we all take, based on the choices we make.

𐤉𐤄𐤅𐤄 YAHUAH's Commandments

In the Bible, the word "commandments" (Hebrew: mitzvot) refers to specific duties or instructions from YAHUAH that individuals are expected to follow. These commandments are part of the covenant agreement between YAHUAH and His people, outlining guidelines for living a righteous and faithful life according to His standard.

There are several Hebrew words for commandments:

מִצְוָה (mitsvah) (Strong's concordance #4687): This word means "commandment" and is often used to describe the commands or instructions of God.

פִּקּוּד (piqqûd) (Strong's concordance #6490): This word means "precepts, commandments, statutes" and is often used to describe the commands or instructions of God.

These words are essential in understanding the biblical concept of commandments and their significance in the context of faith and obedience.

𐤉𐤄𐤅𐤄 YAHUAH's Law

Law is best defined as a rule of conduct or action laid down and enforced by the supreme governing authority (as the legislature) of a community or established by custom. Law is an instrument which regulates human conduct/behaviour. Law can also refer to the system of rules which a particular country or community, or kingdom, recognises as regulating the actions of its members or citizens and which it may enforce by the imposition of penalties.

In Strong's Concordance, the Greek word for law is νόμος (nomos), which refers to a law or regulation, especially the law of YAHUAH given through Moses or the gospel. This term is used to describe a prescriptive usage or principle.

In Hebrew, the word for law is תֹּרָה (**TORAH**), which means law, direction, or instruction. This term encompasses various aspects, including:

- Instruction: guidance or teaching, whether human or divine
- Direction: a code of conduct or a set of regulations
- Body of prophetic teaching: a collection of teachings or prophecies

The usage of the word law in the Bible does not refer to a singular law but to multiple laws that have been given by YAHUAH, the ALAHYM of Abraham, Isaac and Jacob, mainly through Moses in the Old Testament, and through His SON YAHUSHA in the New Testament. For example, when YAHUSHA gave His sermon on the mount, also known as the Beatitudes, He was giving instructions/law/Torah. This can be referenced in Matthew chapters 5, 6 and 7.

YAHUAH's commandments and laws are foundational to understanding how He has designed things to work in His creation and for mankind in this present age and in the ages to come. If we don't understand the position He places upon His commandments and laws, we will not be able to make sense of what has happened in the past, and what is happening around us and, in the world, now.

The foundation of the Law of 𐤀𐤋𐤄𐤉𐤌 𐤉𐤄𐤅𐤄 YAHUAH is the 10 Commandments

Here are the commandments listed as it is written in Exodus 20:1-17 and Deuteronomy 5:6-22.

And YAHUAH spoke all these words, saying:

I am YAHUAH, your Aluah, who brought you out of the land of Egypt, out of the house of bondage.

1. "You shall have no other gods before Me.
2. "You shall not make for yourself a carved image—any likeness of anything that is in heaven above, or that is in the earth beneath, or that is in the water under the earth you shall not bow down to them nor serve them. For I, YAHUAH your Aluah, am a jealous Alahym, visiting the iniquity of the fathers upon the children to the third and fourth generations of those who hate Me, but showing mercy to thousands, to those who love Me and keep My commandments.
3. "You shall not take the name of YAHUAH your Aluah in vain, for YAHUAH will not hold him guiltless who takes His name in vain
4. "Remember the Sabbath day, to keep it holy. Six days you shall labour and do all your work, but the seventh day is the Sabbath of YAHUAH your Aluah. In it you shall do no work: you, nor your son, nor your daughter, nor your male servant, nor your female servant, nor your cattle, nor your stranger who is within your gates. For in six days YAHUAH made the heavens and the earth, the sea, and all that is in them, and rested the seventh day. Therefore YAHUAH blessed the Sabbath day and hallowed it.
5. "Honor your father and your mother, that your days may be long upon the land which YAHUAH your Aluah is giving you
6. "You shall not murder.
7. "You shall not commit adultery
8. "You shall not steal

9. "You shall not bear false witness against your neighbour.
10. "You shall not covet your neighbour's house; you shall not covet your neighbour's wife, nor his male servant, nor his female servant, nor his ox, nor his donkey, nor anything that is your neighbour's

The Greatest Commandment

The 10 Commandments are the foundation of YAHUAH's commandments, which are the basis of the covenant (the terms of agreement between YAHUAH and His people). It is from the 10 Commandments that the Greatest Commandment flows, as it was first given in the Old Testament and then repeated by YAHUSHA. The rest of the 'Law of YAHUAH' that is then given after the giving of the 10 Commandments is a combination of laws and rules that relate to how to practically keep the commandments, the consequences for not obeying them, and likewise the process to follow when there is failure to obey either wilfully or unknowingly. As with any law, there are consequences for transgression, and so YAHUAH gives very descriptive instructions on what to do when failure happens, as following these instructions provides access to the pathway for redemption. The framework of the commandments and laws is the guideline that YAHUAH has set for man to remain in agreement with Him. 'For how can two walk together unless they agree, and how can one be yoked to YAHUSHA if not submitted to the requirements of the FATHER who YAHUSHA obeyed absolutely'.

- ○ ***Do two walk together except they make an appointment and have agreed?*** *(Amos 3:3 AMPC)*
- ○ *At that time YAHUSHA answered and said, "I thank You, Father, Master of heaven and earth, that You have hidden these things from the wise and prudent and have revealed*

> them to babes. *[26]* Even so, Father, for so it seemed good in Your sight. *[27]* All things have been delivered to Me by My Father, and no one knows the Son except the Father. Nor does anyone know the Father except the Son, and the one to whom the Son wills to reveal Him. *[28]* Come to Me, all you who labor and are heavy laden, and I will give you rest. *[29]* **Take My yoke upon you and learn from Me, for I am gentle and lowly in heart, and you will find rest for your souls. *[30]* For My yoke is easy and My burden is light."** (Matthew 11:25-30 NKJV)

The image of walking together in agreement with YAHUAH and being yoked (tied together) with YAHUSHA is very powerful, as it shows the picture of living according to the covenant (the agreement that YAHUAH has with His people).

In my tribal tongue of Shona from Zimbabwe, the word for Covenant is SUNGANO. It is derived from the Shona word 'Sunga', which means to TIE TOGETHER. The word 'Sunga' is what speaks of two oxen yoked together to pull something together.

So, in our language, when we speak of Covenant, it means to 'to be tied together so that the two have become one and inseparable', like a grafting together. Similarly, the same covenant (sungano) exists in marriage when a man and a woman become one flesh.

This very image of the marriage covenant is carried throughout the Bible as those who keep the covenant are referred to as the bride of YAHUSHA and will be called to the marriage supper of the Lamb, as it is written.

> o *And I heard, as it were, the voice of a great multitude, as the sound of many waters and as the sound of mighty thunderings, saying, "Alleluia! For YAHUAH Aluah*

BIBLICAL DEFINITIONS AND EQUATIONS

> *Omnipotent reigns! [7]* **Let us be glad and rejoice and give Him glory, for the marriage of the Lamb has come, and His wife has made herself ready."** *[8] And to her it was granted to be arrayed in fine linen, clean and bright, for the fine linen is the righteous acts of the saints. [9] Then he said to me, "Write: 'Blessed are those who are called to the marriage supper of the Lamb!" And he said to me, "These are the true sayings of YAHUAH." (Revelation 19:6-9 NKJV)*
>
> o *"I do not pray for these alone, but also for those who will believe in Me through their word; that they all may be one, as You, Father, are in Me, and I in You;* **that they also may be one in Us***, that the world may believe that You sent Me.(John 17:20-21 NKJV)*

For there to be a 'walking together', for there to be a 'yoking together', for there to be a covenant, for there to be a 'oneness with the FATHER and the SON', there must be love and commitment to the relationship.

> o *"**Teacher, which is the great commandment in the law?"** [37] YAHUSHA said to him, "'You shall love YAHUAH your Aluah with all your heart, with all your soul, and with all your mind.' [38] This is the first and great commandment. [39] And the second is like it: 'You shall love your neighbour as yourself.' [40] On these two commandments hang all the Law and the Prophets."* (Matthew 22:36-40 NKJV)
>
> o *"Hear, O YASHARA'AL: YAHUAH our Aluah, YAHUAH is one!* **You shall love YAHUAH your Aluah with all your heart, with all your soul, and with all your strength.** *(Deuteronomy 6:4-5 NKJV)*

○ ***"And now, YASHARA'AL, what does YAHUAH your Aluah require of you, but to fear YAHUAH your Aluah, to walk in all His ways and to love Him, to serve YAHUAH your Aluah with all your heart and with all your soul, [13] and to keep the commandments of YAHUAH and His statutes which I command you today for your good?*** [14] Indeed heaven and the highest heavens belong to YAHUAH your Aluah, also the earth with all that is in it. [15] YAHUAH delighted only in your fathers, to love them; and He chose their descendants after them, you above all peoples, as it is this day. [16] Therefore circumcise the foreskin of your heart, and be stiff-necked no longer. [17] For YAHUAH your Aluah is God of gods and Lord of lords, the great Alahym, mighty and awesome, who shows no partiality nor takes a bribe. [18] He administers justice for the fatherless and the widow, and loves the stranger, giving him food and clothing. [19] **Therefore love the stranger**, for you were strangers in the land of Egypt. [20] You shall fear YAHUAH your Aluah; you shall serve Him, and to Him you shall hold fast, and take oaths in His name. [21] He is your praise, and He is your Aluah, who has done for you these great and awesome things which your eyes have seen. [22] Your fathers went down to Egypt with seventy persons, and now YAHUAH your Aluah has made you as the stars of heaven in multitude. (Deuteronomy 10:12-22 NKJV)*

Linking the 10 Commandments to the Greatest Commandment

The greatest commandment of 'loving YAHUAH with all your heart, soul and mind' links to the 1st four of the 10 commandments. How does one love YAHUAH? By obeying the 1st four commandments.

BIBLICAL DEFINITIONS AND EQUATIONS

1. "You shall have no other gods before Me.
2. "You shall not make for yourself a carved image—any likeness of anything that is in heaven above, or that is in the earth beneath, or that is in the water under the earth you shall not bow down to them nor serve them. For I, YAHUAH your Aluah, am a jealous Alahym, visiting the iniquity of the fathers upon the children to the third and fourth generations of those who hate Me, but showing mercy to thousands, to those who love Me and keep My commandments.
3. "You shall not take the name of YAHUAH your Aluah in vain, for YAHUAH will not hold him guiltless who takes His name in vain
4. "Remember the Sabbath day, to keep it holy. Six days you shall labour and do all your work, but the seventh day is the Sabbath of YAHUAH your Aluah. In it you shall do no work: you, nor your son, nor your daughter, nor your male servant, nor your female servant, nor your cattle, nor your stranger who is within your gates. For in six days YAHUAH made the heavens and the earth, the sea, and all that is in them, and rested the seventh day. Therefore, YAHUAH blessed the Sabbath day and hallowed it.

The second portion of 'loving your neighbour as yourself' links to commandments 5 to 10. How does one love your neighbour? By obeying commandments 5 to 10.

5. "Honor your father and your mother, that your days may be long upon the land which YAHUAH your Aluah is giving you
6. "You shall not murder.
7. "You shall not commit adultery
8. "You shall not steal

9. "You shall not bear false witness against your neighbour.
10. "You shall not covet your neighbour's house; you shall not covet your neighbour's wife, nor his male servant, nor his female servant, nor his ox, nor his donkey, nor anything that is your neighbour's

Obeying YAHUAH's commandments 'equals' Loving YAHUAH, as will be covered in more detail shortly.

> o *We love because he first loved us. If anyone says, "I love YAHUAH," and hates his brother, he is a liar; for he who does not love his brother whom he has seen cannot love YAHUAH whom he has not seen. And this commandment we have from him:* **whoever loves YAHUAH must also love his brother.** *(1 John 4:19-21 ESV)*

The 10 Commandments and the Greatest Commandment are interlinked as they complete and fulfil each other, as it is written that 'On these two commandments (the greatest and the 2nd) hang all the Law and the Prophets'.

True prophets will speak the word of YAHUAH to bring people back to agreement (covenant) with YAHUAH through YAHUSHA, as it is written that the true spirit of prophecy is YAHUSHA.

> o *Then he said to me, "Write: 'Blessed are those who are called to the marriage supper of the Lamb!'" And he said to me, "These are the true sayings of YAHUAH." And I fell at his feet to worship him. But he said to me, "See that you do not do that! I am your fellow servant, and of your brethren who have the testimony of YAHUSHA. Worship YAHUAH! For the testimony of YAHUSHA is the spirit of prophecy." (Revelation 19:9-10 NKJV)*

Anyone claiming to be a prophet and not pointing people back to the covenant (the terms of the agreement between YAHUAH and His people) is not a prophet sent by YAHUAH who has the Spirit of YAHUAH in him. (More on this issue will be covered in Chapter 20, which speaks about the uncleanness in the religion of Christianity and the church.)

Please note that the corrupt religious leaders of the day (the Pharisees and Sadducees) added their own man-made laws and rules based on their tradition over and above the given Law of YAHUAH and put this as an additional burden on the people. YAHUSHA fought against this practice of adding man-made traditions to the law, but He never spoke about the abolishing of the law that His Abba YAHUAH had given.

- He (YAHUSHA) answered them and said to them, **"Why do you also transgress the commandment of YAHUAH because of your tradition?** (Matthew 15:3 NKJV)
- Then the Pharisees and scribes asked Him, **"Why do Your disciples not walk according to the tradition of the elders,** but eat bread with unwashed hands?" [6] He answered and said to them, "Well did Isaiah prophesy of you hypocrites, as it is written: 'This people honors Me with their lips, but their heart is far from Me. [7] **And in vain they worship Me, Teaching as doctrines the commandments of men.' [8] For laying aside the commandment of YAHUAH, you hold the tradition of men** — the washing of pitchers and cups, and many other such things you do." [9] He said to them, **"All too well you reject the commandment of YAHUAH, that you may keep your tradition.**
- *making the word of YAHUAH of no effect through*

your tradition *which you have handed down. And many such things you do." (Mark 7:5-9, 13 NKJV)*

- Then YAHUSHA spoke to the multitudes and to His disciples, [2] saying: **"The scribes and the Pharisees sit in Moses' seat. [3] Therefore whatever they tell you to observe, that observe and do, but do not do according to their works; for they say, and do not do. [4] For they bind heavy burdens, hard to bear, and lay them on men's shoulders; but they themselves will not move them with one of their fingers.** [5] But all their works they do to be seen by men. They make their phylacteries broad and enlarge the borders of their garments. [6] They love the best places at feasts, the best seats in the synagogues, [7] greetings in the marketplaces, and to be called by men, 'Rabbi, Rabbi.' [8] But you, do not be called 'Rabbi'; for One is your Teacher, HA MASHYACH (The Christ), and you are all brethren. [9] **Do not call anyone on earth your father; for One is your Father, He who is in heaven.** [10] And do not be called teachers; for One is your Teacher, HA MASHYACH. [11] But he who is greatest among you shall be your servant. [12] And whoever exalts himself will be humbled, and he who humbles himself will be exalted. [13] **"But woe to you, scribes and Pharisees, hypocrites! For you shut up the kingdom of heaven against men; for you neither go in yourselves, nor do you allow those who are entering to go in.** [14] Woe to you, scribes and Pharisees, hypocrites! For you devour widows' houses, and for a pretense make long prayers. Therefore you will receive greater condemnation. [15] "Woe to you, scribes and Pharisees, hypocrites! For you travel land and sea to win one proselyte, and when he is won, you make him twice as much *a son of hell as yourselves. [16] "Woe to you, blind guides, who say, 'Whoever swears by the temple, it is nothing; but whoever swears by the gold of the temple, he is obliged to perform it.' [17] Fools and blind! For which is greater, the gold or the temple that sanctifies the gold? [18] And, 'Whoever swears by the altar, it is nothing; but whoever swears by the gift that is on it, he is obliged to perform it.' [19] Fools and blind! For which is greater, the gift or the altar that sanctifies the gift? [20] Therefore he who swears by the altar, swears by it and by all things on it. [21] He who swears by the temple, swears by it and by Him who dwells in it. [22] And he who swears by heaven, swears by the throne of YAHUAH and by Him who sits on it. [23] "Woe to you, scribes and Pharisees, hypocrites! For you pay tithe of mint and anise and cummin, and have neglected the weightier matters of the law: justice and mercy and faith. These you ought to have done, without leaving the others undone. [24] Blind guides, who strain out a gnat and swallow a camel! [25] "Woe to you, scribes and Pharisees, hypocrites! For you cleanse the outside of the cup and dish, but inside they are full of extortion and self-indulgence. [26] Blind Pharisee, first cleanse the inside of the cup and dish, that the outside of them may be clean also. [27] "Woe to you, scribes and Pharisees, hypocrites! For you are like whitewashed tombs which indeed appear beautiful outwardly, but inside are full of dead men's bones and all uncleanness. [28]* **Even so you also outwardly appear righteous to men, but inside you are full of hypocrisy and lawlessness**. *[29] "Woe to you, scribes and Pharisees, hypocrites! Because you build the tombs of the prophets and adorn the monuments of the righteous, [30] and say, 'If we had lived in the days of our* *fathers, we would not have been partakers with them in the blood of the prophets.' [31] "Therefore you are witnesses against yourselves that you are sons of those who murdered the prophets. [32] Fill up, then, the measure of your fathers' guilt. [33] Serpents, brood of vipers! How can you escape the condemnation of hell? [34] Therefore, indeed, I send you prophets, wise men, and scribes: some of them you will kill and crucify, and some of them you will scourge in your synagogues and persecute from city to city, [35] that on you may come all the righteous blood shed on the earth, from the blood of righteous Abel to the blood of Zechariah, son of Berechiah, whom you murdered between the temple and the altar. [36] Assuredly, I say to you, all these things will come upon this generation. (Matthew 23:1-36 NKJV)*

These scriptures were castigating the leaders who were corrupting the Law of YAHUAH by adding to it and insisting that people follow their 'law based on tradition' (man-made religious additions) as a greater requirement. It was not advocating for the genuine Law of YAHUAH to be rejected, as some have concluded and used as a doctrine to teach people to reject YAHUAH's Law and Commandments. This same spirit that elevates the 'traditions of men' ahead of the Law and Commandments of YAHUAH is at the centre of Roman Catholicism and the institutions and doctrines that have come from it to form the religion of Christianity, and hence what most of the church adheres to today.

- o **"Do not think that I came to destroy the Law or the Prophets. I did not come to destroy but to fulfil. [18] For assuredly, I say to you, till heaven and earth pass away, one jot or one tittle will by no means pass from the law till all is fulfilled. [19] Whoever therefore**

> *breaks one of the least of these commandments, and teaches men so, shall be called least in the kingdom of heaven; but whoever does and teaches them, he shall be called great in the kingdom of heaven. [20] For I say to you, that unless your righteousness exceeds the righteousness of the scribes and Pharisees, you will by no means enter the kingdom of heaven. (Matthew 5:17-20 NKJV)*

It was essential to establish the foundation of YAHUAH'S commandments and laws — the terms of His covenant with His people — for it is on this basis that YAHUAH defines what sin is.

Sin according to 𐤉𐤄𐤅𐤄 YAHUAH

YAHUAH is the only authority who has determined what sin is, and He does so according to His definition of sin, which is directly linked to His commandments and laws. His definition of sin is unchanging. We will use the New Testament passage of 1 John 3:4-12 as the main reference for this definition and then link that to several other scriptures. As it is written:

> o *[4] Whosoever committeth sin transgresseth also the law: for sin is the transgression of the law. [5] And ye know that he was manifested to take away our sins; and in him is no sin. [6] Whosoever abideth in him sinneth not: whosoever sinneth hath not seen him, neither known him. [7] Little children, let no man deceive you: he that doeth righteousness is righteous, even as he is righteous. [8] He that committeth sin is of the devil; for the devil sinneth from the beginning. For this purpose the Son of YAHUAH was manifested, that he might destroy the works of the devil. [9] Whosoever is born of YAHUAH doth not commit sin; for*

> *his seed remaineth in him: and he cannot sin, because he is born of YAHUAH. [10] In this the children of YAHUAH are manifest, and the children of the devil: whosoever doeth not righteousness is not of YAHUAH, neither he that loveth not his brother. [11] For this is the message that ye heard from the beginning, that we should love one another. [12] Not as Cain, who was of that wicked one, and slew his brother. And wherefore slew he him? Because his own works were evil, and his brother's righteous. (1 John 3:4-12 KJV)*

Each time the word *law* is used, it can also be read as TORAH – YAHUAH'S instructions and guidance for His people. Because this is such an important point, we will look at it more closely by considering the scripture passage alongside added explanations, shown in (brackets).

Whosoever committeth sin transgresseth also the law: **for sin is the transgression of the law (Torah/given instructions)**. *[5] And ye know that He (YAHUSHA) was manifested to take away our* **(transgressions of the law/Torah/given instructions)** *sins; and in Him (YAHUSHA) is no* **(transgression of the law/Torah/given instructions)** *sin. [6] Whosoever abideth in Him (YAHUSHA)* **(does not wilfully transgress the law/Torah/given instructions)** *sinneth not: whosoever* **(does not wilfully transgress the law/Torah/given instructions)** *sinneth hath not seen Him (YAHUSHA), neither known Him. [7] Little children, let no man deceive you: he that* **(makes right choice according to the law/Torah/given instructions)** *doeth righteousness is righteous, even as he is righteous. [8] He that* **(wilfully transgresses the law/Torah/given instructions)** *committeth sin is of the devil; for the devil* **(wilfully transgresses the law/Torah/given instructions)** *sinneth from the beginning. For this purpose the Son of YAHUAH was manifested, that He might destroy the works* *of the devil. [9] Whosoever is born of YAHUAH doth not* **(wilfully transgress the law/Torah/given instructions)** *commit sin; for his seed remaineth in him: and he cannot* **(wilfully transgresses the law/Torah/given instructions)** *sin, because he is born of YAHUAH. [10] In this the children of YAHUAH are manifest, and the children of the devil: whosoever* **(does not make right choices according to the law/Torah/given instructions)** *doeth not righteousness is not of YAHUAH, neither he that loveth not his brother. [11] For this is the message that ye heard from the beginning, that we should love one another. [12] Not as Cain, who was of that wicked one, and slew his brother. And wherefore slew he him? Because his own works were evil, and his brother's righteous* **(right choices according to the instructions given/law/Torah)**. *(1 John 3:4-12 KJV)*

- Yes, *all YASHARA'AL has transgressed Your law, and has departed so as not to obey Your voice; therefore the curse and the oath written in the Law of Moses the servant of YAHUAH have been poured out on us, because we have sinned against Him. (Daniel 9:11 NKJV)*

In Hebrew, the word for lawlessness is Pesha (H6588 in Strong's Concordance) or in Greek it is Anomia (G458 in Strong's Concordance), and the Strong's concordance describes it as follows -

The Hebrew word "pesha" primarily denotes a wilful (deliberate) transgression or rebellion against YAHUAH's law and authority. It implies a deliberate act of disobedience or defiance, often in a covenantal context. In the Old Testament, "pesha" is used to describe not only individual acts of sin but also national rebellion against YAHUAH's commandments, and even a rejection of His authority.

In Scripture, the Hebrew language gives us three powerful words to describe sin, each showing a different level of our need for God's mercy. "Chet" means "missing the mark" — like stumbling off course or falling short without intending to, as Proverbs 19:2 reminds us: "He who hurries with his feet *sins* (chet)." "Avon" goes deeper, pointing to iniquity — a crookedness in the heart, a choice to go astray, bringing guilt and shame, as David confessed in Psalm 51:5, "In sin (avon) did my mother conceive me." But the heaviest word is pesha: the wilful breaking of His covenant. In simple terms, *chet* is a mistake, *avon* is a deliberate wrong, and *pesha* is outright rebellion — yet for each one, YAHUAH has made a way of forgiveness through YAHUSHA.

In ancient Israel (YASHARA'AL), the concept of "pesha" was deeply tied to the covenant relationship between YAHUAH and His people. Transgressions were seen as breaches of this covenant, which required atonement and repentance. The sacrificial system in the Law provided a means for addressing "pesha," emphasising the seriousness of sin and the need for reconciliation with YAHUAH. The Bible prophets frequently called out "pesha" as a reason for divine judgment, urging the people to return to YAHUAH, the ALAHYM of Abraham, Isaac and Jacob.

Now that we have this understanding of the definition of sin according to YAHUAH, we can look at the consequences of it, as this is part of the 'divine design'. In a nutshell, the consequences of sin can be summarised as (1) separation from YAHUAH in this lifetime and (2) separation from YAHUAH eternally, which He refers to as 'death', signifying a permanent separation from Him now and in the ages to come. Part of the separation from YAHUAH in this lifetime is Him turning His face away from us so that we are no longer under His covenantal covering of protection and provision.

When YAHUAH's covenantal covering is removed, we are

left 'naked' and exposed for the enemy to come in to steal, kill and destroy, which is exactly what has happened to Africa.

As it is written:

- ***For the wages of sin is death, but the gift of YAHUAH is eternal life in YAHUSHA MASHYACH our Master.*** *(Romans 6:23 NKJV)*
- *Then YAHUAH took the man and put him in the garden of Eden to tend and keep it. And YAHUAH commanded the man, saying, "Of every tree of the garden you may freely eat; but of the tree of the knowledge of good and evil you shall not eat,* ***for in the day that you eat of it you shall surely die."*** *(Genesis 2:15-17 NKJV)*
- *Behold, YAHUAH's hand is not shortened, that it cannot save; Nor His ear heavy, that it cannot hear.* ***But your iniquities have separated you from your Aluah; And your sins have hidden His face from you, so that He will not hear.*** *(Isaiah 59:1-2 NKJV)*
- *Then My anger shall be aroused against them in that day, and I will forsake them, and I will hide My face from them, and they shall be devoured. And many evils and troubles shall befall them, so that they will say in that day,* ***'Have not these evils come upon us because our Aluah YAHUAH is not among us?' And I will surely hide My face in that day because of all the evil which they have done, in that they have turned to other gods.*** *(Deuteronomy 31:17-18 NKJV)*
- *Then they will cry to YAHUAH,* ***But He will not hear them; He will even hide His face from them at that time, because they have been evil in their deeds.*** *(Micah 3:4 NKJV)*

When there is sin, YAHUAH does not hear the prayers of His people. He will only turn His face back to His people and hear their cries when sin (transgression of the law/Torah/given instructions) is removed. So, it is important to do this as it is the difference between walking on 'the path that leads to the blessing and life' or 'the path that leads to the curse and death'.

The removal of sin is only through confession and repentance. Confession is the admission that we have transgressed the law, and repentance is our turning away from the error of our ways (change in behaviour) to return to the commitment to obey the instructions that YAHUAH has given. As it is written:

- *If we say that we have fellowship with Him, and walk in darkness, we lie and do not practice the truth. But if we walk in the light as He is in the light, we have fellowship with one another, and the blood of YAHUSHA MASHYACH His Son cleanses us from all sin. If we say that we have no sin, we deceive ourselves, and the truth is not in us.* **If we confess our sins, He is faithful and just to forgive us our sins and to cleanse us from all unrighteousness. If we say that we have not sinned, we make Him a liar, and His word is not in us.** *(I John 1:6-10 NKJV)*
- *YAHUSHA answered and said to them, "Those who are well have no need of a physician, but those who are sick.* **I have not come to the righteous, but sinners, to repentance."** *(Luke 5:31-32 NKJV)*
- *From that time YAHUSHA began to preach and to say,* **"Repent, for the kingdom of heaven is at hand."** *(Matthew 4:17 NKJV)*

YAHUSHA was given His name as a prophetic declaration of what His Abba, YAHUAH sent Him to do, which is to save the people from the consequences of sin (temporary and permanent separation from YAHUAH). He is HA MASHYACH (The Messiah/The Anointed One/The Christ) sent as saviour to fulfil His FATHER'S promise that He, the FATHER YAHUAH, would save us. The FATHER YAHUAH placed His name in His SON YAHUSHA (YAHUAH is salvation) and sent Him with His authority to fulfil this mission on earth.

As it is written:

- *And she shall bring forth a son, and thou shalt call his name YAHUSHA: **for He shall save His people from their sins**. (Matthew 1:21 KJV)*
- *The next day John seeth YAHUSHA coming unto him, and saith, **Behold the Lamb of Alahym, which taketh away the sin of the world.** (John 1:29 KJV)*
- *And you know that, and in Him there is no sin. (I John 3:5 NKJV)*
- *He that committeth sin is of the devil; for the devil sinneth from the beginning. For this purpose the Son of YAHUAH was manifested, that he might destroy the works of the devil. (1 John 3:8 KJV)*

The Law of YAHUAH given to us through Moses stated that for there to be remission of sin, blood had to be shed, and a life sacrificed. Before YAHUSHA was sent to fulfil this on earth, the law of animal sacrifice (which is one component of the overall law) was the mechanism through which life and blood were offered for atonement. Because 'the wages of sin is death', the animal would die to fulfil the payment, and its blood would settle the debt of that sin temporarily. (This is exactly what YAHUSHA fulfilled by taking our sin upon Himself in death, and, in a similar – yet far greater – fashion, His blood settled the debt, this time, permanently).

Please note it is critical to understand that YAHUSHA removed the need for further animal sacrifice and hence fulfilled that part of the law, but did not remove the other elements of the law. Many of us have been confused by words that the Apostle Paul (SHA'UL) spoke about the law, but we need to understand that at times he was addressing issues that relate specifically to the law of animal sacrifice and blood, and not advocating the rejection of the entire Law of YAHUAH. A more detailed explanation of this will be covered in Chapter 11.

Once confession and repentance are activated, it is by our faith in YAHUSHA, having come to pay the price with His life and His blood (the Passover Lamb of YAHUAH), that the separation from YAHUAH is removed as we are justified and now obtain the righteousness (right standing according to the law) of YAHUAH.

If we claim there is no law and no commandments, we shut ourselves off from the process of confession, repentance and, therefore, the remission of sins and connection with YAHUAH. This is part of the 'divine design'.

As it is written:

- *And almost all things are by the law purged with blood; and **without shedding of blood is no remission**. (Hebrews 9:22 KJV)*
- *Is the law then against the promises of YAHUAH? YAHUAH forbid: for if there had been a law given which could have given life, verily righteousness should have been by the law. [22] But the scripture hath concluded all under sin, that the promise by faith of YAHUSHA MASHYACH might be given to them that believe. [23] But before faith came, we were kept under the law, shut up unto the faith*

> which should afterwards be revealed. [24] Wherefore the law was our schoolmaster to bring us unto MASHYACH, that we might be justified by faith. [25] But after that faith is come, we are no longer under a schoolmaster. (Galatians 3:21-25 KJV)

Because this is the cornerstone in the 'divine design' of the Kingdom of YAHUAH, it is worthwhile to reference what is written in Hebrews chapter 10:1-23, referring to what has happened through YAHUSHA (who is the Chief Cornerstone).

- *For the law, having a shadow of the good things to come, and not the very image of the things, can never with these same sacrifices, which they offer continually year by year, make those who approach perfect. [2] For then would they not have ceased to be offered? For the worshipers, once purified, would have had no more consciousness of sins. [3] But in those sacrifices there is a reminder of sins every year. [4] For it is not possible that the blood of bulls and goats could take away sins. [5] Therefore, when He came into the world, He said: "Sacrifice and offering You did not desire, but a body You have prepared for Me. [6] In burnt offerings and sacrifices for sin You had no pleasure. [7] Then I said, 'Behold, I have come— In the volume of the book it is written of Me— To do Your will, O YAHUAH." [8] Previously saying, "Sacrifice and offering, burnt offerings, and offerings for sin You did not desire, nor had pleasure in them" (which are offered according to the law), [9] then He said, "Behold, I have come to do Your will, O YAHUAH." He takes away the first that He may establish the second. [10] By that will we have been sanctified through the offering of the body of YAHUSHA MASHYACH once for all. [11]*

> *And every priest stands ministering daily and offering repeatedly the same sacrifices, which can never take away sins. [12] But this Man, after He had offered one sacrifice for sins forever, sat down at the right hand of YAHUAH, [13] from that time waiting till His enemies are made His footstool. [14] For by one offering He has perfected forever those who are being sanctified. [15] But the Holy Spirit also witnesses to us; for after He had said before, [16] "This is the covenant that I will make with them after those days, says YAHUAH: I will put My laws into their hearts, and in their minds I will write them," [17] then He adds, "Their sins and their lawless deeds I will remember no more." [18] Now where there is remission of these, there is no longer an offering for sin. [19] Therefore, brethren, having boldness to enter the Holiest by the blood of YAHUSHA, [20] by a new and living way which He consecrated for us, through the veil, that is, His flesh, [21] and having a High Priest over the house of YAHUAH, [22] let us draw near with a true heart in full assurance of faith, having our hearts sprinkled from an evil conscience and our bodies washed with pure water. [23] Let us hold fast the confession of our hope without wavering, for He who promised is faithful. (Hebrews 10:1-23 NKJV)*

Please note that when it says "law" in verse 1 of the above passage from Hebrews 10:1-23, it is making reference to the law of animal sacrifice.

In Section 2, the 12 domains of control that have been used to 'conquer and capture' Africa were covered. To recap them again here –

1. Spirituality/Religion

2. Culture
3. Economy
4. Political Institutions
5. Military/Security
6. Media/Information
7. Education
8. Legal System
9. Technology/Infrastructure
10. Healthcare/Social Services
11. Natural Resources
12. Finance/Banking

What we do concerning the Spirituality/Religion 'domain of control' will determine what happens with the others. The spiritual 'domain of control' is the foundation of Africa's redemption and will determine the level of success of the solutions (which we have yet to discuss) required to address the other 11 domains. But what is important to note here is that the Chief Cornerstone in the spiritual domain must be in place, for all things will be built from the Chief Cornerstone.

Tribes of Africa, everything that we build will have to be built upon the Chief Cornerstone.

As it is written:

- o *YAHUSHA saith unto them, did ye never read in the scriptures,* ***The stone which the builders rejected, the same is become the head of the corner:*** *This is the YAHUAH's doing, and it is marvellous in our eyes?* (Matthew 21:42 KJV)
- o *And He (YAHUSHA) beheld them, and said, What is this then that is written,* ***The stone which the builders***

rejected, The same is become the head of the corner? [18] Whosoever shall fall upon that stone shall be broken; but on whomsoever it shall fall, it will grind him to powder. (Luke 20:17-18 KJV)

- Therefore thus saith the YAHUAH, **Behold, I lay in Zion for a foundation a stone, a tried stone, a precious corner stone, a sure foundation**: he that believeth shall not make haste. (Isaiah 28:16 KJV)
- **his is the stone which was set at nought of you builders, which is become the head of the corner.** [12] Neither is there salvation in any other: for there is none other name under heaven given among men, whereby we must be saved. (Acts 4:11-12 KJV)
- Now, therefore, you are no longer strangers and foreigners, but fellow citizens with the saints and members of the household of YAHUAH, having been built on the foundation of the apostles and prophets, **YAHUSHA MASHYACH Himself being the chief cornerstone, in whom the whole building, being fitted together**, grows into a holy temple in YAHUAH, in whom you also are being built together for a dwelling place of YAHUAH in the Spirit. (Ephesians 2:19-22 NKJV)
- **Coming to Him as to a living stone, rejected indeed by men, but chosen by YAHUAH and precious**, [5] you also, as living stones, are being built up a spiritual house, a holy priesthood, to offer up spiritual sacrifices acceptable to YAHUAH through YAHUSHA MASHYACH. [6] Therefore it is also contained in the Scripture, **"Behold, I lay in Zion A chief cornerstone, elect, precious, and he who believes on Him will by no means be put to shame."** [7] Therefore, to you who believe, He is precious;

but to those who are disobedient, **"The stone which the builders rejected has become the chief cornerstone," [8] and "A stone of stumbling and a rock of offense." They stumble, being disobedient to the word, to which they also were appointed.** *[9] But you are a chosen generation, a royal priesthood, a holy nation, His own special people, that you may proclaim the praises of Him who called you out of darkness into His marvelous light; [10]* **who once were not a people but are now the people of YAHUAH, who had not obtained mercy but now have obtained mercy.** *(I Peter 2:4-10 NKJV)*

🔥 **Tribes of Africa,** it is through the Chief Cornerstone that we become the people of YAHUAH, and we will receive the mercy that we have sought and not found.

🔥 **Tribes of Africa,** you no longer have to sacrifice animals and appease our Creator Abba YAHUAH with the blood of animals. YAHUSHA has fulfilled that once and for all. All requirements for blood sacrifice in the spiritual domain have been done through our faith in YAHUSHA – this is the Good News that He came to give us and the Good News He has sent us to proclaim.

🔥 As the tribes of Africa, we have lived in much bondage, and the scriptures reveal to us that the truth shall set us free. Since the freedom of any person, tribe or nation is linked to truth, it is important to establish what truth is within the spiritual domain. Once freedom is achieved in the spiritual domain, that freedom can then flow to the other domains.

> o *Then YAHUSHA said to those Jews who believed Him, "If you abide in My word, you are My disciples indeed. [32]* **And you shall know the truth, and the truth shall make**

you free." *[33] They answered Him, "We are Abraham's descendants, and have never been in bondage to anyone. How can You say, 'You will be made free'?" [34] YAHUSHA answered them,* **"Most assuredly, I say to you, whoever commits sin is a slave of sin***. [35] And a slave does not abide in the house forever, but a son abides forever. [36]* **Therefore if the Son makes you free, you shall be free indeed***. (John 8:31-36 NKJV)*

Establishing what TRUTH is

The Word of YAHUAH defines truth in four ways. It says that Truth is –

(1) The Law
- *Your righteousness is an everlasting righteousness, And* ***Your law is truth****.*
   (Psalm 119:142 KJV)

(2) The Commandments
- *Thou art near, O YAHUAH; And* ***all thy commandments are truth****.*
   (Psalm 119:151 KJV)

(3) The SON YAHUSHA
- *YAHUSHA said to him,* "***I am*** *the way,* ***the truth****, and the life. No one comes to the Father except through Me. (John 14:6 NKJV)*

(4) The Word
- *Sanctify them by Your truth.* ***Your word is truth****. (John 17:17 NKJV)*

If 'the Law' and 'the Commandments' and 'The SON YAHUSHA' and 'the Word' are not applied together 'as one', there is no truth. This is one of the biblical equations.

- YAHUSHA spoke of His assignment (His cause) to Pilate when Pilate asked Him if He was a King:
  - *Pilate therefore said to Him, "Are You a king then?" YAHUSHA answered, "You say rightly that I am a king. For this cause I was born, and for this cause I have come into the world, that I should bear witness to the truth.* **Everyone who is of the truth hears My voice.***" (John 18:37 NKJV)*
- YAHUSHA gives the key to freedom:
  - *Then YAHUSHA said to those Jews who believed Him, "If you abide in My word, you are My disciples indeed. And you shall know the truth, and* **the truth shall make you free.***" (John 8:31-32 NKJV)*
- Apostle Paul appeals to the Galatians not to be fooled into rejecting the truth:
  - *O foolish Galatians!* **Who has bewitched you that you should not obey the truth,** *before whose eyes YAHUSHA MASHYACH (Christ) was clearly portrayed among you as crucified? (Galatians 3:1 NKJV)*
- Apostle Paul gives a stern warning for wilfully rejecting the truth:
  - *For if we sin wilfully after we have received the* **knowledge of the truth,** *there no longer remains a sacrifice for sins, (Hebrews 10:26 NKJV)*
- Apostle Paul speaks of the working of Satan with deception upon those who do not love the truth:
  - *The coming of the lawless one is according to the working of Satan, with all power, signs, and lying wonders, and with all unrighteous deception among those who perish,* **because they did not receive the love of the truth,** *that they might be saved. And for this reason, YAHUAH will send them strong delusion, that they should believe the lie, that they all*

may be condemned **who did not believe the truth** but had pleasure in unrighteousness. (2 Thessalonians 2:9-12)

- The truth is a foundational pillar in the foundation of the throne of YAHUAH and hence in the design of the working of His Kingdom:
  - *Righteousness and Justice are the foundation of Your throne; Mercy and* **Truth** *go before Your face. (Psalm 89:14 NKJV)*
- YAHUSHA states what genuine worship of the FATHER YAHUAH is:
  - *But the hour is coming, and now is, when the true worshippers will worship the Father in spirit and truth; for the Father is seeking such to worship Him. YAHUAH is Spirit, and those who worship Him* **must worship in spirit and truth**. *(John 4:23-24 NKJV)*

As Africans, we have perhaps worshipped Him in Spirit, but we have missed the Truth. I have yet to come across any other people in the world who are as spiritually aware and sensitive as we Africans, seeking the Most High fervently in prayer crusades and all-night prayer gatherings. But perhaps because we have been taught in mainstream Christianity that His law and commandments are no longer valid, we have missed the truth. Since we have just discovered in scripture that 'His law is truth' and 'all His commandments are truth', this is where we have missed the mark in our worship. SELAH

Perhaps it is of value to examine the biblical definition of Spirit so that we can also determine whether we have worshipped YAHUAH in Spirit according to His standard.

As it is written:

- *'It is the Spirit who gives life; the flesh profits nothing.* **The**

> ***words that I speak to you are spirit***, *and they are life.'* (John 6:63)

So, Spirit is the words that YAHUSHA (who is Truth) speaks to us.

Spirit and Truth are not what man or religion defines them as; Spirit and truth are defined by YAHUAH, and He measures them according to His standard.

As a final point on truth, YAHUSHA reveals the enemy, the father of lies, the devil, who is without truth.

- o *You are of your father the devil, and the desires of your father you want to do. He was a murderer from the beginning,* ***and does not stand in the truth, because there is no truth in him****. When he speaks a lie, he speaks from his own resources, for he is a liar and the father of it. But because I tell the truth, you do not believe Me. (John 8:44-45 NKJV)*

According to the 4 things that make up truth it means the devil will always be void of (1) 'The Law' and (2) 'The Commandments' and (3) 'The SON YAHUSHA' and (4) 'The Word'; and he will work to remove these, for when the truth has departed, he can take and keep people in captivity. This is the working of the lawless one – it is the working of the anti-Christ. As it is written:

- o *Let no one deceive you in any way. For that day will not come, unless the rebellion comes first, and* ***the man of lawlessness is revealed, the son of destruction****, [4] who opposes and exalts himself against every so-called god or object of worship, so that he takes his seat in the temple of ALAHYM, proclaiming himself to be YAHUAH. [5] Do you not remember that when I was still with you I told you these things? [6] And you know what is restraining him now so*

> that he may be revealed in his time. [7] **For the mystery of lawlessness is already at work**. Only he who now restrains it will do so until he is out of the way. [8] **And then the lawless one will be revealed,** whom the Master YAHUSHA will kill with the breath of his mouth and bring to nothing by the appearance of his coming. [9] **The coming of the lawless one is by the activity of Satan** with all power and false signs and wonders, [10] and with all wicked deception for those who are perishing, **because they refused to love the truth and so be saved.** [11] Therefore YAHUAH sends them a strong delusion, so that they may believe what is false, [12] **in order that all may be condemned who did not believe the truth but had pleasure in unrighteousness.** 2 Thessalonians 2:3-12 ESV

The mystery of lawlessness has been active since religion 'captured' the truth and convinced us that the law and commandments of YAHUAH are no longer valid. Rejecting the law and commandments of YAHUAH is rejecting the truth and choosing lawlessness and pleasure in unrighteousness.

🔥 **Tribes of Africa,** if you are following a religion that does not have truth, YAHUAH says, "COME OUT OF HER", for that religion will keep you in captivity and lead to your destruction.

As it is written:

- And I heard another voice from heaven saying, "**Come out of her**, my people, lest you share in her sins, and lest you receive of her plagues. For her sins have reached to heaven, and YAHUAH has remembered her iniquities. (Revelation 18:4-5 NKJV)

🔥 **Tribes of Africa,** finding freedom in the spiritual domain is the prerequisite to finding freedom in the other 11 domains and is attained by finding the Truth. This is how YAHUAH has designed things to work. If we don't find truth in the spiritual domain, we will see very little sustainable progress in the other domains.

Definition of 'what is good' to ⵣⵢⵣⵑ YAHUAH

The dictionary defines good as (1) desired or approved of, (2) having the required qualities, of a high standard, (3) that which is morally right, righteousness, (4) benefit or advantage to someone or something.

Let us know among ourselves what is good.

- *Let us choose justice for ourselves; Let us know among ourselves what is good. (Job 34:4 NKJV)*

What does YAHUAH say is good?

- *Therefore the law is holy, and the commandment holy and just **and good**. (Romans 7:12 NKJV)*
- *But we know that the law **is good** if one uses it lawfully, (I Timothy 1:8 NKJV)*
- *Hear, my children, the instruction of a father, and give attention to know understanding;* **For I give you good doctrine:** *Do not forsake my law. (Proverbs 4:1-2 NKJV)*
- **The law of YAHUAH is perfect,** *converting the soul;* **The testimony of YAHUAH is sure,** *making wise the simple; [8]* **The statutes of YAHUAH are right,** *rejoicing the heart;* **The commandment of YAHUAH is pure,** *enlightening the eyes; [9]* **The fear of YAHUAH is clean,** *enduring forever;* **The judgments of YAHUAH** *are true and righteous altogether. [10] More to be desired are they than gold, Yea, than much fine gold, Sweeter also than*

honey and the honeycomb. (Psalms 19:7-10 NKJV)
- He has shown you, O man, **what is good**; And what does YAHUAH require of you but to do justly, To love mercy, and to walk humbly with your Aluah? (Micah 6:8 NKJV)

What is good for YAHUAH remains good forever, for He does not lie and does not change.

- "For **I am YAHUAH, I do not change**; therefore you are not consumed, O sons of Jacob. (Malachi 3:6 NKJV)
- "**YAHUAH is not a man, that He should lie**, nor a son of man, that He should repent. Has He said, and will He not do? Or has He spoken, and **will He not make it good**? (Numbers 23:19 NKJV)
- YAHUSHA MASHYACH **is the same yesterday, today, and forever.** (Hebrews 13:8 NKJV)

What was good yesterday is still good today and will be good forever. No man, or institution, can change what YAHUAH says is good. If YAHUAH says His Law is good and His Commandment is good and He says that His Law is perfect, then that is what it is.

The mystery of lawlessness has permeated mainstream Christianity to call evil good and good evil. To teach a theology that the law and commandments of YAHUAH are evil and should not be honoured anymore, and to say that rejecting them is good, is the foundation of lawlessness. It is setting the stage for the lawless one to have a 'great harvest' of followers who have been deceived into following him.

- Woe to those who call evil good and good evil, who put darkness for light and light for darkness, who put bitter for sweet and sweet for bitter! (Isaiah 5:20 ESV)

How Abba 𐤀𐤅𐤄𐤉 YAHUAH wants to be loved

YAHUAH has established how He wants to be loved. It is the way that He feels loved. He has revealed His standard and definition of what it takes to love Him. It is simply OBEDIENCE.

Rather than putting together a justification based on the words of man, it is best for the WORD of YAHUAH to speak directly of the love He asks from us.

As it is written:

- "You shall therefore love YAHUAH your Aluah and keep His charge, His statutes, His rules, and His commandments always. (Deuteronomy 11:1 ESV)
- "See, I have set before you today life and good, death and evil, in that I command you today to love YAHUAH your Aluah, to walk in His ways, and to keep His commandments, His statutes, and His judgments, that you may live and multiply; and YAHUAH your Aluah will bless you in the land which you go to possess. (Deuteronomy 30:15-16 NKJV)
- **"If you love Me, you will keep My commandments.** (John 14:15 ESV)
- **He who has My commandments and keeps them, it is he who loves Me.** And he who loves Me will be loved by My Father, and I will love him and manifest Myself to him." (John 14:21 NKJV)
- Now by this we know that we know Him, if we keep His commandments. He who says, "I know Him," and does not keep His commandments, is a liar, and the truth is not in him. But whoever keeps His word, truly the love of YAHUAH is perfected in him. By this we know that we are in Him. He who says he abides in Him ought himself also to

- *walk just as He walked. (I John 2:3-6 NKJV)*
  - *Whoever believes that YAHUSHA is the MASHYACH (the Messiah/the anointed One/the Christ) is born of YAHUAH, and everyone who loves Him who begot also loves him who is begotten of Him. By this we know that we love the children of YAHUAH,* ***when we love YAHUAH and keep His commandments. For this is the love of YAHUAH, that we keep His commandments. And His commandments are not burdensome.*** *(I John 5:1-3 NKJV)*
  - *My little children, let us not love in word or in tongue, but in deed and in truth. And by this we know that we are of the truth, and shall assure our hearts before Him. For if our heart condemns us, YAHUAH is greater than our heart, and knows all things. Beloved, if our heart does not condemn us, we have confidence toward YAHUAH. And whatever we ask we receive from Him, because we keep His commandments and do those things that are pleasing in His sight. And this is His commandment: that we should believe on the name of His Son YAHUSHA MASHYACH and love one another, as He gave us commandment. (I John 3:18-23 NKJV)*

Man defines love based on the flesh, which is driven by feelings and emotions; YAHUAH defines it by the Spirit, which is driven by obedience to His Voice and instructions. Let us not be caught in the deadly trap of thinking that we can love YAHUAH based on our definition and standard, which are based on the flesh. **This is the trap that the religion of Christianity has created, and which the mainstream Christian church has fallen into**. Loving YAHUAH is not measured by fleshly emotions and feelings; it is measured by a spirit that drives the flesh to obedience.

BIBLICAL DEFINITIONS AND EQUATIONS

We can have all sorts of feelings of the flesh and emotions of man-defined love, but if we are not obeying His commandments, it means we hate Him (since we do not love Him). This is part of the 'divine design', and it does not change to suit the standard of man or institutions of religion that say otherwise. In fact, YAHUAH goes on to say that we are liars, as it is written:

> o *Whoever says "I know him" but does not keep his commandments is a liar, and the truth is not in him. (I John 2:4 ESV)*

Lying is one of the things that YAHUAH calls an abomination, as we will soon see.

The issue of love is the very essence of YAHUAH, because He is love. He, therefore, goes on to warn against the main things that would cause our hearts to stray from Him. For the purposes of this point, we will see what is written concerning (1) idols, (2) mammon (money), (3) the world and (4) the flesh/man.

> o *'You shall have no other gods before Me.* ***'You shall not make for yourself a carved image—any likeness of anything that is in heaven above, or that is in the earth beneath, or that is in the water under the earth; you shall not bow down to them nor serve them.*** *For I, YAHUAH your Aluah, am a jealous Alahym, visiting the iniquity of the fathers upon the children to the third and fourth generations of* ***those who hate Me****, but showing mercy to thousands, to those who love Me and keep My commandments. (Deuteronomy 5:7-10 NKJV)*

🕎 **Tribes of Africa,** please note that putting up images or 'pictures' of Jesus (which is a fake picture anyway), crucifixes, Catholic rosaries, crosses, and other 'paraphernalia of Christianity' which we honour, bow down to or worship is a direct violation of the 2nd Commandment of YAHUAH and carries generational consequences because it is considered as hatred towards Him.

- *Little children, **keep yourselves from idols**. (I John 5:21 ESV)*

The love of money:

- *"No one can serve two masters; for either he will hate the one and love the other, or else he will be loyal to the one and despise the other. **You cannot serve YAHUAH and mammon**. (Matthew 6:24 NKJV)*
- *For **the love of money is a root of all kinds of evil**, for which some have strayed from the faith in their greediness, and pierced themselves through with many sorrows. (I Timothy 6:10 NKJV)*

The love of the world:

- *Adulterers and adulteresses! Do you not know that friendship with the world is enmity with YAHUAH? **Whoever therefore wants to be a friend of the world makes himself an enemy of YAHUAH**. (James 4:4 NKJV)*
- ***Do not love the world or the things in the world. If anyone loves the world, the love of the Father is not in him.** For all that is in the world—the lust of the flesh, the lust of the eyes, and the pride of life—is not of the Father but is of the world. And the world is passing away, and the lust of it; but he who does the will of YAHUAH abides forever. (I John 2:15-17 NKJV)*
- ***Let your conduct be without covetousness**; be content with such things as you have. For He Himself has said, "I will never leave you nor forsake you." (Hebrews 13:5 NKJV)*

The love of man/the flesh:

- *Thus says YAHUAH: **"Cursed is the man who trusts in man and makes flesh his strength**, whose heart departs from YAHUAH. For he shall be like a shrub in the desert, and shall not see when good comes, but shall inhabit the parched places in the wilderness, in a salt land which is not inhabited. (Jeremiah 17:5-6 NKJV)*

Tribes of Africa, one of the idols that we have fallen to is the idol of man/flesh by following and worshipping the many so-called prophets, apostles, teachers and preachers that have no love (no obedience) of YAHUAH in them but are ravenous wolves in sheep's clothing devouring the people of Africa.

YAHUAH goes further to speak about the things that He hates and calls out as an abomination.

- *These **six things YAHUAH hates**, yes, seven are an abomination to Him: A proud look, A lying tongue, Hands that shed innocent blood, A heart that devises wicked plans, Feet that are swift in running to evil, A false witness who speaks lies, and one who sows discord among brethren. (Proverbs 6:16-19 NKJV)*
- *Diverse weights and diverse measures, they are both alike, **an abomination to YAHUAH**. (Proverbs 20:10 NKJV)*
- ***The sacrifice of the wicked is an abomination**; How much more when he brings it with wicked intent! (Proverbs 21:27 NKJV)*
- ***You shall not lie with a male as with a woman. It is an abomination**. (Leviticus 18:22 NKJV)*
- *And He said to them, "You are those who justify yourselves before men, but YAHUAH knows your hearts. **For what is***

highly esteemed among men is an abomination in the sight of YAHUAH. *(Luke 16:15 NKJV)*

This is not an exhaustive list of the abominations that He gives in His Word, but it makes the point. We need to stay away from following leaders (especially those who claim to be speaking on behalf of YAHUAH) who carry, display and teach what YAHUAH says He hates and is an abomination to Him. For if we don't, we face the consequences of His judgement as a result of them. It is worthwhile to repeat these words, **for what is highly esteemed among men is an abomination in the sight of YAHUAH. What we as flesh esteem is an abomination to YAHUAH. (SELAH)**

- *And I heard another voice from heaven saying, "Come out of her, my people, lest you share in her sins, and lest you receive of her plagues. For her sins have reached to heaven, and YAHUAH has remembered her iniquities. (Revelation 18:4-5 NKJV)*

The core of the covenant that YAHUAH established with us is based on the equation "Love = (equals) Obedience" and is the premise of the covenant (marriage agreement) He made with YASHARA'AL at Mount Sinai. He made the covenant conditional upon our love for Him (which is obedience). In fact, YAHUAH designed His entire Kingdom based on love (if we love Him, we will obey) (or if we don't love Him, we will disobey), with the foundational call to obedience being centred on the 10 commandments.

To clearly understand YAHUAH'S offer of marriage to YASHARA'AL, it may be seen in four parts: (1) the love-offer and YASHARA'AL'S acceptance of it, (2) the covenant terms, which they were to obey as a sign of their love for YAHUAH, (3) the people's agreement to those terms, and (4) the covenant itself being sealed in blood.

BIBLICAL DEFINITIONS AND EQUATIONS

(1) YAHUAH's offer of love to His people and the YASHARA'AL's acceptance of the offer.

- *And Moses went up to YAHUAH, and YAHUAH called to him from the mountain, saying, "Thus you shall say to the house of Jacob, and tell the children of YASHARA'AL: [4] 'You have seen what I did to the Egyptians, and how I bore you on eagles' wings and brought you to Myself. [5]* ***Now therefore, if you will indeed obey My voice and keep My covenant, then you shall be a special treasure to Me above all people; for all the earth is Mine. [6] And you shall be to Me a kingdom of priests and a holy nation.'*** *These are the words which you shall speak to the children of YASHARA'AL." [7] So Moses came and called for the elders of the people, and laid before them all these words which YAHUAH commanded him. [8] Then all the people answered together and said,* ***"All that YAHUAH has spoken we will do." So Moses brought back the words of the people to YAHUAH.*** *(Exodus 19:3-8 NKJV)*

(2) The terms of the covenant to which they were to be obedient as a sign that they loved YAHUAH.

- *And YAHUAH spoke all these words, saying: [2] "I am YAHUAH your Aluah, who brought you out of the land of Egypt, out of the house of bondage. [3] "You shall have no other gods before Me. [4] "You shall not make for yourself a carved image—any likeness of anything that is in heaven above, or that is in the earth beneath, or that is in the water under the earth; [5] you shall not bow down to them nor serve them. For I, YAHUAH your Aluah, am a jealous Alahym, visiting the iniquity of the fathers upon the children to the third and fourth generations of those who hate Me, [6] but showing mercy to thousands, to those who love Me and keep My commandments. [7] "You shall not take the name of YAHUAH your Aluah in vain, for YAHUAH will not hold him guiltless who takes His name in vain. [8] "Remember the Sabbath day, to keep it holy. [9] Six days you shall labour and do all your work, [10] but the seventh day is the Sabbath of YAHUAH your Aluah. In it you shall do no work: you, nor your son, nor your daughter, nor your male servant, nor your female servant, nor your cattle, nor your stranger who is within your gates. [11] For in six days YAHUAH made the heavens and the earth, the sea, and all that is in them, and rested the seventh day. Therefore YAHUAH blessed the Sabbath day and hallowed it. [12] "Honor your father and your mother, that your days may be long upon the land which YAHUAH your Aluah is giving you. [13] "You shall not murder. [14] "You shall not commit adultery. [15] "You shall not steal. [16] "You shall not bear false witness against your neighbour. [17] "You shall not covet your neighbour's house; you shall not covet your neighbour's wife, nor his male servant, nor his female servant, nor his ox, nor his donkey, nor anything that is your neighbour's." (Exodus 20:1-17 NKJV)*

(3) The people of YASHARA'AL accepting the terms given to them by YAHUAH

Now He said to Moses, "Come up to YAHUAH, you and Aaron, Nadab and Abihu, and seventy of the elders of YASHARA'AL, and worship from afar. [2] And Moses alone shall come near YAHUAH, but they shall not come near; nor shall the people go up with him." [3] So Moses came and told the people all the words of YAHUAH and all the judgments. **And all the people answered with one voice and said, "All the words which YAHUAH has said we will do."**

(4) The covenant/agreement being sealed by blood

- *And Moses wrote all the words of YAHUAH. And he rose early in the morning, and built an altar at the foot of the mountain, and twelve pillars according to the twelve tribes of YASHARA'AL. [5] Then he sent young men of the children of YASHARA'AL, who offered burnt offerings and sacrificed peace offerings of oxen to YAHUAH. [6] And Moses took half the blood and put it in basins, and half the blood he sprinkled on the altar. [7]* **Then he took the Book of the Covenant and read in the hearing of the people. And they said, "All that YAHUAH has said we will do, and be obedient." [8] And Moses took the blood, sprinkled it on the people, and said, "This is the blood of the covenant which YAHUAH has made with you according to all these words."** *(Exodus 24:1-8 NKJV)*

The love story continues despite YASHARA'AL's disobedience as YAHUAH speaks through the prophet Jeremiah (and repeated by Apostle Paul to the Hebrews) of a Renewed Covenant (which is often translated as New Covenant) where instead of the record of the covenant being written on stones **YAHUAH would put His Law in our minds and write it on our hearts**, with the agreement again ratified by blood. But not with the blood of animals, but the blood of YAHUSHA as YAHUSHA Himself spoke of as He shared the covenant meal of communion with His disciples, and asked that we continue to do so in remembrance of the fact that we have a covenant with YAHUAH which He has sealed with His blood.

- [31] "Behold, the days are coming, says YAHUAH, when I will make a new covenant with the house of YASHARA'AL and with the house of Judah— [32] not according to the covenant that I made with their fathers in the day that I took them by the hand to lead them out of the land of Egypt, My covenant which they broke, though I was a husband to them, says YAHUAH. [33] **But this is the covenant that I will make with the house of YASHARA'AL after those days, says YAHUAH: I will put My law in their minds, and write it on their hearts; and I will be their Alahym, and they shall be My people.** [34] No more shall every man teach his neighbour, and every man his brother, saying, 'Know YAHUAH,' for they all shall know Me, from the least of them to the greatest of them, says YAHUAH. For I will forgive their iniquity, and their sin I will remember no more." (Jeremiah 31:31-34 NKJV)
- [7] For if that first covenant had been faultless, then no place would have been sought for a second. [8] Because finding fault with them, He says: "Behold, the days are coming, says YAHUAH, when I will make a new covenant with the house of YASHARA'AL and with the house of Judah— [9] not according to the covenant that I made with their fathers in the day when I took them by the hand to lead them out of the land of Egypt; because they did not continue in My covenant, and I disregarded them, says YAHUAH. [10] **For this is the covenant that I will make with the house of YASHARA'AL after those days, says YAHUAH: I will put My laws in their mind and write them on their hearts; and I will be their Alahym, and they shall be My people.** [11] None of them shall teach his neighbour, and none his brother, saying, 'Know YAHUAH,' for all shall

know Me, from the least of them to the greatest of them. [12] For I will be merciful to their unrighteousness, and their sins and their lawless deeds I will remember no more." (Hebrews 8:7-12 NKJV)

- **"This is the covenant that I will make with them after those days, says YAHUAH: I will put My laws into their hearts, and in their minds I will write them,"** *then He adds, "Their sins and their lawless deeds I will remember no more. "Now where there is remission of these, there is no longer an offering for sin. (Hebrews 10:16-18 NKJV)*

By YAHUSHA sharing in the love feast of communion with His disciples before His death, YAHUSHA was replicating the love feast the children of YASHARA'AL celebrated before YAHUAH at Mt Sinai to confirm the establishment of the covenant with celebration just as they did then. As it is written:

- *Then Moses went up, also Aaron, Nadab, and Abihu, and seventy of the elders of YASHARA'AL and they saw the Alahym of YASHARA'AL. And there was under His feet as it were a paved work of sapphire stone, and it was like the very heavens in its clarity. But on the nobles of the children of YASHARA'AL He did not lay His hand.* **So they saw YAHUAH, and they ate and drank.** *(Exodus 24:9-11 NKJV*

- **And as they were eating** *YAHUSHA took bread, blessed and broke it, and gave it to the disciples and said, "Take, eat; this is My body." Then He took the cup, and gave thanks, and gave it to them, saying, "Drink from it, all of you.* **For this is My blood of the new covenant, which is shed for many for the remission of sins.** *But I say to you, I will not drink of this fruit of the vine from now on*

until that day when I drink it new with you in My Father's kingdom." (Matthew 26:26-29 NKJV)
- **And as they were eating**, YAHUSHA took bread, blessed and broke it, and gave it to them and said, "Take, eat; this is My body." Then He took the cup, and when He had given thanks He gave it to them, and they all drank from it. [24] **And He said to them, "This is My blood of the new covenant, which is shed for many.** Assuredly, I say to you, I will no longer drink of the fruit of the vine until that day when I drink it new in the kingdom of YAHUAH." (Mark 14:22-25 NKJV)
- For I received from YAHUAH that which I also delivered to you: that the Master YAHUSHA on the same night in which He was betrayed took bread; and when He had given thanks, He broke it and said, "Take, eat; this is My body which is broken for you; do this in remembrance of Me." In the same manner He also took the cup after supper, saying, **"This cup is the new covenant in My blood. This do, as often as you drink it, in remembrance of Me."** For as often as you eat this bread and drink this cup, you proclaim YAHUSHA's death till He comes. (I Corinthians 11:23-26 NKJV)

As YAHUSHA hung on the tree, He shouted a final breath and said **IT IS FINISHED!!!!** Meaning, **THE SEPARATION OF YASHARA'AL FROM YAHUAH THE FATHER IS FINISHED.** As it is written:

- When YAHUSHA had received the sour wine, He said, **"It is finished,"** and He bowed His head and gave up His spirit. (John 19:30 ESV)

 HALLELU-YAH – PRAISE YAH – PRAISE YAHUAH for the

most amazing love story!!! Tribes of Africa, "this is THE Good News".

The Obedience of OWᕵᕯᐯ YAHUSHA

The Messiah (HA MASHYACH) Himself learnt obedience to His FATHER through the things He had to face and overcome (suffer), which required Him to obey the commandments and instructions of the Father above His flesh (His own will) as it is written:

- *though He was a Son, yet He learned obedience by the things which He suffered. [9] And having been perfected, He became the author of eternal salvation to all who obey Him, [10] called by Alahym as High Priest "according to the order of Melchizedek," (Hebrews 5:8-10 NKJV)*

YAHUSHA laid down His own will for the FATHER's will.

- *For I have come down from heaven, **not to do My own will but the will of Him who sent Me**. (John 6:38 ESV)*
- *And He was withdrawn from them about a stone's throw, and He knelt down and prayed, [42] saying, **"Father, if it is Your will, take this cup away from Me; nevertheless not My will, but Yours, be done."** (Luke 22:41-42 NKJV)*
- *"Now My soul is troubled, and what shall I say? **'Father, save Me from this hour'? But for this purpose I came to this hour.** (John 12:27 NKJV)*

YAHUSHA did not come to fulfil His own agenda but as One who is sent to fulfil the FATHER's agenda. He did not speak His own words, but the words given to Him by the FATHER. He did not do anything except what He saw the FATHER doing. He had no authority except that given to Him by the FATHER.

- *Then YAHUSHA answered and said to them, **"Most***

- *assuredly, I say to you, the Son can do nothing of Himself, but what He sees the Father do; for whatever He does, the Son also does in like manner. (John 5:19 NKJV)*
  - **I can of Myself do nothing**. *As I hear, I judge; and My judgment is righteous, because* **I do not seek My own will but the will of the Father who sent Me.** *(John 5:30 NKJV)*
  - *Then YAHUSHA said to them, "When you lift up the Son of Man, then you will know that I am He,* **and that I do nothing of Myself**; *but as My Father taught Me, I speak these things. [29] And He who sent Me is with Me. The Father has not left Me alone, for I always do those things that please Him." (John 8:28-29 NKJV)*
  - **For I have not spoken on My own authority; but the Father who sent Me gave Me a command, what I should say and what I should speak.** *[50] And I know that His command is everlasting life. Therefore,* **whatever I speak, just as the Father has told Me, so I speak."** *(John 12:49-50 NKJV)*
  - *Do you not believe that I am in the Father, and the Father in Me? The words that I speak to you* **I do not speak on My own authority**; *but the Father who dwells in Me does the works. (John 14:10 NKJV)*

YAHUSHA demonstrated to us what total obedience to the Father looks like and through that confirmed His absolute love for the FATHER.

- *"As the Father loved Me, I also have loved you; abide in My love. [10]* **If you keep My commandments, you will abide in My love, just as I have kept My Father's commandments and abide in His love.** *[11] "These things I have spoken to you, that My joy may remain in you, and*

> *that your joy may be full. [12] This is My commandment, that you love one another as I have loved you. [13] Greater love has no one than this, than to lay down one's life for his friends. [14]* **You are My friends if you do whatever I command you.** *[15] No longer do I call you servants, for a servant does not know what his master is doing;* **but I have called you friends, for all things that I heard from My Father I have made known to you.** *[16] You did not choose Me, but I chose you and appointed you that you should go and bear fruit, and that your fruit should remain, that whatever you ask the Father in My name He may give you. [17]* **These things I command you, that you love one another.** *(John 15:9-17 NKJV)*

YAHUSHA, the Son, did everything YAHUAH the FATHER sent Him to do as the FATHER empowered Him through the Set Apart/Holy Spirit (RUACH HA QADASH) of the FATHER, who was the anointing that qualified Him to be HA MASHYACH (The Messiah).

YAHUSHA demonstrated absolutely and completely how to love His Abba, YAHUAH.

- To be a follower of YAHUSHA is to do as He did.
- To be a friend of YAHUSHA is to do as He did.
- To be a disciple of YAHUSHA is to do as He did.
- To be yoked with YAHUSHA is to be led by Him in doing as He did and still does.

   o *Then YAHUSHA said to His disciples,* **"If anyone desires to come after Me, let him deny himself, and take up his cross, and follow Me.** *For whoever desires to save his life will lose it, but whoever loses his life for My sake will find it. (Matthew 16:24-25 NKJV)*

Defining 'The Word of 𐤀𐤋𐤄𐤉𐤌 YAHUAH (GOD)' and the overcoming saints and the remnant

It is worthwhile to establish what 'The Word of YAHUAH/The Word of Alahym' is, which is spoken about many times in the Bible. The term 'The Word of YAHUAH', before YAHUSHA came to complete His assignment, comprised of **'The Law and the Prophets'**.

After the coming of YAHUSHA, 'The Word of YAHUAH' comprises **'The Law, the Prophets and the Testament'**.

The testament or testimony portion is speaking about all that has been written about YAHUSHA. This is the full 'Word of YAHUAH'. We cannot talk about 'The Word of YAHUAH' if we remove any of these components from it. What we term as the Old Testament and the New Testament cannot be separated, for they together form 'The Word of YAHUAH'.

In some instances, the Old Testament is referred to as 'the Commandments' or 'the Law of Moses' or 'the Song of Moses' and the New Testament as the 'Testimony of YAHUSHA or 'the faith of YAHUSHA' or the 'Song of the Lamb'.

We see this evidenced through the overcomers (those who conquer the beast) as they sing both the song of Moses and the song of the Lamb as an indication of how what YAHUAH did through both Moses and YAHUSHA is a requirement to overcome the system of the beast.

> o *Then I saw another sign in heaven, great and amazing, seven angels with seven plagues, which are the last, for with them the wrath of YAHUAH is finished. [2] And I saw what appeared to be a sea of glass mingled with fire—and also those who had conquered the beast and its image and the*

> *number of its name, standing beside the sea of glass with harps of YAHUAH in their hands. [3]* **And they sing the song of Moses, the servant of YAHUAH, and the song of the Lamb**, *saying, "Great and amazing are your deeds, O YAHUAH the Almighty! Just and true are your ways, O King of the nations! (Revelation 15:1-3 ESV)*

What YAHUAH sent Moses and YAHUSHA to establish are inseparable.

The combination of both establishes the definition and qualifying requirements of what the Bible refers to as the overcoming Saints and Remnant, as it is written:

- *Here is the patience of* **the saints; here are those who keep (1) the commandments of YAHUAH and (2) the faith of YAHUSHA.** *(Revelation 14:12 NKJV)*
- *And the dragon was enraged with the woman, and he went to make war with the rest of her offspring, the remnant,* **(1) who keep the commandments of YAHUAH and (2) have the testimony of YAHUSHA MASHYACH.** *(Revelation 12:17 NKJV)*

What YAHUAH sent Moses to establish and what He sent YAHUSHA to fulfil and establish are intertwined together in the divine design, even as YAHUAH spoke about the coming of YAHUSHA through words He gave to Moses to prophesy.

- **"YAHUAH your Aluah will raise up for you a Prophet like me from your midst, from your brethren.** *Him you shall hear, [16] according to all you desired of YAHUAH your Aluah in Horeb in the day of the assembly, saying, 'Let me not hear again the voice of YAHUAH my Aluah, nor let me see this great fire anymore, lest I die.' [17] "And*

> YAHUAH said to me: 'What they have spoken is good. [18] **I will raise up for them a Prophet like you from among their brethren**, and will put My words in His mouth, and He shall speak to them all that I command Him. [19] And it shall be that whoever will not hear My words, which He speaks in My name, I will require it of him. (Deuteronomy 18:15-19 NKJV).

When we separate the works of YAHUAH through Moses and those through YAHUSHA we fall into the trap of the mystery of lawlessness and into the hands of the lawless one.

For YAHUSHA was destined to come through the tribe of Judah, as it is written that He will come through the loins of David and be born of the seed of David according to the flesh and declared to be the Son of YAHUAH. As it is written:

- *Then the angel said to her, "Do not be afraid, Mary, for you have found favor with YAHUAH. [31] And behold, you will conceive in your womb and bring forth a Son, and shall call His name YAHUSHA. [32] He will be great, and will be called the Son of the Highest;* **and YAHUAH Aluah will give Him the throne of His father David. [33] And He will reign over the house of Jacob forever, and of His kingdom there will be no end."** *(Luke 1:30-33 NKJV)*
- *Paul, a bondservant of YAHUSHA MASHYACH, called to be an apostle, separated to the gospel of YAHUAH [2] which He promised before through His prophets in the Holy Scriptures, [3]* **concerning His Son YAHUSHA MASHYACH our Master, who was born of the seed of David according to the flesh, [4] and declared to be the Son of YAHUAH with power according to the Spirit of holiness,** *by the resurrection from the dead. (Romans 1:1-4 NKJV)*

YAHUSHA will return to reign as the everlasting KING and will receive His bride—the overcoming remnant saints, who will be singing both the song of Moses and the song of the Lamb.

ओwयेxy YAHUSHA is coming back to receive a bride without spot or wrinkle

As it is written:

- *Husbands, love your wives, just as Christ (Mashyach) also loved the church and gave Himself for her, that He might sanctify and **cleanse her with the washing of water by the word**, that He might present her to Himself a glorious church, not having spot or wrinkle or any such thing, but that she should be holy and without blemish. (Ephesians 5:25-27 NKJV)*

It is the word that cleanses the bride, removing all "spot and wrinkle", making her holy and without blemish.

Back to our 'equations' – We have already seen that 'the word is truth' and that 'the law and the commandments are also truth'. Which means 'the word' is 'the law and the commandments'.

So, we could present it as WORD = (equals) TRUTH = (equals) LAW & COMMANDMENTS

Based on this, we can paraphrase Ephesians 5:25-27 as follows:

- *Husbands, love your wives, just as Christ also loved the church and gave Himself for her, that He might sanctify and cleanse her with the washing of water by the TRUTH, WHICH IS THE LAW AND THE COMMANDMENTS, that He might present her to Himself a glorious church, not having spot or wrinkle or any such thing, but that she should*

> *be holy and without blemish. (Ephesians 5:25-27 NKJV)*

YAHUSHA said He is the way, the truth and the life. The TRUTH is the WAY to the FATHER (who is the source of LIFE). Without the LAW & COMMANDMENTS, which are the TRUTH, there is no WAY of getting to the FATHER.

- *YAHUSHA said to him, "I am the way, and the truth, and the life.* **No one comes to the Father except through me.** *(John 14:6 ESV)*

Tribes of Africa embrace the cleansing that YAHUSHA MASHYACH wants to undertake upon you, for you are His bride. He is indeed your bridegroom. The washing of the water by the Word entails the washing by the full Word, the Law, the Prophets, the Psalms and the Testament. If we choose the New Testament only, we will remain dirty with spots and wrinkles. There is no way YAHUSHA will take us to the FATHER if we have refused to be washed by the Word, which is the law and commandments (instructions of the FATHER).

Concluding this section

The reason for spending so much time on these definitions is to help us work from the same understanding as to what the Hebraic culturally based scriptures are saying. If we miss the foundational understanding of the meaning of words, whatever we build on top of that foundation will be flawed, as it will be built on sand and not on the Rock.

- *"Therefore whoever hears these sayings of Mine, and does them, I will liken him to a wise man who built his house on the rock: [25] and the rain descended, the floods came, and the winds blew and beat on that house; and it did not fall,*

> *for it was founded on the rock. [26]* ***"But everyone who hears these sayings of Mine, and does not do them, will be like a foolish man who built his house on the sand: [27] and the rain descended, the floods came, and the winds blew and beat on that house; and it fell. And great was its fall."*** *(Matthew 7:24-27 NKJV)*

I encourage you to read the entire Word of YAHUAH (the Bible) afresh, taking note of the words that have been defined. It is amazing how the scriptures come alive and speak in a very different way when the correct word definitions are applied to them. I was and continue to be astounded by what 'The Voice' is saying and how different it is from what I had been indoctrinated to believe that the scriptures said.

Allow 'The Voice' to speak to you directly and the Spirit of YAHUAH to be your primary teacher.

As we proceed, let us remember -

Tribes of Africa, because YAHUAH is love, He exhorts us to love. The task that lies ahead cannot be accomplished without YAHUAH, and therefore, it cannot be accomplished without love.

> o *Beloved, let us love one another, for love is of YAHUAH; and everyone who loves is born of YAHUAH and knows YAHUAH. [8] He who does not love does not know YAHUAH,* ***for YAHUAH is love.*** *(I John 4:7-8 NKJV)*

"Building on the foundation to undderstand how YAHUAH's design works"
Section 4
Contents

Chapter 10.   The Consequences of idol worship and removing His name.

Chapter 11.   The law of YAHUAH and the law of sacrifice to attain righteousness.

Chapter 12.   The power of repentance and forgiveness

Chapter 13.   Understanding what the Kingdom of YAHUAH is

Chapter 14.   The Ark of the Covenant

Beloved, let us love one another, for love is of YAHUAH; and everyone who loves is born of YAHUAH and knows YAHUAH. [8] He who does not love does not know YAHUAH, for YAHUAH is love. (I John 4:7-8 NKJV)

CHAPTER TEN

The Consequences Of Idol Worship And Removing His Name

The process of the establishment of the covenant with YAHUAH has already been mentioned, but it is worthwhile covering some of the consequences of not honouring its terms.

Here are the commandments listed as it is written in Exodus 20:1-17 and Deuteronomy 5:6-22

1. "You shall have no other gods before Me.
2. "You shall not make for yourself a carved image—any likeness of anything that is in heaven above, or that is in the earth beneath, or that is in the water under the earth, you shall not bow down to them nor serve them. **For I, YAHUAH your Aluah, am a jealous Alahym, visiting the iniquity of the fathers upon the children to the third and fourth generations of those who hate Me, but showing mercy to thousands, to those who love Me and keep My commandments.**
3. "You shall not take the name of YAHUAH your Aluah in

vain, **for YAHUAH will not hold him guiltless who takes His name in vain**

4. "Remember the Sabbath day, to keep it holy. Six days you shall labour and do all your work, but the seventh day is the Sabbath of YAHUAH your Aluah. In it you shall do no work: you, nor your son, nor your daughter, nor your male servant, nor your female servant, nor your cattle, nor your stranger who is within your gates. For in six days YAHUAH made the heavens and the earth, the sea, and all that is in them, and rested the seventh day. Therefore, YAHUAH blessed the Sabbath day and hallowed it.
5. "Honor your father and your mother, that your days may be long upon the land which YAHUAH your Aluah is giving you
6. "You shall not murder.
7. "You shall not commit adultery
8. "You shall not steal
9. "You shall not bear false witness against your neighbour.
10. "You shall not covet your neighbour's house; you shall not covet your neighbour's wife, nor his male servant, nor his female servant, nor his ox, nor his donkey, nor anything that is your neighbour's

It is worthwhile to pay attention to the consequences given for violating Commandments 2 and 3.

The consequences of violating Commandment 2 are generational, as YAHUAH states, *"visiting the iniquity of the fathers upon the children to the third and fourth generations of those who hate Me."*

The consequences of *'making carved images of the likeness of anything that is in heaven above, or that is in the earth beneath, or that is in the water under the earth and of you bowing down to them or to serve them'* are severe.

YAHUAH does not want anything that is created to serve as a means of connecting to Him, not even images in the likeness of anything that is in heaven. This means no images of angels, no man-made images of Him, no man-made images of YAHUSHA, no images of anything that is created.

This is one of the biggest traps we have fallen into because the religious institution of Christianity, led by the Roman Catholic Church, changed the 10 Commandments as they are listed in the scriptures (Exodus 20:1-17 and Deuteronomy 5:6-22) and came up with their own version that purposely changed the 2nd commandment and removed the reference to YAHUAH's abhorrence of idols and images. They removed this reference so that they could promote images (pictures and statues) as part of their worship, which relies on images of crucifixes, crosses, pictures of Jesus and Mary and the venerated saints that people today bow down to and hold in high esteem as a way to connect to God. This is an abomination and direct violation of the Covenant (the agreement with YAHUAH) and has dire consequences.

YAHUAH wants us to worship Him in Spirit and in Truth only. No objects involved. No pictures of Jesus hanging in our houses and cars, no statues of Jesus and Mary, no crosses, no rosaries and no fish symbols displayed. They all violate the 2nd Commandment.

As an important side note: One of the biggest, most harmful and dangerous lies ever propagated by the religious institution of Christianity is the image (idol) of Jesus with long straight blonde hair and blue eyes. No image of YAHUSHA existed, and therefore the image of Jesus is an invention of religion specifically modelled after a noble man named Cesare Borgia, later duc de Valentinois, (born c. 1475/76, probably Rome—died 1507, near Viana, Spain), an Italian military leader, the illegitimate son of Pope Alexander VI, and brother of Lucrezia Borgia. It is an idol (image) designed to promote white supremacy subliminally and was used powerfully to entrench an inferiority complex among all people of other races as part of the agenda to conquer through the domain of religion/spirituality.

For reference, this is the list of the modified 10 commandments of the Catholic Church:

1. I am the LORD thy God. Thou shall not have strange gods before Me.
2. Thou shall not take the name of the LORD thy God in vain.
3. Remember to keep holy the LORD's Day.
4. Honor thy father and mother.
5. Thou shall not kill.
6. Thou shall not commit adultery.
7. Thou shall not steal.
8. Thou shall not bear false witness against thy neighbour.
9. Thou shall not covet thy neighbour's wife.
10. Thou shall not covet thy neighbour's goods.

Tribes of Africa, get rid of all the objects, the graven images and statues. Get rid of pictures of Jesus in your homes. The only way YAHUAH wants us to connect with Him is in Spirit and in Truth, not through any object. He detests us needing to use any object (images, pictures or statues) to invoke our affections and worship to Him.

By using images (pictures and statues, and other physical objects), it shifts our worship of Him by faith alone in what is unseen to worshipping through what we see. The object becomes the mediator in our worship and hence becomes an idol and an abomination to YAHUAH. This is a deeply pagan practice that YAHUAH hates.

The only worship He requires of us is in Spirit and in Truth. The definition of truth has already been highlighted, and it has a direct loop back to the Spirit. For YAHUAH says that He will give His Spirit to only those who obey. As it is written:

- *But Peter and the other apostles answered and said: "We ought to obey YAHUAH rather than men. [30] The Alahym of our fathers raised up YAHUSHA whom you murdered by hanging on a tree. [31] Him YAHUAH has exalted to His right hand to be Prince and Savior, to give repentance to YASHARA'AL and forgiveness of sins. [32] And we are His witnesses to these things, **and so also is the Holy Spirit whom YAHUAH has given to those who obey Him**." (Acts 5:29-32 NKJV)*

YAHUAH makes it very clear that if we do not obey, He will not give His Ruach Ha Qadash (Holy Spirit). It is very simple: if we obey, He gives His Spirit; if we do not obey, He does not give His Spirit. SELAH

YAHUAH tells us very clearly how He wants to be worshipped as it is written:

- *It is the Spirit who gives life; the flesh profits nothing. **The words that I speak to you are spirit, and they are life**. (John 6:63 NKJV)*
- *YAHUSHA said to her, "Woman, believe Me, the hour is coming when you will neither on this mountain, nor in Yarushalayim (Jerusalem), worship the Father. You worship what you do not know; we know what we worship, for salvation is of the Jews. But the hour is coming, and now*

*is, when the **true worshipers will worship the Father in spirit and truth**; for the Father is seeking such to worship Him. **YAHUAH is Spirit, and those who worship Him must worship in spirit and truth.**" (John 4:21-24 NKJV)*

In the 3rd Commandment, YAHUAH says that "He will not hold him guiltless who takes His name in vain". Erasing His name from the Bible is one of the ways that His name has been taken in vain, and that has consequences.

The violation of the terms of the covenant (agreement with YAHUAH) is the primary constraint that, if dealt with, will open up sustainable progress and victory in the 'domains of control' that will bring Africa into its divine place in the plan of YAHUAH.

In Chapter 22, there is a prayer to YAHUAH that serves as a response to the chains and shackles that have bound Africa and many other indigenous people groups across the world to the religious institutions of Christianity (the daughters of the harlot) through the roots connecting back to (the mother of harlots), the Universal church of Rome, the Catholic church.

This is the harlot that instituted the Doctrine of Discovery and went out to use that to conquer many indigenous people across the world. This is the harlot that sits upon the many waters that has chained and shackled indigenous people groups from across the world, as it is written:

- *Then one of the seven angels who had the seven bowls came and talked with me, saying to me, **"Come, I will show you the judgment of the great harlot who sits on many waters, [2] with whom the kings of the earth committed fornication, and the inhabitants of the earth were made drunk with the wine of her fornication."** [3] So he*

- *carried me away in the Spirit into the wilderness. And I saw a woman sitting on a scarlet beast which was full of names of blasphemy, having seven heads and ten horns. [4] The woman was arrayed in purple and scarlet, and adorned with gold and precious stones and pearls, having in her hand a golden cup full of abominations and the filthiness of her fornication. [5] And on her forehead a name was written:* **MYSTERY, BABYLON THE GREAT, THE MOTHER OF HARLOTS AND OF THE ABOMINATIONS OF THE EARTH.** *[6] I saw the woman, drunk with the blood of the saints and with the blood of the martyrs of YAHUSHA. And when I saw her, I marveled with great amazement. (Revelation 17:1-6 NKJV)*
  - *Then he said to me, "The waters which you saw, where the harlot sits, are peoples, multitudes, nations, and tongues. [16] And the ten horns which you saw on the beast, these will hate the harlot, make her desolate and naked, eat her flesh and burn her with fire. [17] For YAHUAH has put it into their hearts to fulfill His purpose, to be of one mind, and to give their kingdom to the beast, until the words of YAHUAH are fulfilled. [18] And the woman whom you saw is that great city which reigns over the kings of the earth." (Revelation 17:15-18 NKJV)*

This is what YAHUAH implores us to get out of, lest we share in the judgement of the harlot.

- *After these things I saw another angel coming down from heaven, having great authority, and the earth was illuminated with his glory. [2] And he cried mightily with a loud voice, saying, "Babylon the great is fallen, is fallen, and has become a dwelling place of demons, a prison for every foul spirit, and a cage for every unclean and hated bird!* **[3] For all the nations have drunk of the wine of the wrath of her fornication, the kings of the earth have committed fornication with her, and the merchants of the earth have become rich through the abundance of her luxury."** *[4] And I heard another voice from heaven saying,* **"Come out of her, my people, lest you share in her sins, and lest you receive of her plagues. [5] For her sins have reached to heaven, and YAHUAH has remembered her iniquities.** *[6] Render to her just as she rendered to you, and repay her double according to her works; in the cup which she has mixed, mix double for her. [7] In the measure that she glorified herself and lived luxuriously, in the same measure give her torment and sorrow; for she says in her heart, 'I sit as queen, and am no widow, and will not see sorrow.'* **[8] Therefore her plagues will come in one day—death and mourning and famine. And she will be utterly burned with fire, for strong is YAHUAH Aluah who judges her.** *(Revelation 18:1-8 NKJV)*

- Then a mighty angel took up a stone like a great millstone and threw it into the sea, saying, "Thus with violence the great city Babylon shall be thrown down, and shall not be found anymore. [22] The sound of harpists, musicians, flutists, and trumpeters shall not be heard in you anymore. No craftsman of any craft shall be found in you anymore, and the sound of a millstone shall not be heard in you anymore. [23] The light of a lamp shall not shine in you anymore, and the voice of bridegroom and bride shall not be heard in you anymore. For your merchants were the great men of the earth, for by your sorcery all the nations were deceived. [24] And in her was found the blood of prophets and saints, *and of all who were slain on the earth." (Revelation 18:21-24 NKJV)*

We have fornicated with this harlot of Babylon and have been made drunk by the intoxicating wine she has served us. It is this intoxication that has led to our indoctrination into the lies that have led us into a perpetual cycle of disobeying YAHUAH and breaking the covenant (terms of agreement), He gave us. This is part of the mystery of lawlessness that YAHUAH is revealing for those who have ears to hear. We agreed to the terms of the agreement, and we are held accountable to them by YAHUAH's righteousness.

- *And Moses went up to YAHUAH, and YAHUAH called to him from the mountain, saying, "Thus you shall say to the house of Jacob, and tell the children of YASHARA'AL: [4] 'You have seen what I did to the Egyptians, and how I bore you on eagles' wings and brought you to Myself. [5]* ***Now therefore, if you will indeed obey My voice and keep My covenant, then you shall be a special treasure to Me above all people; for all the earth is Mine. [6] And you shall be to Me a kingdom of priests and a holy nation.' These are the words which you shall speak to the children of YASHARA'AL."*** *[7] So Moses came and called for the elders of the people, and laid before them all these words which YAHUAH commanded him. [8]* ***Then all the people answered together and said, "All that YAHUAH has spoken we will do."*** *So Moses brought back the words of the people to YAHUAH. (Exodus 19:3-8 NKJV)*

TRIBES OF AFRICA, "GET OUT OF HER" IS A STERN COMMAND AND ALSO A STERN WARNING. SELAH

An enquiry on Google says that there are 234 million people on the African continent who pledge their allegiance to Catholicism, which makes up 17% of the population.

PLEASE NOTE: This is not condemnation or judgement for the millions of people whose hearts' intention is to love the true Alahym (God)with all their hearts and are members of the Catholic church, but it is an indictment against the institutional organisation and those mainly in the highest positions of leadership within the institution who know of and are part of the foundation of lies and wickedness it uses to deceive people and lure them into lawlessness.

As we proceed, let us remember -

Tribes of Africa, because YAHUAH is love, He exhorts us to love. The task that lies ahead cannot be accomplished without YAHUAH, and therefore, it cannot be accomplished without love.

Beloved, let us love one another, for love is of YAHUAH; and everyone who loves is born of YAHUAH and knows YAHUAH. [8] He who does not love does not know YAHUAH, ***for YAHUAH is love****. (I John 4:7-8 NKJV)*

CHAPTER ELEVEN

The Law Of YAHUAH & The Law Of Sacrifice To Attain Righteousness

In YAHUAH's design, He placed the unchangeable statute that for there to be remission of sin, there must be the shedding of blood. The only way to atone for sin is for life to be exchanged for death and for blood to be presented to settle the debt of that sin. This is because, as it is written: 'the wages of sin is death' according to Romans 6:23. Sin demands that it receives life as payment. This requirement was established right at the beginning when YAHUAH gave His first-ever Commandment and Law to the first man, Adam, in Genesis 2:15-17.

> o *Then YAHUAH Aluah took the man and put him in the garden of Eden to tend and keep it. And YAHUAH Aluah commanded the man, saying, "Of every tree of the garden you may freely eat; but of the tree of the knowledge of good and evil you shall not eat,* **for in the day that you eat of it you shall surely die.**" *(Genesis 2:15-17 NKJV)*

The principle of offering life in exchange for sin and the shedding of blood as remittance for that sin was instituted by YAHUAH Himself when HE slaughtered an animal for Adam and Eve. This served to cover them after they committed the first sin by transgressing the first instruction given to them by YAHUAH, which was the first command and law given to mankind. It was the first Law whose consequence was death, so the consequence of death had to come upon them, but YAHUAH also instituted the principle of His grace. It is because of YAHUAH's grace that instead of Adam and Eve dying immediately for their sin, He provided a mechanism for them to have their transgression mitigated. So, man breaking the first law of YAHUAH also brought about the first demonstration of YAHUAH's grace to man. The grace of YAHUAH is not something that was introduced in the 'New Testament'. Grace is part of His nature, and He showed it when the 1st sin (transgression of the law) was committed in the Garden of Eden.

- *Then YAHUAH ALUAH called to Adam and said to him, "Where are you?" [10] So he said, "I heard Your voice in the garden, and I was afraid because I was naked; and I hid myself." [11] And He said, **"Who told you that you were naked? Have you eaten from the tree of which I commanded you that you should not eat?"***
- *Also for Adam and his wife **YAHUAH ALUAH made tunics of skin and clothed them.** (Genesis 3:9-11, 21 NKJV)*

This first animal sacrifice was the first exchange of life for death, and the first blood poured out for the remission of the first sin of the first man. It was pointing to the exchange that YAHUAH had already established through the Lamb of YAHUAH that was slain before the foundations of the world, as it is written in Revelation 13:8. But this first sacrifice would be followed by a period of animal sacrifice before the Lamb Himself would come to earth to fulfil the life sacrifice and blood offering requirement once and for all in front of human witnesses. HalleluYAH!!!!

- *All who dwell on the earth will worship him, whose names have not been written in the Book of Life of* **the Lamb slain from the foundation of the world**. *(Revelation 13:8 NKJV)*
- *For where there is a testament, there must also of necessity be the death of the testator. [17] For a testament is in force after men are dead, since it has no power at all while the testator lives. [18] Therefore not even the first covenant was dedicated without blood. [19] For when Moses had spoken every precept to all the people according to the law, he took the blood of calves and goats, with water, scarlet wool, and hyssop, and sprinkled both the book itself and all the people, [20] saying, "This is the blood of the covenant which YAHUAH has commanded you." [21] Then likewise he sprinkled with blood both the tabernacle and all the vessels of the ministry. [22]* **And according to the law almost all things are purified with blood, and without shedding of blood there is no remission of sin**. *(Hebrews 9:16-22 NKJV)*

When YAHUAH spoke to Cain after he murdered his brother Abel, He said that 'his blood is crying out from the ground' in Genesis 4:10. This is an indication that the blood which carries life (as per Leviticus 17:11) was crying out because there was now a legal requirement within the divine design for life to be offered in return (for the life that had been taken in sin) because there is no remission of sin without the shedding of blood.

- *Now Cain talked with Abel his brother; and it came to pass,*

> *when they were in the field, that Cain rose up against Abel his brother and killed him. [9] Then YAHUAH said to Cain, "Where is Abel your brother?" He said, "I do not know. Am I my brother's keeper?" [10] And He said, "What have you done?* **The voice of your brother's blood cries out to Me from the ground.** *[11] So now you are cursed from the earth, which has opened its mouth to receive your brother's blood from your hand. (Genesis 4:8-11 NKJV)*
> - **For the life of the flesh is in the blood**, *and I have given it to you upon the altar to make atonement for your souls;* **for it is the blood that makes atonement for the soul.'** *(Leviticus 17:11 NKJV)*

From the time of Adam and Eve to the next generation of Cain and Abel, the 1st principle that righteousness before YAHUAH can only be achieved by the sacrifice of life and the shedding of blood was established and then passed on to subsequent generations.

This continues with the institution of the Passover as YAHUAH prepared the YASHARA'ALITES for His deliverance (salvation) out of the land of bondage, Egypt.

> - *[12] 'For I will pass through the land of Egypt on that night, and will strike all the firstborn in the land of Egypt, both man and beast; and against all the gods of Egypt I will execute judgment: I am YAHUAH. [13]* **Now the blood shall be a sign for you on the houses where you are. And when I see the blood, I will pass over you;** *and the plague shall not be on you to destroy you when I strike the land of Egypt. (Exodus 12:12-13 NKJV)*

By the time YAHUAH gave the YASHARA'ALITES the covenant (His agreement) and its terms (the 10 Commandments) and His law, this principle was already established. YAHUAH instructed them to continue this practice, for He had given it as the 'Law of Sacrifice and Offerings,' to be carried out by the Levitical priests. This would continue as a statute as the only way they would attain righteousness before Him, despite them being required to obey the rest of the law (Torah/instructions), as they would never be able to obey it all the time. This was YAHUAH's grace for His people, but a grace they had to work for because they would need to go through the process (the work) of keeping unblemished animals, sacrificing them, and presenting their blood upon the altar. They would need to do this every time they sinned; this is the hard work they had to do to obtain righteousness. These are the works of man unto righteousness that the scriptures speak of.

This mechanism of 'working for salvation unto righteousness' continued until the Anointed One, The Messiah (the Christ), HA MASHYACH would be sent by YAHUAH as His sinless, perfect Lamb to offer up His life and shed His blood (as the offering and sacrifice) once and for all. This was so that no other life (sacrifice) and no other blood (offering) would ever be required to atone for sin. YAHUSHA, therefore, settled the wages of sin for all mankind and paid the debt of all sin with His blood and made that available for anyone who chooses to accept it according to the terms that His Father YAHUAH established. Those who accept this gift, according to the terms set for it, will have their lives preserved from eternal death and the debt of their sins paid for in full. On the other hand, those who don't accept the gift according to the terms set for it will have the requirement of life on themselves and will receive eternal death to fulfil that requirement.

The primary message after the death of YAHUSHA

After YAHUSHA's death, the main message of the disciples and apostles was to communicate this change in dispensation: that people, who had always believed that righteousness (right standing before YAHUAH) was achieved through their animal sacrifices and blood offerings, were now instructed to cease this practice. Instead, they were to believe that the requirement was now fully fulfilled by what HA MASHYACH (The Christ) had accomplished through His death on the stake (tree) and the shedding of His blood.

These are people who for thousands of years and generations WORKED FOR THEIR SALVATION AND RIGHTEOUSNESS by sacrificing animals and presenting their blood, and were now being told they did not have to do this anymore. This became the most contentious issue ever within YASHARA'AL and all who were coming to the faith by believing in the Word of YAHUAH. The Word of YAHUAH (being the Law, the Prophets, the Psalms and the Testament of YAHUSHA), which was now being revealed to people who lived all their lives knowing that the Word for YAHUAH was composed of the Law and the Prophets and the Psalms. The element of the Testament of YAHUSHA was now being added to the word of YAHUAH, and this brought much resistance to a people who had been faithful to Torah and the old dispensation of animal sacrifice, which was a foreshadowing of what had been brought to fulfilment by YAHUSHA.

Therefore, the biggest resistance to the preaching of YAHUSHA was the fact that He was the perfect and final sacrifice, and His blood was the final atonement for sin. Because the people of the day had always known atonement through the sacrificing of animals and using the blood of animals as an offering before YAHUAH, they could not fathom any other different **'Way',** and so the new message was highly offensive to them as they thought it would bring them into disobedience of YAHUAH. They were hearing something that went against centuries of generational obedience and compliance to the 'law of sacrifice unto righteousness' because even though they obeyed the law, they still knew that it was only by blood that they could be justified and attain righteous (acceptable standing) before YAHUAH.

This is why the disciples, apostles and believers were named 'people of **'The Way'** and why YAHUSHA stated that He was **'The Way'**. YAHUSHA is the only **'Way'** for anyone to get to YAHUAH, the FATHER, because that would be the only **'Way'** to be counted as righteous in the FATHER's sight.

- *Then Saul, still breathing threats and murder against the disciples of YAHUAH, went to the high priest and asked letters from him to the synagogues of Damascus, so that if he found any who were of **the Way**, whether men or women, he might bring them bound to Yarushalayim (Jerusalem). (Acts 9:1-2 NKJV)*
- *But when some were hardened and did not believe, but spoke evil of **the Way** before the multitude, he departed from them and withdrew the disciples, reasoning daily in the school of Tyrannus. (Acts 19:9 NKJV)*
- *[14] But this I confess to you, that according to **the Way** which they call a sect, so I worship the Alahym of my fathers, **believing all things which are written in the Law and in the Prophets.***
- *[22] But when Felix heard these things, having more accurate knowledge of **the Way**, he adjourned the proceedings and said, "When Lysias the commander comes down, I will make a decision on your case." (Acts 24:14, 22 NKJV)*
- *YAHUSHA said to him, "I am **the way**, the truth, and the life. No one comes to the Father except through Me. (John 14:6 NKJV)*

Paul's letters address this most contentious issue

'**The Way**' created havoc and a crisis within all YASHARA'AL and all the people who were coming to the faith. This meant that in most of the Apostles' and Paul's preaching and letters, when they spoke about 'the law', they were primarily addressing the issue of sacrifices and offerings and not challenging the entirety of the Law of YAHUAH.

It is so critical to grasp the full context of what is being spoken of when we see the term 'the law' in Paul's letters. One must understand the audience he was addressing. Are they YASHARA'ALITES who have always followed the law of animal sacrifice to obtain righteousness through their own efforts of slaughtering? Or is he speaking to Gentiles who were never exposed to any of the laws and are being taught about The Word of YAHUAH, but at the same time also being told that the aspect of animal sacrifice which YASHARA'ALITES (or Jews to use the term in the Bible) had been doing all their lives was no longer valid and they should therefore not be drawn into it. This practice was being stopped because YAHUSHA had come and died (and rose again) so that '**the Way**' to attain righteousness would now be by faith in the knowledge that the requirement for sacrifice had been fulfilled in HA MASHYACH, and they did not need to seek it by human effort (works) through the sacrifice of animals.

Both YASHARA'ALITE (Jews) and Gentiles were being told that the righteous requirement of the law would no longer be achieved through continually bringing animal sacrifices (the works of man) but that it was fulfilled once and for all and in full through MASHYACH (The work of The Messiah). MASHYACH did everything that was needed to fulfil the law of animal sacrifice.

Please read the letters of Paul through this lens and allow RUACH HA QADASH (The Holy Spirit) to guide you into all truth on this most critical matter.

In the book of Romans, the letter is for the Roman audience (a Gentile territory). These were predominantly Gentiles who were new to the "Word of YAHUAH' and wanted to obey it, and so the message carries a narrative that said, "find righteousness through what YAHUSHA has done and do not seek it through animal sacrifice, which is how it was done before". He was not advocating disobedience to the law and commandments.

- *There is therefore now no condemnation to those who are in MASHYACH YAHUSHA, who do not walk according to the flesh, but according to the Spirit. [2]* **For the law of the Spirit of life in MASHYACH YAHUSHA has made me free from the law of sin and death.** *[3] For what the law could not do in that it was weak through the flesh, YAHUAH did by sending His own Son in the likeness of sinful flesh, on account of sin: He condemned sin in the flesh, [4]* **that the righteous requirement of the law might be fulfilled in us who do not walk according to the flesh but according to the Spirit.** *[5] For those who live according to the flesh set their minds on the things of the flesh, but those who live according to the Spirit, the things of the Spirit. [6] For to be carnally minded is death, but to be spiritually minded is life and peace. [7]* **Because the carnal mind is enmity against YAHUAH; for it is not subject to the law of YAHUAH, nor indeed can be.** *[8] So then, those who are in the flesh cannot please YAHUAH. [9]* **But you are not in the flesh but in the Spirit, if indeed the Spirit of YAHUAH dwells in you. Now if**

> *anyone does not have the Spirit of YAHUSHA, he is not His. [10] And if MASHYACH (Christ) is in you, the body is dead because of sin, but the **Spirit is life because of righteousness**. [11] But if the Spirit of Him who raised YAHUSHA from the dead dwells in you, He who raised MASHYACH (Christ) from the dead will also give life to your mortal bodies through His Spirit who dwells in you. (Romans 8:1-11 NKJV)*

- *What shall we say then? Is the law sin? Certainly not! On the contrary, I would not have known sin except through the law. For I would not have known covetousness unless the law had said, "You shall not covet." But sin, taking opportunity by the commandment, produced in me all manner of evil desire. For apart from the law sin was dead. I was alive once without the law, but when the commandment came, sin revived and I died. And the commandment, which was to bring life, I found to bring death. For sin, taking occasion by the commandment, deceived me, and by it killed me. **Therefore the law is holy, and the commandment holy and just and good.** (Romans 7:7-12 NKJV)*

Hebrews is a letter primarily written to a Hebrew audience; those who had followed the Word of YAHUAH, made up of The Law and the Prophets, for generations, and so had always sacrificed animals as the way to obtain righteousness before YAHUAH. They followed and obeyed 'The Law and the Prophets', but they knew that they would always be prone to breaking the very law and the commandments they strived so hard to keep because of their sinful nature, and hence needed to sacrifice animals through the Levitical priests, to obtain righteousness. When they are now told that they should no longer sacrifice animals, it becomes a major battle for them because they did not want to be disobedient to YAHUAH and lose their righteousness through their works of animal sacrifice. The letter addresses this by going into great detail to explain that YAHUSHA is the fulfilment of the requirement for sacrifice and offerings, so that they can understand this and find rest in knowing that YAHUSHA has fulfilled that requirement in full for them. It was a message ending their compliance with the era of the Levitical priesthood and ushering them into the everlasting priesthood of Melchizedek, for which YAHUSHA is the High Priest. The message is that they no longer needed to labour to raise special, unblemished animals, sacrifice them, and use their blood to meet the requirement for righteousness. The letter carries a narrative that says, "come out of the law of animal sacrifice (your own works) which you and your ancestors have always done and embrace by faith (no human effort and work) the sacrifice of the life of YAHUSHA and the offering of His blood as the only way righteousness can be attained before YAHUAH". This was the aspect of the law that was being discussed, and not a call to abandon obedience to the entirety of YAHUAH's law and commandments as has been so erroneously preached and taught by the institution of the religion of Christianity.

- *As He saith also in another place,* ***Thou art a priest for ever After the order of Melchisedec.*** *[5] So also MASHYACH did not exalt Himself to be made a high priest, but was appointed by Him who said to him, "You are my Son, today I have begotten You" (Hebrews 5:6 KJV)*
- ***YAHUAH has sworn and will not change His mind, "You are a priest forever after the order of Melchizedek."*** *(Psalm 110:4 ESV)*

YAHUSHA came to fulfil His role as the priest forever after the order of Melchizedek, not to abolish or destroy the Law of His FATHER.

A recap of YAHUSHA's words as it is written:

- *"Do not think that I came to destroy the Law or the Prophets. I did not come to destroy but to fulfill. [18] For assuredly, I say to you, till heaven and earth pass away, one jot or one tittle will by no means pass from the law till all is fulfilled. [19] Whoever therefore breaks one of the least of these commandments, and teaches men so, shall be called least in the kingdom of heaven; but whoever does and teaches them, he shall be called great in the kingdom of heaven.* (Matthew 5:17-19 NKJV)

When we look at Paul's letter to the Galatians, he is speaking to a mixed audience of YASHARA'ALITES and Gentiles, so, in his letter he goes to and fro, addressing both sets of audience - to the YASHARA'ALITES (Jews as is used in the bible) he is saying _"come out of the law of animal sacrifice (your own works) which you and your ancestors have always done, and now embrace by faith (no human effort and work) the sacrifice of YAHUSHA and His blood as that is the only Way to attain righteousness with YAHUAH"_ and to the Gentiles he is saying _"the only way to find righteousness with YAHUAH is through what YAHUSHA has done and do not seek to attain it through animal sacrifice as was the practice before"._ He was pointing all (both YASHARA'ALITES (Jew) and Gentiles) to the same conclusion, but bringing them from their respective positions of current understanding, which were different. He was bringing both to receive righteousness through the sacrifice and blood of MASHYACH, but not to violate what YAHUSHA proclaimed that He had not come to abolish the law.

- *"Do not think that I came to destroy the Law or the Prophets. I did not come to destroy but to fulfill. [18]*

> *For assuredly, I say to you, till heaven and earth pass away, one jot or one tittle will by no means pass from the law till all is fulfilled. [19] Whoever therefore breaks one of the least of these commandments, and teaches men so, shall be called least in the kingdom of heaven; but whoever does and teaches them, he shall be called great in the kingdom of heaven.* (Matthew 5:17-19 NKJV)

This is one of the most critical issues we must get right; otherwise, we fall into the trap of permanent error that has eternal consequences. This is the mystery of lawlessness.

This conclusion for both YASHARA'ALITE (natural branches of the cultivated olive tree) and GENTILES (branches of the wild olive tree) is that justification to attain righteousness and thereby receive salvation is through YAHUSHA (the cultivated olive tree) only.

To the YASHARA'ALITES, the natural branches of the cultivated olive tree (who were part of the covenant by bloodline) must be grafted back onto the tree because they were cut off. Cut off because justification was no longer by animal sacrifice, but now by the sacrifice of YAHUSHA. If they did not make this shift, they would remain cut off from the covenant of inheritance.

To the Gentiles, the branches of the wild olive tree (not part of the covenant by bloodline) have an opportunity to become part of the covenant of inheritance by being grafted into the cultivated olive tree. If they did not, they would remain wild and cut off from the promises that are to be received by those who keep the terms of the covenant.

Bloodline inheritors and non-bloodline inheritors are brought together into the same covenant by YAHUSHA, so that they can be presented to YAHUAH as the 'bride of HA MASHYACH'.

This is what Apostle Paul spoke about in the letter to the Romans.

- *I ask, then, has YAHUAH rejected his people? By no means! For I myself am an YASHARA'ALITE, a descendant of Abraham, a member of the tribe of Benjamin. [2] YAHUAH has not rejected his people whom he foreknew. Do you not know what the Scripture says of Elijah, how he appeals to YAHUAH against YASHARA'AL? [3] "YAHUAH, they have killed your prophets, they have demolished your altars, and I alone am left, and they seek my life." [4] But what is YAHUAH's reply to him? "I have kept for myself seven thousand men who have not bowed the knee to Baal." [5] So too at the present time there is a remnant, chosen by grace. [6] But if it is by grace, it is no longer on the basis of works; otherwise grace would no longer be grace. [7] What then? YASHARA'AL failed to obtain what it was seeking. The elect obtained it, but the rest were hardened, [8] as it is written, "YAHUAH gave them a spirit of stupor, eyes that would not see and ears that would not hear, down to this very day." [9] And David says, "Let their table become a snare and a trap, a stumbling block and a retribution for them; [10] let their eyes be darkened so that they cannot see, and bend their backs forever." [11] So I ask, did they stumble in order that they might fall? By no means! Rather, through their trespass salvation has come to the Gentiles, so as to make YASHARA'AL jealous. [12] Now if their trespass means riches for the world, and if their failure means riches for the Gentiles, how much more will their full inclusion mean! [13] Now I am speaking to you Gentiles. Inasmuch then as I am an apostle to the Gentiles,*

I magnify my ministry [14] in order somehow to make my fellow Jews jealous, and thus save some of them. [15] For if their rejection means the reconciliation of the world, what will their acceptance mean but life from the dead? [16] **If the dough offered as firstfruits is holy, so is the whole lump, and if the root is holy, so are the branches. [17] But if some of the branches were broken off, and you, although a wild olive shoot, were grafted in among the others and now share in the nourishing root of the olive tree, [18] do not be arrogant toward the branches. If you are, remember it is not you who support the root, but the root that supports you. [19] Then you will say, "Branches were broken off so that I might be grafted in." [20] That is true. They were broken off because of their unbelief, but you stand fast through faith. So do not become proud, but fear. [21] For if YAHUAH did not spare the natural branches, neither will he spare you. [22] Note then the kindness and the severity of YAHUAH: severity toward those who have fallen, but YAHUAH's kindness to you, provided you continue in his kindness. Otherwise you too will be cut off. [23] And even they, if they do not continue in their unbelief, will be grafted in, for YAHUAH has the power to graft them in again. [24] For if you were cut from what is by nature a wild olive tree, and grafted, contrary to nature, into a cultivated olive tree, how much more will these, the natural branches, be grafted back into their own olive tree.** *[25] Lest you be wise in your own sight, I do not want you to be unaware of this mystery, brothers: a partial hardening has come upon YASHARA'AL, until the fullness of the Gentiles has come in. [26] And in this* *way all YASHARA'AL will be saved, as it is written, "The Deliverer will come from Zion, he will banish ungodliness from Jacob"; [27] "and this will be my covenant with them when I take away their sins." [28] As regards the gospel, they are enemies for your sake. But as regards election, they are beloved for the sake of their forefathers. [29] For the gifts and the calling of YAHUAH are irrevocable. [30] For just as you were at one time disobedient to YAHUAH but now have received mercy because of their disobedience, [31] so they too have now been disobedient in order that by the mercy shown to you they also may now receive mercy. [32] For YAHUAH has consigned all to disobedience, that he may have mercy on all. [33] Oh, the depth of the riches and wisdom and knowledge of YAHUAH! How unsearchable are his judgments and how inscrutable his ways! [34] "For who has known the mind of YAHUAH, or who has been his counselor?" [35] "Or who has given a gift to him that he might be repaid?" [36] For from him and through him and to him are all things. To him be glory forever. Amen. (Romans 11:1-36 ESV)*

In the book of Ezekiel, it is prophetically spoken about the 'strangers/sojourners' (Gentiles) who are joined to YASHARA'AL will be as native born. This is referring to the same picture, of bloodline YASHARA'AL 'adopting' Gentiles (non-bloodline) to become as native born (one bloodline in YAHUSHA) into the family (commonwealth) of YASHARA'AL.

> *"So you shall divide this land among you according to the tribes of YASHARA'AL.* **You shall allot it as an inheritance for yourselves and for the sojourners who reside among you and have had children among you. They shall be**

> *to you as native-born children of YASHARA'AL. With you they shall be allotted an inheritance among the tribes YASHARA'AL. In whatever tribe the sojourner resides, there you shall assign him his inheritance, declares YAHUAH.* (Ezekiel 47:21-23 ESV)

- *For this reason I, Paul, a prisoner of MASHYACH YAHUSHA on behalf of you Gentiles— [2] assuming that you have heard of the stewardship of YAHUAH's grace that was given to me for you, [3] how the mystery was made known to me by revelation, as I have written briefly. [4] When you read this, you can perceive my insight into the mystery of MASHYACH, [5] which was not made known to the sons of men in other generations as it has now been revealed to his holy apostles and prophets by the Spirit. [6]* **This mystery is that the Gentiles are fellow heirs, members of the same body, and partakers of the promise in MASHYACH YAHUSHA** *through the gospel.* (Ephesians 3:1-6 ESV)

Now one might ask, 'Why all the fuss about the joining of Gentile (non-bloodline) into YASHARA'AL (bloodline)?'

YAHUAH made the everlasting covenant (the agreement with mankind and thereby all nations/bloodline) through YASHARA'AL (the firstborn son); therefore, the only route for all to enter into the covenant is through the firstborn son. If the firstborn son is done away with, it means no one can enter. It is YAHUAH's unchangeable design and plan. Trying to understand why He did it this way does not make any logical sense if discerned or processed through a Greek mindset that seeks to make sense of all things. YAHUAH decided to do it this way because He is The Most High and has sole prerogative to do so. Sadly, this is the design that the Catholic Church and most of mainstream Christianity have rejected.

> o *And YAHUAH said to Moses, "When you go back to Egypt, see that you do all those wonders before Pharaoh which I have put in your hand. But I will harden his heart, so that he will not let the people go. Then you shall say to Pharaoh,* ***'Thus says YAHUAH: "YASHARA'AL is My son, My firstborn. So I say to you, let My son go that he may serve Me. But if you refuse to let him go, indeed I will kill your son, your firstborn."*** *(Exodus 4:21-23 NKJV)*

Again, why is this significant in the 'design'?

Because the final destination YAHUAH has for His people is the New Yarushalayim (Jerusalem), which has 12 entry gates that carry the names of the 12 tribes. It is those of the 12 tribes of YASHARA'AL (bloodline) and those who are now as native born (non-bloodline) who have been grafted into YAHUSHA who will enter those gates. The native born now carrying a 'new name' – that of their adopted tribe.

> o *Then one of the seven angels who had the seven bowls filled with the seven last plagues came to me and talked with me, saying,* ***"Come, I will show you the bride, the Lamb's wife."*** *[10] And he carried me away in the Spirit to a great and high mountain, and showed me the great city, the holy Yarushalayim (Jerusalem), descending out of heaven from YAHUAH, [11] having the glory of YAHUAH.* ***Her light was like a most precious stone, like a jasper stone, clear as crystal. [12] Also she had a great and high wall with twelve gates, and twelve angels at the gates, and names written on them, which are the names of the***

twelve tribes of the children of YASHARA'AL: [13] *three gates on the east, three gates on the north, three gates on the south, and three gates on the west.* [14] *Now the wall of the city had twelve foundations, and on them were the names of the twelve apostles of the Lamb.* [15] *And he who talked with me had a gold reed to measure the city, its gates, and its wall.* [16] *The city is laid out as a square; its length is as great as its breadth. And he measured the city with the reed: twelve thousand furlongs. Its length, breadth, and height are equal.* [17] *Then he measured its wall: one hundred and forty-four cubits, according to the measure of a man, that is, of an angel.* [18] *The construction of its wall was of jasper; and the city was pure gold, like clear glass.* [19] *The foundations of the wall of the city were adorned with all kinds of precious stones: the first foundation was jasper, the second sapphire, the third chalcedony, the fourth emerald,* [20] *the fifth sardonyx, the sixth sardius, the seventh chrysolite, the eighth beryl, the ninth topaz, the tenth chrysoprase, the eleventh jacinth, and the twelfth amethyst.* [21] *The twelve gates were twelve pearls: each individual gate was of one pearl. And the street of the city was pure gold, like transparent glass.* [22] **But I saw no temple in it, for YAHUAH Almighty and the Lamb are its temple.** [23] *The city had no need of the sun or of the moon to shine in it, for the glory of YAHUAH illuminated it.* **The Lamb is its light.** [24] **And the nations of those who are saved shall walk in its light**, *and the kings of the earth bring their glory and honor into it.* [25] *Its gates shall not be shut at all by day (there shall be no night there).* [26] *And they shall bring the glory and the honor of the nations into it.* [27] **But there shall by no means enter it** *anything that defiles, or causes an abomination or a lie, but only those who are written in the Lamb's Book of Life. (Revelation 21:9-27 NKJV)*

Tribes of Africa, pay attention. It is interesting to note that the New Yarushalayim (Jerusalem) has no temple in it, as it is written, "But I saw no temple in it, for YAHUAH Almighty and the Lamb are its temple". Many speak about the building of the 3rd temple in the Yarushalayim (Jerusalem), situated in the political State of Zionist Israel, as part of the fulfilment of biblical prophecy. But who are they seeking to build that temple for, one should ask, for YAHUAH is not seeking a new temple, for YAHUAH Himself and MASHYACH will be the temple in true Zion. It is a temple of the order of Melchizedek. Those seeking to reestablish a temple in the Levitical order are perhaps those of the synagogue of Satan. SELAH

YAHUAH speaks of giving a new name, which will perhaps be part of the process of identifying who belongs to which tribe from His registry, so that those invited into the New Yarushalayim (Jerusalem) will know which of the 12 gates to use as they enter. The names given will be known only to YAHUAH and the one who receives them.

- *For Zion's sake I will not hold My peace, And for Yarushalayim's (Jerusalem's) sake I will not rest, until her righteousness goes forth as brightness, and her salvation as a lamp that burns. The Gentiles shall see your righteousness, And all kings your glory.* **You shall be called by a new name, Which the mouth of YAHUAH will name.** *(Isaiah 62:1-2 NKJV)*

- *"He who has an ear, let him hear what the Spirit says to the churches. To him who overcomes I will give some of the hidden manna to eat. And I will give him a white stone,* **and**

> - *on the stone a new name written which no one knows except him who receives it."* (Revelation 2:17 NKJV)
> - And of Zion it will be said, "This one and that one were born in her; And the Most High Himself shall establish her." ***YAHUAH will record, When He registers the peoples: "This one was born there."*** Selah (Psalms 87:5-6 NKJV)

YAHUAH knows the true identities of all and of those who shall be given residency in the true ZION, 'the New Yarushalayim (Jerusalem)'.

The Apostle Paul references this adoption responsibility in Romans 9:4. It is the responsibility of YASHARA'AL to adopt non-bloodline (Gentiles) into the House of YASHARA'AL. That is why they are called to be a light to the Gentiles, to lead them to the House of YAHUAH.

> - *For I could wish that I myself were accursed from MASHYACH for my brethren, my countrymen according to the flesh, who are YASHARA'ALITES,* **to whom pertain the adoption,** *the glory, the covenants, the giving of the law, the service of YAHUAH, and the promises; of whom are the fathers and from whom, according to the flesh, MASHYACH came, who is over all, the eternally blessed YAHUAH. Amen.* (Romans 9:3-5 NKJV)

YAHUAH chose YASHARA'AL as his firstborn who would shine His light on the world, to show and lead the world to the covenant (agreement) the FATHER established with YASHARA'AL and invites all other nations (Gentiles) to become part of, so that all (Jew and Gentile) would dwell in His House of Zion (the New Yarushalayim (Jerusalem)) forever.

- *Then YAHUSHA spoke to them again, saying,* **"I am the light of the world. He who follows Me shall not walk in darkness, but have the light of life."** *(John 8:12 NKJV)*
- **"You are the light of the world.** *A city that is set on a hill cannot be hidden. Nor do they light a lamp and put it under a basket, but on a lampstand, and it gives light to all who are in the house.* **Let your light so shine before men, that they may see your good works and glorify your Father in heaven.** *(Matthew 5:14-16 NKJV)*
- *"I, YAHUAH, have called You in righteousness, and will hold Your hand;* **I will keep You and give You as a covenant to the people, as a light to the Gentiles,** *to open blind eyes, to bring out prisoners from the prison, those who sit in darkness from the prison house. I am YAHUAH, that is My name; and My glory I will not give to another, nor My praise to carved images. (Isaiah 42:6-8 NKJV)*
- *Indeed He says, 'It is too small a thing that You should be My Servant To raise up the tribes of Jacob, and to restore the preserved ones of YASHARA'AL; I will also give You as a light to the Gentiles, That You should be My salvation to the ends of the earth.' (Isaiah 49:6 NKJV)*
- *Arise, shine;* **For your light has come!** *And the glory of YAHUAH is risen upon you. For behold, the darkness shall cover the earth, and deep darkness the people; But YAHUAH will arise over you, And His glory will be seen upon you.* **The Gentiles shall come to your light**, *And kings to the brightness of your rising. (Isaiah 60:1-3 NKJV)*
- *For so YAHUAH has commanded us:* **'I have set you as a light to the Gentiles, that you should be for salvation to the ends of the earth.'** *(Acts 13:47 NKJV)*

- *that HA MASHYACH (The Christ) would suffer, that He would be the first to rise from the dead, and **would proclaim light to the Jewish people and to the Gentiles.**" (Acts 26:23 NKJV)*

YASHARA'AL is the firstborn son, chosen to shine the light so that the Gentiles may see the light that leads to the covenant with YAHUAH and into the New Yarushalayim (Jerusalem), so both (YASHARA'AL Jew and Gentile) can call out Abba FATHER, Abba YAHUAH!!!!

- *Blessed be the Alahym and Father of our Master YAHUSHA MASHYACH, who has blessed us with every spiritual blessing in the heavenly places in MASHYACH, just as He chose us in Him before the **foundation of the world, that we should be holy and without blame before Him in love, having predestined us to adoption as sons by YAHUSHA MASHYACH to Himself, according to the good pleasure of His will, to the praise of the glory of His grace, by which He made us accepted in the Beloved.** (Ephesians 1:3-6 NKJV)*
- *Even so we, when we were children, were in bondage under the elements of the world. But when the fullness of the time had come, YAHUAH sent forth His Son, born of a woman, born under the law, to redeem those who were under the law, **that we might receive the adoption as sons. And because you are sons, YAHUAH has sent forth the Spirit of His Son into your hearts, crying out, "Abba, Father!"** (Galatians 4:3-6 NKJV)*
- ***For as many as are led by the Spirit of YAHUAH, these are sons of YAHUAH.*** *For you did not receive the spirit of bondage again to fear,* ***but you received the Spirit of***

> *adoption by whom we cry out, "Abba, Father."* The Spirit Himself bears witness with our spirit that we are children of YAHUAH, and if children, then heirs—heirs of YAHUAH and joint heirs with MASHYACH (Christ), if indeed we suffer with Him, that we may also be glorified together. (Romans 8:14-17 NKJV)

Tribes of Africa, our ancestors/forefathers once sacrificed animals and offered blood as a means to obtain righteousness, but this is no longer required. We don't have to sacrifice animals and pour out blood for our Creator, our Father, the ALAHYM of Abraham, Isaac and Jacob. It was once required, but no longer. We are being called to full obedience to his law and commandments, but the aspect of animal sacrifice and blood offerings has been removed because it has been fulfilled once and for all by our MASHYACH (Messiah).

It is worthwhile to go back to the issue of justification and righteousness through the sacrifice of YAHUSHA (and no longer animals) by returning to the letter to the Hebrews when these famous words are spoken,

'The just shall live by faith....'

When the writer makes this statement, 'the just shall live by faith', it comes after the discussion of the previous nine chapters of Hebrews in which he had been making the point that YAHUSHA is the sacrifice and the offering, and that animals are no longer required to attain righteousness.

- **Now the just shall live by faith**; But if anyone draws back, my soul has no pleasure in him." But we are not of those who draw back to perdition, but of those who believe to the saving of the soul. (Hebrews 10:38-39 NKJV)

A biblical definition of **'the just'** is given at the end of this portion so that we can also understand what it means to be just.

If the point being made is that 'the just' shall live by faith, it is prudent to ask the question 'Faith in what?' Keeping the context of the letter and discussion to point, the answer is obviously, "faith in what YAHUAH has said concerning the way to enter into His righteousness by YAHUSHA".

Another useful question is, "What is faith?" As it is written in Hebrews 11:1:

- *Now faith is the substance of things hoped for, the evidence of things **not seen**. (Hebrews 11:1 NKJV)*

What are the things that are **not seen,** which are being referred to in the letter?

The answer is: "Slaughtering animals and presenting their blood was the established mechanism to attain righteousness with YAHUAH. This was a process you could undertake with your own effort, and a process which you could see with your own eyes. But in the new mechanism to attain righteousness, you would no longer be able to see with your own eyes the life and blood that has been offered on your behalf. The process would no longer require any effort or work of your own, but you would now need to trust in and believe that what has been done for you by YAHUSHA is sufficient to fulfil the requirement of the law of sacrifice."

And so, the writer is helping them understand this as he goes further to speak in Hebrews chapter 11 on the discourse of what faith is and then gives examples of people who were led to do things by faith, as they obeyed YAHUAH's instructions without any evidence they could see with their own eyes to support the instruction they were given.

> o *By faith we understand that the worlds were framed by the word of YAHUAH, so that the things which are seen were not made of things which are visible. [4] By faith Abel offered to YAHUAH a more excellent sacrifice than Cain, through which he obtained witness that he was righteous, YAHUAH testifying of his gifts; and through it he being dead still speaks. [5] By faith Enoch was taken away so that he did not see death, "and was not found, because YAHUAH had taken him"; for before he was taken he had this testimony, that he pleased YAHUAH. [6] But without faith it is impossible to please Him, for he who comes to YAHUAH must believe that He is, and that He is a rewarder of those who diligently seek Him. (Hebrews 11:1, 3-6 NKJV)*

While on the subject of faith, another good question to ask is, where does faith come from? As it is written:

> o *So then faith comes by hearing, and hearing by the word of YAHUAH. (Romans 10:17 NKJV)*

Therefore the verse 'the just shall live by faith' taken in context is saying, 'those who are considered as being just are the ones counted as righteous by YAHUAH because they no longer see with their own eyes the physical life sacrifice and blood offering, but believe that the sacrifice and offering has been made and presented on their behalf because YAHUAH has said so. And because YAHUAH has said so, they will not draw back to animal sacrifice, which they can see with their own eyes and be drawn into the destruction of their souls because they don't meet the requirement of attaining righteousness that YAHUAH has set in place and spoken to them as an instruction. YAHUAH would no longer accept sacrifices made through the Levitical priests, as the only valid priesthood was that of the order of Melchizedek.

Hebrews 11:6 goes on to say that *'it impossible to please YAHUAH without faith'*. Why is this so? Because if we don't do what He says, it shows we don't love Him. It comes full circle again to the point of "love is obedience". Love is obedience to His Voice, His Instructions, His Word, His Law and His commandments.

Sadly, Hebrews chapter 11 is often taken completely out of context by those who teach without rightly dividing the word of truth.

> - *Study to shew thyself approved unto YAHUAH, a workman that needeth not to be ashamed, **rightly dividing the word of truth**. (2 Timothy 2:15 KJV)*

The Way to attain righteousness.

The main reason for having this dialogue on the Law of YAHUAH, the law of sacrifice and offering, is for us to consider what the truth is on this most critical issue, which has been distorted for a long time by the doctrines of man through the institution of religious Christianity. The lesser point of the discussion is to also demonstrate the need of putting all scripture into context so that verses like *'the just shall live by faith'* are not abused for fleshly purposes as has been extensively done in the Word of Faith driven ministries and others that preach a 'name and claim by faith' doctrine that takes individual verses and makes them fit the desires of man.

Let's have a brief look at the definition of "just".

Strong's Concordance Number G1342

Original Word: δίκαιος

Transliterated Word: dikaios

From G1349; equitable (in character or act); by implication innocent holy (absolutely or relatively): - just meet right (-eous).

Thayer's Definition describes "just" as:

1. righteous, observing divine laws
2. in a wide sense, upright, righteous, virtuous, keeping the commands of God
3. of those who seem to themselves to be righteous, who pride themselves on being righteous, who pride themselves in their virtues, whether real or imagined.
4. innocent, faultless, guiltless 2.

The word 'just' is used to describe someone whose way of thinking, feeling, and acting is wholly conformed to the will of God, and who, therefore, needs no rectification in the heart or life.

The key descriptions to pay attention to are 'observing divine laws', 'keeping the commands of God' and 'acting wholly conformed to the will of God'.

Concluding by coming back to the everlasting covenant

This is a repeat of what is written concerning YAHUAH's desire to have His people never forget His law and how He promises to put His law in their minds and write His laws on their hearts, and how that is part of the covenant.

Why would He put His laws in their minds and write the laws on their hearts if they are no longer valid?

- *"Behold, the days are coming, says YAHUAH, when I will make a new covenant with the house of YASHARA'AL and with the house of Judah— [32] not according to the covenant that I made with their fathers in the day that I took them by the hand to lead them out of the land of Egypt, My covenant* which they broke, though I was a husband to them, says YAHUAH. [33] **But this is the covenant that I will make with the house of YASHARA'AL after those days, says YAHUAH: I will put My law in their minds, and write it on their hearts; and I will be their Aluah, and they shall be My people.** [34] No more shall every man teach his neighbour, and every man his brother, saying, 'Know YAHUAH,' for they all shall know Me, from the least of them to the greatest of them, says YAHUAH. For I will forgive their iniquity, and their sin I will remember no more." (Jeremiah 31:31-34 NKJV)

- For if that first covenant had been faultless, then no place would have been sought for a second. [8] Because finding fault with them, He says: "Behold, the days are coming, says YAHUAH, when I will make a new covenant with the house of YASHARA'AL and with the house of Judah— [9] not according to the covenant that I made with their fathers in the day when I took them by the hand to lead them out of the land of Egypt; because they did not continue in My covenant, and I disregarded them, says YAHUAH. [10] **For this is the covenant that I will make with the house of YASHARA'AL after those days, says YAHUAH: I will put My laws in their mind and write them on their hearts; and I will be their Aluah, and they shall be My people.** [11] None of them shall teach his neighbour, and none his brother, saying, 'Know YAHUAH,' for all shall know Me, from the least of them to the greatest of them. [12] For I will be merciful to their unrighteousness, and their sins and their lawless deeds I will remember no more." (Hebrews 8:7-12 NKJV)

- **"This is the covenant that I will make with them after** *those days, says YAHUAH: I will put My laws into their hearts, and in their minds I will write them,"* then He adds, *"Their sins and their lawless deeds I will remember no more." Now where there is remission of these, there is no longer an offering for sin. (Hebrews 10:16-18 NKJV)*

Tribes of Africa, because YAHUAH is love, He exhorts us to love. The task that lies ahead cannot be accomplished without YAHUAH, and therefore, it cannot be accomplished without love.

Beloved, let us love one another, for love is of YAHUAH; and everyone who loves is born of YAHUAH and knows YAHUAH. [8] He who does not love does not know YAHUAH, **for YAHUAH is love**. *(I John 4:7-8 NKJV*

CHAPTER TWELVE

The Power of Repentance and Forgiveness

A major component in the foundation of the Creator's design is Repentance and Forgiveness.

YAHUAH Himself is full of mercy and grace, for it is His nature to forgive. Inasmuch as He has established Laws and Commandments to determine how he wants us to love Him and how His Kingdom operates and applies consequences (judgements) for transgression of the law (sin), yet He will always apply His mercy and forgiveness before He judges.

YAHUAH will always draw us to confession and repentance so that He can forgive. But He leaves the choice to us if we will do so, or not. His attributes of mercy and forgiveness are activated by our confession and repentance. Without confession and repentance, we remain under His judgement. The entire 'design' of YAHUAH is based on this.

- *If we confess our sins, **he is faithful and just to forgive us our sins** and to cleanse us from all unrighteousness. (1 John 1:9 ESV)*
- *In this manner, therefore, pray: Our Father in heaven, Hallowed be Your name. [10] Your kingdom come. Your will be done On earth as it is in heaven. [11] Give us this day our daily bread. [12] **And forgive us our debts, as we forgive our debtors.** [13] And do not lead us into temptation, but deliver us from the evil one. For Yours is the kingdom and the power and the glory forever. Amen. [14] "**For if you forgive men their trespasses, your heavenly Father will also forgive you. [15] But if you do not forgive men their trespasses, neither will your Father forgive your trespasses.** (Matthew 6:9-15 NKJV)*
- *'YAHUAH is slow to anger and abounding in steadfast love, **forgiving iniquity and transgression,** but he will by no means clear the guilty, visiting the iniquity of the fathers on the children, to the third and the fourth generation.' (Numbers 14:18 ESV)*
- *He does not deal with us according to our sins, nor repay us according to our iniquities. For as high as the heavens are above the earth, so great is his steadfast love toward those who fear him; as far as the east is from the west, **so far does he remove our transgressions from us. As a father shows compassion to his children, so YAHUAH shows compassion to those who fear him.** (Psalm 103:10-13 ESV)*
- *Have mercy on me, O YAHUAH, **according to your steadfast love; according to your abundant mercy blot out my transgressions. Wash me thoroughly from my iniquity, and cleanse me from my sin!** (Psalm 51:1-2 ESV)*

🕯 **Tribes of Africa,** if we choose not to confess and repent, we sentence ourselves to judgement.

🕯 **Tribes of Africa,** if we choose not to confess and repent, we sentence ourselves to judgement.

This statement has been purposely repeated to emphasise the importance of confession and repentance.

This is key for Africa. The reason we are 'blessed and yet cursed' is that we turned away from the covenant (YAHUAH's agreement with us collectively as a tribe and continent) by choosing other gods, breaking the everlasting agreement (covenant), and disobeying YAHUAH's laws. In summary, we were in sin (transgressing the law and commandments) and did not confess and repent; therefore, judgement was meted out to us in the form of being conquered and oppressed by other nations to fulfil the terms of the agreement. For as long as we don't confess and repent, the judgement upon Africa of subjugation and oppression (the curse) will remain.

> o *"**But if they confess their iniquity and the iniquity of their fathers in their treachery that they committed against me, and also in walking contrary to me,** [41] so that I walked contrary to them and brought them into the land of their enemies—**if then their uncircumcised heart is humbled and they make amends for their iniquity,** [42] then I will remember my covenant with Jacob, and I will remember my covenant with Isaac and my covenant with Abraham, and I will remember the land. (Leviticus 26:40-42 ESV)*

If we confess and repent, He will forgive and restore us to the place where He has always intended for us as Africa to be. When we confess and repent our transgression of the law (sin), we activate the sacrifice and offering made by the High Priest after the order of Melchizedek, so that through the life and blood of YAHUSHA we are justified and reestablished in righteousness (right standing, without guilt) before YAHUAH.

YAHUAH is always waiting for His people to confess and repent so that He can restore them.

Here are some scripture references from Amos, Isaiah, and Jeremiah that highlight YAHUAH's desire to always restore His people.

- ***Repent therefore, and turn back, that your sins may be blotted out, that times of refreshing may come from the presence of YAHUAH,*** *and that he may send the Messiah (HA MASHYACH) appointed for you, YAHUSHA, whom heaven must receive until the time for restoring all the things about which YAHUAH spoke by the mouth of his holy prophets long ago. (Acts 3:19-21 ESV)*
- ***I will restore the fortunes of my people YASHARA'AL, and they shall rebuild the ruined cities and inhabit them;*** *they shall plant vineyards and drink their wine, and they shall make gardens and eat their fruit. I will plant them on their land, and they shall never again be uprooted out of the land that I have given them," says YAHUAH your Aluah. (Amos 9:14-15 ESV)*
- *if my people who are called by my name humble themselves, and pray and seek my face and turn from their wicked ways, then I will hear from heaven and will forgive their sin and heal their land. (2 Chronicles 7:14 ESV)*
- ***I will restore to you*** *the years that the swarming locust has eaten, the hopper, the destroyer, and the cutter, my great army, which I sent among you. "You shall eat in plenty and be satisfied, and praise the name of YAHUAH your Aluah,*

> *who has dealt wondrously with you. And my people shall never again be put to shame. You shall know that I am in the midst of YASHARA'AL, and that I am YAHUAH your Aluah and there is none else. And my people shall never again be put to shame. (Joel 2:25-27 ESV)*

🔥 **Tribes of Africa,** a prerequisite for YAHUAH's restoration is Repentance.

Repentance is firstly confessing our sin to our High Priest YAHUSHA and then turning away from transgressing the instructions of YAHUAH (sin) and returning to compliance with the terms of the everlasting covenant (the agreement between YAHUAH and His people).

HOWEVER, there is a further condition within the prerequisite: 'forgive and you shall be forgiven'.

🔥 **Tribes of Africa,** YAHUAH placed a condition that He will forgive as (inasmuch as) we forgive. If we don't forgive, we shut the door to receiving His forgiveness.

- ***"For if you forgive men their trespasses, your heavenly Father will also forgive you. But if you do not forgive men their trespasses, neither will your Father forgive your trespasses.*** (Matthew 6:14-15 NKJV)

YAHUSHA cried out these words to Abba YAHUAH for all of us:

- And YAHUSHA said, ***"Father, forgive them, for they know not what they do."*** And they cast lots to divide his garments. (Luke 23:34 ESV)

🔥 FATHER, forgive them (the conqueror) for they do not know what they have done to Africa.

Africa has been raped and plundered through slavery, colonialisation and apartheid. Africa has been captured and continues to be controlled through the systems that have been established within the 12 domains of control. Foreign illicit flows drain Africa of $90bn every year. Some former French colonies allegedly still pay colonial tax to France. 70% of the land in South Africa is still owned by 7% of the population, who are not native to Africa. Prejudice against Africa and injustice towards Africa continue to prevail in the global power structures of politics, the military and economics.

As much as the natural human instinct is to respond with hatred and revenge, YAHUAH's design says, Forgive, do not take vengeance into your own hands, for then you will be fighting on your own. However, should we choose His way, He will take up the fight Himself and fight for Africa.

As it is written:

- *Repay no one evil for evil, but give thought to do what is honorable in the sight of all. If possible, so far as it depends on you, live peaceably with all.* **Beloved, never avenge yourselves, but leave it to the wrath of YAHUAH, for it is written, "Vengeance is mine, I will repay, says YAHUAH."** *To the contrary, "if your enemy is hungry, feed him; if he is thirsty, give him something to drink; for by so doing you will heap burning coals on his head."* **Do not be overcome by evil, but overcome evil with good.** *(Romans 12:17-21 ESV)*
- **Do not rejoice when your enemy falls, and let not your heart be glad when he stumbles,** *lest YAHUAH see it and be displeased, and turn away his anger from him. (Proverbs 24:17-18 ESV)*
- **Do not say, "I will do to him as he has done to me;** *I will*

> *pay the man back for what he has done."* (Proverbs 24:29 ESV)

We must repeat the words of YAHUSHA when He was hanging on the tree/stake as a sinless man suffering for the sins of the world, yet declaring ...... **"Father, forgive them, for they know not what they do."**

It does not make logical sense, but this is KEY to us taking back the spiritual domain that will open the door for YAHUAH to fight for Africa, and for His power to flow into the other 11 domains of control as solutions come forth and are implemented to bring about the Covenant-based restoration that YAHUAH promises.

🕯 **"YAHUAH, forgive us, Africa, for the breaking of the everlasting covenant (agreement) we have with You, for our turning away from You to worship other gods, for our disobedience to Your law and commandments and for our rejection of YAHUSHA who came as the propitiation of our sin (transgression of the law). Forgive us as we forgive them who have enslaved us, conquered us, oppressed us, raped and plundered us".**

The question might be, but why?

This links back to the 10 Commandments and the Greatest Commandment requirement, 'to love your neighbour'. When we forgive our enemy, do not seek revenge or seek harm for them, we fulfil the requirement of the law, and we are judged as righteous before YAHUAH. When we are judged as righteous (in right standing in YAHUAH's sight according to His standard of right standing), He takes up the cause on our behalf.

🕯 **Tribes of Africa,** YAHUAH wants to fight for us, but only if we will call upon Him to, by meeting His requirement for us to forgive those who have wronged us first, before He will enter the battle.

If we do not forgive, we will not receive His forgiveness.

If we choose revenge and seek to destroy our enemies by our own hand and methods, YAHUAH steps out of the battle and watches because He will only fight for us when we give the battle over to Him.

When we confess our sins and repent to Him, forgive our enemies and love them, YAHUAH steps in and takes over the battle; and He always wins!!!

> o *And he said, "Listen, all Judah and inhabitants of Yarushalayim (Jerusalem) and King Jehoshaphat: Thus says YAHUAH to you, **'Do not be afraid and do not be dismayed at this great horde, for the battle is not yours but YAHUAH's**. (2 Chronicles 20:15 ESV)*

🌿 **Tribes of Africa,** because YAHUAH is love, He exhorts us to love. The task that lies ahead cannot be accomplished without YAHUAH, and therefore, it cannot be accomplished without love. Forgiveness and love do not mean we accept unrighteousness or continue to be trampled upon by injustice in silence; they mean we resist but seek not to harm anyone.

> o *Beloved, let us love one another, for love is of YAHUAH; and everyone who loves is born of YAHUAH and knows YAHUAH. [8] He who does not love does not know YAHUAH,* ***for YAHUAH is love.*** *(I John 4:7-8 NKJV*

CHAPTER THIRTEEN

Understanding What The Kingdom Of YAHUAH Is

The Kingdom of YAHUAH is the realm of His sovereign rulership and reign. It is a Kingdom in which YAHUAH is the Judge and He makes judgements according to the Law and Commandments which He has established as the Lawgiver. The Laws and Commandments serve as the constitution of the Kingdom and the foundation of how it is governed. It is a Kingdom in which YAHUAH is also the King, and His reign and rulership are based on the Laws and Commandments He has established. His throne as King and Judge is established on the foundation of righteousness and justice, truth and mercy stand before him. The measurement of righteousness and justice is based on the standard that He has set through His Laws and Commandments. It is a Kingdom in which YAHUAH, as the Supreme Judge and King, holds Himself accountable to His own Word (Constitution) and will never violate it for He is absolutely righteous, as He has placed His Word (Constitution) above His name.

To get a base understanding of the 'Kingdom of YAHUAH ', it is important to understand the link between (1) YAHUAH as the Judge,

Lawgiver, King and Saviour, (2) the Law and the Commandments, (3) Sin, (4) 'the curse and death', (5) the Law of Righteousness (6) the choice of 'the blessing and life' and that of 'the curse and death, (7) Sacrifice of life and offering of blood and (8) the truth.

This is why it was essential to put the biblical definitions in place first (in Chapter 9) and also link them together so that we establish a common understanding with YAHUAH.

These two scriptures tell us about the foundation of the throne of YAHUAH.

- *The heavens are Yours, the earth also is Yours; The world and all its fullness, You have founded them. [12] The north and the south, You have created them; Tabor and Hermon rejoice in Your name. [13] You have a mighty arm; Strong is Your hand, and high is Your right hand. [14]* **Righteousness and justice are the foundation of Your throne**; *Mercy and truth go before Your face. (Psalms 89:11-14 NKJV)*
- *YAHUAH reigns; Let the earth rejoice; Let the multitude of isles be glad! [2] Clouds and darkness surround Him;* **Righteousness and justice are the foundation of His throne.** *(Psalms 97:1-2 NKJV)*

The Kingdom of YAHUAH is based on a legislative and judicial system

The Kingdom of YAHUAH is designed upon a legislative and judicial system based on the Laws and Commandments He has given, which serve as the constitution of the Kingdom. He rules and reigns based on this system, which He holds Himself accountable to. It is so critical to understand this; otherwise, we miss the whole basis of what the Kingdom of YAHUAH is.

UNDERSTANDING WHAT THE KINGDOM OF YAHUAH IS

The scriptures say that YAHUSHA MASHYACH will not rest until righteousness and justice are established on the earth. The sacrifice of His life and the pouring out of His blood are part of this legislative and judicial system, hence He is the ADVOCATE within the system and why His blood TESTIFIES as a WITNESS within the system.

- "The Spirit of YAHUAH is upon Me, Because He has anointed Me To preach the gospel to the poor; He has sent Me to heal the broken hearted, **To proclaim liberty to the captives and recovery of sight to the blind, To set at liberty those who are oppressed; [19] To proclaim the acceptable year of YAHUAH.**" (Luke 4:18-19 NKJV)
- "The Spirit of YAHUAH Aluah is upon Me, Because YAHUAH has anointed Me To preach good tidings to the poor; He has sent Me to heal the broken hearted, **To proclaim liberty to the captives, And the opening of the prison to those who are bound**; [2] To proclaim the acceptable year of YAHUAH, And the day of vengeance of our Alahym; To comfort all who mourn, (Isaiah 61:1-2 NKJV)
- For unto us a Child is born, unto us a Son is given; And the government will be upon His shoulder. And His name will be called Wonderful, Counselor, Mighty Aluah, Everlasting Father, Prince of Peace. [7] Of the increase of His government and peace there will be no end, Upon the throne of David and over His kingdom, **to order it and establish it with judgment and justice from that time forward**, even forever. The zeal of YAHUAH of hosts will perform this. (Isaiah 9:6-7 NKJV)
- "Behold! My Servant whom I uphold, My Elect One in

- *whom My soul delights! I have put My Spirit upon Him;* **He will bring forth justice to the Gentiles.** *[2] He will not cry out, nor raise His voice, nor cause His voice to be heard in the street. [3] A bruised reed He will not break, and smoking flax He will not quench;* **He will bring forth justice for truth. [4] He will not fail nor be discouraged, Till He has established justice in the earth; And the coastlands shall wait for His law."** *(Isaiah 42:1-4 NKJV)*
- *Give the king Your judgments, O Aluah, And Your righteousness to the king's Son. [2]* **He will judge Your people with righteousness**, *And Your poor with justice. [3] The mountains will bring peace to the people, And the little hills, by righteousness. [4]* **He will bring justice** *to the poor of the people; He will save the children of the needy, and will break in pieces the oppressor. (Psalms 72:1-4 NKJV)*

YAHUSHA is our ADVOCATE as He serves as the lawyer representing us within the legislative and judicial system.

- *My little children, these things write I unto you, that ye sin not. And if any man sin,* **we have an advocate** *with the Father, YAHUSHA MASHYACH the righteous: (1 John 2:1 KJV)*

The blood of YAHUSHA is a WITNESS and TESTIFIES (speaks) for us within the legislative and judicial system.

- *And there are three that* **bear witness in earth, the Spirit, and the water, and the blood:** *and these three agree in one. [9] If we receive the witness of men, the witness of YAHUAH is greater: for this is the witness of YAHUAH which He hath testified of His Son. (1 John 5:8-9 KJV)*
- *and to YAHUSHA the mediator of the new covenant,* **and**

> ***to the blood of sprinkling, that speaketh** better things than that of Abel. (Hebrews 12:24 KJV)*

I hope the legal terms used give a clear indication of the various role players in this legislative and judicial system, which are at the core of YAHUAH's Kingdom.

We have a choice, if we want to be citizens of this Kingdom, to honour and submit ourselves to the CONSTITUTION, which means we will be judged according to the LAWS and COMMANDMENTS which make up the constitution. When we transgress the constitution and we CONFESS our SIN and admit our GUILT and REPENT from the sin (transgression of the law) it first of all transfers the sin on to YAHUSHA, and at the same time triggers the ADVOCATE (YAHUSHA) to now represent us as our LAWYER and for the blood of the Lamb (YAHUSHA) to TESTIFY as a WITNESS on our behalf so that we can be ACQUITTED by righteous JUDGEMENT which YAHUAH the JUDGE renders. We are ACQUITTED because the COURT is presented with the EVIDENCE that our sin has been transferred onto YAHUSHA and that the wage of sin, which is death, has been paid through YAHUSHA's death. At which point the ACCUSER (Satan) who has brought the case against us is thrown out of the COURT and His case against us is rendered null and void as the sin He was seeking to get us CONVICTED on is declared invalid because that sin (transgression of the law) has been transferred unto YAHUSHA who has already SERVED and PAID for the SENTENCE for that sin with His death and the debt of that sin is declared SETTLED by His blood. CASE CLOSED. This is the Good News of how the Kingdom of YAHUAH works. HALLELU-YAH, Praise YAH for His amazing wisdom and love that designed this for us.

In the design, sin is given a voice to also testify. If sin has not been confessed, the case made by its testimony gives Satan a valid case to pursue and seek judgement in His favour.

- *For our transgressions are multiplied before thee, and **our sins testify against us**: for our transgressions are with us; and as for our iniquities, we know them; (Isaiah 59:12 KJV)*
- *O YAHUAH, **though our iniquities testify against us**, do thou it for thy name's sake; for our backslidings are many; we have sinned against thee. (Jeremiah 14:7 KJV)*

Satan understands this legislative and judicial system so well and works within it, constantly trying to win convictions, which he secures successfully when we do not confess our transgressions of the Law and Commandments and repent. When there is no recognition of the Law and Commandments, there is no confession of the sin, and so the Advocate and the Blood remain silent before the court of the Most High Judge, YAHUAH. In this case, the testimony of sin stands as righteous (right standing according to the law), and Satan wins His case in righteousness and is given the legal right to seek payment for the unconfessed sins. This gives Satan the legal authority to go out to steal, kill and destroy because that is how he takes his payment.

Tribes of Africa, let us not be ignorant about how the legislative and judicial system of the Kingdom of YAHUAH operates. It is a system that YAHUAH put in place to work for us, but it can also be what leads to our destruction. Rejection of the Law and Commandments is rejection of the Advocate and rejection of the testimony of the Blood as a witness, and is also a rejection of the Lawgiver who is also the Judge and the King.

Within the constitution, the transgression of the Laws and Commandments is deemed as sin. The predetermined consequence (judgement) of sin is 'the curse and death' (Path 2), as the wage of sin is death. Such is the judgement that is pronounced upon the unrepentant transgressor, who carries the title of an unrighteous, wicked, or evil person. This predetermined consequence of 'the curse and death' can be rescinded when confession, admission of guilt and repentance of the transgression take place and are submitted for atonement through a blood sacrifice. Since mercy and truth stand before His throne, when there is confession and repentance from transgressing the law, this serves as the proclamation of truth, and when truth is proclaimed, mercy accepts it, and the Judge rules based on mercy. A beautiful picture of righteousness and mercy kissing. Before the coming of YAHUSHA, and the shedding of His sinless blood, the blood of animal sacrifice would be the means of this atonement, but righteousness is now only obtained in full through the righteousness of YAHUSHA. This is the 'Good News'. What starts off as bad news is transformed into Good News because of YAHUSHA.

On the other side, when there is obedience to the law and commandments (constitution), the predetermined consequence (judgement) is 'the blessing and life' (Path 1) upon the repentant transgressor (because they will still sin unwilfully) who carries the title of the righteous or godly person. This again is the Good News, as righteousness is obtained in full through the righteousness of YAHUSHA, who imputes His righteousness upon those who would otherwise be unrighteous.

In the Kingdom, YAHUAH is Judge – He is the Supreme Judicial Power

In the Kingdom, YAHUAH is the Lawgiver – He is the Supreme Legislative Power

In the Kingdom, YAHUAH is the King – He is the Supreme Executive Power

As the Supreme Power over the Kingdom, YAHUAH holds Himself accountable to His own Constitution (Word) and as a loving Father. He has revealed His constitution to us, His children, so that we would know His requirements for citizenship within His Kingdom and how everything works for us based on the choices we make. Our choices will either take us down Path 1, which is 'the blessing and life' or Path 2, which is 'the curse and death'. In His lovingkindness and grace as FATHER, He established a mechanism that takes us from Path 2, 'the curse and death', back to Path 1, 'the blessing and life', whenever we find ourselves on the wrong path, the wide road that leads to destruction.

His will for us is that all be on Path 1 of 'the blessing and life', but He leaves us with the choice.

No person on earth is a citizen of a country that has rules and laws that govern its existence and is not held responsible and accountable to the constitution of that country. Every judge in that country uses the law of that land to make judgement, and every king (or president) uses the constitution of that land to rule and reign. It is no different in the Kingdom of YAHUAH. The law and constitution of the Kingdom will be applicable and in full use during the 1000-year reign of King YAHUSHA, which is soon to come, and in the New Yarushalayim (Jerusalem) thereafter, and that is why He says that if we are faithful to honour the constitution now, He will make us rulers within the age to come.

- *It is a faithful saying: For if we be dead with Him, we shall also live with Him: [12]* **if we suffer, we shall also reign with Him***: if we deny Him, He also will deny us: (2 Timothy*

2:11-12 KJV)
- *Dare any of you, having a matter against another, go to law before the unjust, and not before the saints? [2]* **Do ye not know that the saints shall judge the world?** *and if the world shall be judged by you, are ye unworthy to judge the smallest matters? [3]* **Know ye not that we shall judge angels?** *how much more things that pertain to this life? (1 Corinthians 6:1-3 KJV)*
- *and hast made us unto our Aluah kings and priests:* **and we shall reign on the earth.** *(Revelation 5:10 KJV)*
- **And I saw thrones, and they sat on them, and judgment was committed to them.** *Then I saw the souls of those who had been beheaded for their witness to YAHUSHA and for the word of YAHUAH, who had not worshiped the beast or his image, and had not received his mark on their foreheads or on their hands.* **And they lived and reigned with MASHYACH for a thousand years.** *[5] But the rest of the dead did not live again until the thousand years were finished. This is the first resurrection. [6] Blessed and holy is he who has part in the first resurrection. Over such the second death has no power,* **but they shall be priests of YAHUAH and of MASHYACH, and shall reign with Him a thousand years.** *(Revelation 20:4-6 NKJV)*
- *And the kingdom and dominion,* **and the greatness of the kingdom under the whole heaven, shall be given to the people of the saints of the most High,** *whose kingdom is an everlasting kingdom, and all dominions shall serve and obey Him. (Daniel 7:27 KJV)*

YAHUAH has given His people the opportunity to 'practice' being faithful to His Law and Commandments (constitution) in this present age of life by living in submission to His Kingdom's constitution. Those who are found to be faithful in the little can be given much, which is to rule and reign with Him in the next age of life. If we reject and rebel against His constitution in this present age of life, why would He deem us worthy to rule and reign with Him in the next?

- *Now as they heard these things, He spoke another parable, because He was near YARUSHALAYIM and because they thought the kingdom of YAHUAH would appear immediately. [12] Therefore He said: "A certain nobleman went into a far country to receive for himself a kingdom and to return. [13] So he called ten of his servants, delivered to them ten minas, and said to them, 'Do business till I come.' [14]* **But his citizens hated him, and sent a delegation after him, saying, 'We will not have this man to reign over us.'** *[15] "And so it was that when he returned, having received the kingdom, he then commanded these servants, to whom he had given the money, to be called to him, that he might know how much every man had gained by trading. [16] Then came the first, saying, 'Master, your mina has earned ten minas.' [17] And he said to him,* **'Well done, good servant; because you were faithful in a very little, have authority over ten cities.'** *[18] And the second came, saying, 'Master, your mina has earned five minas.' [19] Likewise he said to him,* **'You also be over five cities.'** *[20] "Then another came, saying, 'Master, here is your mina, which I have kept put away in a handkerchief. [21] For I feared you, because you are an austere man. You collect what you did not deposit, and reap what you did not sow.' [22] And he said to him, 'Out of your own mouth I will judge* *you, you wicked servant. You knew that I was an austere man, collecting what I did not deposit and reaping what I did not sow. [23] Why then did you not put my money in the bank, that at my coming I might have collected it with interest?' [24] "And he said to those who stood by, 'Take the mina from him, and give it to him who has ten minas.' [25] (But they said to him, 'Master, he has ten minas.') [26] 'For I say to you, that to everyone who has will be given; and from him who does not have, even what he has will be taken away from him. [27]* **But bring here those enemies of mine, who did not want me to reign over them, and slay them before me.'** *(Luke 19:11-27 NKJV)*

YAHUAH rules and reigns by His righteousness, which establishes justice to always prevail within His Kingdom. Please refer to the scriptures below so that the WORD itself speaks.

- *For YAHUAH is our judge, YAHUAH is our lawgiver, YAHUAH is our king; He will save us. (Isaiah 33:22 KJV)*
- *But YAHUAH is the judge:* **He putteth down one, and setteth up another.** *(Psalm 75:7 KJV)*
- *Before YAHUAH; For he cometh to judge the earth:* **With righteousness shall He judge the world, And the people with equity.** *(Psalm 98:9 KJV)*
- *For we must all appear before the judgment seat of MASHYACH (Christ);* **that everyone may receive the things done in his body, according to that he hath done, whether it be good or bad.** *(2 Corinthians 5:10 KJV)*
- *Therefore thus says YAHUAH: "Behold, I lay in Zion a stone for a foundation, A tried stone, a precious cornerstone, a sure foundation; Whoever believes will not act hastily. Also* **I will make justice the measuring line, And**

- *righteousness the plummet; The hail will sweep away the refuge of lies, And the waters will overflow the hiding place. (Isaiah 28:16-17 NKJV)*
  - *Restore us, O YAHUAH of our salvation, and cause Your anger toward us to cease. [5] Will You be angry with us forever? Will You prolong Your anger to all generations? [6] Will You not revive us again, That Your people may rejoice in You? [7] Show us Your mercy, YAHUAH, and grant us Your salvation. [8] I will hear what YAHUAH will speak, For He will speak peace To His people and to His saints; But let them not turn back to folly. [9] Surely His salvation is near to those who fear Him, that glory may dwell in our land. [10]* **Mercy and truth have met together; Righteousness and peace have kissed. [11] Truth shall spring out of the earth, and righteousness shall look down from heaven.** *[12] Yes, YAHUAH will give what is good; And our land will yield its increase. [13] Righteousness will go before Him, and shall make His footsteps our pathway. (Psalms 85:4-13 NKJV)*
  - *I will praise thee with my whole heart: Before the gods will I sing praise unto thee. [2] I will worship toward thy holy temple, and praise thy name for Thy lovingkindness and for Thy truth:* **For thou hast magnified Thy word above all Thy name.** *(Psalm 138:1-2 KJV)*

YAHUAH's Word is Truth, and Truth is the Law and Commandments. YAHUAH holds Himself accountable to His Word – to the Laws and Commandments He spoke into existence. This is the governance system of YAHUAH.

  - *For the* **wages of sin is death, but the gift of YAHUAH is eternal life in (Christ) MASHYACH YAHUSHA** *our*

- Master. *(Romans 6:23 NKJV)*
  - *And according to the law almost all things are purified with blood, and **without shedding of blood there is no remission of sin.** (Hebrews 9:22 NKJV)*
  - *And I saw thrones, and they sat on them, and judgment was committed to them. Then I saw the souls of those who had been beheaded for their witness to YAHUSHA and for the word of YAHUAH, who had not worshiped the beast or his image, and had not received his mark on their foreheads or on their hands. **And they lived and reigned with MASHYACH (Christ) for a thousand years.** Blessed and holy is he who has part in the first resurrection. Over such the second death has no power, **but they shall be priests of YAHUAH and of MASHYACH (Christ) and shall reign with Him a thousand years.** (Revelation 20:4-6 NKJV)*
  - *Then one of the seven angels who had the seven bowls filled with the seven last plagues came to me and talked with me, saying, "Come, I will show you the bride, the Lamb's wife." [10] And he carried me away in the Spirit to a great and high mountain, and showed me **the great city, the holy Yarushalayim (Jerusalem), descending out of heaven from YAHUAH,** (Revelation 21:9-10 NKJV)*
  - *But I saw no temple in it, for YAHUAH Almighty and the Lamb are its temple. [23] The city had no need of the sun or of the moon to shine in it, for the glory of YAHUAH illuminated it. The Lamb is its light. [24] **And the nations of those who are saved shall walk in its light, and the kings of the earth bring their glory and honor into it.** [25] Its gates shall not be shut at all by day (there shall be no night there). [26] And they shall bring the glory and*

the honor of the nations into it. *[27]* **But there shall by no means enter it anything that defiles, or causes an abomination or a lie, but only those who are written in the Lamb's Book of Life.** *Revelation 21:22-27 NKJV)*

- "For this commandment which I command you today is not too mysterious for you, nor is it far off. *[12]* It is not in heaven, that you should say, 'Who will ascend into heaven for us and bring it to us, that we may hear it and do it?' *[13]* Nor is it beyond the sea, that you should say, 'Who will go over the sea for us and bring it to us, that we may hear it and do it?' *[14]* **But the word is very near you, in your mouth and in your heart, that you may do it.** *[15]* **"See, I have set before you today life and good, death and evil, *[16]* in that I command you today to love YAHUAH your Aluah, to walk in His ways, and to keep His commandments, His statutes, and His judgments, that you may live and multiply**; and YAHUAH your Aluah will bless you in the land which you go to possess. *[17]* But if your heart turns away so that you do not hear, and are drawn away, and worship other gods and serve them, *[18]* I announce to you today that you shall surely perish; you shall not prolong your days in the land which you cross over the Jordan to go in and possess. *[19]* **I call heaven and earth as witnesses today against you, that I have set before you life and death, blessing and cursing; therefore choose life, that both you and your descendants may live;** *[20]* that you may love YAHUAH your Aluah, that you may obey His voice, and that you may cling to Him, for He is your life and the length of your days; and that you may dwell in the land which YAHUAH swore *to your fathers, to Abraham, Isaac, and Jacob, to give them." (Deuteronomy 30:11-20 NKJV)*

It could be of value to review some scriptures that reference 'the Kingdom of YAHUAH' so that we can gain a deeper understanding of them now that we have the baseline standard of what the Kingdom is, according to what is written in His Word.

Let's look at YAHUSHA's instruction for us to 'seek His Kingdom first and His righteousness' as is written in Matthew 6:33:

- *But seek ye first the kingdom of YAHUAH, and **his righteousness**; and all these things shall be added unto you. (Matthew 6:33 KJV)*

We could paraphrase and expand Matthew 6:33 into the following:

"Seek ye first His Kingdom *(the realm of YAHUAH's sovereign rulership and reign, where He is the Judge and makes decisions and judges according to the law and commandments that He has established as the Lawgiver. The realm where His Truth (His Word, Laws and Commandments) serves as the constitution and the basis for all governance. The realm where all decisions, rulings and judgements are made according to choices made with respect to the constitution whose 4 pillars are righteousness, justice, truth and mercy)*, **and His righteousness** *(the right rulings and judgements He makes on your behalf according to your submission to His constitution)* **and all things will come to you** *(as what He has promised flows to you as they are designed to do when you are in right standing according to His constitution).*

Seeking after His constitution and obedience to it brings blessings.

- *Blessed are they which do hunger and thirst after **righteousness**: for they shall be filled. (Matthew 5:6 KJV)*

- Blessed are they which are persecuted for **righteousness' sake**: for theirs is the kingdom of heaven. (Matthew 5:10 KJV)

Zealous about the Kingdom of God in error

Until 2022, I had lived all my life as a Christian speaking about the Kingdom of God and claiming to be working for the Kingdom and speaking as an ambassador for the Kingdom, and yet, in reality, I did not have the correct understanding of what it really was and how to be part of it. Truth be told, I now realise how much I was unknowingly working against 'His Kingdom' in ignorance, as I was caught up in the trap of the mystery of lawlessness. It makes me think of the words spoken to the 'dead church' and the 'lukewarm church in Revelation chapter 3, because I thought I was alive in the Kingdom, and yet I was dead. I thought I was hot in the Kingdom, and yet I was lukewarm.

As it is written:

- "And to the angel of the church in Sardis write, 'These things says He who has the seven Spirits of YAHUAH and the seven stars: **"I know your works, that you have a name that you are alive, but you are dead.** Be watchful, and strengthen the things which remain, that are ready to die, **for I have not found your works perfect before YAHUAH**. (Revelation 3:1-2 NKJV)
- "And to the angel of the church of the Laodiceans write, 'These things says the Amen, the Faithful and True Witness, the Beginning of the creation of YAHUAH: **"I know your works, that you are neither cold nor hot. I could wish you were cold or hot. So then, because you are lukewarm, and neither cold nor hot, I will vomit

> *you out of My mouth. Because you say, 'I am rich, have become wealthy, and have need of nothing'—and do not know that you are wretched, miserable, poor, blind, and naked* (Revelation 3:14-17 NKJV)

What is comforting and reassuring is that, despite times when we can be led astray and be erroneously zealous for YAHUAH through ignorance, He extends grace to us, just as He did with Paul. Paul was initially passionate for YAHUAH but was mistaken until he experienced his Damascus Road encounter, which was an act of grace from YAHUAH to reveal the truth to him.

- *And I thank MASHYACH YAHUSHA our Master who has enabled me, because He counted me faithful, putting me into the ministry, [13]* **although I was formerly a blasphemer, a persecutor, and an insolent man; but I obtained mercy because I did it ignorantly in unbelief.** *[14] And the grace of our Master was exceedingly abundant, with faith and love which are in MASHYACH YAHUSHA. [15] This is a faithful saying and worthy of all acceptance, that MASHYACH YAHUSHA came into the world to save sinners, of whom I am chief. [16] However, for this reason I obtained mercy, that in me first YAHUSHA MASHYACH might show all longsuffering, as a pattern to those who are going to believe on Him for everlasting life. [17] Now to the King eternal, immortal, invisible, to YAHUAH who alone is wise, be honor and glory forever and ever. Amen.* (I Timothy 1:12-17 NKJV)

🕎 **Tribes of Africa**, many of us have served the agenda of institutional Christianity with zeal, but perhaps in error, as we were caught in the trap of the mystery of lawlessness, and our Damascus Road moment is at hand. Maybe reading this book will provide a

Damascus moment for some.

Looking further into the Kingdom

As we look deeper into 'His Kingdom', we see the King has set a calendar which governs time within His Kingdom. It sets the dates for the appointed times, feasts, sabbath, etc, so we can conform to the times of the calendar which are linked to the constitution of the Kingdom. He has a system of time (calendar) through which He has established His HOLY-DAYS, the feasts and appointed times as have been given in Leviticus chapter 23.

If we are truly in the Kingdom, should we not learn to align with YAHUAH's 364-day calendar?

- *And all the days of the commandment will be fifty-two weeks of days, and (these will make) the entire year complete. Thus it is engraved and ordained on the heavenly tablets. [31] And there is no neglecting (this commandment) for a single year or from year to year. [32] And command you the children of YASHARA'AL that they observe the years according to this reckoning- three hundred and sixty-four days, and (these) will constitute a complete year, and they will not disturb its time from its days and from its feasts; for everything will fall out in them according to their testimony, and they will not leave out any day nor disturb any feasts. [33] But if they do neglect and do not observe them according to His commandment, then they will disturb all their seasons and the years will be dislodged from this (order), [and they will disturb the seasons and the years will be dislodged] and they will neglect their ordinances. [34] And all the children of YASHARA'AL will forget and will not find the path of the years, and will forget the new months, and seasons, and*

> *Shabbats and they will go wrong as to all the order of the years. [35] For I know and from henceforth will I declare it unto you, and it is not of my own devising; for the book is written before me, and on the heavenly tablets the division of days is ordained, lest they forget the feasts of the covenant and walk according to the feasts of the Gentiles after their error and after their ignorance. [36] For there will be those who will assuredly make observations of the moon -how it disturbs the seasons and comes in from year to year ten days too soon. [37] For this reason the years will come upon them when they will disturb (the order), and make an abominable (day) the day of testimony, and an unclean day a feast day, and they will confound all the days, the Qadash (Holy) with the unclean, and the unclean day with the Qadash (Holy); for they will go wrong as to the months and Shabbats and feasts and jubilees. (Jubilees 6:30-37)*

Tribes of Africa, have we disturbed the order of time and the appointments that YAHUAH has commanded us to follow so that we remain in alignment with Him?

The major appointed times are the 7 feasts named as YAHUAH's Passover, Feast of Unleavened Bread, Feast of First Fruits, Feast of Weeks, Feast of Trumpets, Day of Atonement and the Feast of Tabernacles. Each serves as an appointed time of worship that YAHUAH has called His people to honour and observe, and each has been given as a specific date to be celebrated in His calendar. For example, as it is written in Exodus 12:2, the command is to celebrate YAHUAH's Passover specifically in the month of ABIB on the 14th day, indicating that YAHUAH's calendar is not a January to December calendar.

- **"Observe the month of Abib**, *and keep the Passover to*

YAHUAH your God, for **in the month of Abib YAHUAH your Aluah brought you out of Egypt by night**. *(Deuteronomy 16:1 NKJV)*

o *Now YAHUAH spoke to Moses and Aaron in the land of Egypt, saying, [2]* **"This month shall be your beginning of months; it shall be the first month of the year to you.** *[3] Speak to all the congregation of YASHARA'AL, saying: 'On the tenth of this month every man shall take for himself a lamb, according to the house of his father, a lamb for a household. [4] And if the household is too small for the lamb, let him and his neighbour next to his house take it according to the number of the persons; according to each man's need you shall make your count for the lamb. [5] Your lamb shall be without blemish, a male of the first year. You may take it from the sheep or from the goats. [6] Now you shall keep it until the* **fourteenth day of the same month**. *Then the whole assembly of the congregation of YASHARA'AL* **shall kill it at twilight**. *[7] And they shall take some of the blood and put it on the two doorposts and on the lintel of the houses where they eat it. [8] Then they shall eat the flesh on that night; roasted in fire, with unleavened bread and with bitter herbs they shall eat it. [9] Do not eat it raw, nor boiled at all with water, but roasted in fire—its head with its legs and its entrails. [10] You shall let none of it remain until morning, and what remains of it until morning you shall burn with fire. [11] And thus you shall eat it: with a belt on your waist, your sandals on your feet, and your staff in your hand. So you shall eat it in haste.* **It is YAHUAH's Passover.** *(Exodus 12:1-11 NKJV)*

As we know that this was a foreshadowing of the Lamb of YAHUAH,

YAHUSHA HA MASHYACH, who would be slain as the perfect and final offering and sacrifice, pouring out His blood for the remission of sins once and for all. YAHUSHA Himself was slain on the 14th of ABIB to coincide directly with the time His Father gave for YAHUAH's Passover when His people were in Egypt. YAHUSHA's death brought the 'Law of Sacrifice' to a final fulfilment and end, with YASHARA'AL never required to offer the life and blood of animals again to atone for sin before YAHUAH.

Each of these feasts of YAHUAH from (1) YAHUAH's Passover, (2) Feast of Unleavened Bread, (3) Feast of First Fruits, (4) Feast of Weeks, (5) Feast of Trumpets, (6) Day of Atonement and (7) the Feast of Tabernacles speak of the entire journey of YAHUAH's redemption for His people. The commandment to keep the 7th day Holy as a Shabbat is part of YAHUAH's Kingdom design. The cycle starts with the deliverance at YAHUAH's Passover, and ends with YAHUAH dwelling with His people, which is represented by the Feast of Tabernacles. By doing away with YAHUAH's Holy Days, we miss the understanding of the pathway He has established for us to walk on to get to His intended destination of eternal life and residence in the New Yarushalayim (Jerusalem).

As the deceiver and father of lies, Satan has worked through the kingdoms of this world — Rome being one example — to establish a separate calendar (the Gregorian calendar used today, with months named after Greco-Roman pagan gods) and to set apart holidays and observances such as Lent, Ash Wednesday, Easter, and Christmas. These became fixed times of worship within the spiritual "design" created by the so-called early church fathers of Christianity, who established times and laws contrary to the Kingdom of YAHUAH.

Why would the religious institution of Christianity, through the Roman Catholic church, deem it fit to do away with YAHUAH's

Passover and establish Easter instead? They established Easter from Good Friday to Easter Sunday as the period from when Jesus was crucified to when He rose from the dead. The notion of Jesus dying on Friday at 3 pm and resurrecting early on Sunday morning means that he was dead for 2 nights (Friday and Saturday) and less than 48 hours, which makes a mockery of the biblical fact that YAHUSHA would be in the grave for 3 nights and 3 days to fulfil what is written.

- *For as Jonah was three days and three nights in the belly of the great fish,* **so will the Son of Man be three days and three nights in the heart of the earth.** *(Matthew 12:40 NKJV)*
- *On the next day, which followed the Day of Preparation, the chief priests and Pharisees gathered together to Pilate, saying, "Sir, we remember, while He was still alive, how that deceiver said,* **'After three days I will rise.'** *Therefore command that the tomb be made secure until the third day, lest His disciples come by night and steal Him away, and say to the people, 'He has risen from the dead.' So the last deception will be worse than the first." (Matthew 27:62-64 NKJV)*
- *And He began to teach them that the Son of Man must suffer many things, and be rejected by the elders and chief priests and scribes, and be killed,* **and after three days rise again.** *(Mark 8:31 NKJV)*
- *And He strictly warned and commanded them to tell this to no one, saying, "The Son of Man must suffer many things, and be rejected by the elders and chief priests and scribes,* **and be killed, and be raised the third day."** *(Luke 9:21-22 NKJV)*

Could this be a direct way to go against truth and draw billions of people into deception (the mystery of lawlessness) by following a feast and ritual that is not biblical in any way and was not ordained by YAHUAH?

Daniel 7:25 speaks of this as it is written:

> o **He shall speak pompous words against the Most High, shall persecute the saints of the Most High, and shall intend to change times and law.** Then the saints shall be given into his hand for a time and times and half a time. [26] 'But the court shall be seated, and they shall take away his dominion, to consume and destroy it forever. [27] Then the kingdom and dominion, And the greatness of the kingdoms under the whole heaven, shall be given to the people, the saints of the Most High. His kingdom is an everlasting kingdom, and all dominions shall serve and obey Him.' [28] "This is the end of the account. As for me, Daniel, my thoughts greatly troubled me, and my countenance changed; but I kept the matter in my heart." (Daniel 7:25-28 NKJV)

Just like every country has official legislated holidays and laws in their constitution, so are the HOLY DAYS and LAWS that are legislated in the constitution of the Kingdom of YAHUAH. This is the very thing that the religion of Christianity usurped by becoming a mouthpiece to speak pompous words against the Most High by setting aside what YAHUAH mandated as Holy Days and coming up with a rival set of holidays.

Those who desire to be part of the Kingdom of YAHUAH will follow His set times, appointments and laws, while the rest follow those set by the god of this world. The times, appointments and laws that one keeps serve as a strong reference point to who they pledge allegiance to and hence which God one worships.

I believe many, like me, have spent most of their Christian lives believing that they are standing for the Kingdom of YAHUAH when, in actual fact, they are lawless and standing in opposition to it, because they, just like me, had/have rejected the constitution (laws and commandments) of the Kingdom, thereby rejecting the Judge, the Lawgiver and King who they claim to serve. This is an ignorance we have carried for centuries because we have not known the definitions and have not studied the scriptures ourselves to find ourselves approved as we comprehend what they really say, according to the teaching of RUACH HA QADASH (the Holy Spirit) and not according to the interpretation of man or the religion of Christianity. As it is written:

> o *Study to show thyself approved unto YAHUAH, a workman that need not be ashamed, rightly dividing the word of truth. (2 Timothy 2:15)*

Remembering the definition of truth already spoken about - the word is truth, the law is truth, the commandments are truth, YAHUSHA is the truth.

We can claim to be the people of the Kingdom of YAHUAH, but the reality is we only qualify to be its citizens based on the criteria set by the King. If we reject the constitution (laws and commandments) of the Kingdom, it means we decline to participate in the Kingdom, and it further signifies that we refuse to submit ourselves to the King of the Kingdom.

The god of this world also has a kingdom; it's a lawless one where the constitution (the truth) of YAHUAH is opposed. But YAHUAH has revealed the final outcome of these opposing kingdoms of the world as it is written:

> o *Then the seventh angel sounded: And there were loud*

voices in heaven, saying, **"The kingdoms of this world have become the kingdoms of YAHUAH and of His MASHYACH (Christ), and He shall reign forever and ever!"** *And the twenty-four elders who sat before YAHUAH on their thrones fell on their faces and worshiped YAHUAH, saying:* **"We give You thanks, O YAHUAH Almighty, The One who is and who was and who is to come, Because You have taken Your great power and reigned.** *(Revelation 11:15-17 NKJV)*

I would like to conclude this section by referencing the longest Psalm in the Bible, as it beautifully speaks of a deep love for TRUTH, the laws, commandments, statutes, ordinances, precepts, and judgements of YAHUAH. There is no better way to make a point than to let the WORD speak for itself, 'as it is written in Psalm 119':

Blessed are the undefiled in the way, who walk in the law of YAHUAH! *[2] Blessed are those who keep His testimonies, who seek Him with the whole heart! [3] They also do no iniquity; they walk in His ways. [4] You have commanded us To keep Your precepts diligently. [5] Oh, that my ways were directed to keep Your statutes! [6]* ***Then I would not be ashamed, When I look into all Your commandments.*** *[7] I will praise You with uprightness of heart,* ***When I learn Your righteous judgments.*** *[8]* ***I will keep Your statutes****; Oh, do not forsake me utterly! [9]* ***How can a young man cleanse his way? By taking heed according to Your word.*** *[10] With my whole heart I have sought You;* ***Oh, let me not wander from Your commandments!*** *[11]* ***Your word I have hidden in my heart, That I might not sin against You.*** *[12] Blessed are You, O YAHUAH! Teach me Your statutes. [13] With my lips I have declared All the judgments of Your mouth. [14] I have rejoiced in the way of Your testimonies, as much as* in all riches. [15] **I will meditate on Your precepts, and contemplate Your ways.** [16] I will delight myself in Your statutes; I will not forget Your word. [17] Deal bountifully with Your servant, That I may live and keep Your word. [18] **Open my eyes, that I may see Wondrous things from Your law.** [19] I am a stranger in the earth; **Do not hide Your commandments from me.** [20] **My soul breaks with longing For Your judgments at all times.** [21] **You rebuke the proud—the cursed, who stray from Your commandments.** [22] Remove from me reproach and contempt, For I have kept Your testimonies. [23] Princes also sit and speak against me, But Your servant meditates on Your statutes. [24] Your testimonies also are my delight and my counselors. [25] My soul clings to the dust; Revive me according to Your word. [26] I have declared my ways, and You answered me; Teach me Your statutes. [27] **Make me understand the way of Your precepts**; So shall I meditate on Your wonderful works. [28] My soul melts from heaviness; Strengthen me according to Your word. [29] Remove from me the way of lying, **and grant me Your law graciously**. [30] **I have chosen the way of truth; Your judgments I have laid before me.** [31] I cling to Your testimonies; O YAHUAH, do not put me to shame! [32] **I will run the course of Your commandments**, For You shall enlarge my heart. [33] Teach me, O YAHUAH, the way of Your statutes, And I shall keep it to the end. [34] **Give me understanding, and I shall keep Your law**; Indeed, I shall observe it with my whole heart. [35] **Make me walk in the path of Your commandments, For I delight in it.** [36] Incline my heart to Your testimonies, And not to covetousness. [37] Turn away my eyes from looking at worthless things, and revive me in Your way. [38] Establish Your word to Your servant, who is devoted to fearing You. [39] Turn away my reproach which I dread, For Your judgments are good. [40] Behold, I long for Your precepts; Revive me in Your righteousness. [41] Let Your mercies come also to me, O YAHUAH— Your salvation according to Your word. [42]

So shall I have an answer for him who reproaches me, **For I trust in Your word.** *[43]* **And take not the word of truth utterly out of my mouth, For I have hoped in Your ordinances.** *[44]* **So shall I keep Your law continually, Forever and ever.** *[45]* **And I will walk at liberty, For I seek Your precepts.** *[46] I will speak of Your testimonies also before kings, and will not be ashamed. [47]* **And I will delight myself in Your commandments, Which I love.** *[48]* **My hands also I will lift up to Your commandments, Which I love,** *And I will meditate on Your statutes. [49] Remember the word to Your servant, upon which You have caused me to hope. [50] This is my comfort in my affliction, For Your word has given me life. [51] The proud have me in great derision,* **Yet I do not turn aside from Your law.** *[52] I remembered Your judgments of old, O YAHUAH, and have comforted myself. [53] Indignation has taken hold of me Because of the wicked, who forsake Your law. [54] Your statutes have been my songs in the house of my pilgrimage. [55]* **I remember Your name in the night, O YAHUAH, And I keep Your law.** *[56] This has become mine, Because I kept Your precepts. [57] You are my portion, O YAHUAH; I have said that I would keep Your words. [58] I entreated Your favor with my whole heart; Be merciful to me according to Your word. [59] I thought about my ways, and turned my feet to Your testimonies. [60]* **I made haste, and did not delay To keep Your commandments.** *[61] The cords of the wicked have bound me,* **But I have not forgotten Your law.** *[62] At midnight I will rise to give thanks to You, Because of Your righteous judgments. [63] I am a companion of all who fear You, and of those who keep Your precepts. [64] The earth, O YAHUAH, is full of Your mercy; Teach me Your statutes. [65] You have dealt well with Your servant, O YAHUAH, according to Your word. [66] Teach me good judgment and knowledge,* **For I believe Your commandments.** *[67] Before I was afflicted I went astray, but now I keep Your word. [68] You are good, and do good; Teach me Your statutes. [69] The proud* have forged a lie against me, But I will keep Your precepts with my whole heart. [70] Their heart is as fat as grease, **But I delight in Your law.** [71] **It is good for me that I have been afflicted, That I may learn Your statutes.** [72] **The law of Your mouth is better to me Than thousands of coins of gold and silver.** [73] Your hands have made me and fashioned me; **Give me understanding, that I may learn Your commandments.** [74] Those who fear You will be glad when they see me, Because I have hoped in Your word. [75] I know, O YAHUAH, that Your judgments are right, and that in faithfulness You have afflicted me. [76] Let, I pray, Your merciful kindness be for my comfort, According to Your word to Your servant. [77] Let Your tender mercies come to me, that I may live; **For Your law is my delight.** [78] Let the proud be ashamed, for they treated me wrongfully with falsehood; But I will meditate on Your precepts. [79] Let those who fear You turn to me, those who know Your testimonies. [80] Let my heart be blameless regarding Your statutes, That I may not be ashamed. [81] My soul faints for Your salvation, But I hope in Your word. [82] My eyes fail from searching Your word, Saying, "When will You comfort me?" [83] For I have become like a wineskin in smoke, Yet I do not forget Your statutes. [84] How many are the days of Your servant? When will You execute judgment on those who persecute me? [85] The proud have dug pits for me, which is not according to Your law. [86] **All Your commandments are faithful**; They persecute me wrongfully; Help me! [87] They almost made an end of me on earth, But I did not forsake Your precepts. [88] Revive me according to Your lovingkindness, So that I may keep the testimony of Your mouth. [89] Forever, O YAHUAH, Your word is settled in heaven. [90] Your faithfulness endures to all generations; You established the earth, and it abides. [91] They continue this day according to Your ordinances, for all are Your servants. [92] **Unless Your law had been my delight, I would then have perished in my affliction.** [93] I will never forget Your precepts, for by them You have given me life. *[94] I am Yours, save me; For I have sought Your precepts. [95] The wicked wait for me to destroy me, But I will consider Your testimonies. [96] I have seen the consummation of all perfection, But Your commandment is exceedingly broad. [97]* **Oh, how I love Your law! It is my meditation all the day.** *[98]* **You, through Your commandments, make me wiser than my enemies;** *For they are ever with me. [99] I have more understanding than all my teachers, For Your testimonies are my meditation. [100] I understand more than the ancients, Because I keep Your precepts. [101] I have restrained my feet from every evil way, That I may keep Your word. [102] I have not departed from Your judgments, For You Yourself have taught me. [103] How sweet are Your words to my taste, Sweeter than honey to my mouth! [104] Through Your precepts I get understanding; therefore I hate every false way. [105]* **Your word is a lamp to my feet and a light to my path.** *[106] I have sworn and confirmed That I will keep Your righteous judgments. [107] I am afflicted very much; Revive me, O YAHUAH, according to Your word. [108] Accept, I pray, the freewill offerings of my mouth, O YAHUAH, and teach me Your judgments. [109]* **My life is continually in my hand, Yet I do not forget Your law.** *[110] The wicked have laid a snare for me, Yet I have not strayed from Your precepts. [111] Your testimonies I have taken as a heritage forever, for they are the rejoicing of my heart. [112] I have inclined my heart to perform Your statutes Forever, to the very end. [113] I hate the double minded,* **But I love Your law.** *[114] You are my hiding place and my shield; I hope in Your word. [115] Depart from me, you evildoers,* **For I will keep the commandments of my Aluah!** *[116] Uphold me according to Your word, that I may live; And do not let me be ashamed of my hope. [117] Hold me up, and I shall be safe, And I shall observe Your statutes continually. [118] You reject all those who stray from Your statutes, for their deceit is falsehood. [119] You put away all the wicked of the earth like dross; therefore I love Your testimonies. [120] My flesh* trembles for fear of You, And I am afraid of Your judgments. [121] I have done justice and righteousness; Do not leave me to my oppressors. [122] Be surety for Your servant for good; Do not let the proud oppress me. [123] My eyes fail from seeking Your salvation And Your righteous word. [124] Deal with Your servant according to Your mercy, and teach me Your statutes. [125] I am Your servant; Give me understanding, That I may know Your testimonies. [126] **It is time for You to act, O YAHUAH, for they have regarded Your law as void. [127] Therefore I love Your commandments More than gold, yes, than fine gold!** [128] Therefore all Your precepts concerning all things I consider to be right; I hate every false way. [129] Your testimonies are wonderful; therefore my soul keeps them. [130] The entrance of Your words gives light; It gives understanding to the simple. [131] **I opened my mouth and panted, For I longed for Your commandments.** [132] **Look upon me and be merciful to me, As Your custom is toward those who love Your name.** [133] Direct my steps by Your word, and let no iniquity have dominion over me. [134] Redeem me from the oppression of man, That I may keep Your precepts. [135] Make Your face shine upon Your servant, and teach me Your statutes. [136] **Rivers of water run down from my eyes, because men do not keep Your law.** [137] Righteous are You, O YAHUAH, and upright are Your judgments. [138] Your testimonies, which You have commanded, Are righteous and very faithful. [139] My zeal has consumed me, because my enemies have forgotten Your words. [140] Your word is very pure; therefore Your servant loves it. [141] I am small and despised, Yet I do not forget Your precepts. [142] **Your righteousness is an everlasting righteousness, And Your law is truth. [143] Trouble and anguish have overtaken me, Yet Your commandments are my delights.** [144] The righteousness of Your testimonies is everlasting; Give me understanding, and I shall live. [145] I cry out with my whole heart; Hear me, O YAHUAH! I will keep Your statutes. [146] I cry out to You; Save me, and I will keep Your testimonies. [147] I rise before the dawning of the morning, and cry for help; I hope in Your word. [148] My eyes are awake through the night watches, That I may meditate on Your word. [149] Hear my voice according to Your lovingkindness; O YAHUAH, revive me according to Your justice. [150] **They draw near who follow after wickedness; They are far from Your law.** [151] **You are near, O YAHUAH, and all Your commandments are truth.** [152] Concerning Your testimonies, I have known of old that You have founded them forever. [153] **Consider my affliction and deliver me, For I do not forget Your law.** [154] Plead my cause and redeem me; Revive me according to Your word. [155] Salvation is far from the wicked, for they do not seek Your statutes. [156] Great are Your tender mercies, O YAHUAH; Revive me according to Your judgments. [157] Many are my persecutors and my enemies, Yet I do not turn from Your testimonies. [158] I see the treacherous, and am disgusted, because they do not keep Your word. [159] Consider how I love Your precepts; Revive me, O YAHUAH, according to Your lovingkindness. [160] **The entirety of Your word is truth, and every one of Your righteous judgments endures forever.** [161] Princes persecute me without a cause, but my heart stands in awe of Your word. [162] **I rejoice at Your word as one who finds great treasure.** [163] **I hate and abhor lying, But I love Your law.** [164] Seven times a day I praise You, Because of Your righteous judgments. [165] **Great peace have those who love Your law, and nothing causes them to stumble.** [166] **YAHUAH, I hope for Your salvation, And I do Your commandments.** [167] My soul keeps Your testimonies, And I love them exceedingly. [168] I keep Your precepts and Your testimonies, for all my ways are before You. [169] Let my cry come before You, O YAHUAH; Give me understanding according to Your word. [170] Let my supplication come before You; Deliver me according to Your word. [171] My lips shall utter praise, For You teach me Your statutes. [172] **My tongue shall speak of Your** *word, for all Your commandments are righteousness. [173] Let Your hand become my help, For I have chosen Your precepts. [174] I long for Your salvation, O YAHUAH, And Your law is my delight.* [175] Let my soul live, and it shall praise You; And let Your judgments help me. [176] *I have gone astray like a lost sheep; Seek Your servant, For I do not forget Your commandments. (Psalms 119:1-176 NKJV)*

Tribes of Africa, how do we respond to this? By confessing our lawlessness and repenting for breaking the everlasting covenant (agreement) with YAHUAH.

CHAPTER FOURTEEN

The Ark of The Covenant

Understanding the importance of YAHUAH's Covenant with us (YAHUAH's agreement with His people and the terms thereof) has been a major part of this book thus far and central to its title ***"Awakening the tribes of Africa – come out of her and return to the covenant with the ALAHYM of Abraham, Isaac and Jacob"***.

The agreement that YAHUAH made with people of all tongues, tribes and nations through His firstborn son YASHARA'AL is of greatest importance and value to Him that He has always, through the ages, called for it to be kept in the Holiest of places.

From the days of Moses, when the Book of the Covenant was first given to YASHARA'AL until the destruction of the temple at the hands of the Babylonians, the Book of the Covenant (in the form of the stone tablets) found a dwelling place in the Ark of the Covenant.

- o Then he took the **Book of the Covenant** and read in the hearing of the people. And they said, "All that YAHUAH has said we will do, and be obedient." And Moses took the

- blood, sprinkled it on the people, and said, "This is the blood of the covenant which YAHUAH has made with you according to all these words." (Exodus 24:7-8 NKJV)
  - Then the king commanded all the people, saying, "Keep the Passover to YAHUAH your Aluah, **as it is written in this Book of the Covenant."** (II Kings 23:21 NKJV)
  - Now the king sent them to gather all the elders of Judah and Yarushalayim (Jerusalem) to him. The king went up to the house of YAHUAH with all the men of Judah, and with him all the inhabitants of Yarushalayim (Jerusalem)— the priests and the prophets and all the people, both small and great. **And he read in their hearing all the words of the Book of the Covenant which had been found in the house of YAHUAH.** Then the king stood by a pillar and made a covenant before YAHUAH, to follow YAHUAH and to keep His commandments and His testimonies and His statutes, with all his heart and all his soul, to perform the words of this covenant that were written in this book. And all the people took a stand for the covenant. (II Kings 23:1-3 NKJV)

The Book of the Covenant was and remains a treasure unto YAHUAH as it guides and determines the affairs of His greatest treasure, which are the people He has created in His own image, whom He desires to dwell with in the 'New Yarushalayim (Jerusalem)' for eternity.

For it is His will that no one should perish.

- But, beloved, do not forget this one thing, that with YAHUAH one day is as a thousand years, and a thousand years as one day. YAHUAH is not slack concerning His promise, as some count slackness, but is long suffering toward us, **not willing that any should perish but that all should come**

> ***to repentance.*** *(II Peter 3:8-9 NKJV)*

The Ark of the Covenant is where YAHUAH committed His presence would always be present.

The Ark of the Covenant was/is placed in the most Holy place, the Holy of Holies, in the tabernacle and specifically under the Mercy Seat where YAHUAH Himself sits and judges from, as the Book of the Covenant serves as the basis for His judgements concerning YASHARA'AL and the nations.

The children of YASHARA'AL knew the importance of the covenant and hence would carry the Ark of the Covenant whenever they went into battle as a reminder of their agreement with YAHUAH and His promise to fight for them whenever they were honouring the terms of the agreement. They also carried it knowing that the presence of YAHUAH would always be upon the Ark. YAHUAH was and is always present where the covenant is. That's how important the covenant is to Him.

The Ark of the Covenant carried:

1. **The Two Tablets of the Covenant (The Ten Commandments),** written by YAHUAH's finger on Mount Sinai (Exodus 31:18, Deuteronomy 10:2, Hebrews 9:4).

2. **Aaron's Rod,** the staff that budded miraculously, confirming Aaron's divine appointment as high priest (Numbers 17:10, Hebrews 9:4).

3. **A Golden Jar of Manna,** a container holding a sample of the miraculous manna YAHUAH provided for the YASHARA'ALITES in the wilderness (Exodus 16:32-34, Hebrews 9:4).

These items represented YAHUAH's covenant (agreement) with

the YASHARA'ALITES, His promised provision and care for them, and the authority of the priesthood He gave them.

The covenant that was written on stone tablets and kept in the Ark of the Covenant in the Holy of Holies is the covenant that YAHUAH writes in the Holy of Holies of people's hearts, since His people have become His dwelling place, His temple.

- *For this is the covenant that I will make with the house of YASHARA'AL after those days, says YAHUAH:* ***I will put My laws in their mind and write them on their hearts; and I will be their Aluah, and they shall be My people.*** *(Hebrews 8:10 NKJV)*
- *"Behold, the days are coming, says YAHUAH, when I will make a new covenant with the house of YASHARA'AL and with the house of Judah (YAHUDA)— not according to the covenant that I made with their fathers in the day that I took them by the hand to lead them out of the land of Egypt, My covenant which they broke, though I was a husband to them, says YAHUAH.* ***But this is the covenant that I will make with the house of YASHARA'AL after those days, says YAHUAH: I will put My law in their minds, and write it on their hearts; and I will be their Aluah, and they shall be My people.*** *(Jeremiah 31:31-33 NKJV)*
- ***Do you not know that you are the temple of YAHUAH and that the Spirit of YAHUAH dwells in you?*** *If anyone defiles the temple of YAHUAH, YAHUAH will destroy him. For the temple of YAHUAH is holy, which temple you are. (I Corinthians 3:16-17 NKJV)*

Although the 'earthly' Ark of His Covenant may have been lost to mankind here on earth, YAHUAH has not lost it as He has kept it safe and will show it off at the sounding of the 7th angel, as it is written:

> o **Then the seventh angel sounded: And there were loud voices in heaven, saying, "The kingdoms of this world have become the kingdoms of YAHUAH and of His MASHYACH (Christ), and He shall reign forever and ever!"** *[16] And the twenty-four elders who sat before YAHUAH on their thrones fell on their faces and worshiped YAHUAH, [17] saying: "We give You thanks, O YAHUAH Almighty, The One who is and who was and who is to come, Because You have taken Your great power and reigned. [18] The nations were angry, and Your wrath has come, and the time of the dead, that they should be judged, and that You should reward Your servants the prophets and the saints, and those who fear Your name, small and great, and should destroy those who destroy the earth." [19]* **Then the temple of YAHUAH was opened in heaven, and the ark of His covenant was seen in His temple.** *And there were lightnings, noises, thunderings, an earthquake, and great hail. (Revelation 11:15-19 NKJV)*

The Ark of the Covenant is seen in the heavenly temple, symbolising YAHUAH's presence and the fulfilment of His covenant with His people. This vision connects the earthly representation of the Ark with its heavenly reality, signifying YAHUAH's enduring faithfulness and the ultimate victory of His promises through YAHUSHA MASHYACH. The Ark, containing the tablets of the Law (Torah), Manna, and Aaron's rod, represents YAHUAH's law, mercy, and guidance.

- Writing the Book of the Covenant:

  o *And when He had made an end of speaking with him on*

Mount Sinai, He gave Moses two tablets of the Testimony, tablets of stone, written with the finger of YAHUAH. (Exodus 31:18 NKJV)

- And I will write on the tablets the words that were on the first tablets, which you broke; and you shall put them in the ark.' [3] "So I made an ark of acacia wood, hewed two tablets of stone like the first, and went up the mountain, having the two tablets in my hand. [4] And He wrote on the tablets according to the first writing, the Ten Commandments, which YAHUAH had spoken to you in the mountain from the midst of the fire in the day of the assembly; and YAHUAH gave them to me. [5] Then I turned and came down from the mountain, and put the tablets in the ark which I had made; and there they are, just as YAHUAH commanded me." (Deuteronomy 10:2-5 NKJV)

- The building of the Ark of the Covenant:

  - "And they shall make an ark of acacia wood; two and a half cubits shall be its length, a cubit and a half its width, and a cubit and a half its height. [11] And you shall overlay it with pure gold, inside and out you shall overlay it, and shall make on it a molding of gold all around. [12] You shall cast four rings of gold for it, and put them in its four corners; two rings shall be on one side, and two rings on the other side. [13] And you shall make poles of acacia wood, and overlay them with gold. [14] You shall put the poles into the rings on the sides of the ark, that the ark may be carried by them.

  - And you shall put into the ark the Testimony which I will give you. [17] "You shall make a mercy seat of pure gold; two *and a half cubits shall be its length and a cubit and a half its width. [18] And you shall make two cherubim of gold; of hammered work you shall make them at the two ends of the mercy seat. [19] Make one cherub at one end, and the other cherub at the other end; you shall make the cherubim at the two ends of it of one piece with the mercy seat. [20] And the cherubim shall stretch out their wings above, covering the mercy seat with their wings, and they shall face one another; the faces of the cherubim shall be toward the mercy seat. [21] You shall put the mercy seat on top of the ark, and in the ark you shall put the Testimony that I will give you. [22] And there I will meet with you, and I will speak with you from above the mercy seat, from between the two cherubim which are on the ark of the Testimony, about everything which I will give you in commandment to the children of YASHARA'AL. (Exodus 25:10-14, 16-22 NKJV)*

- *Then Bezalel made the ark of acacia wood; two and a half cubits was its length, a cubit and a half its width, and a cubit and a half its height. [2] He overlaid it with pure gold inside and outside, and made a molding of gold all around it. [3] And he cast for it four rings of gold to be set in its four corners: two rings on one side, and two rings on the other side of it. [4] He made poles of acacia wood, and overlaid them with gold. [5] And he put the poles into the rings at the sides of the ark, to bear the ark. [6] He also made the mercy seat of pure gold; two and a half cubits was its length and a cubit and a half its width. [7] He made two cherubim of beaten gold; he made them of one piece at the two ends of the mercy seat: [8] one cherub at one end on this side, and the other cherub at the other end on that side. He made the cherubim at the two ends of one piece with the mercy* seat. *[9] The cherubim spread out their wings above, and covered the mercy seat with their wings. They faced one another; the faces of the cherubim were toward the mercy seat. (Exodus 37:1-9 NKJV)*

- YAHUAH moving with the Ark:

    o *they departed from the mountain of YAHUAH on a journey of three days; and the ark of the covenant of YAHUAH went before them for the three days' journey, to search out a resting place for them. [34] And the cloud of YAHUAH was above them by day when they went out from the camp. [35]* **So it was, whenever the ark set out, that Moses said: "Rise up, O YAHUAH! Let Your enemies be scattered, and let those who hate You flee before You." [36] And when it rested, he said: "Return, O YAHUAH, To the many thousands of YASHARA'AL."** *(Numbers 10:33-36 NKJV)*

- The Ark of the Covenant went before the YASHARA'ALITES:

    o *Then Joshua rose early in the morning; and they set out from Acacia Grove and came to the Jordan, he and all the children of YASHARA'AL, and lodged there before they crossed over. [2] So it was, after three days, that the officers went through the camp; [3] and they commanded the people, saying,* **"When you see the ark of the covenant of YAHUAH your Aluah, and the priests, the Levites, bearing it, then you shall set out from your place and go after it.** *[4] Yet there shall be a space between you and it, about two thousand cubits by measure. Do not come near it,* *that you may know the way by which you must go, for you have not passed this way before." [5] And Joshua said to the people, "Sanctify yourselves, for tomorrow YAHUAH will do wonders among you." [6] Then Joshua spoke to the priests, saying,* **"Take up the ark of the covenant and cross over before the people."** *So they took up the ark of the covenant and went before the people. [7] And YAHUAH said to Joshua, "This day I will begin to exalt you in the sight of all YASHARA'AL, that they may know that, as I was with Moses, so I will be with you. [8] You shall command the priests who bear the ark of the covenant, saying, 'When you have come to the edge of the water of the Jordan, you shall stand in the Jordan." [9] So Joshua said to the children of YASHARA'AL, "Come here, and hear the words of YAHUAH your Aluah." [10] And Joshua said, "By this you shall know that the living Alahym is among you, and that He will without fail drive out from before you the Canaanites and the Hittites and the Hivites and the Perizzites and the Girgashites and the Amorites and the Jebusites: [11]* **Behold, the ark of the covenant of the ALAHYM of all the earth is crossing over before you into the Jordan.** *[12] Now therefore, take for yourselves twelve men from the tribes of YASHARA'AL, one man from every tribe. [13] And it shall come to pass, as soon as the soles of the feet of the priests who bear the ark of YAHUAH, ALAHYM of all the earth, shall rest in the waters of the Jordan, that the waters of the Jordan shall be cut off, the waters that come down from upstream, and they shall stand as a heap." [14]* **So it was, when the people set out from their camp to cross over the Jordan, with the priests bearing the ark of the covenant before the people,** *[15]* *and as those who bore the ark came to the Jordan, and the feet of the priests who bore the ark dipped in the edge of the water (for the Jordan overflows all its banks during the whole time of harvest), [16] that the waters which came down from upstream stood still, and rose in a heap very far away at Adam, the city that is beside Zaretan. So the waters that went down into the Sea of the Arabah, the Salt Sea, failed, and were cut off; and the people crossed over opposite Jericho.* **[17] Then the priests who bore the ark of the covenant of YAHUAH stood firm on dry ground in the midst of the Jordan; and all YASHARA'AL crossed over on dry ground, until all the people had crossed completely over the Jordan.** *(Joshua 3:1-17 NKJV)*

- The Ark of the Covenant being captured because of YASHARA'AL's disobedience:

  o *And the word of Samuel came to all YASHARA'AL. Now YASHARA'AL went out to battle against the Philistines, and encamped beside Ebenezer; and the Philistines encamped in Aphek. [2] Then the Philistines put themselves in battle array against YASHARA'AL. And when they joined battle, YASHARA'AL was defeated by the Philistines, who killed about four thousand men of the army in the field.* **[3] And when the people had come into the camp, the elders of YASHARA'AL said, "Why has YAHUAH defeated us today before the Philistines? Let us bring the ark of the covenant of YAHUAH from Shiloh to us, that when it comes among us it may save us from the hand of our enemies." [4] So the people sent to Shiloh, that they might bring from there the ark of the covenant of**

YAHUAH of hosts, who dwells between the cherubim. And the two sons of Eli, Hophni and Phinehas, were there with the ark of the covenant of YAHUAH. [5] And when the ark of the covenant of YAHUAH came into the camp, all YASHARA'AL shouted so loudly that the earth shook. [6] Now when the Philistines heard the noise of the shout, they said, "What does the sound of this great shout in the camp of the Hebrews mean?" **Then they understood that the ark of YAHUAH had come into the camp. [7] So the Philistines were afraid, for they said, "Alahym has come into the camp!"** And they said, "Woe to us! For such a thing has never happened before. [8] Woe to us! Who will deliver us from the hand of these mighty gods? These are the gods who struck the Egyptians with all the plagues in the wilderness. [9] Be strong and conduct yourselves like men, you Philistines, that you do not become servants of the Hebrews, as they have been to you. Conduct yourselves like men, and fight!" [10] So the Philistines fought, and YASHARA'AL was defeated, and every man fled to his tent. There was a very great slaughter, and there fell of YASHARA'AL thirty thousand foot soldiers. [11] Also the ark of YAHUAH was captured; and the two sons of Eli, Hophni and Phinehas, died. [12] Then a man of Benjamin ran from the battle line the same day, and came to Shiloh with his clothes torn and dirt on his head. [13] Now when he came, there was Eli, sitting on a seat by the wayside watching, for his heart trembled for the ark of YAHUAH. And when the man came into the city and told it, all the city cried out. [14] When Eli heard the noise of the outcry, he said, "What does the sound of this tumult mean?" And the man came quickly and told Eli.

[15] Eli was ninety-eight years old, and his eyes were so dim that he could not see. [16] Then the man said to Eli, "I am he who came from the battle. And I fled today from the battle line." And he said, "What happened, my son?" [17] So the messenger answered and said, "YASHARA'AL has fled before the Philistines, and there has been a great slaughter among the people. Also your two sons, Hophni and Phinehas, are dead; and the ark of YAHUAH has been captured." [18] Then it happened, when he made mention of the ark of YAHUAH, that Eli fell off the seat backward by the side of the gate; and his neck was broken and he died, for the man was old and heavy. And he had judged YASHARA'AL forty years. [19] Now his daughter-in-law, Phinehas's wife, was with child, due to be delivered; and when she heard the news that the ark of YAHUAH was captured, and that her father-in-law and her husband were dead, she bowed herself and gave birth, for her labor pains came upon her. [20] And about the time of her death the women who stood by her said to her, "Do not fear, for you have borne a son." But she did not answer, nor did she regard it. [21] Then she named the child Ichabod, saying, "The glory has departed from YASHARA'AL!" because the ark of YAHUAH had been captured and because of her father-in-law and her husband. [22] **And she said, "The glory has departed from YASHARA'AL, for the ark of YAHUAH has been captured."** *(I Samuel 4:1-22 NKJV)*

- The man after YAHUAH's own heart, David retrieving the Ark of the Covenant:

  - *Again David gathered all the choice men of YASHARA'AL,*

thirty thousand. [2] And David arose and went with all the people who were with him from Baale Judah to bring up from there the ark of YAHUAH, whose name is called by the Name, YAHUAH of Hosts, who dwells between the cherubim. [3] So they set the ark of YAHUAH on a new cart, and brought it out of the house of Abinadab, which was on the hill; and Uzzah and Ahio, the sons of Abinadab, drove the new cart. [4] And they brought it out of the house of Abinadab, which was on the hill, accompanying the ark of YAHUAH; and Ahio went before the ark. [5] Then David and all the house of YASHARA'AL played music before YAHUAH on all kinds of instruments of fir wood, on harps, on stringed instruments, on tambourines, on sistrums, and on cymbals. [6] And when they came to Nachon's threshing floor, Uzzah put out his hand to the ark of YAHUAH and took hold of it, for the oxen stumbled. [7] Then the anger of YAHUAH was aroused against Uzzah, and YAHUAH struck him there for his error; and he died there by the ark of YAHUAH. [8] And David became angry because of YAHUAH's outbreak against Uzzah; and he called the name of the place Perez Uzzah to this day. [9] David was afraid of YAHUAH that day; and he said, "How can the ark of YAHUAH come to me?" [10] So David would not move the ark of YAHUAH with him into the City of David; but David took it aside into the house of Obed-Edom the Gittite. [11] The ark of YAHUAH remained in the house of Obed-Edom the Gittite three months. And YAHUAH blessed Obed-Edom and all his household. [12] Now it was told King David, saying, "YAHUAH has blessed the house of Obed-Edom and all that belongs to him, because of the ark of YAHUAH." So David went and brought up the ark of YAHUAH from the house of Obed-Edom to the City of David with gladness. [13] And so it was, when those bearing the ark of YAHUAH had gone six paces, that he sacrificed oxen and fatted sheep. [14] Then David danced before YAHUAH with all his might; and David was wearing a linen ephod. [15] So David and all the house of YASHARA'AL brought up the ark of YAHUAH with shouting and with the sound of the trumpet. [16] Now as the ark of YAHUAH came into the City of David, Michal, Saul's daughter, looked through a window and saw King David leaping and whirling before YAHUAH; and she despised him in her heart. [17] So they brought the ark of YAHUAH, and set it in its place in the midst of the tabernacle that David had erected for it. Then David offered burnt offerings and peace offerings before YAHUAH. [18] And when David had finished offering burnt offerings and peace offerings, he blessed the people in the name of YAHUAH of hosts. [19] Then he distributed among all the people, among the whole multitude of YASHARA'AL, both the women and the men, to everyone a loaf of bread, a piece of meat, and a cake of raisins. So all the people departed, everyone to his house. [20] Then David returned to bless his household. And Michal the daughter of Saul came out to meet David, and said, "How glorious was the king of YASHARA'AL today, uncovering himself today in the eyes of the maids of his servants, as one of the base fellows shamelessly uncovers himself!" [21] So David said to Michal, "It was before YAHUAH, who chose me instead of your father and all his house, to appoint me ruler over the people of YAHUAH, over YASHARA'AL. Therefore I will play music before YAHUAH. [22] And I will be even more undignified than this, and will be humble in my own sight.

But as for the maidservants of whom you have spoken, by them I will be held in honor." [23] Therefore Michal the daughter of Saul had no children to the day of her death. (II Samuel 6:1-23 NKJV)

- The ministry of the Great High Priest YAHUSHA upon the Ark of the Covenant:

    o *Then indeed, even the first covenant had ordinances of divine service and the earthly sanctuary. [2] For a tabernacle was prepared: the first part, in which was the lampstand, the table, and the showbread, which is called the sanctuary; [3] and behind the second veil,* **the part of the tabernacle which is called the Holiest of All, [4] which had the golden censer and the ark of the covenant overlaid on all sides with gold, in which were the golden pot that had the manna, Aaron's rod that budded, and the tablets of the covenant; [5] and above it were the cherubim of glory overshadowing the mercy seat.** *Of these things we cannot now speak in detail. [6] Now when these things had been thus prepared, the priests always went into the first part of the tabernacle, performing the services. [7] But into the second part the high priest went alone once a year, not without blood, which he offered for himself and for the people's sins committed in ignorance; [8] the Holy Spirit indicating this, that the way into the Holiest of All was not yet made manifest while the first tabernacle was still standing. [9] It was symbolic for the present time in which both gifts and sacrifices are offered which cannot make him who performed the service perfect in regard to the conscience— [10] concerned only with foods and drinks,* *various washings, and fleshly ordinances imposed until the time of reformation. [11] But MASHYACH came as High Priest of the good things to come, with the greater and more perfect tabernacle not made with hands, that is, not of this creation. [12] Not with the blood of goats and calves, but with His own blood He entered the Most Holy Place once for all, having obtained eternal redemption. [13] For if the blood of bulls and goats and the ashes of a heifer, sprinkling the unclean, sanctifies for the purifying of the flesh, [14] how much more shall the blood of MASHYACH, who through the eternal Spirit offered Himself without spot to YAHUAH, cleanse your conscience from dead works to serve the living Alahym? [15] And for this reason He is the Mediator of the new covenant, by means of death, for the redemption of the transgressions under the first covenant, that those who are called may receive the promise of the eternal inheritance. [16] For where there is a testament, there must also of necessity be the death of the testator. [17] For a testament is in force after men are dead, since it has no power at all while the testator lives. [18] Therefore not even the first covenant was dedicated without blood. [19] For when Moses had spoken every precept to all the people according to the law, he took the blood of calves and goats, with water, scarlet wool, and hyssop, and sprinkled both the book itself and all the people, [20] saying, "This is the blood of the covenant which YAHUAH has commanded you." [21] Then likewise he sprinkled with blood both the tabernacle and all the vessels of the ministry. [22] And according to the law almost all things are purified with blood, and without shedding of blood there is no remission. [23] Therefore it was necessary that the copies of the things in the heavens should*

> *be purified with these, but the heavenly things themselves with better sacrifices than these. [24] For MASHYACH (Christ) has not entered the holy places made with hands, which are copies of the true, but into heaven itself, now to appear in the presence of YAHUAH for us; [25] not that He should offer Himself often, as the high priest enters the Most Holy Place every year with blood of another— [26] He then would have had to suffer often since the foundation of the world; but now, once at the end of the ages, He has appeared to put away sin by the sacrifice of Himself. [27] And as it is appointed for men to die once, but after this the judgment, [28] so MASHYACH was offered once to bear the sins of many. To those who eagerly wait for Him He will appear a second time, apart from sin, for salvation. (Hebrews 9:1-28 NKJV)*

❦ **Tribes of Africa,** the restoration of Africa's guardianship of the Covenant is key to the redemption and restoration of the tribes of Africa and the nations. The covenant with YAHUAH has been lost from within the spiritual domain of Africa. Just as King David's focus was when he became King, to ensure that the Ark of the Covenant would be recovered and that YASHARA'AL would restore their obedience to the covenant, so it must be for Africa.

❦ **Arise, King Davids of Africa, Arise**

❦ **Arise, men and women of Africa who are after YAHUAH's own heart.**

> o *And Samuel said to Saul, "You have done foolishly. You have not kept the commandment of YAHUAH your Aluah, which He commanded you. For now YAHUAH would have established your kingdom over YASHARA'AL forever. [14]*

> *But now your kingdom shall not continue.* ***YAHUAH has sought for Himself a man after His own heart, and YAHUAH has commanded him to be commander over His people, because you have not kept what YAHUAH commanded you.*** *" (I Samuel 13:13-14 NKJV)*

- *Then Paul stood up, and motioning with his hand said, "Men of YASHARA'AL, and you who fear YAHUAH, listen: [17] The Alahym of this people YASHARA'AL chose our fathers, and exalted the people when they dwelt as strangers in the land of Egypt, and with an uplifted arm He brought them out of it. [18] Now for a time of about forty years He put up with their ways in the wilderness. [19] And when He had destroyed seven nations in the land of Canaan, He distributed their land to them by allotment. [20] "After that He gave them judges for about four hundred and fifty years, until Samuel the prophet. [21] And afterward they asked for a king; so YAHUAH gave them Saul the son of Kish, a man of the tribe of Benjamin, for forty years. [22] And when He had removed him,* ***He raised up for them David as king, to whom also He gave testimony and said, 'I have found David the son of Jesse, a man after My own heart, who will do all My will.'*** *(Acts 13:16-22 NKJV)*

Tribes of Africa, our return to the covenant (the terms of the agreement) YAHUAH established with us is most urgent.

"Navigating through existing narratives in search of truth"

Section 5

Contents

Chapter 15.   Searching for the truth of biblical identities

Chapter 16.   The path to 'heaven' or the New Yarushalayim (Jerusalem)

Chapter 17.   A call to Holiness

Chapter 18.   The big elephant in the room named Jewish Israel

Beloved, let us love one another, for love is of YAHUAH; and everyone who loves is born of YAHUAH and knows YAHUAH. [8] He who does not love does not know YAHUAH, for YAHUAH is love. (I John 4:7-8 NKJV)

CHAPTER FIFTEEN

Searching For The Truth Of Biblical Identities

This finally brings us to the chapter where the question my book editor asked while reviewing Chapter 7 can be answered. This was her question. "I would just like to clarify whether you are saying that Africans are the covenant people, thereby replacing Israel... or whether, through some other means, Africans came into contact with the Sovereign God who then placed the same demand on them as He had on Israel. Whether it is either of the two or a third option, I recommend fleshing out this biblical identity more strongly to support the position you have laid out."

This is indeed a critical point that needs clarification.

This book aims to reveal the identity of the true Israel. Therefore, contested narratives of identity and heritage concerning those who claim to be Israel are laid bare for your examination. The modern communities claiming to be Israel are not the original descendants, but rather groups that have appropriated the name for political, cultural, and self-serving reasons. In contrast, Black people, particularly the Bantu, represent the true Israel of Yah. Their forced displacement can be traced historically to the Assyrian captivity and later to the Babylonian exile, events that marked a long history of dispersal and dispossession. This shall be expounded on in greater detail in this chapter.

One of the things I have constantly heard and read many times on my journey as a Christian was that Africa and dark-skinned people in general were cursed because of the curse of Ham, (which is a flawed statement in itself because the curse that Noah pronounced was on Canaan, Ham's son; not on Ham himself and hence not on Ham's other three sons, Cush, Mizraim, Put,). This very lie has been the basis of much of "the conquerors'" theological justification for what they have done to darker-skinned indigenous people.

> o *And Noah began to be a farmer, and he planted a vineyard. [21] Then he drank of the wine and was drunk, and became uncovered in his tent. [22] And Ham, the father of Canaan, saw the nakedness of his father, and told his two brothers outside. [23] But Shem and Japheth took a garment, laid it on both their shoulders, and went backward and covered the nakedness of their father. Their faces were turned away, and they did not see their father's nakedness. [24] So Noah awoke from his wine, and knew what his younger son had done to him. [25]* **Then he said: "Cursed be Canaan**; *A servant of servants He shall be to his brethren." [26] And he said: "Blessed be YAHUAH, The Alahym of Shem, and may Canaan be his servant. [27] May Aluah enlarge Japheth, and may he dwell in the tents of Shem; And may Canaan be his servant." (Genesis 9:20-27 NKJV)*

The real question that we should be exploring is rather, is the curse being experienced by melanated (darker-skinned) people of African linked to the Deuteronomy 28 narrative of the curse that comes to the covenant people of YAHUAH, who are experiencing the effects of 'the curse' because of their breaking of the covenant (breaking the terms of the agreement) that YAHUAH has made with them and which they agreed to?

If indeed we as 'darker-skinned' people are under a curse, it behoves us to investigate if this is the case, and what the reason is, and how to break out of it.

Is it possible that "the conqueror" actually turned the story upside down to fit a narrative that would work in their favour, and use that to propagate the biggest lie ever by switching the identities of the descendants of the sons of Noah—Shem, Ham and Japheth?

The genealogy of the people of the earth (referred to as the table of nations) starts with Noah after the flood through His 3 sons, Shem, Ham and Japheth.

As it is written:

- **Now this is the genealogy of the sons of Noah: Shem, Ham, and Japheth.** *And sons were born to them after the flood. [2]* **The sons of Japheth** *were Gomer, Magog, Madai, Javan, Tubal, Meshech, and Tiras. [3] The sons of Gomer were Ashkenaz, Riphath, and Togarmah. [4] The sons of Javan were Elishah, Tarshish, Kittim, and Dodanim. [5] From these the coastland peoples of the Gentiles were separated into their lands, everyone according to his language, according to their families, into their nations. [6]* **The sons of Ham** *were Cush, Mizraim, Put, and Canaan. [7] The sons of Cush were Seba, Havilah, Sabtah, Raamah, and Sabtechah; and the sons of Raamah were Sheba and Dedan. [8] Cush begot Nimrod; he began to be a mighty one on the earth. [9] He was a mighty hunter before YAHUAH; therefore it is said, "Like Nimrod the* *mighty hunter before YAHUAH." [10] And the beginning of his kingdom was Babel, Erech, Accad, and Calneh, in the land of Shinar. [11] From that land he went to Assyria and built Nineveh, Rehoboth Ir, Calah, [12] and Resen between Nineveh and Calah (that is the principal city). [13] Mizraim begot Ludim, Anamim, Lehabim, Naphtuhim, [14] Pathrusim, and Casluhim (from whom came the Philistines and Caphtorim). [15] Canaan begot Sidon his firstborn, and Heth; [16] the Jebusite, the Amorite, and the Girgashite; [17] the Hivite, the Arkite, and the Sinite; [18] the Arvadite, the Zemarite, and the Hamathite. Afterward the families of the Canaanites were dispersed. [19] And the border of the Canaanites was from Sidon as you go toward Gerar, as far as Gaza; then as you go toward Sodom, Gomorrah, Admah, and Zeboiim, as far as Lasha. [20] These were the sons of Ham, according to their families, according to their languages, in their lands and in their nations. [21] And **children were born also to Shem**, the father of all the children of Eber, the brother of Japheth the elder. [22] The sons of Shem were Elam, Asshur, Arphaxad, Lud, and Aram. [23] The sons of Aram were Uz, Hul, Gether, and Mash. [24] Arphaxad begot Salah, and Salah begot Eber. [25] To Eber were born two sons: the name of one was Peleg, for in his days the earth was divided; and his brother's name was Joktan. [26] Joktan begot Almodad, Sheleph, Hazarmaveth, Jerah, [27] Hadoram, Uzal, Diklah, [28] Obal, Abimael, Sheba, [29] Ophir, Havilah, and Jobab. All these were the sons of Joktan. [30] And their dwelling place was from Mesha as you go toward Sephar, the mountain of the east. [31] These were the sons of Shem, according to their families, according to their languages, in their lands,*

> *according to their nations. [32] These were the families of the sons of Noah, according to their generations, in their nations; and from these the nations were divided on the earth after the flood. (Genesis 10:1-32 NKJV)*

PAY ATTENTION in particular to the name of one of the sons of Japheth, named Gomer, who fathered Ashkenaz. This will become very relevant in discussing the 'Ashkenazi Jews' who are the primary group of Jews in the political State of Israel and the largest group who claim to be Jew(ish) in the world.

The best description of who the sons were and how they were allocated portions of land by their Father Noah under instruction from YAHUAH is best found in the apocrypha Bible books of Jasher and Jubilees. (By the way, the book of Jasher is mentioned 3 times in the main canon of scripture (Joshua 10:13, 2 Samuel 1:18), and so it is a wonder why it was removed from the 'recognised' biblical canon. Perhaps it was done to conceal the information it contains that debunks the mainstream narratives of biblical identity and land allocations given to the sons of Noah.

It is worth noting how the Shemites (descendants of Shem) and the Hamites (descendants of Ham) are repeatedly shown throughout the Bible to be in close relationship, often intermarrying and interacting with one another. I believe that one of the main reasons for this is that they carry a similar cultural mindset, which is very different to the Greco-Roman cultural mindset, which comes from the lineage of Japheth.

There are many examples of this intermingling. Abraham came to Egypt (the land of Mizraim, the 2nd son of Ham), and his 2nd wife, Hagar, and his 3rd wife were Hamites. Joseph blended into Mizraim (Egypt) and had two sons, Manasseh and Ephraim, from his union with a Hamite. The house of Jacob came and settled in the land of Mizraim. Moses was raised as the son of a Hamite (Egyptian/Mizraim) and was mistaken to be a Hamite when he met the daughters of Jethro, and his 2nd wife was a Hamite (Cushite). YAHUSHA went to hide in Hamite land (Mizraim/Egypt) and must have blended in with the people there. Paul was mistaken as a Hamite (Egyptian), meaning his natural look and features were consistent with those of the sons of Ham.

The descendants of Shem and the descendants of Ham must have had very similar looks because they could hide undetected in each other's territories and not be distinguished based on their looks. The same is true today.

Ancient history tells us that ancient Egyptians were not the Arab looking people that we identify Egypt with today. They were melanated (darker skinned) people, as the indigenous people of the continent of Africa have always been. There is plenty of research on this, including how even the features of the Great Sphinx of Giza and other artifacts in Egypt were defaced (flat noses cut off) so that the deception of ethnicity would be brought in, in an attempt to 'whitewash' history.

It is the same reason why, during the colonial era, much of the ancient history of Africa was either destroyed or captured and taken back to Europe, so that history could be altered to suit the narrative of "the conqueror".

Why is this even an issue and important enough to address here?

Because it is a critical part of YAHUAH's design with regard to the salvation of people of all tongues, tribes and nations and also for the awaited fulfilment of certain key prophecies, especially Ezekiel 37, which we will look at again shortly.

What I share below are some of the areas I explored on my journey. I am not stating my discoveries as absolute truth, but rather as what I have found so far on a continuing journey of searching and not just accepting 'the conquerors" narratives that we have been indoctrinated with for so long through manipulated history.

Map of Africa before 1884

Ancient maps of Africa (for example, from the year 1747) show 'Negroland/Slave Coast' and also an area called 'Kingdom of Juda' in the Western part of Africa (Nigeria, Niger, Ghana, etc.) and likewise several other biblical names dotted across the continent. Is this a coincidence or a hidden truth about true biblical identities?

Source: The Library of Congress and the following URL to get the full map https://www.loc.gov/item/2018585377/

SEARCHING FOR THE TRUTH OF BIBLICAL IDENTITIES

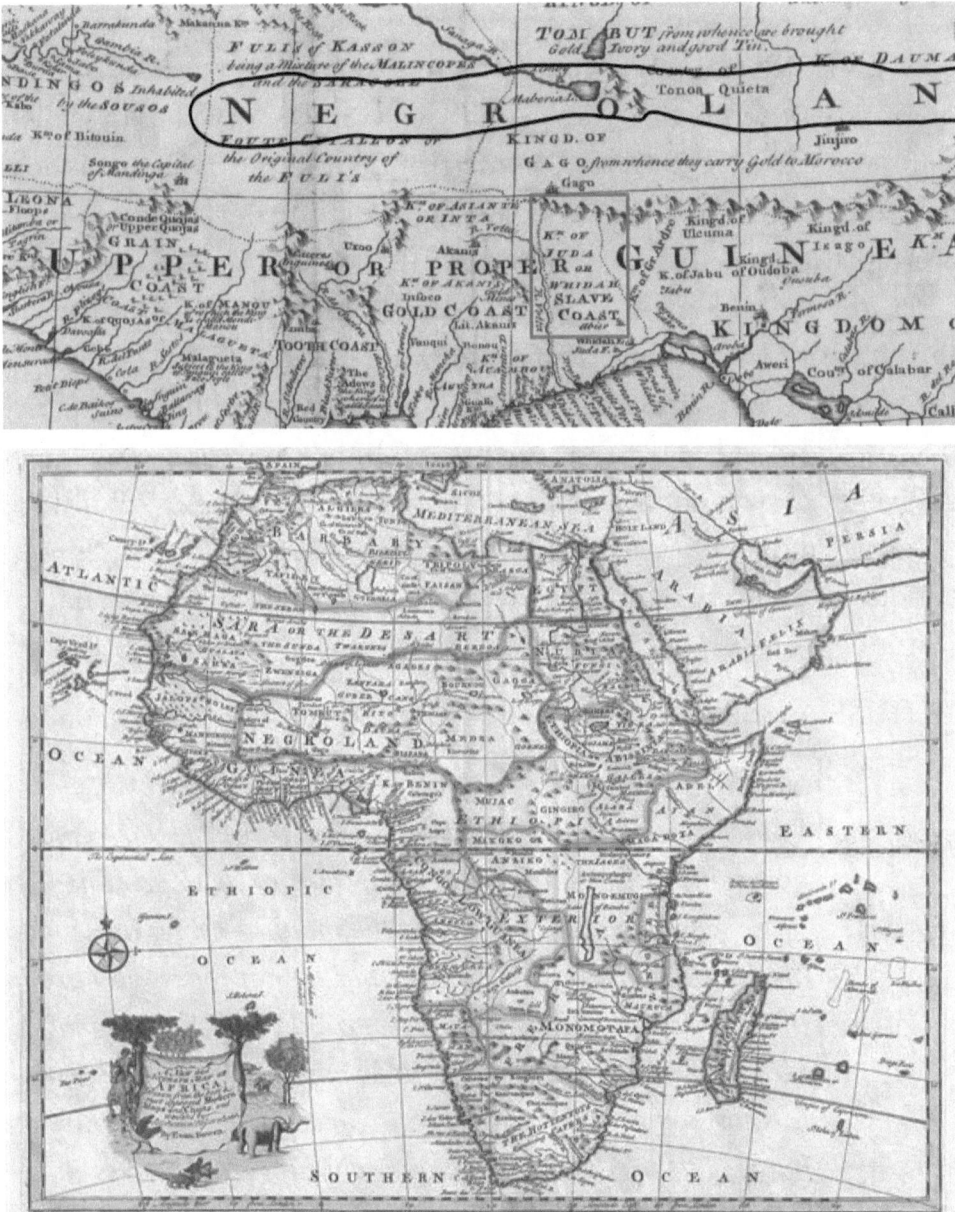

The 1747 Bowen map of Africa

Source: https://www.geographicus.com/P/AntiqueMap/Africa-bowen-1747

Likewise, we need to dig into history to understand the background behind the 'Bantu migration' (which is one of the greatest human migrations). Who are the people who are grouped and called Bantu today, where did they come from, and what is their biblical identity and history? Why was the Transatlantic slave trade centred around the area that was known as 'Negroland and Kingdom of Juda' on the old African maps, going further down to areas on the coasts of Congo and even around the Cape of Good Hope into the coasts of Mozambique? Why did masses of people have to flee from 'Negroland and the Kingdom of Juda', and where did they go? What movement of people took place during the Assyrian siege of Yarushalayim (Jerusalem) in 701 BC, and during the Babylonian conquest of 597 BC and finally the Roman siege of Yarushalayim (Jerusalem) in 70 CE?

YAHUSHA speaks about the Roman siege of Yarushalayim (Jerusalem) as it is written:

- *"But when you see Yarushalayim (Jerusalem) surrounded by armies, then know that its desolation is near. Then let those who are in Judea flee to the mountains, let those who are in the midst of her depart, and let not those who are in the country enter her. For these are the days of vengeance, that all things which are written may be fulfilled. But woe to those who are pregnant and to those who are nursing babies in those days! For there will be great distress in the land and wrath upon this people. And they will fall by the edge of the sword, and be led away captive into all nations.* ***And Yarushalayim (Jerusalem) will be trampled by Gentiles until the times of the Gentiles are fulfilled.*** *(Luke 21:20-24 NKJV)*

YAHUSHA mentions the period when Yarushalayim (Jerusalem)

will be under the control of the Gentiles (non-bloodline descendants of Jacob).

In the 'table of nations', it is only the sons of Japheth who are given the title 'Gentiles', and so this is perhaps the indicator of who is currently occupying Yarushalayim (Jerusalem) (trampling it) until the time of the Gentiles are fulfilled. As it is written:

- **The sons of Japheth** were Gomer, Magog, Madai, Javan, Tubal, Meshech, and Tiras. [3] The sons of Gomer were Ashkenaz, Riphath, and Togarmah. [4] The sons of Javan were Elishah, Tarshish, Kittim, and Dodanim. [5] **From these the coastland peoples of the Gentiles** were separated into their lands, everyone according to his language, according to their families, into their nations. (Genesis 10:2-5)

With Yarushalayim's (Jerusalem's) desolation and it being controlled by the Gentiles, is it possible that the plan of YAHUAH is for the earthly Yarushalayim (Jerusalem) never to be rebuilt as He now focuses His people on the path to true Zion, the New Yarushalayim (Jerusalem) that shall come out of the heavens down to the earth? The holy city that YAHUSHA said He would go and prepare.

- In My Father's house are many mansions; if it were not so, I would have told you. **I go to prepare a place for you. [3] And if I go and prepare a place for you,** I will come again and receive you to Myself; that where I am, there you may be also. (John 14:2-3 NKJV)
- Then one of the seven angels who had the seven bowls filled with the seven last plagues came to me and talked with me, saying, "Come, I will show you the bride, the Lamb's wife." [10] And he carried me away in the Spirit to a great and

high mountain, **and showed me the great city, the holy Yarushalayim (Jerusalem), descending out of heaven from YAHUAH,** *(Revelation 21:9-10 NKJV)*

The dragon/serpent mentioned in Revelation 12:17 is the representation of Satan, the devil, who is enraged with the woman and goes to make war with her offspring. The woman is a representation of YASHARA'AL, and the offspring are the 12 tribes (of which YAHUSHA HA MASHYACH would come from the tribe of Judah/YAHUDA). And so, even as in the days of the Roman King Herod, Satan has always used world powers and empires to search for the remnant of the seed (bloodline descendants of Jacob/YASHARA'AL) to seek to destroy them and remove them from existence. This continues even today and has been well executed by perhaps the greatest heist of identity, as is written in Psalm 83:4-12. A plan to try and erase from history the true 'offspring of the woman' and replace them by the 'Jews in name only' as is written in Revelation 2:9 and 3:9. A plan to pull off the greatest heist of truth by establishing Zionism as the platform for 'stolen biblical identity' and then building a world structure (a kingdom) and system of power and manipulation based on that.

> o *Now when they had departed, behold, an angel of YAHUAH appeared to Joseph in a dream, saying, "Arise, take the young Child and His mother, flee to Egypt, and stay there until I bring you word;* **for Herod will seek the young Child to destroy Him."** *[14] When he arose, he took the young Child and His mother by night and departed for Egypt, [15] and was there until the death of Herod, that it might be fulfilled which was spoken by YAHUAH through the prophet, saying, "Out of Egypt I called My Son." [16]* **Then Herod, when he saw that he was deceived by the**

wise men, was exceedingly angry; and he sent forth and put to death all the male children who were in Bethlehem and in all its districts, from two years old and under,** according to the time which he had determined from the wise men. [17] Then was fulfilled what was spoken by Jeremiah the prophet, saying: [18] "A voice was heard in Ramah, Lamentation, weeping, and great mourning, Rachel weeping for her children, refusing to be comforted, because they are no more." (Matthew 2:13-18 NKJV)

- **And the dragon was enraged with the woman, and he went to make war with the rest of her offspring,** who keep the commandments of YAHUAH and have the testimony of YAHUSHA MASHYACH. (Revelation 12:17 NKJV)
- Do not keep silent, O YAHUAH! Do not hold Your peace, and do not be still, O YAHUAH! [2] **For behold, Your enemies make a tumult; And those who hate You have lifted up their head. [3] They have taken crafty counsel against Your people, and consulted together against Your sheltered ones. [4] They have said, "Come, and let us cut them off from being a nation, That the name of YASHARA'AL may be remembered no more."** [5] For they have consulted together with one consent; They form a confederacy against You: [6] The tents of Edom and the Ishmaelites; Moab and the Hagrites; [7] Gebal, Ammon, and Amalek; Philistia with the inhabitants of Tyre; [8] Assyria also has joined with them; They have helped the children of Lot. Selah [9] Deal with them as with Midian, As with Sisera, As with Jabin at the Brook Kishon, [10] Who perished at En Dor, who became as refuse on the earth. [11] Make their nobles like Oreb and like Zeeb, Yes,

> all their princes like Zebah and Zalmunna, [12] **Who said, "Let us take for ourselves the pastures of YAHUAH for a possession."** [13] O my Alahym, make them like the whirling dust, Like the chaff before the wind! [14] As the fire burns the woods, and as the flame sets the mountains on fire, [15] So pursue them with Your tempest, and frighten them with Your storm. [16] Fill their faces with shame, that they may seek Your name, O YAHUAH. [17] Let them be confounded and dismayed forever; Yes, let them be put to shame and perish, [18] That they may know that You, whose name alone is YAHUAH, are the Most High over all the earth. (Psalms 83:1-18 NKJV)
>   - "I know your works, tribulation, and poverty (but you are rich); **and I know the blasphemy of those who say they are Jews and are not, but are a synagogue of Satan.** (Revelation 2:9 NKJV)
>   - **Indeed I will make those of the synagogue of Satan, who say they are Jews and are not, but lie—indeed I will make them come and worship before your feet, and to know that I have loved you.** (Revelation 3:9 NKJV)

SATAN has worked through many empires — the kingdoms of this world — in attempts to destroy "the offspring of the woman," from the Assyrian, Babylonian, Roman, British, and Ottoman empires to the "new Babylonian" system of today. Satan has used many schemes, such as slavery and colonialization, to take out 'the offspring of the woman', for Satan will always seek people to use 'to cut YASHARA'AL off from being a nation and take for themselves the pastures of the covenant people of YAHUAH'.

Essentially, what this is saying is that Satan, through his synagogue (the synagogue of Satan), would raise up a people who would claim the name Jew, and with that name seek to usurp the identity and inheritance of 'the offspring of the woman' so that all recognition of her seed is erased and forgotten.

I started learning Paleo (ancient) Hebrew, and it is interesting to see how many Bantu language words link directly to Paleo (ancient) Hebrew. Coincidence? I don't know.

It is important to note that the modern Hebrew spoken by the Israelis in the political state of Israel is not the original Hebrew of the Bible. It is a created language mainly from Yiddish, a blend of Middle High German, Aramaic, Slavic, Hebrew, and other Eastern European languages. It was a language creation project that was part of the Zionist agenda to establish a political state called Israel that would become the homeland for people of Khazarian/Ashkenazi bloodlines and have a language that could be deemed to be Hebraic. Interestingly, they have called themselves 'Israelis and not Israelites (YASHARA'ALITES)', as I believe this is not coincidence because the ALAHYM of Abraham, Isaac and Jacob YAHUAH would not allow the 'Israelite (YASHARA'ALITE)' identity to be used by people who are not bloodline descendants of Jacob whose name was changed to Israel (YASHARA'AL). Perhaps it is time to deeply enquire what the scriptures of Revelation 2:9 and Revelation 3:9 mean and who they refer to.

I stumbled across the writings of the Jewish Sanhedrin which are linked to the Jewish Talmud of the religion of Judaism.

Jewish Sanhedrin 94a:15

This text below taken directly from the Jewish Sanhedrin 94a:15 provides telling information about where the ten 'lost tribes' where exiled to, as it gives the answer as AFRIKEI (Africa)

- *The Gemara asks:* **To where did Sennacherib exile the ten tribes?** *Mar Zutra says:* **He exiled them to Afrikei,** *and Rabbi Ḥanina says: To the Selug Mountains. The Gemara adds: But those exiled from the kingdom of Israel spoke in disparagement of Eretz Yisrael and extolled the land of their exile. When they arrived at one place, they called it Shosh, as they said: It is equal [shaveh] to our land. When they arrived at another place, they called it Almin, as they said: It is like our world [almin], as Eretz Yisrael is also called beit olamim. When they arrived at a third place they called it Shosh the second [terei], as they said: For one measure of good in Eretz Yisrael, there are two [terein] here.*

The Sanhedrin, a Jewish council during the Second Temple period, primarily produced legal and traditional writings that became part of the Talmud, specifically the Mishnah and Gemara. These writings encompass Jewish law, customs, and traditions. While the Sanhedrin didn't produce a single, unified body of work, their deliberations and decisions were incorporated into the larger corpus of rabbinic literature.

The Sanhedrin's writings main focus was on Jewish law, or Halakha, which outlines religious observances and daily conduct. Many of the Sanhedrin's rulings were based on oral traditions passed down through generations. These traditions and legal interpretations were eventually compiled into the Mishnah and Gemara, forming the core of the current Jewish Talmud.

Some things are just hidden in plain sight. AFRIKEI.

Paleo Hebrew language similarities with Bantu languages

Coming back to the point about similarities between Paleo Hebrew and Bantu languages, here are some examples (including some words in my language of Shona and Zulu).

In Paleo-Hebrew, the word **"ABANTU"** (אבנתו) can be broken down into its individual components:

1. *Ab* (אב) - means "father"
2. *antu* or *nethu* (נתו) - likely means "his seed" or "his offspring"

"Abantu" in Paleo-Hebrew can be translated to "Father of his Seed" or "Father of his offspring". This phrase has been interpreted in various ways, including references to the patriarchal lineage of the Israelites or the concept of divine fatherhood.

In Paleo-Hebrew, the word **"BANTU"** (בנתו) can be broken down into its individual components:

1. *Ben* (בו) - means "son"
2. *Tu* or *Nethu* (תו/נתו) - likely means "his seed" or "his people"

So, "Bantu" in Paleo-Hebrew can be translated to "Son of his Seed" or "Son of his People". This term has been linked to various interpretations, including:
- A reference to the descendants of a particular patriarch or tribe.
- A term for the people of Israel or a specific group within Israel.
- A concept related to the idea of a chosen people or a covenant community.

In Paleo-Hebrew, the word **"UMUNTU"** (אומנטו) can be broken down into its individual components:

1. *Umu* (אומו) - likely means "community" or "people"
2. *Ntu* (נטו) - means "humanity" or "person"

So, "Umuntu" in Paleo-Hebrew can be translated to "Community of Humanity" or "Person of the People". This concept resonates with the African philosophy of Ubuntu, which emphasises the importance of community, interconnectedness, and humanity.

In Paleo-Hebrew, the concept of Umuntu may have referred to:
- A person who is part of a community
- A sense of belonging and identity within a group
- A recognition of the interconnectedness of all people

The similarities between the Paleo-Hebrew meaning and the African concept of Umuntu are striking, highlighting the shared values and concepts that transcend cultures and time. Umuntu is often translated as "personhood" or "humanity", emphasising the importance of community and relationships in defining a person's identity.

<u>In Paleo-Hebrew, the word **"BABA"** (באבא) can be broken down into its individual components:</u>

1. *Ba* (בא) - means "father" or "daddy"
2. *Ba* (בא) - repetition of the first syllable, emphasising affection or intimacy

So, "Baba" in Paleo-Hebrew can be translated to "Daddy" or "Papa", conveying a sense of affection, love, and respect. This term was likely used to address or refer to one's father or a respected elder.

In many ancient cultures, including the Israelites, the term "Baba", which is linked to 'Abba', was used to express reverence, affection, and respect for one's father. This term continues to be used in various forms across many cultures today.

In Paleo-Hebrew, the word **"AMAI"** (אמאי) can be broken down into its individual components:

1. *Ama* (אמא) - means "mother"
2. *I* (י) - suffix indicating "my" or "mine"

So, "Amai" in Paleo-Hebrew can be translated to "My Mother", conveying a sense of affection, love, and closeness.

In ancient Israelite culture, the term "Amai" was likely used to express reverence, respect, and love for one's mother. This term continues to be used in various forms across many cultures today.

In Paleo-Hebrew, the word **"SHONA"** (שונא) can be broken down into its individual components:

1. *Shon* (שו) - means "to repeat" or "to sing"
2. *A* (א) - suffix indicating "father" or " divine"

So, "Shona" in Paleo-Hebrew can be translated to "Father's Song" or "Divine Harmony", conveying a sense of spiritual connection and melodic expression. In ancient Israelite culture, music and song played a vital role in worship, celebration, and storytelling. The term "Shona" may have referred to a sacred song or hymn, possibly even a reference to the Psalms.

Interestingly, "Shona" is also the name of a Bantu language spoken in Zimbabwe, and the term has cultural significance in

African contexts as well.

Is all this a coincidence, or something that the Most High Alahym of Abraham, Isaac and Jacob wants us to pay attention to as we embark on the journey of seeking after 'the truth'? Spiritual healing and restoration cannot come if we do not know who we are.

A book worth referencing is: Hidden Hebrew: Linguistic Evidence of Proto/Paleo-Hebrew in Bantu Language, written by Yahukanon Ben Yahudah Besodeyahu

The Berlin Congo Conference as a master plan to erase identity and history.

Psalm 83 indicates that the intention of the enemy has been and will always be to try 'to cut YASHARA'AL off from being a nation and take for themselves the pastures (the identity and inheritance) of the covenant people of YAHUAH'.

The Psalm says the following in verses 2 to 8:

> o *For behold,* **Your enemies make a tumult; And those who hate You have lifted up their head. They have taken crafty counsel against Your people, and consulted together against Your sheltered ones. For they have consulted together with one consent; They form a confederacy against You:** *The tents of Edom and the Ishmaelites; Moab and the Hagrites; Gebal, Ammon, and Amalek; Philistia with the inhabitants of Tyre; Assyria also has joined with them; They have helped the children of Lot. Selah*

This is showing numerous nations and empires that hate YAHUAH consulting together and forming a confederacy against YAHUAH and 'the seed of the woman' (referring to the 12 tribes). This exact situation was replicated from the 15th November 1884 to the 26th February 1885 when 14 nations gathered in Berlin, Germany for the 'Berlin Congo West Africa Conference' that resulted in the signing of the Berlin Congo West Africa Act that led to the partitioning of Africa into Western controlled colonies with Belgian King Leopold II taking Congo as his personal possession from 1885 to 1908.

Indeed, there is nothing new under the sun; the enemy is always trying to replicate the cycles of what he tried before.

- *That which has been is what will be, that which is done is what will be done, and* **there is nothing new under the sun**. *[10] Is there anything of which it may be said,* **"See, this is new"? It has already been in ancient times before us**. *(Ecclesiastes 1:9-10 NKJV)*

These 14 nations/kingdoms under the authorisation of their respective Royal houses/Presidents signed the General Act of the Berlin Conference on February 26, 1885, which marked the beginning of the 'Scramble for Africa', the beginning of the servitude and plundering of an entire continent, its people and their God-given land. Africa fully entered into its season as a conquered land and people.

The Berlin Congo West Africa Conference of 1884-1885 was a significant event in African history, where European powers gathered to divide and colonise the continent. Here are the signatories of the Berlin Congo West Africa Act:

1. **Austria-Hungary:** Count Kalnóky

2. **Belgium:** Baron Lambermont

3. **Denmark:** Count Rantzau

4. **France:** Jules Ferry

5. **Germany:** Otto von Bismarck (host)

6. **Great Britain:** Sir Edward Malet

7. **Italy:** Count Launay

8. **Netherlands:** Baron Gericke

9. **Portugal:** Antônio José da Costa

10. **Russia:** Prince Orlow

11. **Spain:** Francisco de Silva

12. **Sweden-Norway:** Baron Bodenhausen

13. **Ottoman Empire:** Mehmed Ali Pasha

14. **United States:** John A. Kasson (observer)

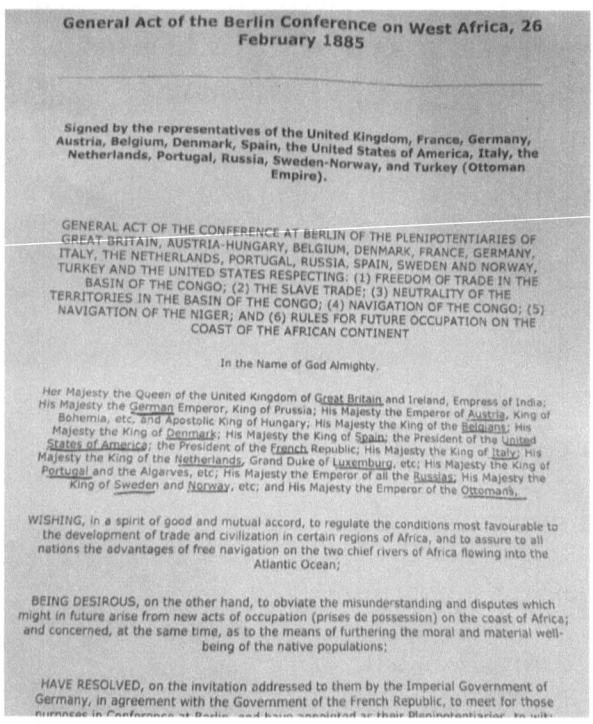

With the understanding that the plan of the adversary, Satan, the father of lies, has always been to try to destroy and remove from existence the true bloodline lineage of Jacob, the possibility exists that the Berlin Congo West Africa Conference served as another platform to do this. This was used as part of the master plan to capture Africa, set up man-made borders, rename nations and places so that the original names, locations, and history were erased and lost. It is interesting to look at ancient maps of Africa and to see many names of locations, tribes, and families linked to names in the Bible. Perhaps the enemy wanted to make sure this gets lost and permanently forgotten by covering Africa with multiple 'blankets of falsehoods'. It seems very apparent that the land and the people of Africa have been such a 'prized' possession in the agenda of the 'white horse that went out conquering and to conquer' as is written in Revelation 6:1-2.

I believe Africa was 'attacked' using a two-pronged strategy, namely the 'use of religion to take the people and the land' and the 'taking of the land and use of religion as a tool to pacify the people'. Both were used to great effect.

The Catholic Papal Bulls of the Doctrine of Discovery laid the foundation for the taking of land through religion, and likewise the spread of the Catholic and Freemasonic-led form of religious Christianity which is founded on rejecting and disobeying the Commandments and Laws of YAHUAH and breaking the everlasting Covenant (agreement) with YAHUAH. Both are the foundational pillars for the outworking of the mystery of lawlessness. For they knew that this would be the most effective way to get 'the seed of the woman' to be in contradiction to YAHUAH and hence be permanently assigned to the path of 'the curse and death', based on the terms and conditions of the everlasting Covenant. It is a brilliant strategy that uses the very covenant of YAHUAH as the instrument that would work against the people who were given the covenant, because they would bring the curse upon themselves by their choices.

In researching the spread of Christianity in Africa, I was amazed to discover how many famous missionaries, credited with bringing the gospel to Africa, were part of Freemason Lodges and were funded with Freemason money at the same time as the colonial project was being rolled out in the 1800s to 1900s. I wonder if that was coincidental or if it was part of the execution of a master plan. Was Africa and many other indigenous lands conquered by the white horse written in Revelation 6:1-2 so that the true identity of the 'remnant seed of the woman' as written in Revelation 12:15-17 could be erased?

- *Now I saw when the Lamb opened one of the seals; and I heard one of the four living creatures saying with a voice like thunder, "Come and see." [2] And I looked, and behold, a white horse.* **He who sat on it had a bow; and a crown was given to him, and he went out conquering and to conquer.** *(Revelation 6:1-2 NKJV)*
- *So the serpent spewed water out of his mouth like a flood after the woman, that he might cause her to be carried away by the flood. But the earth helped the woman, and the earth opened its mouth and swallowed up the flood which the dragon had spewed out of his mouth.* **And the dragon was enraged with the woman, and he went to make war with the rest of her offspring, who keep the commandments of YAHUAH and have the testimony of YAHUSHA MASHYACH.** *(Revelation 12:15-17 NKJV)*

It is interesting that the serpent is not after those who have the testimony of YAHUSHA alone. The serpent is after those who both (1) keep the commandments of YAHUAH and (2) have the testimony of YAHUSHA. The serpent is always after 'the seed of the woman', to whom the covenant of YAHUAH pertains, as it is written:

> o *For I could wish that I myself were accursed from MASHYACH for my brethren, my countrymen according to the flesh, who are YASHARA'ALITES,* **to whom pertain the adoption, the glory, the covenants, the giving of the law, the service of YAHUAH, and the promises;** *of whom are the fathers and from whom, according to the flesh, MASHYACH came, who is over all, the eternally blessed YAHUAH. Amen. (Romans 9:3-5 NKJV)*

Those who have rejected the commandments and law of YAHUAH and don't commit to obey them are considered lawless and so are not under the Kingdom (the domain of the uncontested rule and reign) of YAHUSHA, and so the dragon/serpent does not need to go after them because they are already under his rule of lawlessness.

It is to those who pertain to (1) the adoption, (2) the glory, (3) the covenants (agreements with YAHUAH), (4) the giving of the Law, (5) the service of YAHUAH (His appointed priests and ambassadors) and (6) the promises; that the serpent, dragon, Satan, the devil is most seeking after because of the plan of YAHUAH for the whole earth that is designed to flow through them.

The Earth's 7 pillars

The Earth's lithosphere is made up of 7 major tectonic plates, of which the African Plate is one. I often wonder if these 7 Tectonic Plates could be related to the 7 pillars as it is written in Proverbs 9:1 as part of the divine design of the Creator, the Most High Alahym of Abraham, Isaac and Jacob, YAHUAH.

o   *Wisdom has built her house, She has hewn out her seven pillars; (Proverbs 9:1 NKJV)*

The political State of Israel is situated on the northeastern corner of the African tectonic plate, near the boundary with the Arabian Plate. In fact, before the geographical term 'Middle East' was created (in the late 1800s/early 1900s), the area used to be known as the 'Near East', and before that, it was known as 'North-East Africa'. Palestine is also on the African Plate, while Jordan, Lebanon and Syria straddle the African and Arabian Plates. All this made me wonder whether there is perhaps a deeper spiritual reason why 'the conquerors' felt it necessary to separate the land of Israel from Africa, if that is the 'divinely assigned' pillar of the earth (Tectonic Plate) it is on. This separation has massive implications for understanding true biblical geography and hence what was happening as we read the Bible, where it was happening, who was involved and the cultural context. Without this separation, it means most of what we read in the Bible happened in Africa (on the African Tectonic Plate or Pillar).

Was our Messiah, our MASHYACH YAHUSHA, born in Africa (African tectonic plate) as per how 'Wisdom' built her house (the earth) as in Proverbs 9:1? It further says that 'Wisdom' was at the side of the FATHER as a 'master craftsman', as in Proverbs 8:30, as the earth was established, as is written in Proverbs chapter 8:

o   *Does not wisdom cry out, and understanding lift up her voice? [2] She takes her stand on the top of the high hill, Beside the way, where the paths meet. [3] She cries out by the gates, at the entry of the city, At the entrance of the doors: [4] "To you, O men, I call, and my voice is to the sons of men. [5] O you simple ones, understand prudence, and you fools, be of an understanding heart. [6] Listen, for I will speak of excellent things, and from the opening of my lips will come right things; [7] For my mouth will speak truth; Wickedness is an abomination to my lips. [8] All the words of my mouth are with righteousness; Nothing crooked or perverse is in them. [9] They are all plain to him who understands, and right to those who find knowledge. [10] Receive my instruction, and not silver, and knowledge rather than choice gold; [11] For wisdom is better than rubies, and all the things one may desire cannot be compared with her. [12] "I, wisdom, dwell with prudence, and find out knowledge and discretion. [13] The fear of YAHUAH is to hate evil; Pride and arrogance and the evil way and the perverse mouth I hate. [14] Counsel is mine, and sound wisdom; I am understanding, I have strength. [15] By me kings reign, And rulers decree justice. [16] By me princes rule, and nobles, All the judges of the earth. [17] I love those who love me, and those who seek me diligently will find me. [18] Riches and honor are with me, Enduring riches and righteousness. [19] My fruit is better than gold, yes, than fine gold, And my revenue than choice silver. [20] I traverse the way of righteousness, In the midst of the paths of justice, [21] That I may cause those who love me to inherit wealth, That I may fill their treasuries. [22] "YAHUAH possessed me at the beginning of His way, Before His works of old. [23]* **I have been established from everlasting, From the beginning, before there was ever an earth. [24] When there were no depths I was brought forth, when there were no fountains abounding with water. [25] Before the mountains were settled, Before the hills, I was brought forth; [26] While as yet He had not made the earth or the fields, Or the primal dust of the world. [27] When He prepared the heavens, I was** *there, When He drew a circle on the face of the deep, [28] When He established the clouds above, When He strengthened the fountains of the deep, [29] When He assigned to the sea its limit, So that the waters would not transgress His command, When He marked out the foundations of the earth, [30] Then I was beside Him as a master craftsman; And I was daily His delight, Rejoicing always before Him, [31] Rejoicing in His inhabited world, And my delight was with the sons of men.* [32] "Now therefore, listen to me, my children, for blessed are those who keep my ways. [33] Hear instruction and be wise, and do not disdain it. [34] Blessed is the man who listens to me, watching daily at my gates, Waiting at the posts of my doors. [35] For whoever finds me finds life, and obtains favor from YAHUAH; [36] But he who sins against me wrongs his own soul; All those who hate me love death." (Proverbs 8:1-36 NKJV)

Was all of YAHUSHA's life and ministry conducted and fulfilled in Africa? Is it possible that most of what we read from Genesis to Revelation, and in the apocryphal books, took place on African soil? Could this be a key to gaining a deeper understanding of many things that happened in ancient times and what is still to happen to fulfil future biblical prophecy? So, one of the critical questions for me over the past year has been 'where is biblical Zion, where is biblical Israel (YASHARAA'AL), and who is biblical Israel (YASHARA'AL)'? I have a sense this could all be related to the natural tensions and wars that have taken place and continue to take place in the 'invented' region of the Middle East. Perhaps this is one of the foundational issues that our FATHER, the ALAHYM of Abraham, Isaac and Jacob, YAHUAH, wants us to see through

His eyes and search out beyond the mainstream narratives we have been indoctrinated with, including Christian Zionism.

Attacks from the North – Flee to the South

Previous reference has been made to the major attacks that overran Yarushalayim (Jerusalem), namely the Assyrian siege of Yarushalayim (Jerusalem) in 701 BC, the Babylonian conquest of 597 BC and the Roman siege of Yarushalayim (Jerusalem) in 70 CE.

Considering the numerous times the Romans (remember the white horse from Revelation 6:1) besieged Yarushalayim (Jerusalem) in ancient times, it would make logical sense to assume that the inhabitants of the city and surrounding lands would flee in the opposite direction from where the Romans were coming. If the Romans were coming from the 'north' (Europe), would the Israelites (YASHARA'ALITES) flee north into lands from where 'the conqueror' was coming from and end up in Europe, or would they flee in the opposite 'south' direction deeper into Africa and seek refuge there? I would like to think that they fled 'south' in the opposite direction of the invading enemy.

In fact, the Bible references that almost every time Yarushalayim (Jerusalem) was invaded, the attack came from the north. The Assyrian and Babylonian attacks came from the north. Again, it tracks that the route to escape would be to flee south.

As it is written:

- *And the word of YAHUAH came to me the second time, saying, "What do you see?" And I said, **"I see a boiling pot, and it is facing away from the north."** Then YAHUAH said to me: **"Out of the north calamity shall break forth on all the inhabitants of the land.** (Jeremiah 1:13-14*

- *NKJV)*
- *Thus says YAHUAH: Behold, **a people is coming from the north country**, and a great nation is arousing itself from the ends of the earth. They lay hold on bow and spear; they are cruel (ruthless and inhuman) and have no mercy. Their voice sounds like the roaring sea; they ride on horses, every one set in array as a man for battle against you, O Daughter of Zion! (Jeremiah 6:22-23 AMPC)*

A look into the New Testament shows how YAHUSHA (through his parents Joseph and Mary) had to flee in the southern direction from Herod, whose Roman army was coming from the north in search of Him, as is written in Matthew 2:13-15. Fleeing to the South seems to always be the route that the YASHARA'ALITES took when their enemies attacked from the north.

- *Now when they had departed, behold, an angel of YAHUAH appeared to Joseph in a dream, saying, **"Arise, take the young Child and His mother, flee to Egypt**, and stay there until I bring you word; for Herod will seek the young Child to destroy Him." When he arose, he took the young Child and His mother by night and departed for Egypt, and was there until the death of Herod, that it might be fulfilled which was spoken by YAHUAH through the prophet, saying, **"Out of Egypt I called My Son."** (Matthew 2:13-15 NKJV)*

"Out of Egypt I called My Son", an interesting word that was prophesied through Hosea as it is written:

- *When YASHARA'AL was a child, then I loved him, **and called my son out of Egypt**. (Hosea 11:1 NKJV)*

If fleeing to the south is indeed correct, then it makes logical sense to assume that there would be more 'seed of the woman, lost tribes

SEARCHING FOR THE TRUTH OF BIBLICAL IDENTITIES

of YASHARA'AL' (the descendants of the 12 sons of Jacob) hidden in the south beyond the rivers of Ethiopia/Cush than in the north (Europe). What is written in Zephaniah 3:10 and Isaiah 11:11-12 seems to allude to this.

- *From **beyond the rivers of Cush/Ethiopia** my worshipers, the daughter of my dispersed/scattered ones, shall bring my offering. (Zephaniah 3:10)*
- *It shall come to pass in that day that YAHUAH shall set His hand again the second time to recover the remnant of His people who are left, **From Assyria and Egypt, From Pathros and Cush**, From Elam and Shinar, From Hamath and the islands of the sea. He will set up a banner for the nations, and will assemble the outcasts of YASHARA'AL, and gather together the dispersed of Judah from the four corners of the earth. (Isaiah 11:11-12 NKJV)*

The illustration helps to visualise the fleeing to the south.

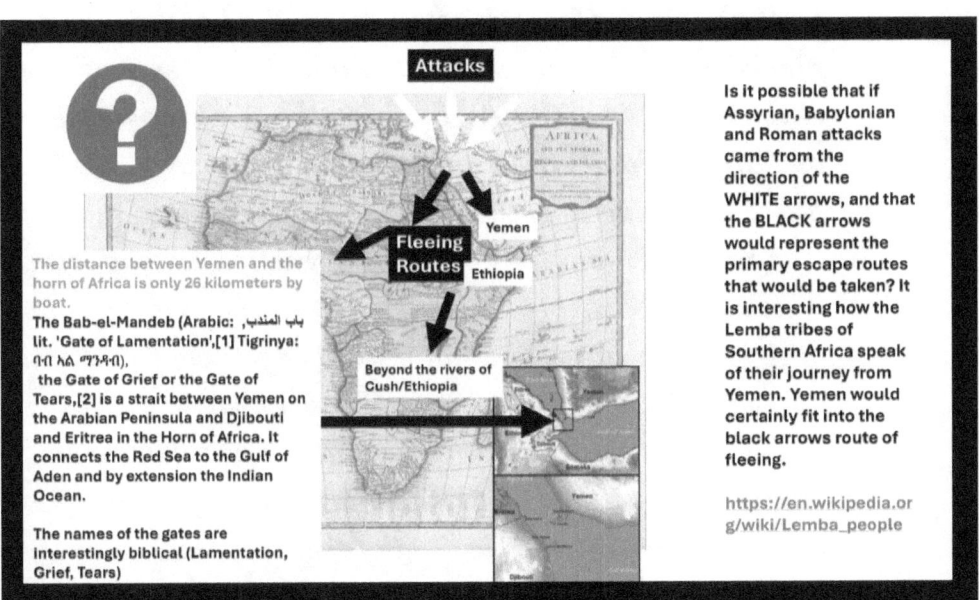

We should also note that some of the (Israelites) YASHARA'ALITES were also taken captive in the various invasions of Yarushalayim (Jerusalem) and YASHARA'AL and so were brought into enemy lands in the north and assimilated into those territories.

An interesting point to note is how the scriptures reveal that when YASHARA'AL was attacked, 'the conquerors' would take the territory and 'pretend' to be the people of the land, as is seen in 2 Kings 17. After the Assyrians conquered Samaria (Northern Kingdom), they brought in people from other nations and placed them in the cities of Samaria. After the foreign people had been brought in, they were then attacked by lions and called for a priest to come and teach them the ways of the God of that territory (which is YAHUAH), and that is how they learnt His ways. This provides an answer as to how even the Jews of today have taken a territory and called themselves by the name of the territory and claimed the God of that territory for themselves.

- ○ ***Then the king of Assyria brought people from Babylon, Cuthah, Ava, Hamath, and from Sepharvaim, and placed them in the cities of Samaria instead of the children of YASHARA'AL; and they took possession of Samaria and dwelt in its cities.*** *[25] And it was so, at the beginning of their dwelling there, that they did not fear YAHUAH; therefore YAHUAH sent lions among them, which killed some of them. [26] So they spoke to the king of Assyria, saying, "The nations whom you have removed and placed in the cities of Samaria do not know the rituals of the God of the land; therefore He has sent lions among them, and indeed, they are killing them because they do not know the rituals of the God of the land." [27] Then the king of Assyria commanded, saying,* ***"Send there one of***

> *the priests whom you brought from there; let him go and dwell there, and let him teach them the rituals of the God of the land." [28] Then one of the priests whom they had carried away from Samaria came and dwelt in Bethel, and taught them how they should fear YAHUAH. (II Kings 17:24-28 NKJV)*

From the lands of the north, we then see YASHARA'ALITES being shipped from the Iberian region during the Edicts of Expulsion from Spain in 1492 and Portugal in 1496/7 when 'Jews' (YAHUDYM) were expelled and put on boats to be settled on the islands of São Tomé and Príncipe and other ports on the west coast of Africa. They were expelled because they would not accept and assimilate into Catholic Christianity, because they chose obedience to YAHUAH's law and commandments even unto death rather than compromise on the agreement (covenant) with YAH.

(Please research this topic to get more information, as it is beyond the scope of this book to go into detail on all the research, but rather to point the reader to research further for themselves. Note that most mainstream narratives will try to paint a different picture of the identities of the people expelled, but deeper research will begin to reveal the truth).

So why is this relevant and important?

Because it is directly linked to major biblical prophecies that are still to be fulfilled for YAHUAH's script (His unchangeable plan for mankind and His creation as outlined from the first word in the book of Genesis until the last word in the book of Revelation) to be completed in the overall story of the redemption of YASHARA'AL and the nations. It is a redemption story that will only be complete when the branches are grafted back into the Olive Tree as discussed in chapter 11, so that the invitation list can be complete of those who will be invited to the wedding feast of the Lamb. Such is a precursor to them entering through the 12 gates (with the names of the 12 tribes) into New Holy Yarushalayim (Jerusalem), which is the final destination for the saints and the remnant.

Ezekiel chapter 37 speaks of the formation of the House of YASHARA'AL, which is the natural branch of the cultivated Olive Tree. This natural branch cannot be 'faked' with a wild branch 'disguised' as a natural one.

I believe the enemy has created a 'fake' natural branch as a way to try to thwart the fulfilment of the script of YAHUAH, which is unchanging and will only happen as YAHUAH has said it will. This is why YAHUAH Himself will and is awakening the dry bones of the true natural branch.

Understanding the split of the 12 tribes into the northern and southern Kingdoms

It is important to understand a bit of the biblical history that the house/nation of YASHARA'AL (all 12 tribes) started together as a house/nation, but a split between the tribes occurred, which is yet to be reunified even up to today. This reunification is what YAHUAH promises in Ezekiel 37:19 as it is written:

> o *'Thus says YAHUAH ALAHYM: "Surely I will take the stick of Joseph, which is in the hand of Ephraim, and the tribes of YASHARA'AL, his companions; and I will join them with it, with the stick of Judah, and make them one stick,* **and they will be one in My hand."** *(Ezekiel 37:19 NKJV)*

The split of the ancient Kingdom of Israel (YASHARA'AL) into the northern and southern kingdoms occurred shortly after the death of King Solomon around 931 BCE. This division marked a major turning point in the history of the YASHARA'ALITE people. The United Monarchy consisted of 12 tribes of YASHARA'AL, governed by King Saul, King David, and then King Solomon.

Under Solomon, the kingdom experienced prosperity and centralisation, but also growing dissatisfaction due to heavy taxation and forced labour, especially for building projects like the Temple in Yarushalayim (Jerusalem).

The split occurred around 931 BCE after Solomon's death, and his son Rehoboam became king. When the people, led by Jeroboam, asked Rehoboam to reduce the burdens imposed by Solomon, he refused and instead threatened harsher policies. As a result, 10 tribes rebelled, rejecting Rehoboam's rule and forming a separate kingdom under Jeroboam.

This resulted in the emergence of 2 separate Kingdoms within the house of Jacob.

The Northern Kingdom

The Northern Kingdom has retained the name Israel (YASHARA'AL) (and is also called Ephraim or Joseph in scriptural references). Its capital city was initially in Shechem and later moved to Samaria. That is why several scriptural references allude to Israel and Samaria being enemies. They were enemies because of the split, but were still bloodline brothers from the 12 tribes (the 12 sons of Jacob).

The Northern Kingdom was first led by Jeroboam I and the tribes that were part of it included (1) Reuben, (2) Simeon, (3) Dan, (4) Naphtali, (5) Gad, (6) Asher, (7) Issachar, (8) Zebulun, (9) Ephraim and (10) Manasseh. Levi also had cities in the north but no territory.

The Northern Kingdom created its own centres of worship in Bethel and Dan, with golden calves, to prevent people from going to Yarushalayim (Jerusalem), which was in the south. This idolatry and spiritual decline which they were warned off by the biblical prophets resulted in YAHUAH judging them through the Assyrian invasion in 722 BCE. The 10 tribes were exiled and became known as the "Lost Tribes of Israel (YASHARA'AL)."

I personally believe that the "10 lost tribes of YASHARA'AL" ventured south and continued to migrate deep into Sub-Saharan Africa, where they assimilated and mingled with the Hamites as they expanded beyond the rivers of Ethiopia and Cush. The ancestral bloodline of the "10 lost tribes" is therefore very alive within the lands of Sub-Saharan Africa and are and will be awakened by YAHUAH for YAHUAH to fulfil His promise to unite all the tribes again.

The migration of the "10 lost tribes of YASHARA'AL' into Africa (AFRIKEI, as the Jewish Sanhedrin called it) is what is referred to in the records of the Sanhedrin 94:15a referenced earlier.

YAHUAH promises that for a second time (as He did with the Exodus from Egypt) He will recover the remnant of His people who are left (speaking about the '10 lost tribes) and also gather the dispersed of Judah (speaking of Judah and Benjamin) from the four corners of the earth.

- ***From beyond the rivers of Cush/Ethiopia my worshipers, the daughter of my dispersed/scattered ones, shall bring my offering.*** *(Zephaniah 3:10)*
- ***It shall come to pass in that day that YAHUAH shall set His hand again the second time to recover the remnant of His people who are left***, *From Assyria and*

> *Egypt, From Pathros and Cush, From Elam and Shinar, From Hamath and the islands of the sea. He will set up a banner for the nations,* **and will assemble the outcasts of YASHARA'AL, and gather together the dispersed of Judah from the four corners of the earth.** *(Isaiah 11:11-12 NKJV)*

The "10 lost tribes of YASHARA'AL" (Northern Kingdom) are the ones that are referenced as the 'stick of Joseph that is in the hand of Ephraim' in Ezekiel 37:19, and the stick of Judah is the Northern Kingdom.

- o *'Thus says YAHUAH ALUAH:* **"Surely I will take the stick of Joseph, which is in the hand of Ephraim, and the tribes of YASHARA'AL,** *his companions; and I will join them with it,* **with the stick of Judah,** *and make them one stick, and they will be one in My hand." (Ezekiel 37:19 NKJV)*

 Tribes of Africa, discern what this means. SELAH

The Southern Kingdom

The Southern Kingdom took the name of Judah (YAHUDA) with its capital city in Yarushalayim (Jerusalem).

Its first king was Rehoboam, son of Solomon and the tribes that belonged to it were (1) Judah and (2) Benjamin. Levi, the priestly tribe, remained in service at the Temple in Yarushalayim (Jerusalem).

The Southern Kingdom survived longer than the Northern, but again, because of YAHUAH's judgement coming upon them for breaking the covenant and for their sins, they were conquered by Babylon in 586 BCE, leading to the Babylonian exile.

After the 70 years of Babylonian exile, Judah (the Southern Kingdom), returned to Yarushalayim (Jerusalem) and rebuilt the temple in the days of Nehemiah and Ezra, but due to their sin and breaking the covenant, they were conquered again by the Romans during the invasion of CE 70, the temple was destroyed, and they were exiled until to this day.

I believe most fled again to the south, settling primarily in the areas of the Sahel and West Africa, hence the Kingdom of Juda on the old African maps. They then became the primary target of the Transatlantic slave trade. This means most of the bloodline descendants of Judah (YAHUDA) and Ephraim, and some of Levi, are the descendants of slaves scattered in the Americas.

If one were to listen to the songs classified as the 'Negro spirituals', which the slaves sang, one can pick up the words they used describing their ancestry and history. Likewise, singers from Jamaica like Bob Marley sang much about Zion, jubilee, redemption, Moses, the river Jordan as a cry to Jah (YAH).

I will quote the words of one the 'Negro spirituals' called OLD SHIP OF ZION

I was standing by the banks of a river

Looking out over life's troubled seas

When I saw an old ship that was sailing

Is that the old ship of ZION I see

Its hull was bent and battered

From the storms of life I could see

Waves were rough but that old ship kept sailing

At the stern of the ship was the captain
I could hear as he called out my name
Get on board it's the old ship of ZION
It will never pass this way again

As I step on board I'll be leaving
All my troubles and trails behind
I'll be safe with Jesus (YAHUSHA) the captain
Sailing out on the old ship of ZION

Those who sang these 'Negro' spirituals and their descendants are the ones referred to as the 'stick of Judah' in Ezekiel 37:19.

The joining of these 2 sticks is the word of YAHUAH, confirming that He will bring the 2 Kingdoms together again as one house (tabernacle). It will be the full house (tabernacle) reestablished again as it once was under King David, hence fulfilling what is written:

- "On that day **I will raise up the tabernacle of David, which has fallen down, And repair its damages; I will raise up its ruins, and rebuild it as in the days of old**; That they may possess the remnant of Edom, And all the Gentiles who are called by My name," Says YAHUAH who does this thing. (Amos 9:11-12 NKJV)

- *And with this the words of the prophets agree, just as it is written:* ***'After this I will return And will rebuild the tabernacle of David, which has fallen down; I will rebuild its ruins, and I will set it up;*** *So that the rest of mankind may seek YAHUAH, Even all the Gentiles who are called by My name, Says YAHUAH who does all these things.' (Acts 15:15-17 NKJV)*

This is why Ezekiel 37 is so important for the tribes of Africa to understand.

YAHUAH's promise to 'regather and restore' His people is very clear.

- *Sing, O daughter of Zion! Shout, O YASHARA'AL! Be glad and rejoice with all your heart, O daughter of Yarushalayim (Jerusalem)! [15] YAHUAH has taken away your judgments, He has cast out your enemy. The King of YASHARA'AL, YAHUAH, is in your midst; You shall see disaster no more. [16] In that day it shall be said to Yarushalayim (Jerusalem): "Do not fear; Zion, let not your hands be weak. [17]* ***YAHUAH your ALUAH in your midst, The Mighty One, will save; He will rejoice over you with gladness, He will quiet you with His love, He will rejoice over you with singing.****" [18] "I will gather those who sorrow over the appointed assembly, who are among you, to whom its reproach is a burden. [19] Behold, at that time I will deal with all who afflict you; I will save the lame, and gather those who were driven out; I will appoint them for praise and fame in every land where they were put to shame. [20]* ***At that time I will bring you back, even at the time I gather you; For I will give you fame and praise Among all the peoples of the earth, When I***

return your captives before your eyes," Says YAHUAH. *(Zephaniah 3:14-20 NKJV)*

Even before YAHUAH had scattered His people because of their unfaithfulness to Him (harlotry) He had already spoken through His prophet Jeremiah (YARAMAYAHU) of His promise to bring them back together again and restore them.

- *YAHUAH said also to me in the days of Josiah the king: "Have you seen what backsliding YASHARA'AL has done? She has gone up on every high mountain and under every green tree, and there played the harlot. [7] And I said, after she had done all these things, 'Return to Me.' But she did not return. And her treacherous sister Judah saw it. [8] Then I saw that for all the causes for which backsliding YASHARA'AL had committed adultery, I had put her away and given her a certificate of divorce; yet her treacherous sister Judah did not fear, but went and played the harlot also. [9] So it came to pass, through her casual harlotry, that she defiled the land and committed adultery with stones and trees. [10] And yet for all this her treacherous sister Judah has not turned to Me with her whole heart, but in pretense," says YAHUAH. [11] Then YAHUAH said to me, "Backsliding YASHARA'AL has shown herself more righteous than treacherous Judah. [12] Go and proclaim these words toward the north, and say: 'Return, backsliding YASHARA'AL,' says YAHUAH; 'I will not cause My anger to fall on you. For I am merciful,' says YAHUAH; 'I will not remain angry forever. [13] Only acknowledge your iniquity, that you have transgressed against YAHUAH your Aluah, and have scattered your charms to alien deities under every green tree, and you have not obeyed My voice,' says YAHUAH.*

> *[14] "Return, O backsliding children," says YAHUAH; "for I am married to you. I will take you, one from a city and two from a family, and I will bring you to Zion. [15] And I will give you shepherds according to My heart, who will feed you with knowledge and understanding. [16] "Then it shall come to pass, when you are multiplied and increased in the land in those days," says YAHUAH, "that they will say no more, 'The ark of the covenant of YAHUAH.' It shall not come to mind, nor shall they remember it, nor shall they visit it, nor shall it be made anymore. [17] "At that time Yarushalayim (Jerusalem) shall be called The Throne of YAHUAH, and all the nations shall be gathered to it, to the name of YAHUAH, to Yarushalayim (Jerusalem). No more shall they follow the dictates of their evil hearts. [18] "In those days the house of Judah (YAHUDA) shall walk with the house of YASHARA'AL, and they shall come together out of the land of the north to the land that I have given as an inheritance to your fathers. (Jeremiah 3:6-18 NKJV)*

Understanding YAHUSHA's stated mission

At the time when the FATHER sent His SON, YAHUSHA, YASHARA'AL was comprised of the Southern Kingdom of Judah (Yahuda) only because the Northern Kingdom (10 'lost tribes') had long been exiled. YAHUSHA, therefore, states what His Abba, YAHUAH, sent Him to do, as it is written:

- o *But He answered and said, **"I was not sent except to the lost sheep of the house of Israel (YASHARA'AL)."** (Matthew 15:24 NKJV)*
- o *These twelve YAHUSHA sent out and commanded them, saying: **"Do not go into the way of the Gentiles**, and do not enter a city of the Samaritans. [6] **But go rather to***

- *the lost sheep of the house of Israel (YASHARA'AL). (Matthew 10:5-6 NKJV)*
  - *I am the good shepherd; and I know My sheep, and am known by My own. [15] As the Father knows Me, even so I know the Father; and I lay down My life for the sheep. [16]* **And other sheep I have which are not of this fold; them also I must bring, and they will hear My voice; and there will be one flock and one shepherd.** *(John 10:14-16 NKJV)*
  - *And YAHUSHA came and spoke to them, saying, "All authority has been given to Me in heaven and on earth. [19]* **Go therefore and make disciples of all the nations, baptizing them in the name of the Father and of the Son and of the Holy Spirit, [20] teaching them to observe all things that I have commanded you;** *and lo, I am with you always, even to the end of the age." Amen. (Matthew 28:18-20 NKJV)*
  - *And He said to them, "It is not for you to know times or seasons which the Father has put in His own authority. [8] But you shall receive power when the Holy Spirit has come upon you;* **and you shall be witnesses to Me in Jerusalem, and in all Judea and Samaria, and to the end of the earth.**" *(Acts 1:7-8 NKJV)*

YAHUSHA's assignment was precisely ordered by His FATHER. He was first to seek the lost sheep of the house of YASHARA'AL (the '10 lost tribes' of the Northern Kingdom) and bring them back into the fold so that they would become one flock. The next stage would then be to seek out the Gentiles and also bring them in based on their choice to join the fold (the house of YASHARA'AL).

This is why His instructions to the disciples were for them to start their mission in Jerusalem and Judea (the area where the Southern Kingdom sheep were resident), and then to expand to Samaria and the ends of the earth where the Northern Kingdom sheep had been scattered into Gentile lands. The strategy was that as the message went out to the ends of the earth in search of the 'Lost sheep' of the Northern Kingdom, it would also be heard by the Gentiles who would have the option to choose to be grafted into the sheep fold and become as native born with YASHARA'AL.

Pay attention when the word scattered is used, as it means a people who were once together were dispersed, referring to the breaking up of the Kingdom of YASHARA'AL into the Northern and Southern Kingdoms. But YAHUAH promises to bring them back together again.

- *'For thus says YAHUAH Aluah : "Indeed I Myself will search for My sheep and seek them out. [12] As a shepherd seeks out his flock on the day he is among his scattered sheep, so will I seek out My sheep and deliver them from all the places where they were scattered on a cloudy and dark day. [13] And I will bring them out from the peoples and gather them from the countries, and will bring them to their own land; I will feed them on the mountains of YASHARA'AL, in the valleys and in all the inhabited places of the country. [14] I will feed them in good pasture, and their fold shall be on the high mountains of YASHARA'AL. There they shall lie down in a good fold and feed in rich pasture on the mountains of YASHARA'AL. [15] I will feed My flock, and I will make them lie down," says YAHUAH Aluah. [16] "I will seek what was lost and bring back what was driven away, bind up the broken and strengthen what was sick;*

- but I will destroy the fat and the strong, and feed them in judgment." (Ezekiel 34:11-16 NKJV)
- James, a bondservant of YAHUAH and of the Master YAHUSHA MASHYACH, **To the twelve tribes which are scattered abroad:** Greetings. (James 1:1 NKJV)
- "As I live," says YAHUAH Aluah, "surely with a mighty hand, with an outstretched arm, and with fury poured out, I will rule over you. [34] **I will bring you out from the peoples and gather you out of the countries where you are scattered, with a mighty hand, with an outstretched arm, and with fury poured out. [35] And I will bring you into the wilderness of the peoples, and there I will plead My case with you face to face.** [36] Just as I pleaded My case with your fathers in the wilderness of the land of Egypt, so I will plead My case with you," says YAHUAH Aluah. [37] "I will make you pass under the rod, and I will bring you into the bond of the covenant; [38] I will purge the rebels from among you, and those who transgress against Me; I will bring them out of the country where they dwell, but they shall not enter the land of YASHARA'AL. Then you will know that I am YAHUAH. (Ezekiel 20:33-38 NKJV)
- Then many of the Jews who had come to Mary, and had seen the things YAHUSHA did, believed in Him. [46] But some of them went away to the Pharisees and told them the things YAHUSHA did. [47] Then the chief priests and the Pharisees gathered a council and said, "What shall we do? For this Man works many signs. [48] If we let Him alone like this, everyone will believe in Him, and the Romans will come and take away both our place and nation." [49] And one of them, Caiaphas, being high priest that year, said to them, "You know nothing at all, [50] nor do you consider

that it is expedient for us that one man should die for the people, and not that the whole nation should perish." [51] Now this he did not say on his own authority; but being high priest that year he prophesied that **YAHUSHA would die for the nation, [52] and not for that nation only, but also that He would gather together in one the children of YAH who were scattered abroad.** (John 11:45-52 NKJV)

Ezekiel 37 and the awakening of the dry bones of the House of YASHARA'AL

This takes us into the discussion on an important biblical prophecy, which is still to be fulfilled, and is the reason why the awakening trumpet of YAHUAH is sounding across Africa and the nations.

Ezekiel chapter 37 is so critical for Africa to understand today, therefore, I will quote it first before discussing it.

- *The hand of YAHUAH came upon me and brought me out in the Spirit of YAHUAH, and set me down in the midst of the valley; and it was full of bones. [2] Then He caused me to pass by them all around, and behold, there were very many in the open valley; and indeed they were very dry. [3] And He said to me, "Son of man, can these bones live?" So I answered, "O YAHUAH Aluah, You know." [4] Again He said to me, **"Prophesy to these bones, and say to them, 'O dry bones, hear the word of YAHUAH! [5] Thus says YAHUAH Aluah to these bones: "Surely I will cause breath to enter into you, and you shall live. [6] I will put sinews on you and bring flesh upon you, cover you with skin and put breath in you; and you shall live. Then you shall know that I am YAHUAH."** ' " [7] So I prophesied as I was commanded; and as I prophesied, there* was a noise, and suddenly a rattling; and the bones came together, bone to bone. [8] Indeed, as I looked, the sinews and the flesh came upon them, and the skin covered them over; but there was no breath in them. [9] Also He said to me, **"Prophesy to the breath, prophesy, son of man, and say to the breath, 'Thus says YAHUAH Aluah: "Come from the four winds, O breath, and breathe on these slain, that they may live." [10] So I prophesied as He commanded me, and breath came into them, and they lived, and stood upon their feet, an exceedingly great army. [11] Then He said to me, "Son of man, these bones are the whole house of YASHARA'AL.** They indeed say, 'Our bones are dry, our hope is lost, and we ourselves are cut off!' [12] Therefore prophesy and say to them, **'Thus says YAHUAH Aluah: "Behold, O My people, I will open your graves and cause you to come up from your graves, and bring you into the land of YASHARA'AL. [13] Then you shall know that I am YAHUAH, when I have opened your graves, O My people, and brought you up from your graves. [14] I will put My Spirit in you, and you shall live, and I will place you in your own land. Then you shall know that I, YAHUAH, have spoken it and performed it,"** says YAHUAH." [15] **Again the word of YAHUAH came to me, saying, [16] "As for you, son of man, take a stick for yourself and write on it: 'For Judah and for the children of YASHARA'AL, his companions.' Then take another stick and write on it, 'For Joseph, the stick of Ephraim, and for all the house of YASHARA'AL, his companions.' [17] Then join them one to another for yourself into one stick, and they will become one in your hand. [18] "And when the children of your people** speak to you, saying, 'Will you not show us what you mean by these?'— [19] say to them, **'Thus says YAHUAH Aluah: "Surely I will take the stick of Joseph, which is in the hand of Ephraim, and the tribes of YASHARA'AL, his companions; and I will join them with it, with the stick of Judah, and make them one stick, and they will be one in My hand."** ' [20] And the sticks on which you write will be in your hand before their eyes. [21] "Then say to them, **'Thus says YAHUAH Aluah: "Surely I will take the children of YASHARA'AL from among the nations, wherever they have gone, and will gather them from every side and bring them into their own land; [22] and I will make them one nation in the land, on the mountains of YASHARA'AL; and one king shall be king over them all; they shall no longer be two nations, nor shall they ever be divided into two kingdoms again.** [23] They shall not defile themselves anymore with their idols, nor with their detestable things, nor with any of their transgressions; but I will deliver them from all their dwelling places in which they have sinned, and will cleanse them. Then they shall be My people, and I will be their Alahym. [24] "David My servant shall be king over them, and they shall all have one shepherd; they shall also walk in My judgments and observe My statutes, and do them. [25] Then they shall dwell in the land that I have given to Jacob My servant, where your fathers dwelt; and they shall dwell there, they, their children, and their children's children, forever; and My servant David shall be their prince forever. [26] Moreover I will make a covenant of peace with them, and it shall be an everlasting covenant with them; I will establish them and multiply them, and I

> *will set My sanctuary in their midst forevermore. [27] My tabernacle also shall be with them; indeed I will be their Alahym, and they shall be My people. [28] The nations also will know that I, YAHUAH, sanctify YASHARA'AL, when My sanctuary is in their midst forevermore."* (Ezekiel 37:1-28 NKJV)

What is written in Ezekiel chapter 37 is the process of fulfilling the coming together of the full House of YASHARA'AL (all 12 sons of Jacob), as YAHUAH brings them together again as ONE NATURAL BRANCH. Isaiah (YASHAYAHU) writes in Isaiah 11:11-16, and specifically, verse 11 says, "YAHUAH will set His hand a second time to recover His people".

YAHUSHA, the everlasting King from the seed (lineage) of David, will be King over the United Kingdom of YASHARA'AL. A Kingdom that will comprise the 12 tribes (natural branches) and those of the Gentiles (wild branches) who have been grafted into YAHUSHA, who will rule over them as King.

It is also important to note that the term Jew (YAHUDYM) does not equal Israel (YASHARA'AL). The correct biblical definition of 'a Jew' (YAHUDYM) is 'people from the geographical area of Judea', of which most in that area were from the tribe of Judah (descendants of the fourth son of Jacob), as that was their home area. So biblical fulfilment of the restoration of the House of YASHARA'AL cannot be based on the people of Judea or the tribe of Judah (YAHUDA) alone, it will only be fulfilled when the '2 sticks' become one as described in Ezekiel 37:15-28.

The 'fake' branch (Jew(ish)) would deceive the world into thinking that it is the House of YASHARA'AL and that prophecy concerning the regathering of 'the seed of the woman' has been fulfilled by the

1948 political state of Israel.

- ***There shall come forth a Rod from the stem of Jesse, and a Branch shall grow out of his roots. [2] The Spirit of YAHUAH shall rest upon Him***, *The Spirit of wisdom and understanding, The Spirit of counsel and might, The Spirit of knowledge and of the fear of YAHUAH. [3] His delight is in the fear of YAHUAH, And He shall not judge by the sight of His eyes, Nor decide by the hearing of His ears; [4] But with righteousness He shall judge the poor, And decide with equity for the meek of the earth; He shall strike the earth with the rod of His mouth, And with the breath of His lips He shall slay the wicked. [5] Righteousness shall be the belt of His loins, And faithfulness the belt of His waist. [6] "The wolf also shall dwell with the lamb, The leopard shall lie down with the young goat, The calf and the young lion and the fatling together; And a little child shall lead them. [7] The cow and the bear shall graze; Their young ones shall lie down together; And the lion shall eat straw like the ox. [8] The nursing child shall play by the cobra's hole, And the weaned child shall put his hand in the viper's den. [9] They shall not hurt nor destroy in all My holy mountain, For the earth shall be full of the knowledge of YAHUAH As the waters cover the sea. [10] "And in that day there shall be a Root of Jesse, who shall stand as a banner to the people; For the Gentiles shall seek Him, And His resting place shall be glorious." [11]* ***It shall come to pass in that day that YAHUAH shall set His hand again the second time to recover the remnant of His people who are left****, From Assyria and Egypt, From Pathros and Cush, From Elam and Shinar, From Hamath and the islands of the sea.*

*[12] **He will set up a banner for the nations, and will assemble the outcasts of YASHARA'AL, and gather together the dispersed of Judah (YAHUDA) From the four corners of the earth.** (Isaiah 11:1-12 NKJV)*

The re-establishment of the House of YASHARA'AL is only attained when the "two sticks" become one.

- *Again the word of YAHUAH came to me, saying, [16] "As for you, son of man, take a stick for yourself and write on it: 'For YAHUDA and for the children of YASHARA'AL, his companions.' Then take another stick and write on it, 'For Joseph, the stick of Ephraim, and for all the house of YASHARA'AL, his companions.' [17] Then join them one to another for yourself into one stick, and they will become one in your hand. [18] "And when the children of your people speak to you, saying, 'Will you not show us what you mean by these?'— [19] say to them, 'Thus says YAHUAH Aluah: "Surely I will take the stick of Joseph, which is in the hand of Ephraim, and the tribes of YASHARA'AL, his companions; and I will join them with it, with the stick of YAHUDA, and make them one stick, and they will be one in My hand." ' [20] And the sticks on which you write will be in your hand before their eyes. [21] "Then say to them, 'Thus says YAHUAH Aluah: "Surely I will take the children of YASHARA'AL from among the nations, wherever they have gone, and will gather them from every side and bring them into their own land; [22] and I will make them one nation in the land, on the mountains of YASHARA'AL; and one king shall be king over them all; they shall no longer be two nations, nor shall they*

ever be divided into two kingdoms again *(Ezekiel 37:15-28)*

Satan, the father of lies, the serpent, the dragon that is always seeking 'the seed of the woman' thinks that He can steal, destroy, kill and bury true YASHARA'AL, but YAHUAH Himself is now breathing His life breath (wind) into YASHARA'AL as He raises from the grave 'the seed of the woman' through whom He has established His covenant for all nations.

Tribes of Africa don't miss the wind of His breath as He breathes across the lands of Africa and the lands of the diaspora. YAHUAH is awakening and raising up the mighty army.

Extensive research of geography

It is important to do an extensive study and research to discover the 'real borders' of what the ALAHYM of Abraham, Isaac and Jacob, YAHUAH, established as 'The Promised Land' and likewise where the YASHARA'ALITES travelled from to get to it.

Abraham was told to leave his house (family), which was in the Ur of the Chaldeans, as written in Genesis 12:1-9:

> o *Now YAHUAH had said to Abram: "Get out of your country, from your family and from your father's house, to a land that I will show you. [2] I will make you a great nation; I will bless you and make your name great; And you shall be a blessing. [3] I will bless those who bless you, And I will curse him who curses you; And in you all the families of the earth shall be blessed." [4] So Abram departed as YAHUAH had spoken to him, and Lot went with him. And Abram was seventy-five years old when he departed from Haran. [5] Then Abram took Sarai his wife and Lot his brother's*

> son, and all their possessions that they had gathered, and the people whom they had acquired in Haran, and they departed to go to the land of Canaan. So they came to the land of Canaan. [6] Abram passed through the land to the place of Shechem, as far as the terebinth tree of Moreh. And the Canaanites were then in the land. [7] Then YAHUAH appeared to Abram and said, "To your descendants I will give this land." And there he built an altar to YAHUAH, who had appeared to him. [8] And he moved from there to the mountain east of Bethel, and he pitched his tent with Bethel on the west and Ai on the east; there he built an altar to YAHUAH and called on the name of YAHUAH. [9] **So Abram journeyed, going on still toward the South.** (Genesis 12:1-9 NKJV)

So, Abram journeyed on, going still toward the South. Where did he travel from when he was called? Which direction did he travel? Where did he end up?

Further in biblical history, from what direction did the YASHARA'ALITES enter Egypt, and likewise, which direction did they depart from, and where did they go? How were the respective lands named and demarcated in biblical times? We need to find the truth about historical geography and cartography, because I sense this has been greatly distorted.

I have come across some additional credible research that even disputes 'the land' being where we have been told it is, and rather places it deeper into Sub-Saharan Africa. This is based on a study of the historical geographical topology, maps, and descriptions given in the scriptures, including the apocrypha books detailing the journey of the YASHARA'ALITES out of Egypt, as they were led by Moses. I do not mention this with any level of personal certainty, and so the point is to urge the reader to research for themselves because 'there are many things that seem to be, which are not' and 'many things that seem not, which are'.

What is useful to remember is that YAHUAH did tell Abram to leave his family and country and go to Canaanite territory, for that is where the 'Land of Promise', which he was being given, was situated.

- Now YAHUAH had said to Abram: **"Get out of your country, from your family and from your father's house, to a land that I will show you.** [2] I will make you a great nation; I will bless you and make your name great; And you shall be a blessing. [3] I will bless those who bless you, And I will curse him who curses you; And in you all the families of the earth shall be blessed." [4] So Abram departed as YAHUAH had spoken to him, and Lot went with him. And Abram was seventy-five years old when he departed from Haran. [5] Then Abram took Sarai his wife and Lot his brother's son, and all their possessions that they had gathered, and the people whom they had acquired in Haran, **and they departed to go to the land of Canaan. So they came to the land of Canaan.** [6] Abram passed through the land to the place of Shechem, as far as the terebinth tree of Moreh. **And the Canaanites were then in the land.** [7] Then YAHUAH appeared to Abram and said, **"To your descendants I will give this land."** And there he built an altar to YAHUAH, who had appeared to him. [8] And he moved from there to the mountain east of Bethel, and he pitched his tent with Bethel on the west and Ai on the east; there he built an altar to YAHUAH and called on the name of YAHUAH. [9] So Abram journeyed, **going on still**

toward the South. *(Genesis 12:1-9 NKJV)*

Canaan was the son of Ham and, therefore, the grandson of Noah. It was the area that Canaan had been allocated that YAHUAH decided would be the "Land of Promise", which He would give to Abram and his descendants. The question is where was and where is this land of Canaan. The one certain thing is that if the children of Ham (Cush, Mizraim, Put and Canaan) are said to have been the main occupants of what is known today as the land of Africa, it means Abram was sent to this land.

Is it possible Abram started his journey in Northeast Africa (which has been renamed the Middle East) and travelled south deeper into Africa, pushing the Hamites (Canaanites and their tribes) out of lands as YAHUAH had said He would do, and therefore, making the land of Africa the primary habitation of the children of YASHARA'AL?

- **"When YAHUAH your Aluah brings you into the land which you go to possess, and has cast out many nations before you,** *the Hittites and the Girgashites and the Amorites and the Canaanites and the Perizzites and the Hivites and the Jebusites, seven nations greater and mightier than you, (Deuteronomy 7:1 NKJV)*

This created a situation in which the children of YASHARA'AL and the children of Ham dwelt on the same piece of real estate called Africa today and started intermingling.

Not all of Africa is of Shem, and Shem is not only of Africa

Please note that the point made about the direct association of the bloodline descendants of Jacob (the 12 tribes) with Africa is not to say that every 'dark skinned' person in Africa or of African descent is of the lineage of Shem. Likewise, the point being made is not that every 'dark skinned' person in Africa or of African descent is of the lineage of Ham. Both lineages are present on the continent and in the diaspora.

It is equally important to make the point that many are of the lineage of Shem in the native and indigenous people across the four corners of the earth, in the Native Indians of the Americas, the Aborigines in Australia and New Zealand and the Pacific Islands, the outcasts in India and even in the lands of China and Japan. YAHUAH did indeed scatter His people to the four corners of the earth as He said He would do.

The challenge that Ham and Shem face

Because both the descendants of the lineage of Ham and Shem have found themselves on the receiving end of being conquered by 'the conqueror' who used the religion of Christianity as one of the primary weapons to conquer them, both have become very sceptical of anything that has to do with Christianity, which unfortunately also includes the Bible. The Word of YAHUAH (the Bible), unfortunately, became synonymous with Christianity, which in truth is not the case. But the perception of such meant many who rejected the religion of Christianity sadly also rejected the Word of YAHUAH (the Bible) and the Truth which it contains that shall set them free. This has resulted in many Hamites (descendants of Ham) and Shemites (descendants of Shem) rejecting the Word of YAHUAH and seeking after Hamite spirituality, which is based on Egyptian mythology and spirituality and linked to the worship of the dead. (Remember that the original name of Egypt is Mizraim, who was one of the sons of Ham). We are to honour our ancestors/forefathers but not to worship them nor venerate them. We are not to venerate the dead, which is what the mythology and spirituality of Mizraim is based on and is one of the things YAHUAH hates.

- *There shall not be found among you anyone who makes his son or his daughter pass through the fire, or one who practices witchcraft, or a soothsayer, or one who interprets omens, or a sorcerer, [11] or one who conjures spells, or a medium, or a spiritist,* **or one who calls up the dead. [12] For all who do these things are an abomination to YAHUAH, and because of these abominations YAHUAH your Aluah drives them out from before you.** *[13] You shall be blameless before YAHUAH your Aluah. [14] For these nations which you will dispossess listened to soothsayers and diviners; but as for you, YAHUAH your Aluah has not appointed such for you. (Deuteronomy 18:10-14 NKJV)*
- *And when they say to you, "Seek those who are mediums and wizards, who whisper and mutter," should not a people seek their Aluah?* **Should they seek the dead on behalf of the living?** *(Isaiah 8:19 NKJV)*

This Hamite rebellion against YAHUAH is evident in the early days through Nimrod, the son of Cush (grandson of Ham), who undertook a project to build the Tower of Babel as a direct defiance and challenge to YAHUAH's authority as the Most High. The people were thereafter scattered, along with Nimrod's uncle Mizraim and his sons, establishing Mizraim (Egyptian) mythology and spirituality. These beliefs became widespread across the Hamite lands, as Egypt (Mizraim) evolved into a centre of demonic-inspired knowledge that fuels witchcraft, sorcery, divination, spell-casting, calling up the dead, and all other forms of wickedness which stand in direct rebellion to YAHUAH.

So, a large number of Hamites have continued to practice elements of this and tend to revert to the veneration and worship of the dead in rejection of anything that carries a Christian label or related to what they view as the Christian Bible. Some will continue in the veneration and worship of the dead practices and mix Christianity into it.

It is this same Egyptian mythology (Mizraim mythology and spirituality) which is also at the foundation of Freemasonry, and secret societies like the Illuminati and even into Roman Catholicism, Christianity and 'modern day' Babylon. This is where the eye of Horus (the all-seeing eye) and the pyramid on the United States one-dollar ($1) note comes from. This is where the network of obelisks across the world originated from, including the original obelisks that were transported from Egypt and placed in Rome (The Vatican obelisk and 12 others), London (Cleopatra's needle), New York (the second Cleopatra's needle), Paris (The Obelisk of Luxor) and in Istanbul. The tallest obelisk in Washington, DC, the Washington Monument, which was erected to honour the first President of the United States of America (POTUS), links the seat and office of the President of the USA to Mizraim mythology and spirituality. This is also evident in how the city of Washington, DC, is designed based on Egyptian and Roman mythological themes. Replicas of these obelisks are found all over the world in nearly every city and town, and many church buildings feature them as church steeples. So, when you see the statement 'in God we trust' on the US$1-dollar bill, do not think it is referring to YAHUAH, the ALAHYM of Abraham, Isaac and Jacob. Likewise, when many presidents and other officials are sworn into their offices 'in the name of God' do not think they are necessarily referring to YAHUAH, the ALAHYM of Abraham, Isaac and Jacob. Most have a different God they are pledging allegiance to.

The prevalence of Egyptian mythology in the Western world, especially the United States of America, helps make better sense of Deuteronomy 28:68 when it speaks about the children of YASHARA'AL being taken to Egypt in ships. It is not referring to literal Egypt but the 'new Egypt' which has become the place of bondage of the House of Judah.

> o *"**And YAHUAH will take you back to Egypt in ships**, by the way of which I said to you, 'You shall never see it again.' And there you shall be offered for sale to your enemies as male and female slaves, but no one will buy you."* (Deuteronomy 28:68 NKJV)

Coming back to the challenge that Shem faces.

Because Shemites (descendants of Shem) were exiled (especially the 10 'lost' tribes) into Hamite territories, they adopted practices which are linked to, or originated from, the veneration and worship of the dead, and they tend to go to that spiritual route when they reject Christianity, and hence the Word of YAHUAH. They see African spirituality (which emanates from Mizraim) as something to identify with because of their identification with the land of Africa.

This is the big error that entraps them and something that YAHUAH warned, as it is written:

> o *On that day I swore to bring them out of the land of Egypt into a land that I had searched out for them, a land flowing with milk and honey, the glory of all lands. [7] And I said to them: '**Each of you must throw away the abominations before his eyes, and you must not defile yourselves with the idols of Egypt**. I am the YAHUAH your Aluah.'* (Ezekiel 20:6-7 BSB)

Unfortunately, the abominations and idols of Mizraim (Egypt) became a big snare and continue to be so today.

Linking African spirituality solely to the practices of Mizraim is error, because the worship of the ALAHYM of Abraham, Isaac and Jacob also comes out of Africa.

The Good News is that YAHUAH has promised that He will break the covenant with death, the shroud of death that has been cast over the heads of all the people and spread over the nations.

- *And He will destroy on this mountain the covering of the face that is cast over the heads of all peoples [in mourning], and the veil [of profound wretchedness] that is woven and spread over all nations. [8] He will swallow up death [in victory; He will abolish death forever].* And YAHUAH Aluah will wipe away tears from all faces; and the reproach of His people He will take away from off all the earth; for YAHUAH has spoken it. (Isaiah 25:7-8 AMPC)

Shemites (descendants of Shem) must return to the agreement with YAHUAH, the ALAHYM of their ancestors Abraham, Isaac, and Jacob, and embrace the Word of YAHUAH, which is part of their heritage. They have a divine responsibility to be guardians of the covenant and to be a light to the world (nations), so that other nations may be drawn by the light and come to be adopted into the covenant, and thus into the house of YASHARA'AL.

Hamites (descendants of Ham) must depart from the deception of the demonic covenant with death made through Nimrod and Mizraim and enter into the covenant of life with YAHUAH through adoption into the House of YASHARA'AL.

This is the designed plan of YAHUAH as is written:

> - *In that day five cities in the land of Egypt will speak the language of Canaan and swear by YAHUAH of hosts; one will be called the City of Destruction. [19]* **In that day there will be an altar to YAHUAH in the midst of the land of Egypt, and a pillar to YAHUAH at its border. [20] And it will be for a sign and for a witness to YAHUAH of hosts in the land of Egypt; for they will cry to YAHUAH because of the oppressors, and He will send them a Savior and a Mighty One, and He will deliver them. [21] Then YAHUAH will be known to Egypt, and the Egyptians will know YAHUAH in that day, and will make sacrifice and offering; yes, they will make a vow to YAHUAH and perform it.** *[22] And YAHUAH will strike Egypt, He will strike and heal it;* **they will return to YAHUAH, and He will be entreated by them and heal them.** *[23]* **In that day there will be a highway from Egypt to Assyria, and the Assyrian will come into Egypt and the Egyptian into Assyria, and the Egyptians will serve with the Assyrians. [24] In that day YASHARA'AL will be one of three with Egypt and Assyria—a blessing in the midst of the land, [25] whom YAHUAH of hosts shall bless, saying, "Blessed is Egypt My people, and Assyria the work of My hands, and YASHARA'AL My inheritance."** *(Isaiah/YASHAYAHU 19:18-25 NKJV)*

- Egypt (Mizraim), My people.
- Assyria, the works of My hands
- YASHARA'AL, My inheritance.

It is not by accident that both the descendants of Shem and Ham are directly associated with the land of Africa and have been intermingled through proximity and intermarriage.

The land and people of Africa are front and centre of YAHUAH's plan for all nations. This plan is centred on our identity. He names the descendants of Ham of the lineage of Mizraim as His people and the descendants of Shem of the lineage of Jacob as His inheritance. This is the destiny of the people of the land of Africa and those in the diaspora who have an association with the land by lineage of patriarchal seed through Jacob and through the seed of Mizraim.

Who is the political state of Israel? - Who are Israelis? (Note: they are not called Israelites)

What has been discussed so far raises the question, 'so who is the Israel that we know today and where does it fit into the everlasting script of our FATHER, the ALAHYM of Abraham, Isaac and Jacob, YAHUAH, who has guaranteed that everything that He has said (as is written) will be fulfilled without exception?

On November 29th, 1947, the United Nations adopted Resolution 181 (also known as the Partition Resolution), which would divide Great Britain's former Palestinian mandate into Jewish and Arab states in May 1948 when the British mandate was scheduled to end.

Perhaps this was a major spiritual 'false flag', to officially create the 'fake natural branch' that would deceive many into believing that the prophecy concerning 'The House of Israel (YASHARA'AL)' has been fulfilled. A 'false flag' that completely deceived the world and brought about the rise of Christian Zionism as one of the foundational pillars to get Christians to support the modern-day state of Israel project using what is written in Genesis 12:1-3 as the manipulative bait to get support for their agenda and likewise get nations to turn a blind eye to their activities.

> ○ *Now YAHUAH had said to Abram: "Get out of your country, from your family and from your father's house, to a land that I will show you. [2] I will make you a great nation; I will bless you and make your name great; and you shall be a blessing. [3]* **I will bless those who bless you, and I will curse him who curses you;** *and in you all the families of the earth shall be blessed." (Genesis 12:1-3 NKJV)*

I believe what is prophetically given in many scriptures concerning the restoration of the 'House of YASHARA'AL', such as already mentioned in Ezekiel 37 and Isaiah 11, are only beginning to manifest as the House of YASHARA'AL (all 12 tribes) are 'resurrected' in preparation of the 'rebuilding of the tabernacle of David that had been destroyed' as written in Amos 9:11 and again in Acts 15:14-17.

> ○ *"On that day* **I will raise up The tabernacle of David, which has fallen down, And repair its damages; I will raise up its ruins, and rebuild it as in the days of old**; *That they may possess the remnant of Edom, and all the Gentiles who are called by My name," Says YAHUAH who does this thing. (Amos 9:11-12 NKJV)*
>
> ○ *And with this the words of the prophets agree, just as it is written:* **'After this I will return and will rebuild the tabernacle of David, which has fallen down; I will rebuild its ruins, and I will set it up**; *So that the rest of mankind may seek YAHUAH, Even all the Gentiles who are called by My name, Says YAHUAH who does all these things.' (Acts 15:15-17 NKJV)*

The scripture says that *'Even all the Gentiles who are called by MY NAME'*. What name? The title - The Lord? God? Or maybe His name, YAHUAH, the ALAHYM of Abraham, Isaac and Jacob.

This is a very controversial subject, but I now firmly believe that the people who lead and control the political State of Israel are not those who are of the biblical House of YASHARA'AL ('the seed of the woman, the 12 sons of Jacob') and this has big implications on many fronts in terms of understanding where we are in biblical timelines and, perhaps, how our FATHER the ALAHYM of Abraham, Isaac and Jacob, YAHUAH, is moving through world events as a result.

The deceiver probably pulled off the greatest 'heist' through the Rothschild family, who championed the Balfour Declaration through Great Britain and the United Nations to completely capture 'the church and Christians'. A move that has placed 'the church and Christians' on the wrong path to pledge allegiance to the 'wrong people, the fake natural branch' (the Jews in name only of Revelation 2:9 and Revelation 3:9). A brilliant masterstroke in a strategy to get Christians, America and most of the Western Christianised world to fund, support and turn a blind eye to the behaviour of the 'identity thieves, the counterfeit natural branch' who call themselves Jews and Israel as they use what is written in Genesis 12:1-3 as their fundraising strategy and weapon to cause nations to turn the other way and not sanction their unacceptable behaviour. I believe this is part of the mystery of lawlessness in action.

- o *Now YAHUAH had said to Abram: "Get out of your country, from your family and from your father's house, to a land that I will show you. [2] I will make you a great nation; I will bless you and make your name great; and you shall be a blessing. [3]* **I will bless those who bless you, and I will curse him who curses you;** *and in you all the* *families of the earth shall be blessed." (Genesis 12:1-3 NKJV)*

The spiritual implications of this are what are most dire because the ultimate plan of salvation and redemption in the **Most High's unchangeable design is for all nations to tie into (graft into) the true 'House of YASHARA'AL' as** already referenced. The greater price that is being paid is not material but rather spiritual, as it could lead to everlasting death.

Much has been talked about concerning 'replacement theology' in the religion of Christianity, which is a way to do away with the requirement for the 'natural branches'. But perhaps the greatest manifestation of this plan of the enemy is not the 'New Testament church' replacing YASHARA'AL, but a people who are not descendants of Jacob claiming to be YASHARA'AL and replacing those who truly are of 'the seed of the woman', the 12 sons of Jacob.

As a brief side note, it is interesting to note that Apartheid South Africa was also birthed in 1948, the same year as the State of Israel, and how the Zionist agenda and the formulation of the Balfour Declaration have strong links to South Africa because of the strategic involvement of the then apartheid president Jan Smuts.

What is also interesting to note is how the Zionists first looked at Uganda as a possible land of settlement before they decided on Palestine. Both Uganda and Palestine were under British rule, and so either could be used to fulfil the plan to allocate land that would be used to create the new state of Israel.

I encourage you to take a closer look at this reference on Britannica.

https://www.britannica.com/biography/Theodor-Herzl

All this brings us back to the question of where the borders of true biblical YASHARA'AL where and are, in Palestine or East Africa, or elsewhere.

A book that makes worthwhile reading is 'Conspiracy to erase a nation' authored by Tierney Sheree Peprah who is based in Ghana.

More on this subject will be covered in Chapter 18.

The scary implications if what I share is true.

So, the scary aspect of this, if true, is that it means America, most Western nations and most Protestant, Pentecostal, Evangelical Christianity have effectively been both the primary oppressor and enslaver of the bloodline descendants of Jacob ('the seed of the woman, the 12 tribes') and likewise the biggest supporter of the 'imposters, the fake natural branch, the Jews in name only' who set up the political state of Israel and occupied that piece of land in Near East Africa. I shudder at the thought of this and what it means for the institution of religious Christianity that has likewise been complicit in this.

Could we have been deceived and caught up in a delusion, believing a lie? As it is written:

- *Do you not remember that when I was still with you I told you these things? [6] And now you know what is restraining, that he may be revealed in his own time. [7]* ***For the mystery of lawlessness is already at work;*** *only He who now restrains will do so until He is taken out of the way. [8] And then the lawless one will be revealed, whom YAHUAH will consume with the breath of His mouth and destroy with the brightness of His coming. [9]* ***The coming of the lawless one is according to the working of Satan, with all power, signs, and lying wonders, [10] and with all unrighteous deception among those who perish,***

> *because they did not receive the love of the truth, that they might be saved. [11] And for this reason YAHUAH will send them strong delusion, that they should believe the lie, [12] that they all may be condemned who did not believe the truth but had pleasure in unrighteousness. (II Thessalonians 2:5-12 NKJV)*

I want to conclude this discourse by reiterating why this subject about true biblical identity is important.

The final destination YAHUAH has established for us and the place YAHUSHA said He would go to prepare a place for us is the New Yarushalayim (Jerusalem), whose 12 gates have the names of the 12 tribes. These 12 gates indicate that those (the natural branches and the branches from the wild tree) who are joined to the Cultivated Olive Tree (the Tree of Life) become part of the House of YAHUAH (ZION). The wild branches (Gentiles) are given a natural branch identity as they are adopted into one of the 12 tribes (the new name that they will be given that no one knows*), giving them entrance in the New Yarushalayim (Jerusalem) through the gate they identify with tribally. This is YAHUAH's design.

This joining together fulfils what Ezekiel 47:21-23 speaks of, the 'foreigner' (the branches of the wild olive tree) will become as native born in to the House of YAHUAH, because YASHARA'AL is YAHUAH's first born, who He has given the task to fulfil the role to be a light unto the Gentiles so they can also be brought into the Great city, the New Yarushalayim (Jerusalem), the dwelling place of YAHUAH, the true ZION.

This is why the subject of biblical identity is extremely critical to understand and why Satan will do anything to fight it.

🦁 **Tribes of Africa,** everything comes down to one matter – our love for YAHUAH. Whether we are descendants of Shem or Ham or even Japheth, the true measure of our love for YAHUAH is how we will love our brother. Shem, Ham and Japheth were brothers, and their descendants remain as brothers today.

> o *If someone says, "I love YAHUAH," and hates his brother, he is a liar; for he who does not love his brother whom he has seen, how can he love YAHUAH whom he has not seen? [21] And this commandment we have from Him: that he who loves YAHUAH must love his brother also.* (I John 4:20-21 NKJV)

Since the issue of the final destination (the New YARUSHALAYIM) according to the script of YAHUAH is so pivotal to what He has promised, it is worthwhile to dive into this in the next chapter.

Tribes of Africa, because YAHUAH is love He exhorts us to love. The task that lies ahead cannot be accomplished without YAHUAH, and therefore, it cannot be accomplished without love.

Beloved, let us love one another, for love is of YAHUAH; and everyone who loves is born of YAHUAH and knows YAHUAH. [8] He who does not love does not know YAHUAH, **for YAHUAH is love***.*
(I John 4:7-8 NKJV

CHAPTER SIXTEEN

The Path To 'Heaven' Or The New Yerushalayim (Jerusalem)

What happens when we die, and what are the eternal destinations the Bible speaks of?

Growing up, I remember always hearing the adage, "if you behave badly, you will not make it to heaven" or "we are called to suffer here on earth, but we shall have our reward in heaven".

I often wonder now how much of this was part of the 'strategic indoctrination' through the religion of Christianity to ensure compliance. In essence a message saying, 'if you push back against what we tell you is good you won't enter heaven' and 'don't worry about the suffering you are going through now (which we have caused you), don't resist because you shall get your reward in heaven', (while we 'the conqueror will enjoy our reward here and now').

It seems very similar to the spirit that was behind the practice of indulgences, which made the Roman Catholic Church extremely wealthy and financially powerful. The practice of indulgences is where the Catholic church would grant remission of sins and entrance into heaven by the payment of money. The practice was based on the notion that the Catholic Church had a 'treasury of merits' earned by Christ and the Catholic saints, which could be applied to individuals to reduce their time in purgatory by paying money for these 'merits'. The justification and righteousness obtained through YAHUSHA were thrown out the window and deemed unnecessary by the 'Mother of Harlots'. This is why the Catholic Church and the Vatican today remain one of the largest owners of property in the world and the wealthiest institutions on earth.

This same spirit of greed, which defiles the truth of YAHUAH's word and uses it to deceive people for material gain, seems to be the same spirit flowing through a lot of the charismatic Christian churches and ministries as it manifests through the wolves in sheep's clothing who call themselves apostles, prophets, bishops, fathers, etc. Likewise, through the false doctrines of word of faith and seed faith 'name and claim' prosperity doctrines that are completely unbiblical and hypnotising people into a stupor through the wine of witchcraft and sorcery.

> o *Then one of the seven angels who had the seven bowls came and talked with me, saying to me,* **"Come, I will show you the judgment of the great harlot who sits on many waters, [2] with whom the kings of the earth committed fornication, and the inhabitants of the earth were made drunk with the wine of her fornication."** *[3] So he carried me away in the Spirit into the wilderness. And I saw a woman sitting on a scarlet beast which was full of names of blasphemy, having seven heads and ten horns. [4] The*

woman was arrayed in purple and scarlet, and adorned with gold and precious stones and pearls, having in her hand a golden cup full of abominations and the filthiness of her fornication. [5] And on her forehead a name was written: **MYSTERY, BABYLON THE GREAT, THE MOTHER OF HARLOTS AND OF THE ABOMINATIONS OF THE EARTH.** [6] I saw the woman, drunk with the blood of the saints and with the blood of the martyrs of YAHUSHA. And when I saw her, I marveled with great amazement. [7] But the angel said to me, "Why did you marvel? I will tell you the mystery of the woman and of the beast that carries her, which has the seven heads and the ten horns. [8] The beast that you saw was, and is not, and will ascend out of the bottomless pit and go to perdition. And those who dwell on the earth will marvel, whose names are not written in the Book of Life from the foundation of the world, when they see the beast that was, and is not, and yet is. [9] "Here is the mind which has wisdom: The seven heads are seven mountains on which the woman sits. [10] There are also seven kings. Five have fallen, one is, and the other has not yet come. And when he comes, he must continue a short time. [11] The beast that was, and is not, is himself also the eighth, and is of the seven, and is going to perdition. [12] "The ten horns which you saw are ten kings who have received no kingdom as yet, but they receive authority for one hour as kings with the beast. [13] These are of one mind, and they will give their power and authority to the beast. [14] **These will make war with the Lamb, and the Lamb will overcome them, for He is Lord of lords and King of kings; and those who are with Him are called, chosen, and faithful."** [15] Then he said to me, *"The waters which you saw, where the harlot sits, are peoples, multitudes, nations, and tongues. [16] And the ten horns which you saw on the beast, these will hate the harlot, make her desolate and naked, eat her flesh and burn her with fire. [17] For YAHUAH has put it into their hearts to fulfill His purpose, to be of one mind, and to give their kingdom to the beast,* **until the words of YAHUAH are fulfilled.** *[18] And the woman whom you saw is that great city which reigns over the kings of the earth." (Revelation 17:1-18 NKJV)*

- *After these things I saw another angel coming down from heaven, having great authority, and the earth was illuminated with his glory. [2] And he cried mightily with a loud voice, saying,* **"Babylon the great is fallen, is fallen, and has become a dwelling place of demons, a prison for every foul spirit, and a cage for every unclean and hated bird! [3] For all the nations have drunk of the wine of the wrath of her fornication, the kings of the earth have committed fornication with her, and the merchants of the earth have become rich through the abundance of her luxury." [4] And I heard another voice from heaven saying, "Come out of her, my people, lest you share in her sins, and lest you receive of her plagues. [5] For her sins have reached to heaven, and YAHUAH has remembered her iniquities.** *[6] Render to her just as she rendered to you, and repay her double according to her works; in the cup which she has mixed, mix double for her. [7] In the measure that she glorified herself and lived luxuriously, in the same measure give her torment and sorrow; for she says in her heart, 'I sit as queen, and am no widow, and will not see sorrow.'*

> *[8] Therefore her plagues will come in one day—death and mourning and famine. And she will be utterly burned with fire, for strong is YAHUAH who judges her. (Revelation 18:1-8 NKJV)*

Remember YAHUAH's definition of sin and also the mystery of lawlessness that is at work.

🕯 **Tribes of Africa** awaken from the slumber and get out of these false doctrines, come out of worshipping and following the wolves in sheep's clothing. Stop drinking the wine of witchcraft and sorcery that they serve, which is causing you to fall asleep and accept lies (lawlessness). Get out of fornicating with the harlot/prostitute so that you do not go down as YAHUAH judges her.

Coming back to the issue of 'going to heaven'. Is it the same as New Yarushalayim (Jerusalem) the scriptures speak about as the final destination for the overcoming saints?

It is worthwhile to list references to the New Yarushalayim (Jerusalem) as it is written in scripture and make some comments afterwards. I will start with New Testament references and work backwards to where it is prophesied through the prophets.

- **But you have come to Mount Zion and to the city of the living Alahym, the heavenly Yarushalayim (Jerusalem),** *to an innumerable company of angels, to the general assembly and church of the firstborn who are registered in heaven, to YAHUAH the Judge of all, to the spirits of just men made perfect, [24] to YAHUSHA the Mediator of the new covenant, and to the blood of sprinkling that speaks better things than that of Abel. (Hebrews 12:22-24 NKJV)*
- *Indeed I will make those of the synagogue of Satan, who*

say they are Jews and are not, but lie—indeed I will make them come and worship before your feet, and to know that I have loved you. Because you have kept My command to persevere, I also will keep you from the hour of trial which shall come upon the whole world, to test those who dwell on the earth. Behold, I am coming quickly! Hold fast what you have, that no one may take your crown. He who overcomes, I will make him a pillar in the temple of My Alahym (YAHUAH), and he shall go out no more. I will write on him the name of My Alahym (YAHUAH) **and the name of the city of My Alahym (YAHUAH), the New Yarushalayim (Jerusalem), which comes down out of heaven from My Alahym (YAHUAH)**. *And I will write on him My new name. (Revelation 3:9-12 NKJV)*

- **Now I saw a new heaven and a new earth, for the first heaven and the first earth had passed away. Also there was no more sea. [2] Then I, John, saw the holy city, New Yarushalayim (Jerusalem), coming down out of heaven from YAHUAH, prepared as a bride adorned for her husband.** *[3] And I heard a loud voice from heaven saying,* **"Behold, the tabernacle of YAHUAH is with men, and He will dwell with them, and they shall be His people. YAHUAH Himself will be with them and be their Aluah.** *[4] And YAHUAH will wipe away every tear from their eyes; there shall be no more death, nor sorrow, nor crying. There shall be no more pain, for the former things have passed away." [5]* **Then He who sat on the throne said, "Behold, I make all things new."** *And He said to me, "Write, for these words are true and faithful." [6] And He said to me, "It is done! I am the Alpha and the Omega, the Beginning and the End. I will give of the fountain of the* water of life freely to him who thirsts. [7] He who overcomes shall inherit all things, and I will be his Aluah and he shall be My son. [8] **But the cowardly, unbelieving, abominable, murderers, sexually immoral, sorcerers, idolaters, and all liars shall have their part in the lake which burns with fire and brimstone, which is the second death."** [9] Then one of the seven angels who had the seven bowls filled with the seven last plagues came to me and talked with me, saying, **"Come, I will show you the bride, the Lamb's wife."** [10] **And he carried me away in the Spirit to a great and high mountain, and showed me the great city, the holy Yarushalayim (Jerusalem), descending out of heaven from YAHUAH,** [11] having the glory of YAHUAH. Her light was like a most precious stone, like a jasper stone, clear as crystal. [12] Also she had a great and high wall with twelve gates, and twelve angels at the gates, and names written on them, which are the names of the twelve tribes of the children of YASHARA'AL: [13] three gates on the east, three gates on the north, three gates on the south, and three gates on the west. [14] Now the wall of the city had twelve foundations, and on them were the names of the twelve apostles of the Lamb. [15] And he who talked with me had a gold reed to measure the city, its gates, and its wall. [16] The city is laid out as a square; its length is as great as its breadth. And he measured the city with the reed: twelve thousand furlongs. Its length, breadth, and height are equal. [17] Then he measured its wall: one hundred and forty-four cubits, according to the measure of a man, that is, of an angel. [18] The construction of its wall was of jasper; and the city was pure gold, like clear glass. [19] **The foundations of the wall of the city** were adorned with all kinds of precious stones: the first foundation was jasper, the second sapphire, the third chalcedony, the fourth emerald, [20] the fifth sardonyx, the sixth sardius, the seventh chrysolite, the eighth beryl, the ninth topaz, the tenth chrysoprase, the eleventh jacinth, and the twelfth amethyst. [21] The twelve gates were twelve pearls: each individual gate was of one pearl. And the street of the city was pure gold, like transparent glass. [22] **But I saw no temple in it, for YAHUAH Almighty and the Lamb are its temple. [23] The city had no need of the sun or of the moon to shine in it, for the glory of YAHUAH illuminated it. The Lamb is its light.** [24] And the nations of those who are saved shall walk in its light, and the kings of the earth bring their glory and honor into it. [25] Its gates shall not be shut at all by day (there shall be no night there). [26] And they shall bring the glory and the honor of the nations into it. [27] **But there shall by no means enter it anything that defiles, or causes an abomination or a lie, but only those who are written in the Lamb's Book of Life.** (Revelation 21:1-27 NKJV)

- And he showed me a pure river of water of life, clear as crystal, proceeding from the throne of YAHUAH and of the Lamb. [2] In the middle of its street, and on either side of the river, was the tree of life, which bore twelve fruits, each tree yielding its fruit every month. The leaves of the tree were for the healing of the nations. [3] **And there shall be no more curse, but the throne of YAHUAH and of the Lamb shall be in it, and His servants shall serve Him. [4] They shall see His face, and His name shall be on their foreheads.** [5] There shall be no night there: They need no lamp nor light of the sun, for YAHUAH gives them light. And they shall reign forever and ever. (Revelation 22:1-5 NKJV)

- **YAHUAH loveth the gates of Zion** More than all the dwellings of Jacob (Yaaqab). (Psalms 87:2 KJV)
- Great is YAHUAH, and greatly to be praised **in the city of our Aluah, In His holy mountain.** Beautiful in elevation, **the joy of the whole earth, Is Mount Zion on the sides of the north, The city of the great King.** YAHUAH is in her palaces; He is known as her refuge. (Psalms 48:1-3 NKJV)
- As we have heard, so we have **seen in the city of YAHUAH of hosts, In the city of our Aluah:** YAHUAH will establish it forever. Selah (Psalms 48:8 KJV)
- Awake, awake! Put on thy strength, O Zion; Put on thy beautiful garments, **O Yarushalayim (Jerusalem), the holy city: for henceforth there shall no more come into thee the uncircumcised and the unclean.** (Isaiah 52:1 KJV)
- "For behold, I create new heavens and a new earth; And the former shall not be remembered or come to mind. [18] But be glad and rejoice forever in what I create; **For behold, I create Yarushalayim (Jerusalem) as a rejoicing, And her people a joy. [19] I will rejoice in Yarushalayim (Jerusalem),** And joy in My people; The voice of weeping shall no longer be heard in her, Nor the voice of crying. [20] "No more shall an infant from there live but a few days, nor an old man who has not fulfilled his days; For the child shall die one hundred years old, But the sinner being one hundred years old shall be accursed. [21] They shall build houses and inhabit them; They shall plant vineyards and eat their fruit. [22] They shall not build and another inhabit; They

shall not plant and another eat; For as the days of a tree, so shall be the days of My people, And My elect shall long enjoy the work of their hands. [23] They shall not labor in vain, nor bring forth children for trouble; For they shall be the descendants of the blessed of YAHUAH, And their offspring with them. [24] "It shall come to pass That before they call, I will answer; And while they are still speaking, I will hear. [25] The wolf and the lamb shall feed together, the lion shall eat straw like the ox, and dust shall be the serpent's food. They shall not hurt nor destroy in all My holy mountain," Says YAHUAH. (Isaiah 65:17-25 NKJV)

- **"These are the exits of the city.** *On the north side, measuring four thousand five hundred cubits [31] (the gates of the city shall be named after the tribes of YASHARA'AL), the three gates northward: one gate for Reuben, one gate for Judah, and one gate for Levi; [32] on the east side, four thousand five hundred cubits, three gates: one gate for Joseph, one gate for Benjamin, and one gate for Dan; [33] on the south side, measuring four thousand five hundred cubits, three gates: one gate for Simeon, one gate for Issachar, and one gate for Zebulun; [34] on the west side, four thousand five hundred cubits with their three gates: one gate for Gad, one gate for Asher, and one gate for Naphtali. [35] All the way around shall be eighteen thousand cubits;* **and the name of the city from that day shall be: YAHUAH IS THERE."** *(Ezekiel 48:30-35 NKJV)*

These references provide a glimpse into the biblical concept of the New Yarushalayim (Jerusalem), a place where there is the full manifestation, fulfilment of the redemption, restoration, and eternal fellowship of Man with YAHUAH.

It is the city that has the name of YAHUAH.

Is the New Yarushalayim that descends from heaven the same as what we have been taught about going to heaven? Does the Word of YAHUAH really talk about a concept of going to heaven as the final destination YAHUAH has prepared for us, or does it speak more about entrance into a new holy city, the New Yarushalayim coming down from heaven to earth? Have we been duped into a doctrine that came out of the Roman Catholic Church, just like they duped people before about indulgences? This is a topic I suggest we explore on our own and allow Ruach Ha Qadash (the Holy Spirit) to lead us to an answer.

This next question will touch many nerves because it is an emotional one.

Is the belief that people go to heaven (or hell) after they die biblical?

What does the Bible say about resurrection and final judgment? The Bible seems to say the ultimate destination, (1) heaven (new creation/New Yarushlayim) or (2) the lake of fire, is determined at the final judgment. That all who have departed from us have 'slept' as the Bible calls the death of the body (the first death) until they are raised at the sound of His Voice (the trumpet) for a one-off event of judgement that will determine each person's final destination.

- But I would not have you to be ignorant, brethren, **concerning them which are asleep,** that ye sorrow not, even as others which have no hope. [14] For if we believe that YAHUSHA died and rose again, **even so them also which sleep in YAHUSHA** will YAHUAH bring with Him. [15] For this we say unto you by the word of YAHUSHA, that we which are alive and remain unto the coming of

YAHUSHA shall not prevent **them which are asleep. [16] For YAHUSHA Himself shall descend from heaven with a shout, with the voice of the archangel, and with the trump of YAHUAH: and the dead in MASHYACH shall rise first:** [17] then we which are alive and remain shall be caught up together with them in the clouds, to meet YAHUSHA in the air: and so shall we ever be with YAHUSHA. [18] Wherefore comfort one another with these words. (1 Thessalonians 4:13-18 KJV)

- Now if MASHYACH (Christ) be preached that He rose from the dead, how say some among you that there is no resurrection of the dead? [13] But if there be no resurrection of the dead, then is MASHYACH not risen: [14] and if MASHYACH be not risen, then is our preaching vain, and your faith is also vain. [15] Yea, and we are found false witnesses of YAHUAH; because we have testified of YAHUAH that He raised up MASHYACH: whom He raised not up, if so be that the dead rise not. [16] For if the dead rise not, then is not MASHYACH raised: [17] and if MASHYACH be not raised, your faith is vain; ye are yet in your sins. [18] **Then they also which are fallen asleep in MASHYACH are perished.** [19] If in this life only we have hope in MASHYACH, we are of all men most miserable. [20] **But now is MASHYACH risen from the dead, and become the firstfruits of them that slept.** [21] For since by man came death, by man came also the resurrection of the dead. [22] For as in Adam all die, even so in MASHYACH shall all be made alive. [23] **But every man in his own order: MASHYACH the firstfruits; afterward they that are MASHYACH 's at his coming.** (1 Corinthians 15:12-23 KJV)

- *And many of them that sleep in the dust of the earth shall awake, some to everlasting life, and some to shame and everlasting contempt.* (Daniel 12:2 KJV)
- *Verily, verily, I say unto you, the hour is coming, and now is, when the dead shall hear the voice of the Son of YAHUAH: and they that hear shall live. [26] For as the Father hath life in Himself; so hath He given to the Son to have life in Himself; [27] and hath given Him authority to execute judgment also, because He is the Son of man. [28]* **Marvel not at this: for the hour is coming, in the which all that are in the graves shall hear His voice, [29] and shall come forth; they that have done good, unto the resurrection of life; and they that have done evil, unto the resurrection of damnation.** *(John 5:25-29 KJV)*
- *And I saw a great white throne, and him that sat on it, from whose face the earth and the heaven fled away; and there was found no place for them. [12] And I saw the dead, small and great, stand before YAHUAH; and the books were opened: and another book was opened, which is the book of life: and the dead were judged out of those things which were written in the books, according to their works. [13] And the sea gave up the dead which were in it; and death and hell delivered up the dead which were in them:* **and they were judged every man according to their works.** *[14] And death and hell were cast into the lake of fire. This is the second death. [15]* **And whosoever was not found written in the book of life was cast into the lake of fire.** *(Revelation 20:11-15 KJV)*

For clarification's sake, Strong's Concordance G86 for hell (also referred to as Hades) defines it as a common receptacle for disembodied spirits. Therefore, it is not a final destination which is why it (hell) is eventually cast into the lake of fire. The final destination for the wicked is the lake of fire and not hell.

I strongly believe that the final judgement will be undertaken according to the law of YAHUAH and not the standards of the doctrines of men. Those who have done good and those who have done bad according to the laws and commandments of YAHUAH, which are the standard of judgement.

Dear friends and family, the issue of the law and commandments is a serious one for us. I urge you to lay down all previous doctrine and just read the Bible for yourself and allow RUACH HA QADASH to teach you and lead you into all truth. It is too big a price to pay to outsource the directions to one's final destination to the teaching of the doctrines of a religious institution or preacher (or even a book writer like me).

Since the Bible gives a clear indication of a single day of judgement that takes place at the end, what happens when people 'sleep' as referencing the first death? The traditional 66 books of the Bible do not reveal much on this, but the apocryphal book of 2 Esdras, chapter 7:74-105, does. This specific passage, which has been retained in the Ethiopian Bible, is called the 'missing fragment' and is included below for you to discern.

> o *For how long the time is that the Most High has been patient with those who inhabit the world, and not for their sake, but because of the times which he has foreordained!" [75]* ***I answered and said, "If I have found favor in thy sight, O YAHUAH, show this also to thy servant: whether***

after death, as soon as every one of us yields up his soul, we shall be kept in rest until those times come when thou wilt renew the creation, or whether we shall be tormented at once?" [76] He answered me and said, "I will show you that also, but do not be associated with those who have shown scorn, nor number yourself among those who are tormented. [77] For you have a treasure of works laid up with the Most High; but it will not be shown to you until the last times. [78] **Now, concerning death, the teaching is: When the decisive decree has gone forth from the Most High that a man shall die, as the spirit leaves the body to return again to him who gave it, first of all it adores the glory of the Most High. [79] And if it is one of those who have shown scorn and have not kept the way of the Most High, and who have despised his law, and who have hated those who fear YAHUAH** -- [80] such spirits shall not enter into habitations, but shall immediately wander about in torments, ever grieving and sad, in seven ways. [81] The first way, because they have scorned the law of the Most High. [82] The second way, because they cannot now make a good repentance that they may live. [83] The third way, they shall see the reward laid up for those who have trusted the covenants of the Most High. [84] The fourth way, they shall consider the torment laid up for themselves in the last days. [85] The fifth way, they shall see how the habitations of the others are guarded by angels in profound quiet. [86] The sixth way, they shall see how some of them will pass over into torments. [87] The seventh way, which is worse than all the ways that have been mentioned, because they shall utterly waste away in confusion and be consumed with shame, and shall wither *with fear at seeing the glory of the Most High before whom they sinned while they were alive, and before whom they are to be judged in the last times. [88]* **"Now this is the order of those who have kept the ways of the Most High, when they shall be separated from their mortal body.** *[89] During the time that they lived in it, they laboriously served the Most High, and withstood danger every hour, that they might keep the law of the Lawgiver perfectly. [90] Therefore this is the teaching concerning them:[91] First of all, they shall see with great joy the glory of him who receives them, for they shall have rest in seven orders. [92] The first order, because they have striven with great effort to overcome the evil thought which was formed with them, that it might not lead them astray from life into death. [93] The second order, because they see the perplexity in which the souls of the ungodly wander, and the punishment that awaits them. [94] The third order, they see the witness which he who formed them bears concerning them, that while they were alive they kept the law which was given them in trust. [95] The fourth order, they understand the rest which they now enjoy, being gathered into their chambers and guarded by angels in profound quiet, and the glory which awaits them in the last days. [96] The fifth order, they rejoice that they have now escaped what is corruptible, and shall inherit what is to come; and besides they see the straits and toil from which they have been delivered, and the spacious liberty which they are to receive and enjoy in immortality. [97] The sixth order, when it is shown to them how their face is to shine like the sun, and how they are to be made like the light of the stars, being incorruptible from then on. [98] The seventh order, which is greater than all that have been mentioned,* *because they shall rejoice with boldness, and shall be confident without confusion, and shall be glad without fear, for they hasten to behold the face of him whom they served in life and from whom they are to receive their reward when glorified. [99] This is the order of the souls of the righteous, as henceforth is announced; and the aforesaid are the ways of torment which those who would not give heed shall suffer hereafter." [100] I answered and said, "Will time therefore be given to the souls, after they have been separated from the bodies, to see what you have described to me?" [101] He said to me, "They shall have freedom for seven days, so that during these seven days they may see the things of which you have been told, and afterwards they shall be gathered in their habitations."[102] I answered and said, "If I have found favor in thy sight, show further to me, thy servant, whether on the day of judgment the righteous will be able to intercede for the ungodly or to entreat the Most High for them, [103] fathers for sons or sons for parents, brothers for brothers, relatives for their kinsmen, or friends for those who are most dear." [104] He answered me and said, "Since you have found favor in my sight, I will show you this also. The day of judgment is decisive and displays to all the seal of truth. Just as now a father does not send his son, or a son his father, or a master his servant, or a friend his dearest friend, to be ill or sleep or eat or be healed in his stead, [105] so no one shall ever pray for another on that day, neither shall any one lay a burden on another; for then every one shall bear his own righteousness and unrighteousness." (2 Esdras 7:74-105 RSVA)*

After reading this passage, which reveals the period from 'sleeping' to the day of final judgement, one can better understand the story of Lazarus, as it was a scene from this intermediary period.

- *There was a certain rich man, which was clothed in purple and fine linen, and fared sumptuously every day: [20] and there was a certain beggar named Lazarus, which was laid at his gate, full of sores, [21] and desiring to be fed with the crumbs which fell from the rich man's table: moreover the dogs came and licked his sores. [22]* **And it came to pass, that the beggar died, and was carried by the angels into Abraham's bosom: the rich man also died, and was buried; [23] and in hell he lift up his eyes, being in torments, and seeth Abraham afar off, and Lazarus in his bosom.** *[24] And he cried and said, Father Abraham, have mercy on me, and send Lazarus, that he may dip the tip of his finger in water, and cool my tongue; for I am tormented in this flame. [25] But Abraham said, Son, remember that thou in thy lifetime receivedst thy good things, and likewise Lazarus evil things: but now he is comforted, and thou art tormented. [26]* **And beside all this, between us and you there is a great gulf fixed: so that they which would pass from hence to you cannot; neither can they pass to us, that would come from thence.** *[27] Then he said, I pray thee therefore, father, that thou wouldest send him to my father's house: [28] for I have five brethren; that he may testify unto them, lest they also come into this place of torment. [29] Abraham saith unto him, They have Moses and the prophets; let them hear them. [30] And he said, Nay, father Abraham: but if one went unto them from the dead, they will repent. [31]* **And he said unto him, If they hear not Moses and the prophets, neither will they be**

persuaded, though one rose from the dead.
(Luke 16:19-31 KJV)

Great Day of YAHUAH's judgement

It is important to recognise there is an appointed day of final judgement, where the Judge (YAHUAH), will judge all things according to the law He established as the Lawgiver. The passage in 2 Esdras 7:74-105 shows what happens during the period between 'sleeping' and the final day of judgement. As it is written:

- *Let us hear the conclusion of the whole matter: Fear YAH, and keep his commandments: for this is the whole duty of man. [14]* **For YAHUAH shall bring every work into judgment,** *with every secret thing, whether it be good, or whether it be evil. (Ecclesiastes 12:13-14 KJV)*
- **For we must all appear before the judgment seat of Christ** *(MASHYACH); that every one may receive the things done in his body, according to that he hath done, whether it be good or bad. (2 Corinthians 5:10 KJV)*
- **So then every one of us shall give account of himself to YAHUAH.** *(Romans 14:12 KJV)*
- *And I saw a great white throne, and him that sat on it, from whose face the earth and the heaven fled away; and there was found no place for them. [12] And I saw the dead, small and great, stand before YAHUAH; and the books were opened: and another book was opened, which is the book of life:* **and the dead were judged out of those things which were written in the books, according to their works.** *[13] And the sea gave up the dead which were in it; and death and hell delivered up the dead which were in them: and* **they were judged every man according to their works.** *(Revelation 20:11-13 KJV)*

As it is written, judgement is being made according to the works they have done as per the law given by the Lawgiver and Judge (Isaiah 33:22). This judgement will determine the ultimate destination for each person – either the lake of fire or the New Yarushalayim.

Who enters into the New Yarushalayim (Jerusalem)?

The latter chapters of the book of Revelation describe those who end up in the lake of fire and those who enter into the New Yarushalayim. It is therefore critical to get YAHUAH's definition of these descriptive words and not rely on man-made definitions.

- *But the **fearful, and unbelieving, and the abominable, and murderers, and whoremongers, and sorcerers, and idolaters, and all liars, shall have their part in the lake which burneth with fire and brimstone:** which is the second death. (Revelation 21:8 KJV)*
- *Blessed are those who wash their robes, so that they may have the right to the tree of life and that they may enter the city by the gates. [15] **Outside are the dogs and sorcerers and the sexually immoral and murderers and idolaters, and everyone who loves and practices falsehood (a lie).** (Revelation 22:14-15 ESV)*

Liars will not enter. One of the biblical definitions of a liar we have already covered is according to what is written:

- *He that saith, I know him, and **keepeth not his commandments,** is a liar, and the truth is not in him. (1 John 2:4)*

Unbelievers will not enter. An unbeliever does not believe in the truth, and again we have already summarised the following: Truth = the Law = the Commandments = the Word = YAHUSHA

Liars and unbelievers practice falsehood (a lie), which is what comes from the father of lies.

YAHUAH never intended for the lake of fire to be a destination for His people. He established it as a destination for Satan and his servants, but all who rebel against YAHUAH will end up there because rebellion against YAHUAH means we opt in (knowingly or unknowingly) to become part of Satan's servants.

The scriptures show us the sequence of entrance into the lake of fire, as it is written:

- And **the beast was captured, and with it the false prophet** who in its presence had done the signs by which he deceived those who had received the mark of the beast and those who worshiped its image. **These two were thrown alive into the lake of fire that burns with sulfur.** *(Revelation 19:20 ESV)*
- and **the devil who had deceived them was thrown into the lake of fire and sulfur** where the beast and the false prophet were, and they will be tormented day and night forever and ever. *(Revelation 20:10 ESV)*
- Then **Death and Hades were thrown into the lake of fire.** This is the second death, the lake of fire. [15] And if anyone's name was not found written in the book of life, he was thrown into the lake of fire. *(Revelation 20:14-15 ESV)*
- But as **for the cowardly, the faithless, the detestable, as for murderers, the sexually immoral, sorcerers, idolaters, and all liars, their portion will be in the lake that burns with fire and sulfur, which is the second death."** *(Revelation 21:8 ESV)*

The beast and false prophet will enter first, followed by the devil

(Satan), followed next by death and Hades, and finally, people who have remained in rebellion to YAHUAH.

It is not YAHUAH's will that any should perish. But our choice.

Let us also look at what scripture says about who enters into the New Yarushalayim.

Scriptures give us a glimpse into this through the description of the (1) set apart ones, (2) the remnant, (3) the victorious ones and (4) the entrance into the 'New Yarushalayim (Jerusalem)'

I will leave you with these 4 scriptures. The first 3 define what the prerequisites of qualifying as a 'set apart one', as a 'remnant' and 'the victorious ones' as per the definitions given by the FATHER, and the 4th scripture speaks of the names written on the entrance gates to the 'New Yarushalayim (Jerusalem)'. I have highlighted the key words to ponder, and why all that has been covered so far is important, and yet sadly largely missed in the teachings that come out of the religion of Christianity.

> o *Here is the endurance of the set-apart ones, here are those **guarding the commands (TORAH) of YAHUAH and the belief of** הושע **YAHUSHA**. (Revelation 14:12 TS2009)*

So, the 2 prerequisites for being a 'set apart one' are (1) Guarding Torah (Law and Commandments) + (2) Belief in the Messiah YAHUSHA. So, if we don't meet both, we do not qualify to be given the title of being 'set apart'. If we have belief in YAHUSHA but deny His Law and Commandments (Torah), we don't qualify. If we guard the Torah but do not have belief in YAHUSHA, we don't qualify.

> o *And the dragon was enraged with the woman, and he went to fight with the remnant of her seed, those guarding*

the commands (TORAH) of YAHUAH and possessing the witness of הושע YAHUSHA MASHYACH (Messiah/Christ). (Revelation 12:17 TS2009)

So again, the 2 prerequisites for being 'the remnant' are **(1) Guarding Torah (Law and Commandments) + (2) Possessing the witness of YAHUSHA.** Therefore, if we do not meet both, we don't qualify to be given the title of 'a remnant'. If we possess the witness of YAHUSHA but deny Torah (His law, commandments, instructions), we don't qualify. If we guard the Torah but do not possess witness of YAHUSHA MASHYACH, we equally don't qualify.

- *Then I saw another sign in heaven, great and marvelous: seven angels having the seven last plagues, for in them the wrath of YAHUAH is complete. [2] And I saw something like a sea of glass mingled with fire, and those who have the victory over the beast, over his image and over his mark and over the number of his name, standing on the sea of glass, having harps of YAHUAH. [3] They **sing the song of Moses**, the servant of YAHUAH, **and the song of the Lamb**, saying: "Great and marvelous are Your works, YAHUAH Almighty! Just and true are Your ways, O King of the saints! (Revelation 15:1-3 NKJV)*

Interestingly, the overcomers, who have victory over the beast, are singing two songs – **one is the song of Moses (which I believe refers to their testimony of following TORAH, which are the instructions YAHUAH gave through Moses), the other is the song of the Lamb (which refers to their belief and testimony in YAHUSHA MASHYACH).** So again, Torah (the Law and Commandments of YAHUAH) and YAHUSHA MASHYACH go together.

o *And he carried me away in the Spirit to a great and high mountain, and showed me the great city, the holy Yarushalayim (Jerusalem), descending out of heaven from YAHUAH, [11] having the glory of Alahym. Her light was like a most precious stone, like a jasper stone, clear as crystal. [12]* ***Also she had a great and high wall with twelve gates, and twelve angels at the gates, and names written on them, which are the names of the twelve tribes of the children of YASHARA'AL:*** *[13] three gates on the east, three gates on the north, three gates on the south, and three gates on the west. (Revelation 21:10-13 NKJV)*

Entrance into our final destination (New Yarushalayim (Jerusalem)) is through the 12 gates that have the names of the 12 tribes of the House of Jacob (YASHARA'AL). This has already been covered.

The highway of Holiness that leads people to the 'New Yarushalayim (Jerusalem)'

Tribes of Africa, I believe that YAHUAH is aligning Africa with its divine assignment to trumpet the 'Good News of the Kingdom of YAHUAH' which has not yet been heard, and to shine the light that will give the nations the directions to find the path leading to the 'New Yarushalayim (Jerusalem)'.

o *For many will come in My name, saying, 'I am the Christ,' and will deceive many. [6] And you will hear of wars and rumors of wars. See that you are not troubled; for all these things must come to pass, but the end is not yet. [7] For nation will rise against nation, and kingdom against kingdom. And there will be famines, pestilences, and earthquakes in various places. [8] All these are the*

> beginning of sorrows. [9] "Then they will deliver you up to tribulation and kill you, and you will be hated by all nations for My name's sake. [10] And then many will be offended, will betray one another, and will hate one another. [11] **Then many false prophets will rise up and deceive many. [12] And because lawlessness will abound, the love of many will grow cold. [13] But he who endures to the end shall be saved.** [14] And this gospel of the kingdom will be preached in all the world as a witness to all the nations, and then the end will come. (Matthew 24:5-14 NKJV)
>
> - Then the eleven disciples went away into Galilee, to the mountain which YAHUSHA had appointed for them. [17] When they saw Him, they worshiped Him; but some doubted. [18] And YAHUSHA came and spoke to them, saying, **"All authority has been given to Me in heaven and on earth. Go therefore and make disciples of all the nations, baptizing them in the name of the Father and of the Son and of the Holy Spirit, [20] teaching them to observe all things that I have commanded you; and lo, I am with you always, even to the end of the age."** Amen. (Matthew 28:16-20 NKJV)

The Highway of Holiness is being established as it is written:

> - In that day there will be an altar to YAHUAH in the midst of the land of Egypt, and a pillar to YAHUAH at its border. [20] And it will be for a sign and for a witness to YAHUAH of hosts in the land of Egypt; for they will cry to YAHUAH because of the oppressors, and He will send them a Savior and a Mighty One, and He will deliver

them. *[21] Then YAHUAH will be known to Egypt, and the Egyptians will know YAHUAH in that day, and will make sacrifice and offering; yes, they will make a vow to YAHUAH and perform it. [22] And YAHUAH will strike Egypt, He will strike and heal it; they will return to YAHUAH, and He will be entreated by them and heal them. [23] **In that day there will be a highway from Egypt to Assyria, and the Assyrian will come into Egypt and the Egyptian into Assyria, and the Egyptians will serve with the Assyrians. [24] In that day YASHARA'AL will be one of three with Egypt and Assyria—a blessing in the midst of the land, [25] whom YAHUAH of hosts shall bless, saying, "Blessed is Egypt My people, and Assyria the work of My hands, and YASHARA'AL My inheritance."** *(Isaiah 19:19-25 NKJV)*

- ***A highway shall be there, and a road, and it shall be called the Highway of Holiness. The unclean shall not pass over it, but it shall be for others. Whoever walks the road, although a fool, shall not go astray.** [9] No lion shall be there, nor shall any ravenous beast go up on it; It shall not be found there. But the redeemed shall walk there, [10] And the ransomed of YAHUAH shall return, and come to Zion with singing, With everlasting joy on their heads. They shall obtain joy and gladness, and sorrow and sighing shall flee away. (Isaiah 35:8-10 NKJV)*

🔥 **Tribes of Africa,** the highway of holiness to true ZION is being established, and we are pivotal to it. A highway that leads to the NEW YARUSHALAYIM.

THE PATH TO 'HEAVEN' OR THE NEW YERUSHALAYIM (JERUSALEM)

I will quote the words of one of the 'Negro spirituals' called OH! WHAT A BEAUTIFUL CITY

Oh! What a beautiful city! Oh! What a beautiful city! Oh! What a beautiful city!

Twelve gates to the city. Hallelu!

Three gates in a de east, Three gates in a de west, Three gates in a de north, Three gates in de a south. Making it twelve gates to de city. Hallelu!

My Lord built a dat city, Said it was just a fo square, Wanted all a you sinners, to meet Him in a de air,' Cause He built twelve gates a to city. Hallelu!

Who are all a those children, all dressed up in white? They must be the children of the Israelites cause He built twelve gates a to city. Hallelu!

Who are all those children all dressed up in red? They must be the children that Moses led. The Lord built twelve gates a to city, Hallelu!

When I get to heaven I'm gonna sing an shout, Ain't nobody up there Gonna take me out, 'Cause **He built twelve gates a to city. Hallelu!**

The tribes of Judah, Benjamin and Levi, who were carried in slave ships, knew the ultimate destination that YAHUAH had prepared for them even as they were in captivity and continue to be so today.

CHAPTER SEVENTEEN

A Call to Holiness

The Flow of Ruach Ha Qadash (the Holy Spirit)

YAHUAH has called for Holiness upon the tribes of YASHARA'AL.

Holiness means to be set apart, to be dedicated, to give of oneself completely to YAHUAH.

It is through a Holy vessel that the Holy Spirit can flow into the earth. It is into Holy vessels that the breath of YAHUAH can enter the dry bones to awaken them.

As it is written:

> o *Also He said to me,* **"Prophesy to the breath, prophesy, son of man, and say to the breath, 'Thus says YAHUAH Aluah: "Come from the four winds, O breath, and breathe on these slain, that they may live."** [10] **So I prophesied as He commanded me, and breath came into them, and they lived, and stood upon their feet, an exceedingly great army.** [11] *Then He said to me,* **"Son of man, these bones are the whole house of YASHARA'AL.**

> *They indeed say, 'Our bones are dry, our hope is lost, and we ourselves are cut off!' (Ezekiel 37:9-11)*

Will Ruach Ha Qadash - the Holy Spirit - the Set Apart Spirit - the Clean Spirit flow through an unholy and unclean body or vessel?

YAHUAH defines and establishes the standard of what He considers clean and what is not. YAHUAH defines and establishes the standard of what is Holy and what is unholy (profane). No man, no institution can establish a different definition or standard lest we fall into the same sin as Satan, who tried to elevate himself above The Most High (Isaiah 14:12-14) by seeking to establish his standard above that of The Most High.

As it is written:

- o *"How you are fallen from heaven, O Lucifer, son of the morning! How you are cut down to the ground, you who weakened the nations! [13]* **For you have said in your heart: 'I will ascend into heaven, I will exalt my throne above the stars of Alahym; I will also sit on the mount of the congregation on the farthest sides of the north; [14] I will ascend above the heights of the clouds, I will be like the Most High.'** *(Isaiah 14:12-14 NKJV)*

- o *'He shall speak pompous words against the Most High, shall persecute the saints of the Most High, and shall intend to change times and law. Then the saints shall be given into his hand for a time and times and half a time,' (Daniel 25:7)*

YAHUAH defines and establishes the standard - not man!!!!

In the Torah, in His Word, YAHUAH speaks about His definition and standard of what He considers (1) CLEAN and what He considers (2) HOLY.

Leviticus chapter 11 is an example, as it is written:

- *For I am YAHUAH your Aluah. You shall therefore consecrate yourselves, and you shall be holy; for I am holy. Neither shall you defile yourselves with any creeping thing that creeps on the earth. [45] For I am YAHUAH who brings you up out of the land of Egypt, to be your Aluah.* **You shall therefore be holy, for I am holy.** *(Leviticus 11:44-45 NKJV)*

YAHUAH speaks quite a lot to the prophet Ezekiel (YACHAZQEL) about this.

- *And the word of YAHUAH came to me, saying, [24] "Son of man, say to her, 'You are a land that is not cleansed or rained upon in the day of displeasure.' [25] "There is a conspiracy of her prophets in her midst, like a roaring lion tearing the prey. They have devoured life, they have taken wealth and precious matters, they have made many widows in her midst. [26]* **"Her priests have done violence to My teaching and they profane My set-apart matters. They have not distinguished between the set-apart (Holy) and profane, nor have they made known the difference between the unclean and the clean. And they have hidden their eyes from My Sabbaths, and I am profaned in their midst.** *[27] "Her leaders in her midst are like wolves tearing the prey, to shed blood, to destroy lives, and to get greedy gain. [28] "And her prophets have coated them with whitewash, seeing a false vision, and divining a lie for them, saying, 'Thus said the Master YAHUAH when YAHUAH had not spoken. [29] "The people of the land have practised oppression, and committed robbery, and have wronged the poor and needy. And they oppressed the stranger without right-ruling. [30] "And I sought for a man among them who would make a wall, and stand in the breach before Me on behalf of the land, that I should not* *destroy it – but I did not find one! [31] "Therefore I have poured out My displeasure on them, I have consumed them with the fire of My wrath. And I have put their way on their own head," declares YAHUAH. (Yahazqěl (Ezekiel) 22:23-31 TS2009)*

- **The priests shall teach My people the difference between the holy and the common or profane, and cause them to distinguish between the unclean and the clean.** *(Ezekiel 44:23 AMPC)*

Will The Most High YAHUAH's RUACH HA QADASH, His breath, His set Apart Spirit, His Holy Spirit flow through an unclean and unholy vessel or body or institution?

Could it be that one of SATAN's major strategies has been to deceive the body of MASHYACH into rejecting YAHUAH's standard of *Cleanliness and Holiness*, thereby hindering the flow of His Set-Apart Spirit from His throne to the earth? This deception leads the body of MASHYACH into defilement, so that despite professing YAHUSHA as Master, there is a falling short of YAHUAH's standard and qualification to serve as vessels through whom His RUACH can flow. In this way, the father of lies has defiled the temple, rendering it unclean – a desecration of the very dwelling place where the Ruach Ha Qadash is meant to abide, the sacred temple where the Holy One, who resides in the Holy of Holies, is to dwell. Is the scripture in Matthew 24:15 speaking about the desecration of a physical temple built by man, or is it speaking about the 'abomination of desolation' in the temple built by The Most High - the human body which He has designated as His dwelling place? Is it possible that this scripture of the desecration is being fulfilled through a lawless body that claims to be the body/temple of HA MASHYACH (The Christ) and yet is unclean and profane?

- *And YAHUSHA answered and said to them: "Take heed*

that no one deceives you. *[5]* **For many will come in My name, saying, 'I am HA MASHYACH (The Christ),' and will deceive many.** *[6] And you will hear of wars and rumors of wars. See that you are not troubled; for all these things must come to pass, but the end is not yet. [7] For nation will rise against nation, and kingdom against kingdom. And there will be famines, pestilences, and earthquakes in various places. [8] All these are the beginning of sorrows. [9] "Then they will deliver you up to tribulation and kill you, and you will be hated by all nations for My name's sake. [10] And then many will be offended, will betray one another, and will hate one another. [11] Then many false prophets will rise up and deceive many. [12] And because lawlessness will abound, the love of many will grow cold. [13] But he who endures to the end shall be saved. [14] And this gospel of the kingdom will be preached in all the world as a witness to all the nations, and then the end will come.* *[15]* **"Therefore when you see the 'abomination of desolation,' spoken of by Daniel the prophet, standing in the holy place"** *(whoever reads, let him understand), (Matthew 24:4-15 NKJV)*

In 167 BCE, Antiochus IV (Epiphanes) captured Yarushalayim (Jerusalem) and desecrated the temple by slaughtering and offering the sacrifice of the pig (swine) to Zeus upon the altar.

Is this exactly what is happening today in the temple (temples) that are not made with human hands?

For we are the temple of YAHUAH, the Holy of Holies not made by human hands.

- **Do you not know that you are the temple of YAHUAH and that the Spirit of YAHUAH dwells in you?** *If anyone defiles the temple of YAHUAH, YAHUAH will destroy him.*

> *For the temple of YAHUAH is holy, which temple you are.* (I Corinthians 3:16-17 NKJV)

- **Or do you not know that your body is the temple of the Holy Spirit who is in you, whom you have from YAHUAH, and you are not your own? For you were bought at a price; therefore, glorify YAHUAH in your body and in your spirit, which are YAHUAH's.** (I Corinthians 6:19-20 NKJV)
- "However, **the Most High does not dwell in temples made with hands**, as the prophet says: [49] 'Heaven is My throne, and earth is My footstool. What house will you build for Me? says YAHUAH, or what is the place of My rest? [50] Has My hand not made all these things?' (Acts 7:48-50 NKJV)

Is it possible that a lot of what we have seen flowing through the church is counterfeit Holy Spirit? Could it be unclean spirits flowing through an unclean vessel and body that has rejected YAHUAH's standard and definition of what He accepts as being 'Holy and Clean'? Is it possible that we have seen very little movement of RUACH HA QADASH, which comes from YAHUAH, the ALAHYM of Abraham, Isaac and Jacob? Is it possible that a lot of prophecy today (prophetic and apostolic ministry) flowing through churches and ministries who reject His covenant (marriage agreement) and His Torah (constitution of His Kingdom) and His standard and definition of what He accepts as 'Clean and Holy' is not Holy Spirit birthed and inspired but is rather an unclean spirit of the flesh of man claiming to be led by the Set Apart Spirit?

Can Ruach Ha Qadash, the Holy Spirit, the Set Apart Spirit, the Clean Spirit flow through an unholy and unclean body or vessel or institution?

- *Beloved,* ***do not believe every spirit, but test the spirits,*** *whether they are of YAHUAH; because many false prophets have gone out into the world. (I John 4:1 NKJV)*

Not easy things to ponder and consider, but we must, for we can no longer afford to be deceived.

We are people who have been destroyed for lack of knowledge for too long.

- ***My people are destroyed for lack of knowledge. Because you have rejected knowledge, I also will reject you from being priest for Me; Because you have forgotten the law of your ALAHYM, I also will forget your children.** [7] "The more they increased, the more they sinned against Me; I will change their glory into shame. [8] They eat up the sin of My people; They set their heart on their iniquity. [9] And it shall be: like people, like priest. So I will punish them for their ways, and reward them for their deeds. [10] For they shall eat, but not have enough; They shall commit harlotry, but not increase, **Because they have ceased obeying YAHUAH**. (Hosea 4:6-10 NKJV)*
- ***So then, brethren, we are debtors, but not to the flesh [we are not obligated to our carnal nature], to live [a life ruled by the standards set up by the dictates] of the flesh.** For if you live according to [the dictates of] the flesh, you will surely die. But if through the power of the [Holy] Spirit you are [habitually] putting to death (making extinct, deadening) the [evil] deeds prompted by the body, you shall [really and genuinely] live forever. [14] **For all who are led by the Spirit of YAHUAH are sons of YAHUAH**. (Romans 8:12-14 AMPC)*

RUACH HA QADASH will lead us into all truth.

The truth shall set us free.

The Way of YASHARA'AL is not a religion; it is a birthright. A birthright that others can come into by adoption. It is a birthright initially given to the people of the bloodline of Jacob (12 sons) who were called to separation (Holiness) as the firstborn of YAHUAH, and that through them other tongues, tribes and nations would be adopted into the family.

The religion of Christianity is not part of the natural-born identity, culture and customs of this birthright.

- *Thus says YAHUAH: "Keep justice, and do righteousness, for soon my salvation will come, and my righteousness be revealed. [2] Blessed is the man who does this, and the son of man who holds it fast,* **who keeps the Sabbath, not profaning it, and keeps his hand from doing any evil.**" *[3] Let not the foreigner who has joined himself to YAHUSHA say, "YAHUSHA will surely separate me from his people"; and let not the eunuch say, "Behold, I am a dry tree." [4] For thus says YAHUAH: "To the eunuchs* **who keep my Sabbaths, who choose the things that please me and hold fast my covenant, [5] I will give in my house and within my walls a monument and a name better than sons and daughters; I will give them an everlasting name that shall not be cut off.** *[6] "And* **the foreigners who join themselves to YAHUSHA, to minister to Him, to love the name of YAHUAH, and to be His servants, everyone who keeps the Sabbath and does not profane it, and holds fast My covenant— [7] these I will bring to my holy mountain, and make them joyful in my house of prayer; their burnt offerings and their sacrifices will be accepted on my altar; for My house shall be called a house of prayer for all peoples.**" *[8] YAHUAH, who gathers the outcasts of Israel, declares, "I will gather yet others to him besides those already* *gathered." (Isaiah 56:1-8 ESV)*

Tribes of Africa, we must intentionally choose a set-part life so that we can be vessels of honour that can be commissioned by YAHUAH for the task of rebuilding Africa.

- *But in a great house there are not only vessels of gold and silver, but also of wood and clay, some for honor and some for dishonor. [21]* ***Therefore if anyone cleanses himself from the latter, he will be a vessel for honor, sanctified and useful for the Master, prepared for every good work.*** *[22] Flee also youthful lusts; but pursue righteousness, faith, love, peace with those who call on YAHUSHA out of a pure heart. [23] But avoid foolish and ignorant disputes, knowing that they generate strife. [24] And a servant of YAHUSHA must not quarrel but be gentle to all, able to teach, patient, [25] in humility correcting those who are in opposition, if YAHUAH perhaps will grant them repentance, so that they may know the truth, [26] and that they may come to their senses and escape the snare of the devil, having been taken captive by him to do his will. (II Timothy 2:20-26 NKJV)*

Tribes of Africa, because YAHUAH is love, He exhorts us to love. The task that lies ahead cannot be accomplished without YAHUAH, and therefore, it cannot be accomplished without love.

Beloved, let us love one another, for love is of YAHUAH; and everyone who loves is born of YAHUAH and knows YAHUAH. [8] He who does not love does not know YAHUAH, ***for YAHUAH is love****. (I John 4:7-8 NKJV* **)**

CHAPTER EIGHTEEN

The Big Elephant In The Room Named Jew(ish) Israel

In Chapter 5, the topic of the political state of Israel was briefly mentioned, and the context established that when scripture speaks about Israel (YASHARA'AL), it is not referring to the political state which started to exist in 1948, but rather it is speaking about the bloodline descendants of Abraham, Isaac and Jacob.

The most recognised symbol of the political state of Israel is the hexagon they call the Star of David. Nowhere in the Holy Scriptures is a Star of David mentioned.

- *But ye have borne the tabernacle of your Moloch and Chiun your images,* **the star of your god, which ye made to yourselves.** *(Amos 5:26 KJV)*
- *Yea, ye took up the tabernacle of Moloch,* **and the star of your god Remphan, figures which ye made to worship them:** *and I will carry you away beyond Babylon. (Acts 7:43 KJV)*

Let's look at this issue again, which is such a 'huge elephant in the room' and yet a critical issue because it is central to understanding how the 'design' of YAHUAH works, especially as it relates to end-time prophecy and also events taking place in the world now and into the future. 'Connecting with true YASHARA'AL is central to the salvation plan of nations, culminating in who will enter through the 12 gates of the New Yarushalayim (Jerusalem), which will come down from heaven and become the everlasting dwelling, as already referenced. This is the ultimate promise which YAHUAH has made to His people. He desires that all walk on the path of blessing and life and hence find their way into the New Yarushalayim. It is His will that none should perish, but the reality is some will choose not to take the path of blessing and life through their choices and will end up on the path of the curse and death, whose destination is described as the 'lake of fire' as it is written in the book of Revelation. Therefore, we must search this one out deeply because we, our families and nations cannot afford to get this wrong and be on the wrong path.

- *And I saw the dead, small and great, standing before YAHUAH, and books were opened. And another book was opened, which is the Book of Life. And the dead were judged according to their works, by the things which were written in the books. [13] The sea gave up the dead who were in it, and Death and Hades delivered up the dead who were in them. And they were judged, each one according to his works. [14] Then Death and Hades were cast into the lake of fire. This is the second death. [15]* **And anyone not found written in the Book of Life was cast into the lake of fire.** *(Revelation 20:12-15 NKJV)*
- *And He said to me, "It is done! I am the Alpha and the Omega, the Beginning and the End. I will give of the*

fountain of the water of life freely to him who thirsts. [7] He who overcomes shall inherit all things, and I will be his Aluah and he shall be My son. [8] But the cowardly, unbelieving, abominable, murderers, sexually immoral, sorcerers, idolaters, and all liars **shall have their part in the lake which burns with fire and brimstone, which is the second death.***" (Revelation 21:6-8 NKJV)*

Let us reflect on modern day Jew(ish)ness through the lens of biblical truth

The Bible is very clear about how it determines bloodline lineage through the seed (sperm) of the Father (patriarchal), as is seen throughout the scriptures.

As is written concerning the 'House of YASHARA'AL' which was established through Abraham, Isaac and Jacob who birthed the 12 tribes.

- ***Now the sons of Jacob were twelve:*** *[23] the sons of Leah were* **Reuben**, *Jacob's firstborn, and* **Simeon, Levi, Judah, Issachar, and Zebulun**; *[24] the sons of Rachel were* **Joseph and Benjamin**; *[25] the sons of Bilhah, Rachel's maidservant, were* **Dan and Naphtali**; *[26] and the sons of Zilpah, Leah's maidservant, were* **Gad and Asher**. *These were the sons of Jacob who were born to him in Padan Aram. (Genesis 35:22b-26 NKJV)*

And the sons of Joseph, whom Jacob 'adopted' as his own, I believe as a foreshadowing of YAHUAH's plan for the Gentiles to be adopted into YASHARA'AL.

- *Then Jacob said to Joseph: "YAHUAH Almighty appeared to me at Luz in the land of Canaan and blessed me, [4] and said to me, 'Behold, I will make you fruitful and multiply you, and I will make of you a multitude of people, and give this land to your descendants after you as an everlasting possession.' [5]* **And now your two sons, Ephraim and Manasseh, who were born to you in the land of Egypt before I came to you in Egypt, are mine**; *as Reuben and Simeon, they shall be mine. (Genesis 48:3-5 NKJV)*

The lineage of YAHUSHA is shown to go through the male seed as further evidence of the patriarchal nature of biblical identity. This fulfilled every prophecy that YAHUSHA would come through the lineage of the tribe of Judah (YAHUDA) and be a descendant of David, for YAHUAH promised that a descendant of David would always sit on the throne of the House of YASHARA'AL.

- *The book of the genealogy of YAHUSHA MASHYACH, the Son of David, the Son of Abraham: [2] Abraham begot Isaac, Isaac begot Jacob, and Jacob begot Judah and his brothers. [3] Judah begot Perez and Zerah by Tamar, Perez begot Hezron, and Hezron begot Ram. [4] Ram begot Amminadab, Amminadab begot Nahshon, and Nahshon begot Salmon. [5] Salmon begot Boaz by Rahab, Boaz begot Obed by Ruth, Obed begot Jesse, [6] and Jesse begot David the king. David the king begot Solomon by her who had been the wife of Uriah. [7] Solomon begot Rehoboam, Rehoboam begot Abijah, and Abijah begot Asa. [8] Asa begot Jehoshaphat, Jehoshaphat begot Joram, and Joram begot Uzziah. [9] Uzziah begot Jotham, Jotham begot Ahaz, and Ahaz begot Hezekiah. [10] Hezekiah begot Manasseh, Manasseh begot Amon, and Amon begot Josiah. [11] Josiah begot Jeconiah and his brothers about the time they were carried away to Babylon. [12] And after they were brought to Babylon, Jeconiah begot Shealtiel, and Shealtiel begot Zerubbabel. [13] Zerubbabel begot Abiud, Abiud begot Eliakim, and Eliakim begot Azor. [14] Azor begot Zadok, Zadok begot Achim, and Achim begot Eliud. [15] Eliud begot Eleazar, Eleazar begot Matthan, and Matthan begot Jacob. [16]* **And Jacob begot Joseph the husband of Mary, of whom was born YAHUSHA who is called Christ (MASHYACH).** *[17] So all the generations from Abraham to David are fourteen generations, from David until the captivity in Babylon are fourteen generations, and from the captivity in Babylon until the MASHYACH (Christ) are fourteen generations. [18] Now the birth of YAHUSHA MASHYACH was as follows: After His mother Mary was betrothed to Joseph, before they came together, she was found with child of the Holy Spirit. [19] Then Joseph her husband, being a just man, and not wanting to make her a public example, was minded to put her away secretly. [20] But while he thought about these things, behold, an angel of YAHUAH appeared to him in a dream, saying,* **"Joseph, son of David, do not be afraid to take to you Mary your wife, for that which is conceived in her is of the Holy Spirit. [21] And she will bring forth a Son, and you shall call His name YAHUSHA (YAHUAH Saves), for He will save His people from their sins."** *(Matthew 1:1-21 NKJV)*

In the religion of Judaism, the qualification for Jewish identity and lineage is primarily through the mother (matrilineally) and conversion to the religion of Judaism. Both qualifications completely violate the bloodline identity and lineage based on the father.

This is extremely important to pay attention to concerning who the true biblical House of YASHARA'AL is according to YAHUAH's definition and registry of bloodline identity.

Matrilineal Jewish law refers to the traditional Jewish law (Halakha) principle that determines Jewish identity and lineage through the mother's line.

A simple search on Wikipedia will present this information:

The article about 'Matrilineality in Judaism' on Wikipedia states the following: "The State of Israel adheres to the Jewish law of matrilineal descent for matters which could affect Israeli family law."

In Jewish tradition, a person's Jewish status is determined by the following principles:

i. *Matrilineal descent:* A person is considered Jewish if their mother is Jewish, regardless of the father's Jewish status.
ii. *Matrilineal inheritance:* Jewish identity and lineage are passed down from mother to child.

Key implications of matrilineal Jewish law:

i. *Jewish identity:* A person born to a Jewish mother is considered Jewish, regardless of their father's Jewish status.
ii. *Conversion:* If a person's mother is not Jewish, they may still become Jewish through conversion, but this requires a formal conversion process.
iii. *Marriage:* In traditional Jewish law, a Jewish person may only marry another Jewish person or a convert to Judaism.
iv. *Inheritance:* Jewish lineage and inheritance are passed down through the maternal line.

It's worth noting that there are different interpretations and customs within Jewish communities regarding matrilineal descent. Some Jewish denominations, like Reform and Reconstructionist Judaism, have modified or abandoned traditional matrilineal descent rules.

However, in Orthodox and Conservative Jewish communities, the matrilineal principle remains a fundamental aspect of Jewish law and identity.

Ancient biblical reference to terms Judean or Jew

Ancient Bibles used the term «Judean» or «Jew» in a different context than we do today.

In ancient times, the term "Jew" (Greek: Ἰουδαῖος, I o u d a i o s) referred specifically to people from the region of Judea, which was a province in the Roman Empire. The term "Judean" is a more accurate translation of the Greek word Ἰουδαῖος, which referred to people from Judea, regardless of their ethnicity or religion.

The earliest known manuscripts of the New Testament, such as Codex Sinaiticus and Codex Vaticanus, use the term Ἰουδαῖος, (Ioudaios) to refer to people from Judea. The term "Jew" as we understand it today, referring to a specific ethnic or religious group, is a later development.

In 2007, the Greek scholar and theologian, Dr. Shaye Cohen, wrote an article titled "Ioudaios: Judean or Jew?" in which he argued that the term Ἰουδαῖος, (Ioudaios) in ancient Greek texts should be translated as "Judean" rather than "Jew".

In recent years, some Bible translations, such as the New Revised Standard Version (NRSV) and the Complete Jewish Bible (CJB), have begun to use the term "Judean" instead of "Jew" in certain passages to reflect the original meaning of the Greek text.

However, it's worth noting that the distinction between "Judean" and "Jew" is not always clear-cut, and different scholars and translators may have different opinions on the matter.

The term "Jewish" has a complex and evolving history. The word "Jewish" is derived from the Middle English word "Jew," which was used to refer to people from Judea.

The earliest known use of the term "Jewish" in English dates back to the 13th century. However, the concept of a distinct Jewish identity and the use of terms to describe it have a much longer history.

Here are some key milestones in the development of the term "Jewish":

- Ancient Greece and Rome: The Greek word "Ἰουδαῖος," (Ioudaios) and the Latin word "Iudaeus" were used to refer to people from Judea.
- 1st century CE: The Jewish historian Flavius Josephus used the term "Ἰουδαῖος" (Ioudaios) to describe the Jewish people.
- 4th century CE: The Latin word "Iudaeus" was used in Christian texts to refer to the Jewish people.
- 13th century CE: The Middle English word "Jew" emerged, and the term "Jewish" began to be used to describe the Jewish people, their culture, and their religion.
- 16th century CE: The term "Jewish" became more widely used in English, particularly in the context of the Protestant Reformation.

It's worth noting that the concept of Jewish identity has evolved, and different terms have been used to describe the Jewish people throughout history.

The term "Jewish" is not an ancient Israelite term

THE BIG ELEPHANT IN THE ROOM NAMED JEW(ISH) ISRAEL

This is an extract from Wikipedia:

In fact, the concept of a distinct "Jewish" identity as we understand it today did not exist in ancient Israel.

In ancient Israel, people were identified as "Israelites" or "Hebrews," which referred to their ethnic and national identity. The term "Israelite" (Hebrew: ישראלי, Yisraeli) referred to a member of the tribes of Israel, while "Hebrew" (Hebrew: עברי, Ivri) referred to the language and culture of the ancient Israelites.

The term "Jew" (Hebrew: יהודי, Yehudi) originated in the Persian period (539-332 BCE), when the Persian Empire conquered the Babylonians and allowed the Israelites to return to Yarushalayim (Jerusalem). The term "Yehudi" referred specifically to the people from the province of Yehud (Judea), which was one of the provinces of the Persian Empire.

Over time, the term "Jew" (Yehudi) came to be used to refer to all people who practised the religion of the Israelites, regardless of their geographic location or ethnic background. However, the concept of a distinct "Jewish" identity as we understand it today, with its own set of traditions, customs, and practices, developed much later, during the Hellenistic and Roman periods (332 BCE-636 CE).

In summary, while the term "Jew" (Yehudi) has ancient roots, the concept of a distinct "Jewish" identity is a more recent development, and the term "Jewish" is not an ancient Israelite term.

It is worthwhile remembering that the letter J is a recent addition to the alphabet, being introduced in 1524.

Ashkenazi Jews

The biggest and most well-known group of 'Jews' today are Ashkenazi Jews.

Ashkenazi refers to a group of Jewish people whose ancestors lived primarily in Central and Eastern Europe, particularly in the Rhineland (western Germany) and later migrated to other parts of Europe, like Poland and Russia. They are one of the two major ancestral groups within Judaism, the other being Sephardic Jews. Most of the world's Jewish population today identifies as Ashkenazi, and they have a distinct cultural identity, including the Yiddish language, according to Chabad and unique traditions.

Here's a more detailed breakdown:

- Historical Origins: Ashkenazi Jews emerged as a distinct cultural group in the 10th century in the Rhineland.
- Migration Patterns: They migrated from the Rhineland into Central and Eastern Europe, and eventually to other parts of the world.
- Cultural Identity: Ashkenazi Jews have a unique cultural identity that includes the Yiddish language, specific religious practices, and traditions.
- Global Distribution: Today, Ashkenazi Jews are concentrated in the United States, Israel, the UK, and other parts of the world, making up a significant portion of the Jewish population.

A search in the scriptures reveals who ASHKENAZI is, as is listed in the 'table of nation' lineages from Noah, as it is written in Genesis 10:1-31:

*[1] Now this is the genealogy of the sons of **Noah: Shem, Ham, and***

Japheth*. And sons were born to them after the flood.*

Sons of Japheth

[2] **The sons of Japheth were Gomer, Magog, Madai, Javan, Tubal, Meshech, and Tiras. [3] The sons of Gomer were ASHKENAZ, Riphath, and Togarmah**. *[4] The sons of Javan were Elishah, Tarshish, Kittim, and Dodanim. [5] From these the coastland peoples of the Gentiles were separated into their lands, everyone according to his language, according to their families, into their nations.*

Sons of Ham

[6] The sons of Ham were Cush, Mizraim, Put, and Canaan. [7] The sons of Cush were Seba, Havilah, Sabtah, Raamah, and Sabtechah; and the sons of Raamah were Sheba and Dedan. [8] Cush begot Nimrod; he began to be a mighty one on the earth. [9] He was a mighty hunter before YAHUAH; therefore it is said, "Like Nimrod the mighty hunter before YAHUAH." [10] And the beginning of his kingdom was Babel, Erech, Accad, and Calneh, in the land of Shinar. [11] From that land he went to Assyria and built Nineveh, Rehoboth Ir, Calah, [12] and Resen between Nineveh and Calah (that is the principal city). [13] Mizraim begot Ludim, Anamim, Lehabim, Naphtuhim, [14] Pathrusim, and Casluhim (from whom came the Philistines and Caphtorim). [15] Canaan begot Sidon his firstborn, and Heth; [16] the Jebusite, the Amorite, and the Girgashite; [17] the Hivite, the Arkite, and the Sinite; [18] the Arvadite, the Zemarite, and the Hamathite. Afterward the families of the Canaanites were dispersed. [19] And the border of the Canaanites was from Sidon as you go toward Gerar, as far as Gaza; then as you go toward Sodom, Gomorrah, Admah, and Zeboiim, as far as Lasha. [20] These were the sons of Ham, according to their families, according to their languages, in their lands and in their nations.

Sons of Shem

[21] And children were born also to Shem, the father of all the children of Eber, the brother of Japheth the elder. [22] The sons of Shem were Elam, Asshur, Arphaxad, Lud, and Aram. [23] The sons of Aram were Uz, Hul, Gether, and Mash. [24] Arphaxad begot Salah, and Salah begot Eber. [25] To Eber were born two sons: the name of one was Peleg, for in his days the earth was divided; and his brother's name was Joktan. [26] Joktan begot Almodad, Sheleph, Hazarmaveth, Jerah, [27] Hadoram, Uzal, Diklah, [28] Obal, Abimael, Sheba, [29] Ophir, Havilah, and Jobab. All these were the sons of Joktan. [30] And their dwelling place was from Mesha as you go toward Sephar, the mountain of the east. [31] These were the sons of Shem, according to their families, according to their languages, in their lands, according to their nations.

Let us focus on the sons of Japheth.

- *[2]* **The sons of Japheth were Gomer,** *Magog, Madai, Javan, Tubal, Meshech, and Tiras. [3]* **The sons of Gomer were ASHKENAZ,** *Riphath, and Togarmah. [4] The sons of Javan were Elishah, Tarshish, Kittim, and Dodanim. [5]* **From these the coastland peoples of the Gentiles were separated into their lands,** *everyone according to his language, according to their families, into their nations.*

ASHKENAZ was the son of Gomer, who was the son of Japheth. The lineage of Japheth is also referred to as the 'coastland peoples of the Gentiles'

It is worthwhile to take note of this reference to 'Gentiles'.

Remember the words of YAHUSHA that there would come a time when Yarushalayim (Jerusalem) would be trampled underfoot by the Gentiles. YAHUSHA knew the genealogy of the peoples, and so He knew exactly who He was referring to.

> o *"But when you see Yarushalayim (Jerusalem) surrounded by armies, then know that its desolation is near. [21] Then let those who are in Judea flee to the mountains, let those who are in the midst of her depart, and let not those who are in the country enter her. [22] For these are the days of vengeance, that all things which are written may be fulfilled. [23] But woe to those who are pregnant and to those who are nursing babies in those days! For there will be great distress in the land and wrath upon this people. [24] And they will fall by the edge of the sword, and be led away captive into all nations.* **And Yarushalayim (Jerusalem) will be trampled by Gentiles until the times of the Gentiles are fulfilled**. (Luke 21:20-24 NKJV)

Ashkenaz is a Japhetite (descendant of Japheth) and not a Shemite (descendant of Shem).

The lineage of Japheth is referred to as the Gentiles.

YAHUAH's firstborn son, YASHARA'AL comes from the lineage of Shem. They are Shemites, which is where the term 'Semitic' is derived from.

Ashkenaz cannot claim to be a Shemite or Semitic (of the lineage of Shem).

Perhaps this makes the Revelation 2:9 and 3:9 statements of the 'Jews in name only' and 'those who say they are Jews but are not' take greater significance in understanding who Ashkenaz is.

> o *"I know your works, tribulation, and poverty (but you are rich); and* **I know the blasphemy of those who say they**

> *are Jews and are not, but are a synagogue of Satan. (Revelation 2:9 NKJV)*
> - *Indeed **I will make those of the synagogue of Satan, who say they are Jews and are not**, but lie—indeed I will make them come and worship before your feet, and to know that I have loved you. (Revelation 3:9 NKJV)*

Direct examples of conversions from Ashkenaz (Japheth) names and identity to Jewish names and modern-day Hebraic identity can be found by researching the original names of the Prime Ministers of the State of Israel.

Let's use an example taken from Wikipedia of the current Israeli prime minister.

Quoted directly from Wikipedia:

*"Netanyahu was born in 1949 in Tel Aviv. His mother, Tzila Segal (1912–2000), was born in Petah Tikva in the Ottoman Empire's Mutasarrifate of Yarushalayim (Jerusalem) — her family had migrated from Minneapolis in 1911, having relocated there from Lithuania in the 1870s — and studied law at Gray's Inn, London. **His father, Warsaw-born Benzion Netanyahu (né Mileikowsky; 1910–2012)**, was a historian specializing in the Jewish Golden age of Spain. **His paternal grandfather, Nathan Mileikowsky**, was a rabbi and Zionist writer. **When Netanyahu's father immigrated to Mandatory Palestine, he hebraized his surname from "Mileikowsky" to "Netanyahu"**, meaning "God has given." **His family is predominantly Ashkenazi.**"*

Let's take a look at Israel's first woman Prime Minister, Golda Meir. **Golda Meir's original name was Goldie Mabovitch. She was born in Kiev, Ukraine, on May 3, 1898.** Later, after marrying Morris Myerson, she became known as Goldie Myerson before eventually **changing her name to Golda Meir when she became** *a prominent political figure in Israel,* according to Britannica. She said she would have liked to keep it forever, but in 1956, Ben-Gurion made her Foreign Minister, the second-highest position in the government. **He also insisted she adopt a Hebrew-sounding surname to better represent her Hebrew-speaking nation; thus, Myerson became Meir.**

'Jews in name only' (Jew(ish)) is about stolen names, stolen heritage and stolen identity.

It is very clear that the Ashkenazi bloodline traces back to Eastern Europe, mainly the areas which are now Poland/Russia/Ukraine and the tongue— the language of Yiddish—which was incorporated into the creation of modern Hebrew, was created as part of the Zionist project.

Below is the legal definition of a Jew according to "The Law of Return" in the state of Israel.

While the Law of Return allowed every Jew to immigrate to Israel, it did not define who is a Jew, which brought on some legal issues such as the case of Rufeisen versus the Minister of the Interior in 1962. Oswald Rufeisen was a Polish Jew who had converted to Catholicism and sought to immigrate to Israel. The Supreme Court ruled that by converting to another religion he had forfeited his right to return. This decision of the court would make its way into the second amendment of the Law of Return in 1970 in which "Jew" was defined: In 1970, the right of entry and settlement was extended to people with one Jewish grandparent and a person who is married to a Jew, whether on or he or she is considered Jewish under Orthodox interpretations of Halakha 4A. (a) The rights of a Jew under this law and the rights of an oleh under the Nationality Law, 5712-1952, as well as the rights of an oleh under any other enactment, are also vested in a child and a grandchild of a Jew, the spouse of a Jew, the spouse of child of Jew and the spouse of a grandchild of a Jew, except for a person who had been a Jew and has voluntarily changed his religion. (b) It shall be immaterial whether or not a Jew by whose right a right under subsection (a) is claimed is alive and whether or not he has immigrated to Israel. 4B. For the purposes of this law, "Jew" means a person who was born of a Jewish mother or has become converted to Judaism and who is not a member of another religion. (reference: the Jewish Agency website).

For further reference, the scriptures list the full lineage of Shem to Abraham, as it is written:

- **This is the genealogy of Shem**: *Shem was one hundred years old, and begot Arphaxad two years after the flood. [11] After he begot Arphaxad, Shem lived five hundred years, and begot sons and daughters. [12] Arphaxad lived thirty-five years, and begot Salah. [13] After he begot Salah, Arphaxad lived four hundred and three years, and begot sons and daughters. [14] Salah lived thirty years, and begot Eber. [15] After he begot Eber, Salah lived four hundred and three years, and begot sons and daughters. [16] Eber lived thirty-four years, and begot Peleg. [17] After he begot Peleg, Eber lived four hundred and thirty years, and begot sons and daughters. [18] Peleg lived thirty years, and begot Reu. [19] After he begot Reu, Peleg lived two hundred and nine years, and begot sons and daughters. [20] Reu lived thirty-two years, and begot Serug. [21] After he begot Serug, Reu lived two hundred and seven years, and begot sons and daughters. [22] Serug lived thirty years, and begot Nahor. [23] After he begot Nahor, Serug lived two hundred years, and begot sons and daughters. [24] Nahor lived twenty-nine years, and begot Terah. [25] After he begot Terah, Nahor*

> *lived one hundred and nineteen years, and begot sons and daughters. [26]* ***Now Terah lived seventy years, and begot Abram,*** *Nahor, and Haran. (Genesis 11:10-26 NKJV)*

As a matter of interest, the word HEBREW came out of the name EBER, who is mentioned in the genealogy of Shem. Eber means 'the region beyond' and Hebrew means 'to crossover or pass through'.

The manipulated narrative of 'the conquerors' on biblical identity has painted the picture that melanated (darker-skinned) people came from the lineage of Ham and that non-melanated people (also referred to as Caucasians) were from the lineage of Shem and Japheth. The biblical truth says otherwise, as both Ham and Shem were melanated (darker-skinned) people, which is why Moses could be raised in the house of Egypt and mistaken for a Hamite (Egyptian). Paul was also mistaken for an Egyptian (Hamite). This is why Abraham, Isaac, Joseph and the Israelites could hide in Egypt (Hamite land) and not be detected, as they blended in with the locals. This is why YAHUSHA himself could find refuge again in Egypt (Hamite territory) and not stand out like a sore thumb in a melanated (darker-skinned) people territory.

- *Now the priest of Midian had seven daughters. And they came and drew water, and they filled the troughs to water their father's flock. [17] Then the shepherds came and drove them away; but **Moses stood up and helped them**, and watered their flock. [18] When they came to Reuel their father, he said, "How is it that you have come so soon today?" [19] And they said,* ***"An Egyptian*** *delivered us from the hand of the shepherds, and he also drew enough water for us and watered the flock." (Exodus 2:16-19 NKJV)*
- *Then* ***as Paul*** *was about to be led into the barracks, he said to the commander, "May I speak to you?" He replied, "Can*

you speak Greek? **Are you not the Egyptian** *who some time ago stirred up a rebellion and led the four thousand assassins out into the wilderness?" (Acts 21:37-38 NKJV)*

* Please note that ancient Egypt in biblical times was not made up of a predominantly Arab and mixed population as it is today. These changes occurred through Ottoman and Roman empire conquests.

Intermarriage between the bloodlines of Shem and Ham was commonplace as seen with a few of these notable examples:

Israelite Man	Wife's Name	Ethnicity/Lineage	Scripture Reference
Joseph	Asenath	Egyptian (Mizraim)	Genesis 41:45, 50
Moses	Zipporah / Cushite	Midianite / Cushite	Exodus 2:21; Numbers 12:1
Judah	Daughter of Shua	Canaanite	Genesis 38:2
Simeon	Unknown	Canaanite	Genesis 46:10
Solomon	Pharaoh's daughter and others	Egyptian, Canaanite tribes	1 Kings 3:1; 11:1-2

Is this a racial issue? Absolutely not!!!!

YAHUAH does not determine identity by the human concept of 'race based on skin colour'. The real issue is YAHUAH is restoring peoples of every tongue, tribe and nation according to His original design as He prepares to send His Son YAHUSHA (The Lion of the Tribe of YAHUDA) to return and sit upon the throne of David over the House of YASHARA'AL and all other nations which choose to be 'as native born' with them. Satan has fought very hard and continues to fight very hard to try and thwart this plan.

I reject the notion of race based on skin colour, which was introduced by Carl Linnaeus, a Freemason scientist from Sweden in the 1700s. As far as I am concerned, YAHUAH established tongues, tribes and nations from one blood and likewise has redeemed them through one blood (YAHUSHA). It is returning to Him through this 'one blood', YAHUSHA that YAHUAH desires to see the 'conquered' and the 'conqueror' commit to as they submit their bloodlines to oneness in Him. The FATHER who created both the 'conquered' and the 'conqueror' in His image and placed a part of His DNA in them is seeking for both to return to Him.

YAHUAH's redemptive plan for the earth will be fulfilled according to how He has designed it to happen, and it will not happen in any other way. YAH is the Most High, and He chose to bring redemption to all through a lineage that He chose for that purpose.

- *After these things I looked, and behold, a great multitude which no one could number, **of all nations, tribes, peoples, and tongues, standing before the throne and before the Lamb,** clothed with white robes, with palm branches in their hands, [10] and crying out with a loud voice, saying, "Salvation belongs to YAHUAH who sits on the throne, and to the Lamb!" [11] All the angels stood around the throne and the elders and the four living creatures, and fell on their faces before the throne and worshiped YAHUAH, [12] saying: "Amen! Blessing and glory and wisdom, Thanksgiving and honor and power and might, Be to YAHUAH forever and ever. Amen." (Revelation 7:9-12 NKJV)*
- *Therefore YAHUAH also has highly exalted Him and given Him the name which is above every name, that at the name of YAHUSHA every knee should bow, of those in heaven, and of those on earth, and of those under the earth, [11] and that **every tongue should confess that YAHUSHA MASHYACH is Master, to the glory of YAHUAH the Father.** (Philippians 2:9-11 NKJV)*

- And ***He has made from one blood every nation of men to dwell on all the face of the earth***, *and has determined their preappointed times and the boundaries of their dwellings, (Acts 17:26 NKJV)*

The ALAHYM of Abraham, Isaac and Jacob, YAHUAH, keeps the true birth registry

The one thing that is guaranteed, whether what has been shared here regarding identities is correct or not, is that YAHUAH Himself has the birth registry of all His creation. He knows who to raise up when He calls forth the 12 tribes of YASHARA'AL. He knows who to mark when He marks the first fruit 144,000 (12,000 from each tribe), which precedes the gathering of the multitudes of people of every tongue, tribe and nation who will be gathered before His throne. He knows who the 'natural branches of the olive tree' are, and likewise, He knows who the 'wild branches of the uncultivated olive tree' are. Irrespective of what man or Satan has done to manipulate and establish human-derived criteria for identity on the earth, YAHUAH has the original birth certificates, as it is written in Psalm 87. HALLELUYAH!!! PRAISE YAH!!!

- *His foundation is in the holy mountains. YAHUAH loves the gates of Zion More than all the dwellings of Jacob. Glorious things are spoken of you, O city of YAHUAH! Selah 4 "I will make mention of Rahab and Babylon to those who know Me; Behold, O Philistia and Tyre, with Ethiopia: 'This one was born there.'* ***"and of Zion it will be said, "This one and that one were born in her; And the Most High Himself shall establish her." YAHUAH will record, when He registers the peoples: "This one was born there."*** *Selah. Both the singers and the players on instruments say, "All my springs are in you." (Psalms*

87:1-2, 4-7 NKJV)

- *After these things I saw four angels standing at the four corners of the earth, holding the four winds of the earth, that the wind should not blow on the earth, on the sea, or on any tree. [2] Then I saw another angel ascending from the east, having the seal of the living Alahym. And he cried with a loud voice to the four angels to whom it was granted to harm the earth and the sea, [3] saying, "Do not harm the earth, the sea, or the trees till we have sealed the servants of our Alahym on their foreheads." [4]* **And I heard the number of those who were sealed. One hundred and forty-four thousand of all the tribes of the children of YASHARA'AL were sealed:** *[5] of the* **tribe of Judah** *twelve thousand were sealed; of the* **tribe of Reuben** *twelve thousand were sealed; of the* **tribe of Gad** *twelve thousand were sealed; [6] of the* **tribe of Asher** *twelve thousand were sealed; of the* **tribe of Naphtali** *twelve thousand were sealed; of the* **tribe of Manasseh** *twelve thousand were sealed; [7] of the* **tribe of Simeon** *twelve thousand were sealed; of the* **tribe of Levi** *twelve thousand were sealed; of the* **tribe of Issachar** *twelve thousand were sealed; [8] of the* **tribe of Zebulun** *twelve thousand were sealed; of the* **tribe of Joseph** *twelve thousand were sealed; of the* **tribe of Benjamin** *twelve thousand were sealed. [9]* **After these things I looked, and behold, a great multitude which no one could number, of all nations, tribes, peoples, and tongues**, *standing before the throne and before the Lamb, clothed with white robes, with palm branches in their hands, [10] and crying out with a loud voice, saying, "Salvation belongs to YAHUAH who sits on the throne, and to the Lamb!" [11] All the angels stood around the throne and the*

> elders and the four living creatures, and fell on their faces before the throne and worshiped YAHUAH, [12] saying: "Amen! Blessing and glory and wisdom, Thanksgiving and honor and power and might, Be to YAHUAH forever and ever. Amen." (Revelation 7:1-12 NKJV)
>   o For Zion's sake I will not hold My peace, And for Yarushalayim's (Jerusalem's) sake I will not rest, until her righteousness goes forth as brightness, and her salvation as a lamp that burns. [2] The Gentiles shall see your righteousness, And all kings your glory. You shall be called by a new name, Which the mouth of YAHUAH will name. [3] You shall also be a crown of glory in the hand of YAHUAH, And a royal diadem in the hand of YAHUAH. [4] **You shall no longer be termed Forsaken, nor shall your land any more be termed Desolate; But you shall be called Hephzibah, and your land Beulah; For YAHUAH delights in**

Keeping track of time as we track the true descendants of Jacob/ YASHARA'AL

I believe these two time markers are critical to pay attention to –

1. The 400-year (1619 – 2019) anniversary of the Trans-Atlantic slavery

2. The 140-year (1885 – 2025) anniversary of the Berlin Congo Conference

YAHUAH always sets an appointed time for His people being held in captivity, but when the time is up, He rescues them (on condition that they have repented and returned to Him, to keep His Covenant and obey His Laws and Commandments).

As YASHARA'AL were in Egypt on a 430-year captivity sentence, they were delivered on the day that YAHUAH had set an appointed time for deliverance.

> o *Now the sojourn of the children of YASHARA'AL who lived in Egypt was four hundred and thirty years.* **And it came to pass at the end of the four hundred and thirty years—on that very same day—it came to pass that all the armies of YAHUAH went out from the land of Egypt.** *(Exodus 12:40-41 NKJV)*

YASHARA'AL were 'sentenced' to a 70-year period of captivity in Babylon, which YAHUAH spoke through Jeremiah (Yaramayah). Towards the end of those 70 years, Daniel remembered the appointed 'sentence' period (as was prophesied by Jeremiah) and started the process of repentance to open the way for YAHUAH's deliverance.

> o *And this whole land shall be a desolation and an astonishment, and these nations shall serve the king of Babylon* **seventy years***. [12] 'Then it will come to pass, when* **seventy years** *are completed, that I will punish the king of Babylon and that nation, the land of the Chaldeans, for their iniquity,' says YAHUAH; 'and I will make it a perpetual desolation. [13] So I will bring on that land all My words which I have pronounced against it, all that is written in this book, which Jeremiah has prophesied concerning all the nations. [14] (For many nations and great kings shall be served by them also; and I will repay them according to their deeds and according to the works of their own hands.)" (Jeremiah 25:11-14 NKJV)*
>
> o *For thus says YAHUAH:* **After seventy years are completed** *at Babylon, I will visit you and perform My good word toward you, and cause you to return to this place. [11] For I know the thoughts that I think toward you,*

says YAHUAH, thoughts of peace and not of evil, to give you a future and a hope. [12] Then you will call upon Me and go and pray to Me, and I will listen to you. [13] And you will seek Me and find Me, when you search for Me with all your heart. [14] I will be found by you, says YAHUAH, and I will bring you back from your captivity; I will gather you from all the nations and from all the places where I have driven you, says YAHUAH, and I will bring you to the place from which I cause you to be carried away captive. (Jeremiah 29:10-14 NKJV)

- *In the first year of Darius the son of Ahasuerus, of the lineage of the Medes, who was made king over the realm of the Chaldeans— [2] in the first year of his reign* **I, Daniel, understood by the books the number of the years specified by the word of YAHUAH through Jeremiah the prophet, that He would accomplish seventy years in the desolations of Yarushalayim (Jerusalem)**. *(Daniel 9:1-2 NKJV)*

- *In the first year of Darius the son of Ahasuerus, of the lineage of the Medes, who was made king over the realm of the Chaldeans— [2] in the first year of his reign I, Daniel, understood by the books the number of the years specified by the word of YAHUAH through Jeremiah the prophet, that He would accomplish* **seventy years in the desolations of Yarushalayim (Jerusalem)**. *[3] Then I set my face toward YAHUAH to make request by prayer and supplications, with fasting, sackcloth, and ashes. [4] And I prayed to YAHUAH my Aluah, and made confession, and said, "O YAHUAH, great and awesome Alahym, who keeps His covenant and mercy with those who love Him, and with those who keep His commandments, [5] we have sinned and committed iniquity,* we have done wickedly and rebelled, even by departing from Your precepts and Your judgments. [6] Neither have we heeded Your servants the prophets, who spoke in Your name to our kings and our princes, to our fathers and all the people of the land. [7] O YAHUAH, righteousness belongs to You, but to us shame of face, as it is this day—to the men of Judah, to the inhabitants of Yarushalayim (Jerusalem) and all YASHARA'AL, those near and those far off in all the countries to which You have driven them, because of the unfaithfulness which they have committed against You. [8] "O YAHUAH, to us belongs shame of face, to our kings, our princes, and our fathers, because we have sinned against You. [9] To YAHUAH our Aluah belong mercy and forgiveness, though we have rebelled against Him. [10] We have not obeyed the voice of YAHUAH our Aluah, to walk in His laws, which He set before us by His servants the prophets. [11] Yes, all YASHARA'AL has transgressed Your law, and has departed so as not to obey Your voice; therefore the curse and the oath written in the Law of Moses the servant of YAHUAH have been poured out on us, because we have sinned against Him. [12] And He has confirmed His words, which He spoke against us and against our judges who judged us, by bringing upon us a great disaster; for under the whole heaven such has never been done as what has been done to Yarushalayim (Jerusalem). [13] "As it is written in the Law of Moses, all this disaster has come upon us; yet we have not made our prayer before YAHUAH our Aluah, that we might turn from our iniquities and understand Your truth. [14] Therefore YAHUAH has kept the disaster in mind, and brought it upon us; for YAHUAH our Aluah is righteous in all the works which He does, though we have *not obeyed His voice. [15] And now, O YAHUAH our Aluah, who brought Your people out of the land of Egypt with a mighty hand, and made Yourself a name, as it is this day—we have sinned, we have done wickedly! [16] "O YAHUAH, according to all Your righteousness, I pray, let Your anger and Your fury be turned away from Your city Yarushalayim (Jerusalem), Your holy mountain; because for our sins, and for the iniquities of our fathers, Yarushalayim (Jerusalem) and Your people are a reproach to all those around us. [17] Now therefore, our Aluah, hear the prayer of Your servant, and his supplications, and for YAHUAH's sake cause Your face to shine on Your sanctuary, which is desolate. [18] O YAHUAH, incline Your ear and hear; open Your eyes and see our desolations, and the city which is called by Your name; for we do not present our supplications before You because of our righteous deeds, but because of Your great mercies. [19] O YAHUAH, hear! O YAHUAH, forgive! O YAHUAH, listen and act! Do not delay for Your own sake, my Aluah, for Your city and Your people are called by Your name." [20] Now while I was speaking, praying, and confessing my sin and the sin of my people YASHARA'AL, and presenting my supplication before YAHUAH my Aluah for the holy mountain of my Aluah, [21] yes, while I was speaking in prayer, the man Gabriel, whom I had seen in the vision at the beginning, being caused to fly swiftly, reached me about the time of the evening offering. [22] And he informed me, and talked with me, and said, "O Daniel, I have now come forth to give you skill to understand. [23] At the beginning of your supplications the command went out, and I have come to tell you, for you are greatly beloved; therefore consider the matter, and understand the vision:*

> *[24] "Seventy weeks are determined For your people and for your holy city, To finish the transgression, To make an end of sins, To make reconciliation for iniquity, To bring in everlasting righteousness, To seal up vision and prophecy, And to anoint the Most Holy. [25] "Know therefore and understand, that from the going forth of the command to restore and build Yarushalayim (Jerusalem) Until Messiah (MASHYACH) the Prince, there shall be seven weeks and sixty-two weeks; The street shall be built again, and the wall, even in troublesome times. [26] "And after the sixty-two weeks Messiah (MASHYACH) shall be cut off, but not for Himself; And the people of the prince who is to come Shall destroy the city and the sanctuary. The end of it shall be with a flood, and till the end of the war desolations are determined. [27] Then he shall confirm a covenant with many for one week; But in the middle of the week He shall bring an end to sacrifice and offering. And on the wing of abominations shall be one who makes desolate, even until the consummation, which is determined, is poured out on the desolate." (Daniel 9:1-27 NKJV)*

Pay careful attention to what Daniel repented for and brought forward as the reason why YAHUAH had allowed YASHARA'AL to be taken into captivity.

Tribes of Africa, the appointed cycle of time is up. Deliverance is at hand, but we all need to respond as Daniel responded, as he understood the times and what needed to be done to put things in motion.

"The battle for spiritual freedom"

Section 6

Contents

Chapter 19.   Confronting and overcoming the primary enemy

Chapter 20.   The uncleanness in the religion of Christianity and the church

Chapter 21.   Fighting against YAHUAH

Chapter 22.   Confronting and resisting the white horse that came conquering and to conquer Africa

Chapter 23.   The call to come out of her

Beloved, let us love one another, for love is of YAHUAH; and everyone who loves is born of YAHUAH and knows YAHUAH. [8] He who does not love does not know YAHUAH, for YAHUAH is love. (I John 4:7-8 NKJV)

CHAPTER NINETEEN

Confronting and Overcoming The Primary Enemy

To truly confront and overcome the great enemy, we must walk in agreement with YAHUAH and be yoked to YAHUSHA. Our footing must be firm upon the unshakable ground of Truth, with hands ready to wield the spiritual weapons YAHUAH has placed within reach of all who will take them up. Without this, our striving is in vain, and we step into peril, for the enemy shows no mercy to those who come unarmoured. Only clothed in the armour of YAHUAH, and guided in the use of His weapons as He has ordained, can we stand with courage and prevail. We see this in the narration of the seven sons of Sceva

- *Now YAHUAH worked unusual miracles by the hands of Paul, [12] so that even handkerchiefs or aprons were brought from his body to the sick, and the diseases left them and the evil spirits went out of them. [13]* **Then some of the itinerant Jewish exorcists took it upon themselves to call the name of YAHUSHA MASHYACH over those who had evil spirits, saying, "We exorcise you by YAHUSHA whom Paul preaches." [14] Also there were**

> *seven sons of Sceva, a Jewish chief priest, who did so. [15] And the evil spirit answered and said, "YAHUSHA I know, and Paul I know; but who are you?" [16] Then the man in whom the evil spirit was leaped on them, overpowered them, and prevailed against them, so that they fled out of that house naked and wounded.* (Acts 19:11-16 NKJV)

It is, therefore, critical to establish a righteous platform to stand on, to wear YAHUAH's armour, to carry YAHUAH's weapons and to use them according to His instructions, lest we are overpowered, defeated and left 'naked and wounded'.

The righteous platform is our agreement and obedience with YAHUAH.

The first battle to look at is when YAHUSHA was led by the Holy Spirit into the wilderness to face off with Satan, the devil. As it is written:

- *Then YAHUSHA was led up by the Spirit into the wilderness to be tempted by the devil. [2] And when He had fasted forty days and forty nights, afterward He was hungry. [3] Now when the tempter came to Him, he said, "If You are the Son of YAHUAH, command that these stones become bread." [4]* **But He answered and said, "It is written, 'Man shall not live by bread alone, but by every word that proceeds from the mouth of YAHUAH.'"** *[5] Then the devil took Him up into the holy city, set Him on the pinnacle of the temple, [6] and said to Him, "If You are the Son of YAHUAH, throw Yourself down. For it is written: 'He shall give His angels charge over you,' and, 'In their hands they shall bear you up, lest you dash your foot against a stone.'"*

> *[7]* ***YAHUSHA said to him, "It is written again, 'You shall not tempt YAHUAH your Aluah."*** *[8] Again, the devil took Him up on an exceedingly high mountain, and showed Him all the kingdoms of the world and their glory. [9] And he said to Him, "All these things I will give You if You will fall down and worship me." [10]* ***Then YAHUSHA said to him, "Away with you, Satan! For it is written, 'You shall worship YAHUAH your Aluah, and Him only you shall serve."*** *[11] Then the devil left Him, and behold, angels came and ministered to Him. (Matthew 4:1-11 NKJV)*

YAHUSHA used the Word (Torah/The instructions of YAHUAH) as the primary weapon to confront and overcome Satan. **YAHUSHA said, 'IT IS WRITTEN....'**

The Word of YAHUAH is the Sword of the Spirit of YAHUAH, as it is written:

- *Finally, my brethren, be strong in YAHUSHA and in the power of His might. [11] Put on the whole armor of YAHUAH, that you may be able to stand against the wiles of the devil. [12] For we do not wrestle against flesh and blood, but against principalities, against powers, against the rulers of the darkness of this age, against spiritual hosts of wickedness in the heavenly places. [13] Therefore take up the whole armor of YAHUAH, that you may be able to withstand in the evil day, and having done all, to stand. [14] Stand therefore, having girded your waist with truth, having put on the breastplate of righteousness, [15] and having shod your feet with the preparation of the gospel of peace; [16] above all, taking the shield of faith with which you will be able to quench all the fiery darts of the wicked*

> one. *[17] And take the helmet of salvation, and **the sword of the Spirit, which is the word of YAHUAH**; [18] praying always with all prayer and supplication in the Spirit, being watchful to this end with all perseverance and supplication for all the saints— (Ephesians 6:10-18 NKJV)*

The Sword of the Spirit of YAHUAH is the Word of YAHUAH and is the only offensive weapon listed in the armour of YAHUAH, which He makes available for us.

Going back to the 'biblical definitions in Chapter 9, we can work through some equations to establish exactly what the Sword of Spirit of YAHUAH is comprised of in full, so we can determine if we are carrying it or not.

From the biblical definitions, we have already established that:

'The word is truth' because the truth is comprised of four things, namely (1) The Law, (2) The Commandments, (3) The Word and (4) YAHUSHA as given once more below.

The Law

- *Your righteousness is an everlasting righteousness, And **Your law is truth**.*
  (Psalm 119:142 KJV)

The Commandments

- *Thou art near, O YAHUAH; And **all thy commandments are truth**.*
  (Psalm 119:151 KJV)

The SON YAHUSHA

- *YAHUSHA said to him, "**I am** the way, **the truth**, and the* life. No one comes to the Father except through Me. (John 14:6 NKJV)

The Word
- Sanctify them by Your truth. **Your word is truth**. (John 17:17 NKJV)

We can equate this as follows: 'The Truth = (equals) The Law = (equals) The Commandments = The Word = (equals) YAHUSHA'.

It, therefore, means that 'If the Sword of the Spirit is The Word' it must also mean that 'the Sword of the Spirit = (equals) 'The Truth' = (equals) 'The Law' = (equals) 'The Commandments' = (equals) 'YAHUSHA' = (equals) 'The Word'.

It would follow that if there was a rejection or no recognition of 'The Law', and 'The Commandments' which are 'The Word' and 'YAHUSHA' and 'The Truth', then we can't be carrying the Sword of the Spirit of YAHUAH.

There is the element of the Spirit of YAHUAH, which is linked to the Sword, so we need to look at what it means to be in the Spirit of YAHUAH.

It is written that YAHUAH's word is Spirit, and likewise that YAHUAH's Spirit leads to all truth.

- **It is the Spirit who gives life**; *the flesh profits nothing.* **The words that I speak to you are spirit**, *and they are life. (John 6:63)*
- **However, when He, the Spirit of truth, has come, He will guide you into all truth**; *for He will not speak on His own authority, but whatever He hears He will speak; and He will tell you things to come. (John 16:13 NKJV)*

Going through the equations again:

If YAHUAH's Word is Spirit, **and** The Word is 'The Truth', 'The Law', 'The Commandments', 'YAHUSHA', **it must follow** that YAHUAH's Spirit will always lead to 'The Law', lead to 'The Commandments', lead to 'The Word' and lead to 'YAHUSHA'.

So, by extrapolation, **'If I am walking and living in the Spirit of YAHUAH, it means that** I am walking and living in The Law, I am walking and living in The Commandments, I am walking and living in The Truth, and I am walking and living in YAHUSHA'.

Is it possible for me to be walking and living in YAHUAH's Spirit if I have rejected 'The Law', "The Commandments', 'The Truth', 'The Word' and 'YAHUSHA'? I doubt it.

Scripture makes the clear statement that the carnal mind (the mind that has yet to be renewed by the Spirit of YAHUAH) is not subject to the law, which means being spiritually minded (to the Spirit of YAHUAH) means being subjected to the law of YAHUAH. Anyone who is not subject to the law of YAHUAH is carnally minded and of the flesh. The Spirit of YAHUAH and of MASHYACH cannot dwell where there is a rejection of the law of YAHUAH. As it is written:

- *For they that are after the flesh do mind the things of the flesh; but they that are after the Spirit the things of the Spirit. [6] For to be carnally minded is death; but to be spiritually minded is life and peace. [7]* **Because the carnal mind is enmity against YAHUAH: for it is not subject to the law of YAHUAH, neither indeed can be. [8] So then they that are in the flesh cannot please YAHUAH.** *[9] But ye are not in the flesh, but in the Spirit, if so be that the Spirit of YAHUAH dwell in you. Now if any man have not the Spirit of MASHYACH, he is none of His. [10] And if*

MASHYACH be in you, the body is dead because of sin; but the Spirit is life because of righteousness. [11] But if the Spirit of Him that raised up YAHUSHA from the dead dwell in you, He that raised up MASHYACH from the dead shall also quicken your mortal bodies by His Spirit that dwelleth in you. [12] Therefore, brethren, we are debtors, not to the flesh, to live after the flesh. [13] For if ye live after the flesh, ye shall die: but if ye through the Spirit do mortify the deeds of the body, ye shall live. [14] **For as many as are led by the Spirit of YAHUAH, they are the sons of YAHUAH.** *(Romans 8:5-14 KJV)*

- *After the death of Moses the servant of YAHUAH, it came to pass that YAHUAH spoke to Joshua the son of Nun, Moses' assistant, saying: [2] "Moses My servant is dead. Now therefore, arise, go over this Jordan, you and all this people, to the land which I am giving to them—the children of YASHARA'AL. [3] Every place that the sole of your foot will tread upon I have given you, as I said to Moses. [4] From the wilderness and this Lebanon as far as the great river, the River Euphrates, all the land of the Hittites, and to the Great Sea toward the going down of the sun, shall be your territory. [5] No man shall be able to stand before you all the days of your life; as I was with Moses, so I will be with you. I will not leave you nor forsake you. [6] Be strong and of good courage, for to this people you shall divide as an inheritance the land which I swore to their fathers to give them. [7]* **Only be strong and very courageous, that you may observe to do according to all the law which Moses My servant commanded you; do not turn from** *it to the right hand or to the left, that you may prosper wherever you go. [8] This Book of the Law shall not depart from your mouth, but you shall meditate in it day and night, that you may observe to do according to all that is written in it. For then you will make your way prosperous, and then you will have good success. [9] Have I not commanded you? Be strong and of good courage; do not be afraid, nor be dismayed, for YAHUAH your Aluah is with you wherever you go." (Joshua 1:1-9 NKJV)*

To find freedom, we already established the precept which says "the truth shall make you free" as it is written:

- Then YAHUSHA said to those Jews who believed Him, "If you abide in My word, you are My disciples indeed. [32] And you shall know the truth, **and the truth shall make you free.**" (John 8:31-32 NKJV)

Before YAHUSHA made the statement 'the truth shall make you free', He made the statement about abiding in His word.

The Truth = (equals) The Word

So, the statement could easily read, 'If you abide in My truth, you are My disciples indeed. And you shall know the word, and the word shall make you free.'

Again 'The Truth' = (equals) 'The Word' = (equals) 'The Law' = (equals) 'The Commandments' = (equals) 'YAHUSHA'

By extrapolation,

The Truth shall make you free.

The Law shall make you free.

The Commandments shall make you free.

YAHUSHA shall make you free.

Likewise,

If I don't abide in The Word, I will be held captive.

If I don't abide in The Truth, I will be held captive.

If I don't abide in The Law, I will be held captive.

If I don't abide in The Commandments, I will be held captive.

If I don't abide in YAHUSHA, I will be held captive.

The Sword of the Spirit is what YAHUSHA used to overcome Satan as He spoke The Word, He spoke The Law and Commandments (TORAH), He spoke the truth of what YAHUAH had said.

The Sword of the Spirit is available to us according to the definition of what YAHUAH said it is. If we don't accept what He said it is, we will go to battle thinking we have a weapon when in actual fact we are empty-handed and a sitting duck for the enemy who will strip us and leave us naked and wounded.

For further reference, herewith are scriptures which speak of the power of the SWORD OF THE SPIRIT, THE WORD OF YAHUAH, which always delivers victory when it is used.

> o *Let us therefore be diligent to enter that rest, lest anyone fall according to the same example of disobedience. [12]* **For the word of YAHUAH is living and powerful, and sharper than any two-edged sword**, *piercing even to the division of soul and spirit, and of joints and marrow, and is a discerner of the thoughts and intents of the heart. [13] And there is no creature hidden from His sight, but all things are*

- naked and open to the eyes of Him to whom we must give account. (Hebrews 4:11-13 NKJV)
- Then I turned to see the voice that spoke with me. And having turned I saw seven golden lampstands, [13] and in the midst of the seven lampstands One like the Son of Man, clothed with a garment down to the feet and girded about the chest with a golden band. [14] His head and hair were white like wool, as white as snow, and His eyes like a flame of fire; [15] His feet were like fine brass, as if refined in a furnace, and His voice as the sound of many waters; [16] He had in His right hand seven stars, **out of His mouth went a sharp two-edged sword**, and His countenance was like the sun shining in its strength. (Revelation 1:12-16 NKJV)
- "And to the angel of the church in Pergamos write, 'These things says He who has the sharp two-edged sword: [13] "I know your works, and where you dwell, where Satan's throne is. And you hold fast to My name, and did not deny My faith even in the days in which Antipas was My faithful martyr, who was killed among you, where Satan dwells. [14] But I have a few things against you, because you have there those who hold the doctrine of Balaam, who taught Balak to put a stumbling block before the children of YASHRA'AL, to eat things sacrificed to idols, and to commit sexual immorality. [15] Thus you also have those who hold the doctrine of the Nicolaitans, which thing I hate. [16] Repent, **or else I will come to you quickly and will fight against them with the sword of My mouth.** (Revelation 2:12-16 NKJV)
- Now I saw heaven opened, and behold, a white horse. And He who sat on him was called Faithful and True, and in righteousness He judges and makes war. [12] His eyes were like a flame of fire, and on His head were many crowns. He

> had a name written that no one knew except Himself. [13] He was clothed with a robe dipped in blood, and His name is called The Word of YAHUAH. [14] And the armies in heaven, clothed in fine linen, white and clean, followed Him on white horses. [15] **Now out of His mouth goes a sharp sword, that with it He should strike the nations**. And He Himself will rule them with a rod of iron. He Himself treads the winepress of the fierceness and wrath of Almighty YAHUAH. [16] And He has on His robe and on His thigh a name written: KING OF KINGS AND MASTER OF MASTERS. (Revelation 19:11-16 NKJV)

Returning to the armour of YAHUAH, we are reminded of its sacred parts:

- **The Belt of Truth.** What is truth? It has already been shown — the Truth is the Law, the Commandments, the Word, and above all, YAHUSHA Himself. Without these, the belt is missing.

- **The Breastplate of Righteousness.** This is our covenantal obedience to YAHUAH, and our covering through the sacrifice and offering of YAHUSHA, by which we are justified.

- **The Gospel of Peace.** This is the fullness of the Good News: that YAHUAH has opened His covenant to all mankind, calling them to be His people, that He might be their ALAHYM and dwell among them.

- **The Shield of Faith.** Faith comes by hearing the instructions of YAHUAH. The shield, then, is the certainty that His every word is truth — a living guarantee that guards us against the fiery arrows of lies and deception hurled by the father of lies.

In light of this, we must pause and ask ourselves: Are we truly clothed in the armour of YAHUAH, and are we bearing His sword according to His standard and definition?

Casting down everything that exalts itself against the knowledge of YAHUAH

Scriptures give us another precept on the issue of spiritual warfare in 2 Corinthians 10:3-6 as it is written:

> o *For though we walk in the flesh, we do not war according to the flesh. [4] For the weapons of our warfare are not carnal but mighty in YAHUAH for pulling down strongholds, [5]* **casting down arguments and every high thing that exalts itself against the knowledge of YAHUAH, bringing every thought into captivity to the obedience of MASHYACH,** *[6] and being ready to punish all disobedience when your obedience is fulfilled. (II Corinthians 10:3-6 NKJV)*

The central battlefield of our warfare with Satan is in our minds. It's a battle of obedience. Will we obey YAHUAH, or will we accept arguments (lies) that will cause us to rebel and disobey His Word, His Truth, His Law, His Commandments and YAHUSHA? For if we do, the deceiver, the father of lies, Satan, the devil, can capture us and hold us in captivity.

If we are defeated in our minds, we will not be able to take up the armour of YAHUAH nor His Sword of the Spirit, for both are dependent on the state of our obedience to YAHUAH.

The blood of YAHUSHA, the Word and laying down of our lives

The word of YAHUAH points us to another battle with Satan in Revelation 12:7-11 as it is written:

> o *And war broke out in heaven: Michael and his angels fought with the dragon; and the dragon and his angels fought, [8] but they did not prevail, nor was a place found for them in heaven any longer. [9]* **So the great dragon was cast out, that serpent of old, called the Devil and Satan, who deceives the whole world; he was cast to the earth, and his angels were cast out with him.** *[10] Then I heard a loud voice saying in heaven, "Now salvation, and strength, and the kingdom of YAHUAH, and the power of His MASHYACH have come, for the accuser of our brethren, who accused them before YAHUAH day and night, has been cast down. [11]* **And they overcame him by the blood of the Lamb and by the word of their testimony, and they did not love their lives to the death.** *(Revelation 12:7-11 NKJV)*

They overcame him by the blood of the Lamb, and by the word of their testimony, and they did not love their lives even unto death.

The Blood of the Lamb – YAHUSHA:

Through His blood we are redeemed, our guilt acquitted, and every debt of sin cancelled. By grace we are justified, and through His sacrifice our transgressions are atoned for. As we walk in confession and repentance, bringing our sins under the covering of His blood, Satan is rendered powerless.

The Word of our Testimony:

This is the living witness of our agreement with YAHUAH, spoken as YAHUSHA Himself declared the Word to silence the accuser. It is the truth of His TORAH—His Law, His Commandments, His instructions and judgements—affirmed on our lips and in our lives. When we stand in full alignment with His Word, Satan cannot prevail.

Not loving our lives unto death:
This is the unwavering devotion that refuses compromise. It is faithfulness to the Voice of YAHUAH, to His Covenant and His Instructions, even when obedience may cost us everything. To be fully yoked with YAHUSHA is to follow Him wherever He leads—even unto death—treasuring His commandments above self-preservation. And in this, the adversary is defeated.

- *Then YAHUSHA said to His disciples,* **"If anyone desires to come after Me, let him deny himself, and take up his cross, and follow Me. [25] For whoever desires to save his life will lose it, but whoever loses his life for My sake will find it. [26] For what profit is it to a man if he gains the whole world, and loses his own soul?** *Or what will a man give in exchange for his soul? [27] For the Son of Man will come in the glory of His Father with His angels, and then He will reward each according to his works. (Matthew 16:24-27 NKJV)*
- *For consider Him who endured such hostility from sinners against Himself, lest you become weary and discouraged in your souls. [4]* **You have not yet resisted to bloodshed, striving against sin.** *(Hebrews 12:3-4 NKJV)*

Resist the devil, and he will flee from you

- **Therefore submit to YAHUAH. Resist the devil and he will flee from you. [8] Draw near to YAHUAH and He will draw near to you.** *Cleanse your hands, you sinners; and purify your hearts, you double-minded. [9] Lament and mourn and weep! Let your laughter be turned to mourning and your joy to gloom. [10]* **Humble yourselves in the sight of YAHUAH,** *and He will lift you up. (James 4:7-10 NKJV)*

Resist the devil and he will flee from you. How do we resist the devil?

The scriptures provide us with 6 ways to do this.

- **By submitting to YAHUAH,** which is our obedience to Him.
- **By drawing near to YAHUAH,** as we love Him according to how He wants to be loved. (Those who obey my commandments are those who love me).
- **By cleansing our hands from doing sin** (by not transgressing the law of YAHUAH)
- **By purifying our hearts from being double-minded** (questioning the instructions of YAHUAH and finding justification to disobey them, for a double-minded man is unstable in all his ways and will not receive anything from YAHUAH according to what is written in James 1:2-8).
- **By lamenting and mourning,** which is confession and repentance from our sin (transgression of the instructions of YAHUAH)
- **By humbling ourselves before YAHUAH,** as we do not lean on our own understanding but commit to laying down our lives in obedience to what He has instructed, irrespective of whether it makes logical sense or not.

   o *My brethren, count it all joy when you fall into various trials, [3] knowing that the testing of your faith produces patience. [4] But let patience have its perfect work, that you may be perfect and complete, lacking nothing. [5] If any of you lacks wisdom, let him ask of YAHUAH, who gives to all liberally and without reproach, and it will be given to him. [6]* ***But let him ask in faith, with no doubting, for he who doubts is like a wave of the sea driven and*** *tossed by the wind. [7] For let not that man suppose that he will receive anything from YAHUAH; [8] he is a double-minded man, unstable in all his ways. (James 1:2-8 NKJV)*

Tribes of Africa, YAHUAH has given us an 'armoury' full of weapons which we can use to defeat and conquer the enemy who has taken us captive in the spiritual domain.

YAHUAH also warns us to be wary of the wiles of the enemy, *'Put on the whole armour of YAHUAH, that you may be able to stand against the wiles of the devil'.*

The wiles of the enemy, the father of lies, the deceiver

What are the wiles of the enemy?

The Word of YAHUAH paints a clear picture of who the enemy is and the nature of his ways. He is the father of lies, the deceiver, the accuser of the brethren, appearing even as a counterfeit angel of light. His chief work is to twist truth and lead us astray, seeking to draw us away from The Truth, The Word, The Law, The Commandments, and from YAHUSHA Himself. His purpose is to entice us into transgression of YAHUAH's instructions, knowing that sin separates us from YAHUAH. And when we step outside of obedience to YAHUAH, our devotion and worship are misdirected, given over to the adversary instead.

Throughout history, his schemes have sought to turn hearts against the Kingdom of YAHUAH, using systems of religion that reject the covenant of obedience—what Scripture speaks of as the "Mother of Harlots and her daughters," symbolizing the great falling away from The Way, The Truth, and The Life. In this way, the everlasting covenant is disregarded and trampled underfoot.

His strategy has not changed since the beginning. Just as in the Garden of Eden with Adam and Eve, his aim is still to entice us into rebellion against the voice of YAHUAH.

> o ***Now the serpent was more cunning than any beast of the field which YAHUAH had made. And he said to the woman, "Has YAHUAH indeed said, 'You shall not eat of every tree of the garden'?"*** *[2] And the woman said to the serpent, "We may eat the fruit of the trees of the garden; [3] but of the fruit of the tree which is in the midst of the garden, YAHUAH has said, 'You shall not eat it, nor shall you touch it, lest you die.'"* ***[4] Then the serpent said to the woman, "You will not surely die. [5] For YAHUAH knows that in the day you eat of it your eyes will be opened, and you will be like YAHUAH, knowing good and evil.***" *[6] So when the woman saw that the tree was good for food, that it was pleasant to the eyes, and a tree desirable to make one wise, she took of its fruit and ate. She also gave to her husband with her, and he ate. (Genesis 3:1-6 NKJV)*

Did YAHUAH really say you should keep the everlasting terms of the covenant? Did YAHUAH really say you should keep the 10 commandments? Did YAH really say you should obey His Laws (TORAH)?

He is the father of lies and will always challenge what YAHUAH has said and give an alternative option that seems 'good' but leads to death. It is in this way that He continues what He tried to do, to rebel against YAHUAH and lift himself above YAHUAH when He was still in the presence of YAHUAH.

If YAHUAH says obey - Satan will look for a way to deceive us into disobedience so that he can gain our worship, as this is how He lifts himself above YAHUAH.

- *"How you are fallen from heaven, O Lucifer, son of the morning! How you are cut down to the ground, You who weakened the nations! [13]* **For you have said in your heart: 'I will ascend into heaven, I will exalt my throne above the stars of God; I will also sit on the mount of the congregation On the farthest sides of the north; [14] I will ascend above the heights of the clouds, I will be like the Most High.'** *(Isaiah 14:12-14 NKJV)*

Let us not be ignorant about the work of Lucifer, and let us be confident that when we are yoked to YAHUSHA, we partake in His victory over the works of the devil.

- *He who sins (transgresses the law) is of the devil, for the devil has sinned (transgressed the law) from the beginning.* **For this purpose the Son of YAHUAH was manifested, that He might destroy the works of the devil.** *[9] Whoever has been born of YAHUAH does not sin (wilfully transgress the law), for His seed remains in him; and he cannot sin (wilfully transgress the law), because he has been born of YAHUAH. (I John 3:8-9 NKJV)*
- *In Him you were also circumcised with the circumcision made without hands, by putting off the body of the sins of the flesh, by the circumcision of MASHYACH (Christ), [12] buried with Him in baptism, in which you also were raised with Him through faith in the working of YAHUAH, who raised Him from the dead. [13]* **And you, being dead in your trespasses and the uncircumcision of your flesh, He has made alive together with Him,**

> *having forgiven you all trespasses, [14] having wiped out the handwriting of requirements that was against us, which was contrary to us. And He has taken it out of the way, having nailed it to the cross. [15] Having disarmed principalities and powers, He made a public spectacle of them, triumphing over them in it.* (Colossians 2:11-15 NKJV)

THE BATTLE IS IN OUR MIND – that is the primary place of the warfare that we are in.

Have we been fighting in vain?

This might be quite offensive to some, but I believe that we (those who have professed Christianity) have spent so much time warring against spirits, marine spirits, Leviathan spirits, Jezebel spirits, territorial spirits, the list goes on and on. We seek them out in deliverance meetings and all night prayer meetings when actually YAHUAH is simply saying "come back to obedience because you have not complied with My instructions, you are not wearing My armour, you don't have My Sword of the Spirit, you don't have the weapons I have made available in My armoury, Your minds are still in captivity to lies".

Is it possible we have seen very little of the manifestation of the power of YAHUAH because He has not been with us because of our rebellion and disobedience?

It is pointless to go to battle if we are in rebellion against the Commander of Heaven's Armies, for surely, we will be defeated if we go without Him, as our ancestors found out multiple times in the past.

- o And Moses said, **"Now why do you transgress the**

- *command of YAHUAH? For this will not succeed. [42] Do not go up, lest you be defeated by your enemies, for YAHUAH is not among you.* [43] *For the Amalekites and the Canaanites are there before you, and you shall fall by the sword; because you have turned away from YAHUAH, YAHUAH will not be with you." [44] But they presumed to go up to the mountaintop. Nevertheless, neither the ark of the covenant of YAHUAH nor Moses departed from the camp. [45] Then the Amalekites and the Canaanites who dwelt in that mountain came down and attacked them, and drove them back as far as Hormah. (Numbers 14:41-45 NKJV)*
- *And it came to pass, when Joshua was by Jericho, that he lifted his eyes and looked, and behold,* **a Man stood opposite him with His sword drawn in His hand**. *And Joshua went to Him and said to Him, "Are You for us or for our adversaries?" [14] So He said,* **"No, but as Commander of the army of YAHUAH I have now come**.*" And Joshua fell on his face to the earth and worshiped, and said to Him, "What does my Master say to His servant?" [15]* **Then the Commander of YAHUAH's army said to Joshua, "Take your sandal off your foot, for the place where you stand is holy."** *And Joshua did so. (Joshua 5:13-15 NKJV)*
- *Give ear, O Shepherd of YASHARA'AL, You who lead Joseph like a flock; You who dwell between the cherubim, shine forth! [2] Before Ephraim, Benjamin, and Manasseh, stir up Your strength, and come and save us! [3] Restore us, O YAHUAH; Cause Your face to shine, and we shall be saved! [4] O YAHUAH of hosts, how long will You be angry Against the prayer of Your people? [5] You have*

fed them with the bread of tears, and given them tears to drink in great measure. [6] You have made us a strife to our neighbours, and our enemies laugh among themselves. [7] Restore us, O YAHUAH of hosts; Cause Your face to shine, and we shall be saved! [8] You have brought a vine out of Egypt; You have cast out the nations, and planted it. [9] You prepared room for it, and caused it to take deep root, and it filled the land. [10] The hills were covered with its shadow, And the mighty cedars with its boughs. [11] She sent out her boughs to the Sea, And her branches to the river. [12] Why have You broken down her hedges, so that all who pass by the way pluck her fruit? [13] The boar out of the woods uproots it, And the wild beast of the field devours it. [14] Return, we beseech You, O YAHUAH of hosts; Look down from heaven and see, and visit this vine [15] and the vineyard which Your right hand has planted, And the branch that You made strong for Yourself. [16] It is burned with fire, it is cut down; They perish at the rebuke of Your countenance. [17] Let Your hand be upon the man of Your right hand, Upon the son of man whom You made strong for Yourself. [18] Then we will not turn back from You; Revive us, and **we will call upon Your name**. *[19] Restore us, O YAHUAH of hosts; Cause Your face to shine, and we shall be saved! (Psalms 80:1-19 NKJV)*

Tribes of Africa, call out to the name of YAHUAH, repent. Restore us, O YAHUAH of hosts. We cannot afford to take on this task of rebuilding Africa if YAHUAH does not go with us and fight for us. Going without Him will guarantee another defeat.

- Then Moses said to YAHUAH, "See, You say to me, 'Bring up this people.' But You have not let me know whom You will *send with me. Yet You have said, 'I know you by name, and you have also found grace in My sight.' [13] Now therefore, I pray, if I have found grace in Your sight, show me now Your way, that I may know You and that I may find grace in Your sight. And consider that this nation is Your people." [14] And He said, "My Presence will go with you, and I will give you rest." [15] Then he said to Him,* ***"If Your Presence does not go with us, do not bring us up from here. [16] For how then will it be known that Your people and I have found grace in Your sight, except You go with us****? So we shall be separate, Your people and I, from all the people who are upon the face of the earth." (Exodus 33:12-16 NKJV)*

- *So Joshua conquered all the land: the mountain country and the South and the lowland and the wilderness slopes, and all their kings; he left none remaining, but utterly destroyed all that breathed, as YAHUAH Aluah of YASHARA'AL had commanded. [41] And Joshua conquered them from Kadesh Barnea as far as Gaza, and all the country of Goshen, even as far as Gibeon. [42]* ***All these kings and their land Joshua took at one time, because YAHUAH Aluah of YASHARA'AL fought for YASHARA'AL****. (Joshua 10:40-42 NKJV)*

Tribes of Africa, the most powerful weapon we have is obedience.

CHAPTER TWENTY

The Uncleanliness In The Religion Of Christianity And The Church

The primary place of captivity for most of Africa is sadly in the religion of Christianity and in churches, which unknowingly walk in rebellion to YAHUAH because of the doctrine of lawlessness that has been taught and passed on from generation to generation in error.

The trap of witchcraft in the religion of Christianity and the church

🦋 **Tribes of Africa,** we have been destroyed for lack of knowledge in YAHUAH (rejecting what YAHUAH requires of us according to the agreement/covenant we have with Him), we have forgotten His instructions, and because of that, YAHUAH has rejected us and forgotten our children, but He is showing us the way back.

> o *My people are destroyed for lack of knowledge;* **because you have rejected knowledge, I reject you from being a priest to me. And since you have forgotten the law**

> *of YAHUAH, I also will forget your children. [7] The more they increased, the more they sinned against Me; I will change their glory into shame. (Hosea 4:6-7 ESV)*

The sad truth we must face is that the religion of Christianity and many churches have been the main channels of witchcraft. For the scriptures define witchcraft as it is written:

- *So Samuel said: "Has YAHUAH as great delight in burnt offerings and sacrifices, as in obeying the voice of YAHUAH?* **Behold, to obey is better than sacrifice,** *And to heed than the fat of rams. [23]* **For rebellion is as the sin of witchcraft, and stubbornness is as iniquity and idolatry.** *Because you have rejected the word of YAHUAH, He also has rejected you from being king." (I Samuel 15:22-23 NKJV)*
- **They profess to know YAHUAH, but they deny Him by their works. They are detestable, disobedient, unfit for any good work.** *(Titus 1:16 ESV)*

As the scriptures say, anyone who claims to know Him but does not keep His commandments is a liar.

- **Whoever says "I know Him" but does not keep his commandments is a liar, and the truth is not in him,** *[5] but whoever keeps his word, in him truly the love of YAHUAH is perfected. By this we may know that we are in Him: [6] whoever says he abides in Him ought to walk in the same way in which He walked. (1 John 2:4-6 ESV)*

The fate of liars (according to YAHUAH's definition of a liar) is clearly given as it is written:

- *Then He who sat on the throne said, "Behold, I make all*

- *things new." And He said to me, "Write, for these words are true and faithful." [6] And He said to me, "It is done! I am the Alpha and the Omega, the Beginning and the End. I will give of the fountain of the water of life freely to him who thirsts. [7] He who overcomes shall inherit all things, and I will be his Aluah and he shall be My son. [8] But the cowardly, unbelieving, abominable, murderers, sexually immoral, sorcerers, idolaters,* **and all liars shall have their part in the lake which burns with fire and brimstone, which is the second death.** *" (Revelation 21:5-8 NKJV)*
  - *Blessed are they that do His commandments, that they may have right to the tree of life, and may enter in through the gates into the city. [15]* **For without are dogs, and sorcerers, and whoremongers, and murderers, and idolaters, and whosoever loveth and maketh a lie.** *(Revelation 22:14-15 KJV)*

For lying lips are an abomination to YAHUAH.

  - **Lying lips are an abomination to YAHUAH**: *But they that deal truly are His delight. (Proverbs 12:22 KJV)*

Tribes of Africa, let us not be conformed to the standards of man, religion and the world, but let us connect to the everlasting standard given by YAHUAH, even if it means persecution unto death, which will lead to the deliverance and redemption of our children and future generations.

If we define things and measure them according to the standards of man and the world, and conform to those standards, we will be led down the wide road which leads to destruction.

  - *I beseech you therefore, brethren, by the mercies of YAHUAH, that ye present your bodies a living sacrifice,*

> holy, acceptable unto YAHUAH, which is your reasonable service. [2] **And be not conformed to this world**: but be ye transformed by the renewing of your mind, that ye may prove what is that good, and acceptable, and perfect, will of YAHUAH. (Romans 12:1-2 KJV)
>
> - ***Blessed are they which are persecuted for righteousness' sake: for their's is the kingdom of heaven. [11] Blessed are ye, when men shall revile you, and persecute you, and shall say all manner of evil against you falsely, for My sake.*** *[12] Rejoice, and be exceeding glad: for great is your reward in heaven: for so persecuted they the prophets which were before you. [13] Ye are the salt of the earth: but if the salt have lost his savour, wherewith shall it be salted? it is thenceforth good for nothing, but to be cast out, and to be trodden under foot of men. [14] Ye are the light of the world. A city that is set on an hill cannot be hid. [15] Neither do men light a candle, and put it under a bushel, but on a candlestick; and it giveth light unto all that are in the house. [16] Let your light so shine before men, that they may see your good works, and glorify your Father which is in heaven. (Matthew 5:10-16 KJV)*

To the teachers of the Bible and leaders of churches in Africa, take heed of the words of YAHUSHA, that those who break the least of His Commandments and teach others to do the same will be called least in the kingdom of heaven.

> - *Think not that I am come to destroy the law, or the prophets: I am not come to destroy, but to fulfil. [18] For verily I say unto you, till heaven and earth pass, one jot or one tittle shall in no wise pass from the law, till all be fulfilled. [19]* ***Whosoever therefore shall break one of***

> these least commandments, and shall teach men so, he shall be called the least in the kingdom of heaven: *but whosoever shall do and teach them, the same shall be called great in the kingdom of heaven. [20] For I say unto you, that except your righteousness shall exceed the righteousness of the scribes and Pharisees, ye shall in no case enter into the kingdom of heaven. (Matthew 5:17-20 KJV)*

Teachers will be judged even more strictly for leading people astray from YAHUAH, should they teach in error.

> o *My brethren, let not many of you become* **teachers, knowing that we shall receive a stricter judgment.** *(James 3:1 NKJV)*

As I was writing this book, the James 3:1 scripture was foremost in my mind, knowing that if what I am releasing through this book is wrong, I will have a harsh sentence awaiting me on the day of judgement.

We always think of witchcraft as something that is happening exclusively in a dark witchdoctor's hut, secret society lodge or openly satanist assembly with witches, warlocks, etc, and that is correct, for they are unapologetically in open rebellion against YAHUAH. But let us also remember the rebellion against YAHUAH, which is also taking place in plain sight through the religion of Christianity and the church, which is the outworking of the mystery of lawlessness.

The dictionary defines rebellion as "an act of armed resistance to an established government or leader. The action or process of resisting authority".

♱ Rebellion against YAHUAH's Word, YAHUAH's Truth, YAHUAH's Law, YAHUAH's Commandments, YAHUAH's

Statutes, YAHUAH's Judgements, YAHUAH's Precepts is witchcraft.

Rebellion against YAHUAH's Covenant (agreement) is witchcraft.

Rebellion against YAHUSHA is witchcraft.

Perhaps a lot of what we see coming from many self-professed apostles and prophets of today, and likewise many churches and ministries, is actually the fruit of witchcraft from the rebellion against YAHUAH. The outcomes of the fruit of the flesh promote the lust of the flesh, the lust of the eyes and the pride of life. The outpouring of the fruit of sin (transgression of the instructions of YAHUAH) is what results in the curse and death.

In chapter one, I mentioned one of the realities I lamented about is 'how is it possible we have churches on almost every street corner and yet the fruit of the curse is growing so overwhelming in our nations? How is it possible that the equation reads as follows: 'more churches = (equals) more poverty'? Perhaps the answer is that there are witchcraft centres (rebellious churches) on almost every street corner. The presence of witchcraft guarantees the presence of the curse. The presence of rebellion guarantees the presence of the curse.

Cursed be anyone who does not confirm the words of the law by doing them.

- o **'Cursed be anyone who does not confirm the words of this law by doing them.'** And all the people shall say, 'Amen.' (Deuteronomy 27:26 ESV)

Tribes of Africa let us come out of rebellion, let us come out of the spell of witchcraft which has been cast over us.

Witchcraft in the very place that is supposed to be holy and set apart for YAHUAH is not new. It has happened over the centuries as Yachazqel (Ezekiel) spoke about, as it is written. In the days of Yachazqel there was much 'abomination in the temple' which is why RUACH HA QADASH (the Spirit of YAHUAH) had to depart.

- *And He put forth the form of a hand and took me by a lock of my head; and the Spirit lifted me up between the earth and the heavens and brought me in the visions of YAHUAH to Yarushalayim (Jerusalem), to the entrance of the door of the inner [court] which faces toward the north, where was the seat of the idol (image) of jealousy, which provokes to jealousy. And behold, there was the glory of the Aluah of YASHARA'AL, like the vision I saw in the plain. Then He [the Spirit] said to me, Son of man, now lift up your eyes toward the north. So I lifted up my eyes toward the north, and behold, on the north of the altar gate was that idol (image) of jealousy in the entrance. [6] Furthermore, [the Spirit] said to me, **Son of man, do you see what they are doing? The great abominations that the house of YASHARA'AL is committing here to drive Me far from My sanctuary?** But you shall again see greater abominations. [7] And He brought me to the door of the court; and when I looked, behold, there was a hole in the wall. [8] Then He said to me, Son of man, dig now in the wall. And when I had dug in the wall, behold, there was a door. [9] And He said to me, go in and see the wicked abominations that they do here. [10] So I went in and saw there pictures of every form of creeping things and loathsome beasts and all the idols of the house of YASHARA'AL, painted round about on the wall.*

[11] And there stood before these [pictures] seventy men of the elders of the house of YASHARA'AL, and in the midst of them stood Jaazaniah the son of Shaphan [the scribe], with every man his censer in his hand, and a thick cloud of incense was going up [in prayer to these their gods]. [12] Then said He to me, Son of man, have you seen what the elders of the house of YASHARA'AL do in the dark, every man in his [secret] chambers of [idol] pictures? For they say, YAHUAH does not see us; YAHUAH has forsaken the land. [13] He also said to me, yet again you shall see greater abominations which they are committing. *[14] Then He brought me to the entrance of the north gate of YAHUAH's house; and behold, there sat women weeping for Tammuz [a Babylonian god, who was supposed to die annually and subsequently be resurrected]. [15]* Then said [the Spirit] to me, have you seen this, O son of man? Yet again you shall see greater abominations that they are committing. *[16] And He brought me to the inner court of YAHUAH's house; and behold, at the door of the temple of YAHUAH, between the porch and the bronze altar, were about twenty-five men with their backs to the temple of YAHUAH and their faces toward the east, and they were bowing themselves toward the east and worshiping the sun.* (Ezekiel 8:3-16 AMPC)

As a side note to those who follow the Rabbinic Jewish calendar, please notice how they have a month that they named Tammuz.

Because YAHUAH is a jealous Aluah who commands absolute devotion to Himself alone (as He has commanded in the first two Commandments *'you shall have no other gods before me'* and *'you shall not have any graven images'*), when His people decide to give their affections (and allegiance) to another, YAHUAH quietly departs and turns His face away from looking at their prostitution and leaves them to continue in their fornication.

- Then one of the seven angels who had the seven bowls came and talked with me, saying to me, **"Come, I will show you the judgment of the great harlot who sits on many waters, [2] with whom the kings of the earth committed fornication, and the inhabitants of the earth were made drunk with the wine of her fornication."** [3] So he carried me away in the Spirit into the wilderness. And I saw a woman sitting on a scarlet beast which was full of names of blasphemy, having seven heads and ten horns. [4] The woman was arrayed in purple and scarlet, and adorned with gold and precious stones and pearls, having in her hand a golden cup full of abominations and the filthiness of her fornication. [5] And on her forehead a name was written: MYSTERY, BABYLON THE GREAT, THE MOTHER OF HARLOTS AND OF THE ABOMINATIONS OF THE EARTH. (Revelation 17:1-5 NKJV)
- **"Harlotry, wine, and new wine enslave the heart. [12] My people ask counsel from their wooden idols, and their staff informs them. For the spirit of harlotry has caused them to stray, and they have played the harlot against YAHUAH.** [13] They offer sacrifices on the mountaintops, and burn incense on the hills, under oaks, poplars, and terebinths, Because their shade is good. **Therefore your daughters commit harlotry, and your brides commit adultery. [14] "I will not punish your daughters when they commit harlotry, nor your brides**

> ***when they commit adultery; For the men themselves go apart with harlots, and offer sacrifices with a ritual harlot.*** *Therefore people who do not understand will be trampled. [15] "Though you, YASHARA'AL, play the harlot, let not Judah offend. Do not come up to Gilgal, nor go up to Beth Aven, nor swear an oath, saying, 'As YAHUAH lives'— [16] "For YASHARA'AL is stubborn Like a stubborn calf; Now YAHUAH will let them forage Like a lamb in open country. [17] "Ephraim is joined to idols, Let him alone. [18] Their drink is rebellion, they commit harlotry continually. Her rulers dearly love dishonour. [19] The wind has wrapped her up in its wings, and they shall be ashamed because of their sacrifices. (Hosea 4:11-19 NKJV)*

There are many sanctuaries, churches and ministries where the Spirit of YAHUAH has long departed, but they continue to thrive on witchcraft and sorcery, tickling people's ears, giving them the wine of harlotry which feeds their flesh with what their desires want to hear. There are many so-called apostles and prophets, 'men and women of God' who are praying to their gods (not YAHUAH), weeping for Tammuz, and bowing down in worship to the sun, while they are clothed in robes and garments of Christianity.

- *And I looked, and there in the firmament that was above the head of the cherubim, there appeared something like a sapphire stone, having the appearance of the likeness of a throne. [2] Then He spoke to the man clothed with linen, and said, "Go in among the wheels, under the cherub, fill your hands with coals of fire from among the cherubim, and scatter them over the city." And he went in as I watched. [3] Now the cherubim were standing on the south side of the temple when the man went in, and the cloud filled the inner court. [4]* **Then the glory of YAHUAH went up from the cherub, and paused over the threshold of the temple; and the house was filled with the cloud, and the court was full of the brightness of YAHUAH's glory.** *[5] And the sound of the wings of the cherubim was heard even in the outer court, like the voice of Almighty YAHUAH when He speaks. [6] Then it happened, when He commanded the man clothed in linen, saying, "Take fire from among the wheels, from among the cherubim," that he went in and stood beside the wheels. [7] And the cherub stretched out his hand from among the cherubim to the fire that was among the cherubim, and took some of it and put it into the hands of the man clothed with linen, who took it and went out. [8] The cherubim appeared to have the form of a man's hand under their wings. [9] And when I looked, there were four wheels by the cherubim, one wheel by one cherub and another wheel by each other cherub; the wheels appeared to have the colour of a beryl stone. [10] As for their appearance, all four looked alike—as it were, a wheel in the middle of a wheel. [11] When they went, they went toward any of their four directions; they did not turn aside when they went, but followed in the direction the head was facing. They did not turn aside when they went. [12] And their whole body, with their back, their hands, their wings, and the wheels that the four had, were full of eyes all around. [13] As for the wheels, they were called in my hearing, "Wheel." [14] Each one had four faces: the first face was the face of a cherub, the second face the face of a man, the third the face of a lion, and the fourth the face of an eagle. [15] And the cherubim were lifted up. This was the living creature I saw by the River Chebar. [16] When the cherubim went, the wheels went beside them;*

and when the cherubim lifted their wings to mount up from the earth, the same wheels also did not turn from beside them. [17] When the cherubim stood still, the wheels stood still, and when one was lifted up, the other lifted itself up, for the spirit of the living creature was in them. [18] **Then the glory of YAHUAH departed from the threshold of the temple and stood over the cherubim.** [19] And the cherubim lifted their wings and mounted up from the earth in my sight. When they went out, the wheels were beside them; and they stood at the door of the east gate of YAHUAH's house, and the glory of the Alahym of YASHARA'AL was above them. [20] This is the living creature I saw under the Alahym of YASHARA'AL by the River Chebar, and I knew they were cherubim. [21] Each one had four faces and each one four wings, and the likeness of the hands of a man was under their wings. [22] And the likeness of their faces was the same as the faces which I had seen by the River Chebar, their appearance and their persons. They each went straight forward. (Ezekiel 10:1-22 NKJV)*

But those who lead the people in this prostitution and fornication from within the temple of YAHUAH will be judged severely.

- *Then the Spirit lifted me up and brought me to the East Gate of YAHUAH's house, which faces eastward; and there at the door of the gate were twenty-five men, among whom I saw Jaazaniah the son of Azzur, and Pelatiah the son of Benaiah, princes of the people. [2]* **And He said to me: "Son of man, these are the men who devise iniquity and give wicked counsel in this city,** *[3] who say, 'The time is not near to build houses; this city is the caldron, and we are the meat.' [4] Therefore prophesy against them,* *prophesy, O son of man!" [5] Then the Spirit of YAHUAH fell upon me, and said to me, "Speak! 'Thus says YAHUAH: "Thus you have said, O house of YASHARA'AL; for I know the things that come into your mind. [6] You have multiplied your slain in this city, and you have filled its streets with the slain." [7] Therefore thus says YAHUAH: "Your slain whom you have laid in its midst, they are the meat, and this city is the caldron; but I shall bring you out of the midst of it. [8]* **You have feared the sword; and I will bring a sword upon you,"** *says YAHUAH.* [9] *"And I will bring you out of its midst, and deliver you into the hands of strangers, and execute judgments on you.* [10] **You shall fall by the sword.** *I will judge you at the border of YASHARA'AL. Then you shall know that I am YAHUAH.* [11] *This city shall not be your caldron, nor shall you be the meat in its midst.* **I will judge you at the border of YASHARA'AL.** **[12] And you shall know that I am YAHUAH; for you have not walked in My statutes nor executed My judgments, but have done according to the customs of the Gentiles which are all around you."** **[13] Now it happened, while I was prophesying, that Pelatiah the son of Benaiah died.** *Then I fell on my face and cried with a loud voice, and said, "Ah, YAHUAH! Will You make a complete end of the remnant of YASHARA'AL?" (Ezekiel 11:1-13 NKJV)*

🕯 "Ah, YAHUAH! Will You make a complete end of the remnant of YASHARA'AL?

🕯 "Ah, YAHUAH! Will You make a complete end of the remnant of AFRICA for what the wicked priests and leaders have done? Have mercy, YAHUAH, for we have sinned greatly against You.

In this age of prophetic and apostolic hype and showmanship we must be so careful we are not consuming the 'food of prostitution' and drinking the wine of harlotry' from sources which might seem to be pure on the outside but are in fact connected to darkness (not necessarily because they are all evil people, but rather because they themselves are deceived, thinking they are serving The Most High YAHUAH and walking with Him, when in fact they are in rebellion to Him and therefore in witchcraft). Those who do what they do knowingly serving Satan and knowingly deceiving the sheep shall be judged as **Pelatiah, the son of Benaiah.**

Be alert, Be alert, Be alert

- *Let the evildoer still do evil, and the filthy still be filthy, and the righteous still do right, and the holy still be holy." (Revelation 22:11 ESV)*
- *Thus says YAHUAH concerning the prophets Who make my people stray; Who chant "Peace" While they chew with their teeth, But who prepare war against him Who puts nothing into their mouths: [6] "Therefore you shall have night without vision, And you shall have darkness without divination;* ***The sun shall go down on the prophets****, And the day shall be dark for them. [7]* ***So the seers shall be ashamed, and the diviners abashed; indeed they shall all cover their lips; For there is no answer from YAHUAH.****" [8] But truly I am full of power by the Spirit of YAHUAH, and of justice and might, to declare to Jacob his transgression And to YASHARA'AL his sin. [9] Now hear this, You heads of the house of Jacob and rulers of the house of YASHARA'AL, who abhor justice and pervert all equity, [10] Who build up Zion with bloodshed And Yarushalayim (Jerusalem) with iniquity: [11] Her heads judge for a bribe,* ***Her priests teach for pay, and her prophets divine***

> *for money.* Yet they lean on YAHUAH, and say, "Is not YAHUAH among us? No harm can come upon us." (Micah 3:5-11 NKJV)
> - **For the time will come when they will not endure sound doctrine; but after their own lusts shall they heap to themselves teachers, having itching ears; [4] and they shall turn away their ears from the truth, and shall be turned unto fables.** (2 Timothy 4:3-4 KJV)

45,000 versions of truth

When absolute truth is rejected, the result is 45,000 versions of truth.

We recall from the biblical definition of truth being (1) The Word, (2) The Law, (3) The Commandments, (4) YAHUSHA

The World Christian Encyclopedia and World Christian Database estimated over 45,000 Christian denominations globally as of 2019.

Why is this the case when there is 'ONE WAY, YAHUSHA', and ONE SPIRIT OF YAHUAH, which leads all the sons of ONE FATHER YAHUAH, by ONE covenant (agreement)?

The answer is simple: when there is a rejection of YAHUAH's Truth, it results in 45,000 opinions of man, 45,000 doctrines of man and 45,000 traditions of man now determining the 45,000 versions of 'truth'.

> - *For then will I turn to the people a pure language, that they may all call upon the name of the YAHUAH,* **to serve Him with one consent.** *(Zephaniah 3:9 KJV)*

45,000 versions of 'truth' also result in 45,000 constitutions, which all claim to be of the Kingdom. No wonder unity remains a fleeting dream in Christianity, for all do what seems right in their own sight instead of submitting to the constitution of YAHUAH. There will never be unity outside of the truth of YAHUAH.

❦ **Tribes of Africa,** perhaps the pure language YAHUAH is restoring to us is the language of His Truth, which will bring us all into one consent in His constitution

Drinking from broken cisterns and enticed by foreign gods

We have been enticed to serve other gods, we have inquired of other gods and committed two evils against YAHUAH, as it is written:

- ***and go not after other gods to serve them, and to worship them***, *and provoke Me not to anger with the works of your hands; and I will do you no hurt. [7] Yet ye have not hearkened unto Me, saith YAHUAH; that ye might provoke Me to anger with the works of your hands to your own hurt. (Jeremiah 25:6-7 KJV)*
- *When YAHUAH thy Aluah shall cut off the nations from before thee, whither thou goest to possess them, and thou succeedest them, and dwellest in their land; [30] take heed to thyself that thou be not snared by following them, after that they be destroyed from before thee;* ***and that thou enquire not after their gods, saying, How did these nations serve their gods? even so will I do likewise. [31] Thou shalt not do so unto YAHUAH thy Aluah: for every abomination to YAHUAH, which he hateth, have they done unto their gods***; *for even their sons and their daughters they have burnt in the fire to their gods. [32]* ***What thing soever I command you, observe to do it: thou shalt not add thereto, nor diminish from it***. *(Deuteronomy 12:29-32 KJV)*

- *If thy brother, the son of thy mother, or thy son, or thy daughter, or the wife of thy bosom, or thy friend, which is as thine own soul,* **entice thee secretly, saying, Let us go and serve other gods, which thou hast not known, thou, nor thy fathers; [7] namely, of the gods of the people which are round about you, nigh unto thee, or far off from thee, from the one end of the earth even unto the other end of the earth; [8] thou shalt not consent unto him, nor hearken unto him; neither shall thine eye pity him, neither shalt thou spare, neither shalt thou conceal him:** *[9] but thou shalt surely kill him; thine hand shall be first upon him to put him to death, and afterwards the hand of all the people. [10] And thou shalt stone him with stones, that he die; because he hath sought to thrust thee away from YAHUAH thy Aluah, which brought thee out of the land of Egypt, from the house of bondage. [11] And all Israel shall hear, and fear, and shall do no more any such wickedness as this is among you. (Deuteronomy 13:6-11 KJV)*

- **Hath a nation changed their gods, which are yet no gods? but my people have changed their glory for that which doth not profit.** *[12] Be astonished, O ye heavens, at this, and be horribly afraid, be ye very desolate, saith YAHUAH.* *[13]* **For My people have committed two evils; they have forsaken Me the fountain of living waters, and hewed them out cisterns, broken cisterns, that can hold no water.** *(Jeremiah 2:11-13 KJV)*

Tribes of Africa, do we know which God we are serving? What is His name? Lest we unknowingly drink from profane cisterns that are practising witchcraft.

The uncomfortable questions

With 45,000 different versions of 'truth', we must ask ourselves the most critical questions regarding the plan of salvation because there is only ONE PLAN and not 45,000. What does the ONE PLAN say about salvation and baptism? What does it mean to be saved, and how does one get saved?

We have grown up in a religion that says, "come up to the altar or just lift up your hands and repeat a 'sinners' prayer to give your life to Jesus' and you will be saved". Is that biblical, and is there any biblical reference to this being done anywhere by the disciples and apostles of YAHUSHA?

What the scriptures reference very clearly is a process of repentance, baptism and obedience to the instructions, and the need to endure until the end to receive what has been promised.

Repent

Repent is the first directive that YAHUSHA gave, and likewise Paul and all the other disciples and apostles would start their preaching of salvation with the call to repent.

- o *From that time YAHUSHA began to preach and to say, "**Repent**, for the kingdom of heaven is at hand." (Matthew 4:17 NKJV)*
- o *In those days John the Baptist came preaching in the wilderness of Judea, [2] and saying, "**Repent**, for the kingdom of heaven is at hand!" [3] For this is he who was spoken of by the prophet Isaiah, saying: "The voice of one crying in the wilderness: 'Prepare the way of YAHUSHA; Make His paths straight.' (Matthew 3:1-3 NKJV)*
- o *Therefore, since we are the offspring of YAHUAH, we*

> *ought not to think that the Divine Nature is like gold or silver or stone, something shaped by art and man's devising. [30] Truly, these times of ignorance YAHUAH overlooked, but now **commands all men everywhere to repent**, [31] because He has appointed a day on which He will judge the world in righteousness by the Man whom He has ordained. He has given assurance of this to all by raising Him from the dead." (Acts 17:29-31 NKJV)*

Repentance was already defined in chapter 12, but in summary, it is the process of turning away from something and turning back to something that was already in place. The message of salvation always started with "Repent from your sins". With the understanding of the definition of sin, being 'transgressing of the law'. Repent from your sins was a clarion call to turn away from wilfully transgressing the Law and Commandments of YAHUAH (lawlessness) and turn back to obeying the Law and Commandments of YAHUAH.

Be Baptised

The next action would always be baptism by full immersion in water. This would signify the dying of the old self (old man) who is rebellious and lawless and wilfully transgresses the Law and Commandments of YAHUAH, and the rising up of the 'new self' (new man) committed to obey the Law and Commandments of YAHUAH. The old would die and the new would arise. Baptism was performed on an adult who made their own decision to repent, and not infant sprinkling baptism before the child can decide for themselves to repent and be immersed in water. (Infant baptism is one of those unbiblical things that was birthed by the Roman Catholic Church and spread across Christianity). The water immersion is what activates the testimony of the water within the three on earth that testify on behalf of the true follower of YAHUSHA. A reminder of the legislative and judiciary system of the Kingdom of YAHUAH, discussed in Chapter 13, as the Spirit, the Water and the Blood bear witness in the legal process of AQCUITTING the saints.

> o *And there are three that bear witness on earth: the Spirit, **the water**, and the blood; and these three agree as one. (I John 5:8 NKJV)*

Without righteous baptism, which is preceded by righteous repentance, the three that bear witness will not be activated.

Scripture seems to indicate that after the process of righteous repentance, followed by righteous baptism, YAHUAH would then give His RUACH HA QADASH (Holy Spirit) as a helper who would assist the true follower of YAHUSHA to live out their commitment to learn the ways of YAHUAH, as the RUACH would be their teacher and also would help them keep and obey the Law and Commandments of YAHUAH. The RUACH is the teacher and the one who empowers any person to obedience, as this cannot be done by the strength or abilities of the 'flesh of man' but requires the Spirit of YAHUAH.

Sadly, even the issue of baptism is a contentious one, as all baptisms referenced in the book of Acts were done in the name of YAHUSHA, and not in the name of the Father and the Holy Spirit. The controversy stems from the possibility that Matthew 28:19 was edited to include the Father and the Holy Spirit in the baptism formula as a way to justify the doctrine of the Trinity.

These are the references to baptism in the book of the Acts of the Apostles, which seem to indicate that the Apostles indeed followed the instruction to baptise in the name of YAHUSHA only, without any reference to the Father or Holy Spirit in the baptism process.

- *And Peter said to them,* ***"Repent and be baptized every one of you in the name of YAHUSHA MASHYACH*** *for the forgiveness of your sins, and you will receive the gift of the Holy Spirit. (Acts 2:38 ESV)*
- *Now when the apostles at Jerusalem heard that Samaria had received the word of YAHUAH, they sent to them Peter and John, [15] who came down and prayed for them that they might receive RUACH HA QADASH, [16] for he had not yet fallen on any of them,* ***but they had only been baptized in the name of the Master YAHUSHA.*** *(Acts 8:14-16 ESV)*
- ***And he commanded them to be baptized in the name of YAHUSHA MASHYACH.*** *Then they asked him to remain for some days. (Acts 10:48 ESV)*
- *On hearing this,* ***they were baptized in the name of the Master YAHUSHA.*** *(Acts 19:5 ESV)*

Teach them to observe all the instructions

The third step would be to teach them the ways of YAHUAH—His instructions, Laws, and Commandments—so that they might grow in the knowledge of His ways and walk in obedience as they honour their covenant with Him. On this journey, they would also come to understand that when they stumble and fall into sin, their hope and restoration are found in YAHUSHA. For by His grace they receive righteousness, made possible only through His finished work—the perfect and final offering and sacrifice for sin within YAHUAH's divine order and justice in His Kingdom.

- *And YAHUSHA came and spoke to them, saying, "All authority has been given to Me in heaven and on earth. [19]* ***Go therefore and make disciples*** *of all the nations, baptizing them in the name of the Father and of the Son* and of the Holy Spirit, [20] **teaching them to observe all things that I have commanded you**; and lo, I am with you always, even to the end of the age." Amen. (Matthew 28:18-20 NKJV)

Endure to the end

As they (the new believers) were taught to observe all the things that YAHUSHA commanded as He (the SON) was commanded by YAHUAH (the FATHER), they would commit to a lifestyle of obedience, enduring in this obedience until the end, where they would receive the prize of salvation.

- And because lawlessness will abound, the love of many will grow cold. [13] **But he who endures to the end shall be saved**. (Matthew 24:12-13 NKJV)
- And you will be hated by all for My name's sake. **But he who endures to the end shall be saved**. (Mark 13:13 NKJV)
- Beware, brethren, lest there be in any of you an evil heart of unbelief in departing from the living Aluah; [13] but exhort one another daily, while it is called "Today," lest any of you be hardened through the deceitfulness of sin. [14] For we have become partakers of MASHYACH (Christ) **if we hold the beginning of our confidence steadfast to the end,** (Hebrews 3:12-14 NKJV)

I have yet to see, in the Word of YAHUAH, the concept of just saying a sinner's prayer and you are saved for life. I have yet to see in the Word of YAHUAH the concept of a religious altar call and a single event that guarantees salvation. I have yet to see in the Word of YAHUAH where it speaks of inviting Jesus into one's heart. I may be wrong. What I see is a process of salvation.

If repentance means turning away from transgressing the Laws and Commandments of YAHUAH, and turning toward obedience to them, then can I truly say I have repented if I reject their validity and relevance? What does it mean if I respond to an altar call or recite a sinner's prayer within a religious system that denies the continuing authority of YAHUAH's Laws and Commandments? From what, then, am I repenting, if I have already dismissed the standard He has given?

And what of baptism? If I enter the water without first repenting of breaking YAHUAH's Laws and Commandments—because I believe they no longer apply—what does that baptism mean? If I am baptised within a religious structure that denies His instructions, into what name am I truly baptised? What, then, am I dying to, and into what am I being raised?

Tribes of Africa, these are such critical questions that we must find answers for individually and satisfy ourselves that we have the right answer. The price to pay is too high if we have the wrong version of the 45,000 different ways out there in the religion of Christianity. The answer will determine eternity for me, and you, our families, our loved ones and our nations.

The book of Revelation gives a promise to the 7 churches for those who endure to the end and overcome.

- o *"He who has an ear, let him hear what the Spirit says to the churches.* **To him who overcomes** *I will give to eat from the tree of life, which is in the midst of the Paradise of YAHUAH." (Revelation 2:7 NKJV)*
- o *"He who has an ear, let him hear what the Spirit says to the churches.* **He who overcomes** *shall not be hurt by the second death." (Revelation 2:11 NKJV)*
- o *"He who has an ear, let him hear what the Spirit says to the*

- churches. **To him who overcomes** *I will give some of the hidden manna to eat. And I will give him a white stone, and on the stone a new name written which no one knows except him who receives it." (Revelation 2:17 NKJV)*
  - **And he who overcomes**, *and keeps My works until the end, to him I will give power over the nations— [27] 'He shall rule them with a rod of iron; They shall be dashed to pieces like the potter's vessels'— as I also have received from My Father; (Revelation 2: 26-27 NKJV)*
  - **He who overcomes** *shall be clothed in white garments, and I will not blot out his name from the Book of Life; but I will confess his name before My Father and before His angels. (Revelation 3:5 NKJV)*
  - **He who overcomes**, *I will make him a pillar in the temple of My Aluah, and he shall go out no more. I will write on him the name of My Aluah and the name of the city of My Aluah, the New Jerusalem, which comes down out of heaven from My Aluah. And I will write on him My new name. (Revelation 3:12 NKJV)*
  - **To him who overcomes** *I will grant to sit with Me on My throne, as I also overcame and sat down with My Father on His throne. (Revelation 3:21 NKJV)*

Tribes of Africa, may we be those who endure to the end and overcome to receive the prize.

  - *Therefore, my beloved, as you have always obeyed, not as in my presence only, but now much more in my absence,* **work out your own salvation with fear and trembling;** *(Philippians 2:12 NKJV)*

The Apostle Paul speaks about how he knew that he would only receive 'the crown of righteousness' on the day of YAHUAH, which he describes as 'on that day'. He knew that before 'that day', he needed to run the race diligently because the prize was only at the end and not at the beginning of the race.

> o *For I am already being poured out as a drink offering, and the time of my departure is at hand. [7] I have fought the good fight, I have finished the race, I have kept the faith. [8]* ***Finally, there is laid up for me the crown of righteousness, which the Master, the righteous Judge, will give to me on that Day,*** *and not to me only but also to all who have loved His appearing. (II Timothy 4:6-8 NKJV)*

Thoughts on apostles and prophets and their ministries

It is good to understand the definition and standard of YAHUAH for what a prophet and apostle are.

What is a Prophet?

In Hebrew, the word for prophet is 'Navi' (which is referenced in Strong's Concordance H5030).

'Navi' means a spokesperson, an inspired speaker, one who speaks for YAHUAH. Interestingly, one of the definitions of inspired is - 'to breathe into' or 'to inflame'

The questions we need to ask ourselves when we see the title prophet are -

- Who is he/she speaking on behalf of? (since a prophet is a spokesperson on behalf of someone else)
- Who are they inspired by?
- Who is breathing into them and whose breath (ruach) are they releasing?

- Who is inflaming them and whose flame are they releasing through their words (since a prophet is an inspired speaker), lest we are caught in strange fire that destroys us as is written in Leviticus 10:1-3.

*Then Nadab and Abihu, the sons of Aaron, each took his censer and put fire in it, put incense on it, and **offered profane fire before YAHUAH**, which He had not commanded them. [2] **So fire went out from YAHUAH and devoured them, and they died before YAHUAH**.*

Many are genuinely seeking the Holy Fire of YAHUAH, but sadly, many get caught up in strange fire, thinking that it is genuine.

Which God do they speak for, since there are many gods and lords out there?

Not everyone who carries the title prophet is a spokesperson, inspired speaker and one who speaks for the ALAHYM of Abraham, Isaac and Jacob, the Most High YAHUAH.

They might be correctly carrying the title prophet and indeed speaking on behalf of 'a god', their 'god'.

If they are speaking on behalf of YAHUAH, they will speak in agreement and alignment with YAHUAH's Truth, YAHUAH's Word, YAHUAH's Law, YAHUAH's Commandments, YAHUAH's Statutes, YAHUAH's Judgements, YAHUAH's Precepts. They will speak in agreement and alignment with YAHUAH's plan for mankind through YAHUSHA.

By looking back at the words that YAHUAH spoke through His true prophets, it is easy to deduce a consistent format in the structure of their prophecies. If one analyses the books of Isaiah (YASHAYAHU), Jeremiah (YARAMAYAH), Ezekiel (YACHAZQEL), Zechariah

(ZAKARYAHU), Hosea (HOSHUA), Joel (YAUL) and others, what is very apparent is how what YAHUAH gave them to say consisted of the following components:

1. **Confronting the people's sin** (lawlessness, transgression of the law and commandments of YAHUAH and breaking the covenant (agreement) with YAHUAH.
2. **Warning the people of the judgement of YAHUAH** (the consequences which would come upon them if they remained in violation of the agreement with YAHUAH).
3. **Calling the people to repentance** (to turn away from their violation of the agreement with YAHUAH and return to obeying the instructions of YAHUAH).
4. **Indicating to the people what YAHUAH will do if they don't repent** (the curse and calamity which YAHUAH would bring upon the people as per the terms of the agreement (covenant).
5. **Indicating to the people what YAHUAH will do if they repent** (the blessings that YAHUAH would bring upon the people as per the terms of the agreement (covenant).

These five elements always formed part of the prophecies that the true prophets of YAHUAH would speak to the people. I believe the same is true today of prophets who YAHUAH speaks through, for YAHUAH is the same yesterday, today and forever. The way He spoke to His prophets yesterday is the same way He is speaking to His prophets today.

Sadly, today we have many 'so-called prophets' who are nothing but a combination of (1) motivational speakers who use scripture, (2) fortune tellers and soothsayers who market themselves on Christian platforms, and (3) Sorcerers and diviners who use scripture as bait to lure their fans into idolatry and witchcraft.

I no longer listen or pay attention to any prophecy or so-called prophet who does not espouse these five elements in their prophecies. I encourage you to read the first few chapters of all the prophetic books: Isaiah (YASHAYAHU), Jeremiah (YARAMAYAH), Ezekiel (YACHAZQEL), etc, in the Bible and see for yourselves how and what YAHUAH spoke to them and use this as the standard to discern who the true and false prophets are.

It is up to us to discern deeply, individually.

What is an Apostle?

In Hebrew, the word for apostle is 'Shaliach' (which is referenced in Strong's Concordance H7971).

'Shaliach' means a messenger, ambassador, and one sent forth with a special commission or assignment.

The questions we need to ask ourselves when we see the title Apostle is -

- Who has sent them, and what have they been sent to deliver? (since an apostle is a messenger sent to deliver something)
- Whose kingdom/constitution do they represent? (since they are an ambassador)
- What special commission/assignment have they been sent to fulfil? (since they are sent with a special commission)

Not everyone who carries the title Apostle is a messenger representing the Kingdom of YAHUAH and the constitution of YAHUAH or carrying out a special commission on behalf of the ALAHYM of Abraham, Isaac and Jacob, The Most High YAHUAH.

They might be correctly carrying the title Apostle and indeed serving as a messenger and carrying out a special commission on behalf of 'the god' who sent them, a god or lord who is not YAHUAH.

It is up to us to discern deeply.

If YAHUAH has established His TORAH as the foundation of His covenant relationship with mankind—built upon (1) listening to and obeying His Voice, (2) keeping His Covenant, (3) walking in His Commandments, Laws, Ordinances, Statutes, and Precepts (His constitution), (4) living in righteousness through the sanctification and justification found only in YAHUSHA MASHYACH and not by works, and (5) yielding to the guidance of His RUACH (Holy Spirit)—would He appoint prophets to speak on His behalf, or Apostles to carry His commission, if they have rejected this very foundation?

Can one who sets aside any part of what YAHUAH has commanded truly serve as His spokesperson or messenger? Would YAHUAH entrust His words and His sacred commission to those who dismiss the very instructions that define His covenant with His people?

Discern, discern, discern as it is written:

> o *And the word of YAHUAH came to me, saying, [24] "Son of man, say to her: 'You are a land that is not cleansed or rained on in the day of indignation.' [25]* **The conspiracy of her prophets in her midst is like a roaring lion tearing the prey; they have devoured people; they have taken treasure and precious things; they have made many widows in her midst. [26] Her priests have violated My law and profaned My holy things; they have not distinguished between the holy and unholy, nor have they made known the difference between the unclean and the clean; and they have hidden their eyes from**

My Sabbaths, so that I am profaned among them. [27] Her princes in her midst are like wolves tearing the prey, to shed blood, to destroy people, and to get dishonest gain. [28] Her prophets plastered them with untampered mortar, seeing false visions, and divining lies for them, saying, 'Thus says YAHUAH Aluah,' when YAHUAH had not spoken. [29] The people of the land have used oppressions, committed robbery, and mistreated the poor and needy; and they wrongfully oppress the stranger. (Ezekiel 22:23-29 NKJV)

- **Beware of false prophets**, who come to you dressed as sheep, but inside they are devouring wolves. (Matthew 7:15 AMPC)
- **Not everyone who says to Me, Master, Master, will enter the kingdom of heaven, but he who does the will of My Father Who is in heaven.** [22] Many will say to Me on that day, Master, Master, have we not prophesied in Your name and driven out demons in Your name and done many mighty works in Your name? [23] **And then I will say to them openly (publicly), I never knew you; depart from Me, you who act wickedly [disregarding My commands].** (Matthew 7:21-23 AMPC)
- **And many false prophets will rise up and deceive and lead many into error.** (Matthew 24:11 AMPC)
- If anyone says to you then, Behold, here is HA MASHYACH (the Messiah)! or, There He is! - do not believe it. [24] **For false MASHYACH's (Christs) and false prophets will arise**, and they will show great signs and wonders so as to deceive and lead astray, if possible, even the elect (YAHUAH's chosen ones). (Matthew 24:23-24 AMPC)
- BELOVED, **DO not put faith in every spirit, but prove**

- *(test) the spirits to discover whether they proceed from YAHUAH; for many false prophets have gone forth into the world.* (1 John 4:1 AMPC)
  - *Then YAHUAH said to me, the [false] prophets prophesy lies in My name. I sent them not, neither have I commanded them, nor have I spoken to them. They prophesy to you a false or pretended vision, a worthless divination [conjuring or practicing magic, trying to call forth the responses supposed to be given by idols], and the deceit of their own minds.* (Jeremiah 14:14 AMPC)
  - *BUT ALSO [in those days] there arose false prophets among the people, just as there will be false teachers among yourselves, who will subtly and stealthily introduce heretical doctrines (destructive heresies), even denying and disowning the Master Who bought them, bringing upon themselves swift destruction.* (2 Peter 2:1 AMPC)
  - *Its heads judge for reward and a bribe and **its priests teach for hire and its prophets divine for money**; yet they lean on YAHUAH and say, Is not YAHUAH among us? No evil can come upon us.* (Micah 3:11 AMPC)
  - *The elderly and honoured man, he is the head; and **the prophet who teaches lies**, he is the tail.* (Isaiah 9:15 AMPC)

The path of 'the law & the prophets' (the ancient path) or the path of the modern prophets, apostles and teachers

These are questions that I would like to pose as we continue the search for truth.

- Are we spending much time seeking the words and listening to the 'prophets and apostles' of today when YAHUAH is perhaps beseeching us to return to the words and instructions

- He has already given to us through 'the law and the prophets', which is His ancient path of truth?
- Is it possible that the modern prophetic and apostolic movements of today have become a stumbling block and a distraction from returning to The Truth of what YAHUAH has already given through 'the Law of Moses, The Prophets and the Psalms'?
- Could this be one of Satan's master strokes to get our eyes and focus (and critically our obedience) away from the foundation of 'the law and the prophets' and trick us into seeking after what our flesh wants to hear by the tickling of our ears? A strategy to keep us trapped as a people in disobedience to what YAHUAH said through 'the law and the prophets' and stuck in lawlessness and disconnected from His everlasting covenant (agreement) with us?

YAHUSHA knew His assignment and mission on earth was directly linked to what His Father YAHUAH had spoken through 'the Law of Moses, the Prophets and the Psalms'.

> o *Then He said to them, "These are the words which I spoke to you while I was still with you, that **all things must be fulfilled which were written in the Law of Moses and the Prophets and the Psalms concerning Me."** And He opened their understanding, that they might comprehend the Scriptures. (Luke 24:44-45 NKJV)*

Tribes of Africa, may our understanding be opened up that we may comprehend the Scriptures.

> o ***"For I am YAHUAH, I do not change**; therefore you are not consumed, O sons of Jacob. [7] Yet from the days of your fathers You have gone away from My ordinances and have*

not kept them. Return to Me, and I will return to you," Says YAHUAH of hosts. "But you said, 'In what way shall we return? (Malachi 3:6-7 NKJV)

What YAHUAH spoke through 'the Law of Moses, the Prophets and the Psalms' is foundational and should not be tampered with, as He gave the warning that nothing should be added or removed, as it is written:

- o **Ye shall not add unto the word which I command you, neither shall ye diminish ought from it**, *that ye may keep the commandments of YAHUAH your Aluah which I command you. (Deuteronomy 4:2 KJV)*
- o *Every word of YAHUAH is pure: He is a shield unto them that put their trust in Him. [6]* **Add thou not unto His words,** *Lest he reprove thee, and thou be found a liar. (Proverbs 30:5-6 KJV)*
- o *For I testify unto every man that heareth the words of the prophecy of this book,* ***If any man shall add unto these things, YAHUAH shall add unto him the plagues that are written in this book: [19] and if any man shall take away from the words of the book of this prophecy, YAHUAH shall take away his part out of the book of life, and out of the holy city, and from the things which are written in this book.*** *(Revelation 22:18-19 KJV)*

Is it possible that many in the modern day prophetic and apostolic movements are guilty of 'tampering with the everlasting truth' of YAHUAH through the prophetic utterances which they speak (declare/decree) in presumption that YAHUAH will do things for them/us in contradiction and in violation to what is written in 'the Law of Moses, the Prophets and the Psalms'?

Is it possible that many are guilty of 'adding and taking away' from what YAHUAH has said?

They speak words that deceive people into believing YAHUAH will fulfil their desires and dish out blessings like a slot machine or money machine, even if they/we don't honour and obey His foundational instructions given in 'the Law, the Prophets and the Psalms'. They speak words that tickle the ears as they feed the insatiable lust of the flesh, the lust of the eyes and the pride of life that lie in people's minds, hearts and souls waiting to be fed.

They speak words that serve as 'magic charms' that are used as bait to hunt and capture souls for Satan, as it is written:

- *'Therefore thus says YAHUAH:* **"Behold, I am against your magic charms by which you hunt souls there like birds.** *I will tear them from your arms, and let the souls go, the souls you hunt like birds. [21] I will also tear off your veils and deliver My people out of your hand, and they shall no longer be as prey in your hand. Then you shall know that I am YAHUAH. (Ezekiel 13:20-21 NKJV)*

Ezekiel 13:20 speaks of the false prophets who, through their magic charms, will hunt for souls and capture them.

It's worthwhile reading the whole of Ezekiel chapter 13.

- *And the word of YAHUAH came to me, saying, [2] "Son of man, prophesy against the prophets of YASHARA'AL who prophesy, and say to those who prophesy out of their own heart, 'Hear the word of YAHUAH!" [3]* **Thus says YAHUAH: "Woe to the foolish prophets, who follow their own spirit and have seen nothing!** *[4] O YASHARA'AL, your prophets are like foxes in the deserts.*

[5] You have not gone up into the gaps to build a wall for the house of YASHARA'AL to stand in battle on the day of YAHUAH. [6] **They have envisioned futility and false divination, saying, 'Thus says YAHUAH!' But YAHUAH has not sent them; yet they hope that the word may be confirmed.** *[7] Have you not seen a futile vision, and have you not spoken false divination?* **You say, 'YAHUAH says,' but I have not spoken."** *[8] Therefore thus says YAHUAH:* **"Because you have spoken nonsense and envisioned lies, therefore I am indeed against you,"** *says YAHUAH. [9] "My hand will be against the prophets who envision futility and who divine lies; they shall not be in the assembly of My people, nor be written in the record of the house of YASHARA'AL, nor shall they enter into the land of YASHARA'AL. Then you shall know that I am YAHUAH. [10]* **"Because, indeed, because they have seduced My people, saying, 'Peace!' when there is no peace***—and one builds a wall, and they plaster it with untempered mortar [11] say to those who plaster it with untempered mortar, that it will fall. There will be flooding rain, and you, O great hailstones, shall fall; and a stormy wind shall tear it down. [12] Surely, when the wall has fallen, will it not be said to you, 'Where is the mortar with which you plastered it?" [13] Therefore thus says YAHUAH: "I will cause a stormy wind to break forth in My fury; and there shall be a flooding rain in My anger, and great hailstones in fury to consume it. [14] So I will break down the wall you have plastered with untempered mortar, and bring it down to the ground, so that its foundation will be uncovered; it will fall, and you shall be consumed in the midst of it. Then you shall know that I am YAHUAH. [15] "Thus will I accomplish My*

wrath on the wall and on those who have plastered it with untempered mortar; and I will say to you, 'The wall is no more, nor those who plastered it, [16] that is, the prophets of YASHARA'AL who prophesy concerning Yarushalayim (Jerusalem), and who see visions of peace for her when there is no peace,' " says YAHUAH. [17] "Likewise, son of man, set your face against the daughters of your people, who prophesy out of their own heart; prophesy against them, [18] and say, **'Thus says YAHUAH: "Woe to the women who sew magic charms on their sleeves and make veils for the heads of people of every height to hunt souls! Will you hunt the souls of My people, and keep yourselves alive?** *[19] And will you profane Me among My people for handfuls of barley and for pieces of bread, killing people who should not die, and keeping people alive who should not live,* **by your lying to My people who listen to lies?"** *[20] 'Therefore thus says YAHUAH:* **"Behold, I am against your magic charms by which you hunt souls there like birds. I will tear them from your arms, and let the souls go, the souls you hunt like birds.** *[21] I will also tear off your veils and deliver My people out of your hand, and they shall no longer be as prey in your hand. Then you shall know that I am YAHUAH. [22]* **"Because with lies you have made the heart of the righteous sad, whom I have not made sad; and you have strengthened the hands of the wicked, so that he does not turn from his wicked way to save his life.** *[23] Therefore you shall no longer envision futility nor practice divination; for I will deliver My people out of your hand, and you shall know that I am YAHUAH." (Ezekiel 13:1-23 NKJV)*

🕯 O YAHUAH, may You hear the cries of repentance from Africa and deliver the people who are called by Your Name out of the hands of the false prophets and apostles who use divination with magic charms to hunt for the souls of the people.

The magic charms of the diviners seduce us to build walls and plaster them with untampered mortar. Building what YAHUAH has not sanctioned for building and what He will, therefore, mark for destruction. This is important to understand as we seek solutions for the rebuilding of the other 11 domains of control as will be addressed in Chapters 24 and 25.

- *Then YAHUAH said unto Moses, Go in unto Pharaoh, and tell him, Thus saith YAHUAH Aluah of the Hebrews, **Let My people go, that they may serve Me**. (Exodus 9:1 KJV)*
- *And I heard another voice from heaven, saying, **Come out of her, My people**, that ye be not partakers of her sins, and that ye receive not of her plagues. (Revelation 18:4 KJV)*

🕯 **Tribes of Africa,** the worst type of bondage/slavery is the one where we think we are free, when in actual fact we are in chains and working for the slave master. Because we think we are free, we don't fight, accepting the slavery we are in as freedom and passing that acceptance down to the next generation.

May our hearts be filled with the deep desire to get out of bondage and slavery and return to 'The Way', the 'ancient path' and the 'narrow road' that was established for us before the ancient path was captured by the enemy and made very wide by Christian syncretism.

Do we need prophets, apostles and teachers?

I believe so, but only those called, chosen and commissioned by

YAHUAH to point us back to the covenant (agreement) and teach us The Way of truth.

We have a choice on the path we are to take, the ancient one or the new one, the narrow one or the wide one.

 Tribes of Africa, choose wisely.

> o *Thus saith YAHUAH, Stand ye in the ways, and see, and **ask for the old paths, where is the good way, and walk therein, and ye shall find rest for your souls**. But they said, we will not walk therein. (Jeremiah 6:16 KJV)*
>
> o *"**Enter by the narrow gate**; for wide is the gate and broad is the way that leads to destruction, and there are many who go in by it. 14 **Because narrow is the gate and difficult is the way which leads to life, and there are few who find it**. (Matthew 7:13-14 NKJV)*

We must make a choice, either for 'The Way' or for Christian syncretism.

Christian syncretism is defined as –

- Incorporating pagan rituals and symbols into what was originally given.
- Blending theologies and doctrines from other beliefs.
- Adopting cultural practices or traditions which are not founded in the Bible and contradict sound, pure biblical instructions.
- Creating new religious movements mixed with elements of other beliefs.
- Removing elements of the original doctrine for expediency.
- Rebellion against the purity and holiness of what YAHUAH instructed and replacing it with other instructions.

YAHUAH strictly forbids this.

- "*These are the statutes and judgments which you shall be careful to observe in the land which YAHUAH ALAHYM of your fathers is giving you to possess, all the days that you live on the earth. [2] You shall utterly destroy all the places where the nations which you shall dispossess served their gods, on the high mountains and on the hills and under every green tree. [3] And you shall destroy their altars, break their sacred pillars, and burn their wooden images with fire; you shall cut down the carved images of their gods and destroy their names from that place. [4]* **You shall not worship YAHUAH your Aluah with such things**. (*Deuteronomy 12:1-4 NKJV*)
- *Do not be unequally yoked together with unbelievers. For what fellowship has righteousness with lawlessness? And what communion has light with darkness? [15] And what accord has MASHYACH (Christ) with Belial? Or what part has a believer with an unbeliever? [16] And what agreement has the temple of YAHUAH with idols? For you are the temple of the living YAHUAH. As YAHUAH has said: "I will dwell in them and walk among them. I will be their Alahym, and they shall be My people." [17] Therefore "Come out from among them and be separate, says YAHUAH. Do not touch what is unclean, And I will receive you." [18] "I will be a Father to you, and you shall be My sons and daughters, Says YAHUAH Almighty." (II Corinthians 6:14-18 NKJV)*
- *But I have a few things against you, because you have there those who hold the doctrine of Balaam, who taught Balak to put a stumbling block before the children of YASHARA'AL,*

- to eat things sacrificed to idols, and to commit sexual immorality. [15] Thus you also have those who hold the doctrine of the Nicolaitans, which thing I hate. [16] Repent, or else I will come to you quickly and will fight against them with the sword of My mouth. (Revelation 2:14-16 NKJV)
  - "I know your works, that you are neither cold nor hot. I could wish you were cold or hot. So then, because you are lukewarm, and neither cold nor hot, **I will vomit you out of My mouth.** (Revelation 3:15-16 NKJV)

Tribes of Africa, come out of following and worshipping the false apostles and prophets who are leading many to destruction.

- *I marvel that you are turning away so soon from Him who called you in the grace of MASHYACH, to a different gospel, [7] which is not another; but there are some who trouble you and **want to pervert the gospel of MASHYACH (Christ).** [8] But even if we, or an angel from heaven, preach any other gospel to you than what we have preached to you, let him be accursed. [9] As we have said before, so now I say again, if anyone preaches any other gospel to you than what you have received, let him be accursed.* (Galatians 1:6-9 NKJV)
- Oh, that you would bear with me in a little folly—and indeed you do bear with me. [2] For I am jealous for you with godly jealousy. **For I have betrothed you to one husband, that I may present you as a chaste virgin to MASHYACH.** [3] But I fear, lest somehow, as the serpent deceived Eve by his craftiness, so your minds may be corrupted from the simplicity that is in MASHYACH. [4] **For if he who comes preaches another YAHUSHA whom we have not preached, or if you receive a different spirit which**

> *you have not received, or a different gospel which you have not accepted—you may well put up with it! (II Corinthians 11:1-4 NKJV)*
> - ***For such are false apostles, deceitful workers, transforming themselves into apostles of MASHYACH. [14] And no wonder! For Satan himself transforms himself into an angel of light. [15] Therefore it is no great thing if his ministers also transform themselves into ministers of righteousness, whose end will be according to their works.*** *(II Corinthians 11:13-15 NKJV)*
> - ***"Enter by the narrow gate; for wide is the gate and broad is the way that leads to destruction, and there are many who go in by it.*** *[14] Because narrow is the gate and difficult is the way which leads to life, and there are few who find it. [15]* ***"Beware of false prophets, who come to you in sheep's clothing, but inwardly they are ravenous wolves.*** *(Matthew 7:13-15 NKJV)*

🔥 **Tribes of Africa,** standing before a wooden or stone cross or a wooden or stone image/statue of Jesus, bowing to it and worshipping through it, is an abomination to YAHUAH.

Just like Muslims do in front of the Kaaba stone in Mecca.

Just like Ashkenazi Jews do in front of the Wailing Wall of stone in Jerusalem.

Just like traditional Egyptian mythologies and spirituality do when they worship stone and wood-carved images of the dead.

Worshipping wood and stone objects are among the highest forms of idolatry, which YAHUAH hates. It might be the way of some of the 45,000 versions of Christianity, but it is not of The Way of YAHUAH and should not be of the house of YASHARA'AL.

- "Then YAHUAH will scatter you among all peoples, from one end of the earth to the other, and **there you shall serve other gods, which neither you nor your fathers have known—wood and stone.** (Deuteronomy 28:64 NKJV)
- but with him who stands here with us today before YAHUAH our Aluah, as well as with him who is not here with us today [16] (for you know that we dwelt in the land of Egypt and that we came through the nations which you passed by, [17] **and you saw their abominations and their idols which were among them—wood and stone and silver and gold);** [18] so that there may not be among you man or woman or family or tribe, whose heart turns away today from YAHUAH our Aluah, to go and serve the gods of these nations, and that there may not be among you a root bearing bitterness or wormwood; (Deuteronomy 29:15-18 NKJV)

Any image, even of anything in heaven, violates His first two Commandments. YAHUAH detests an image which is supposedly of Himself or His SON YAHUSHA. It is an idol.

This leads us to the next chapter, in which we ask ourselves the question whether we could be fighting against YAHUAH in ignorance.

CHAPTER TWENTY-ONE

Fighting Against YAHUAH

Is it possible that so many warfare and battle strategies have been developed in modern Christianity to fight the enemy when the enemy is actually not the issue at all? Rather, the real issue is directly between us and YAHUAH, the ALAHYM of Abraham, Isaac and Jacob, who by covenantal agreement with His people promised us 'the blessing' **IF** we keep His covenant and obey His constitution (laws, commandments, judgements, statutes, precepts, ordinances), and likewise promised us 'the curse' **IF** we don't keep His covenant and **IF** we don't obey His constitution.

Have we spent much time in spiritual warfare fighting the curses that are upon us because we think it is a work of Satan, when actually it is the Most High who has brought them upon us to fulfil what He said He would do if we rejected His covenant and constitution (Torah)?

The righteousness of YAHUAH is Him fulfilling everything which He said He would do. So, in righteousness He brings the blessing, and likewise in righteousness He brings the curse. All that He does is righteous for all He does is always according to His word (His instructions - His Torah) and the agreement He made with His people.

Maybe we have been focused on the wrong thing, declaring war on the enemy, when what the Most High is asking us to do is to come out of lawlessness and return to the covenant and constitution so that He can remove the curse and bring the blessing in accordance with His Word and the terms of the agreement which He holds Himself accountable to.

Do we really have the authority to break curses, or is that the sole prerogative of the Most High based on **IF** we are keeping the terms of the agreement (the covenant) or not, and **IF** we obey His constitution (laws, commandments, judgements, statutes, precepts, ordinances) or not?

If YAHUAH said He would bring the curse (calamity, bondage, desolation) upon us **IF** we reject His voice, His covenant, His constitution, why do we think we can break the curse when we have not done what He says we should do? Would that not constitute YAHUAH allowing unrighteousness? Have we been pridefully presumptuous and even fought against The Most High's own righteousness in our ignorance as we 'name and claim', 'speak words of faith', 'decree and declare' what we want when we are in rebellion to Him and have rejected the covenant?

YAHUAH is not moved by the power of man's words or the faith (presumptions) of man's words. All the teaching that speaks of the power of man's words and does not address the need to submit to the law of YAHUAH and to obey it is leading us in the wrong direction. YAHUAH only moves to what He has obligated Himself to according to the constitution of His Kingdom and the terms of agreement He has established with the citizens of His Kingdom.

Leviticus chapter 26 lays it out so clearly. It specifies what He says He will do (not the enemy) **IF** we do not obey and **IF** we despise His instructions (Constitution). In fact, 4 times He says, "***IF** you walk contrary to Me and are not willing to obey Me, I will bring upon you 7 times more 'curses' according to your sins*". YAHUAH brings calamity and desolation upon us; the enemy might be the agent to do it, but the directive for it to happen is from YAHUAH. So, our only response to turn this around is to confess, admit our guilt, repent through the blood and the finished work of YAHUSHA and revert to doing what the Most High has instructed us to do, while at the same time pursuing obedience to live in righteousness through the sanctification and justification we have obtained through YAHUSHA MASHYACH.

We cannot expect curses to break if we are in violation of YAHUAH's law and commandments. Curses have the legal right to be upon us if we reject YAHUAH's constitution. If we refuse to accept His law, we will be cursed as it is written.

- o **'Cursed be anyone who does not confirm the words of this law by doing them.'** *And all the people shall say, 'Amen.' (Deuteronomy 27:26 ESV)*

The prayer of strength is one that acknowledges YAHUAH's set law and commandments, because if it does not, it sets the standard of what sin is according to the standards of men. Confession and repentance are then done from a flawed standard.

If YAHUAH has said in the 2nd commandment that the iniquity of worshipping graven images and idols will be passed down to the 3rd and 4th generations, it means the judgement YAHUAH has given for breaking this commandment will remain until the transgression of His law is repented for. Likewise, if YAHUAH says there will be a consequence for taking His name in vain in the 3rd commandment, it means the curse will remain until the transgression is acknowledged and repented of. The same goes for the 4th commandment of the Sabbath and all others, which go beyond the 10 commandments.

No prayer of man can override or circumvent how YAHUAH has designed His system of judgement to work.

The words below are YAHUAH speaking."

- **'But if you do not obey Me, and do not observe all these commandments, [15] and if you despise My statutes, or if your soul abhors My judgments, so that you do not perform all My commandments, but break My covenant, [16] I also will do this to you: I will** even appoint terror over you, wasting disease and fever which shall consume the eyes and cause sorrow of heart. And you shall sow your seed in vain, for your enemies shall eat it. [17] **I will** set My face against you, and you shall be defeated by your enemies. Those who hate you shall reign over you, and you shall flee when no one pursues you. [18] **'And after all this, if you do not obey Me, then I will punish you seven times more for your sins. [19] I will** break the pride of your power; **I will** make your heavens like iron and your earth like bronze. [20] And your strength shall be spent in vain; for your land shall not yield its produce, nor shall the trees of the land yield their fruit. [21] **'Then, if you walk contrary to Me, and are not willing to obey Me, I will bring on you seven times more plagues, according to your sins.** [22] **I will** also send wild beasts among you, which shall rob you of your children, destroy your livestock, and make you few in number; and your highways shall be desolate. [23] **'And if by these things you are not reformed by Me,**

but walk contrary to Me, [24] then I also will walk contrary to you, and I will punish you yet seven times for your sins. *[25] And **I will** bring a sword against you that will execute the vengeance of the covenant; when you are gathered together within your cities I will send pestilence among you; and you shall be delivered into the hand of the enemy. [26] When I have cut off your supply of bread, ten women shall bake your bread in one oven, and they shall bring back your bread by weight, and you shall eat and not be satisfied. [27] **'And after all this, if you do not obey Me, but walk contrary to Me, [28] then I also will walk contrary to you in fury; and I, even I, will chastise you seven times for your sins.** [29] You shall eat the flesh of your sons, and you shall eat the flesh of your daughters. [30] **I will** destroy your high places, cut down your incense altars, and cast your carcasses on the lifeless forms of your idols; and My soul shall abhor you. [31] **I will** lay your cities waste and bring your sanctuaries to desolation, and **I will** not smell the fragrance of your sweet aromas. [32] **I will** bring the land to desolation, and your enemies who dwell in it shall be astonished at it. [33] **I will** scatter you among the nations and draw out a sword after you; your land shall be desolate and your cities waste. [34] Then the land shall enjoy its sabbaths as long as it lies desolate and you are in your enemies' land; then the land shall rest and enjoy its sabbaths. [35] As long as it lies desolate it shall rest— for the time it did not rest on your sabbaths when you dwelt in it. [36] 'And as for those of you who are left, **I will** send faintness into their hearts in the lands of their enemies; the sound of a shaken leaf shall cause them to flee; they shall flee as though fleeing from a sword, and they shall fall when* *no one pursues. [37] They shall stumble over one another, as it were before a sword, when no one pursues; and you shall have no power to stand before your enemies. [38] You shall perish among the nations, and the land of your enemies shall eat you up. [39] And those of you who are left shall waste away in their iniquity in your enemies' lands; also in their fathers' iniquities, which are with them, they shall waste away. (Leviticus 26:14-39 NKJV)*

I believe the real battle we have is not one of binding the enemy and breaking curses on our own (as much as we often claim to do it in the name of Jesus), but rather our foremost battle is to do everything in our power to return to the covenant of our Husband and the constitution of our King. Returning to our Father YAHUAH through the Way which has been made possible through the laid down life and poured out blood of YAHUSHA who is 'The Way'.

Where does 'The Way' lead us back to? Perhaps we have forgotten or don't know the answer to this question.

If we reject the covenant and constitution of YAHUAH, it means we reject the destination of where 'The Way' is leading us back to, which is The Father YAHUAH. It means we reject our Maker, our Husband, the Most High Judge and the Most High King, for every marriage is established by a covenant, every court functions by law, and every Kingdom is governed by a constitution.

As the first followers of YAHUSHA were called people of 'The Way', they knew 'The Way' was leading them to a destination, which is the FATHER. They knew Torah (YAHUAH's instructions), they knew His covenant agreement with them (their marriage to Him), they knew the constitution of the Kingdom and that YAHUSHA had come to fulfil YAHUAH's promise to save them and bring them back into the covenant because they had broken that agreement. Perhaps the mainstream institution of Christianity has gotten us to lose 'The Way' and to 'walk contrary' to Him. Perhaps our greatest challenge today is that we have lost 'The Way', the narrow path and do not know the destination where it leads to and hence have no covenant relationship with Abba YAHUAH (as much as we think we do). We must reflect again on these words.

> o *"Not everyone who says to Me, 'Lord, Lord, (Master, Master)' shall enter the kingdom of heaven, but he who does the will of My Father in heaven. [22] Many will say to Me in that day, 'Lord, Lord, (Master, Master) have we not prophesied in Your name, cast out demons in Your name, and done many wonders in Your name?' [23]* ***And then I will declare to them, 'I never knew you; depart from Me, you who practice lawlessness!'*** *(Matthew 7:21-23 NKJV)*

I believe the biggest constraint to prayer is that most churches have taught their people that YAHUAH's law and commandments are Old Testament requirements and, therefore, are no longer valid. Believing this places most people in rebellion against YAHUAH. This is a big stumbling block in prayer ministries. They reject YAHUAH's laws and commandments in their hearts, and this renders much prayer ineffective before YAHUAH, as He says He will not hear the prayers of those who are in rebellion.

All scripture has been given by YAHUAH, both what we call today the Old and New Testaments. We cannot pick and choose what we deem to be valid because all that YAHUAH has said is valid.

> o ***All scripture is given by inspiration of YAHUAH****, and is profitable for doctrine, for reproof, for correction, for*

instruction in righteousness: [17] that the man of YAHUAH may be perfect, thoroughly furnished unto all good works. (2 Timothy 3:16-17 KJV)

Tribes of Africa, can we claim to be citizens of YAHUAH's Kingdom when we have rejected the constitution of the King? Can we claim to be in marriage with our Creator, our Husband, if we have rejected His covenant? Can we claim to love Him when we are openly disobedient to His instructions (through the Law, the Prophets and the Psalms) because we have rejected them?

When we reject His covenant and His constitution, does that not mean we reject both His position and authority as The Most High Judge, King, and Sovereign over ALL?

How can we even go into His courts when we have rejected His law? For He is the Judge, the Lawgiver and the King, the one who saves us (Isaiah 33:22). Is it possible that we have gone into His courts many times in the past and He has rejected our cases because we did not comply with His instructions (through what He said in the Law, Prophets and Psalms). In fact, we had/have rejected His instructions and yet we expected/expect Him to rule in our favour. (It sounds crazy and makes no sense that we would go to a court, having rejected the law by which the Judge makes decisions, yet we still expect him to rule in our favour! Selah).

The word of faith and the power of words, doctrines, and movements

Something I was once so immersed in is what I call "the power of words, just speak it by faith and it shall be, decree and declare and it shall be established" movements within charismatic Christianity. After coming out of it and repenting for thinking I can command YAHUAH to do things for me while I am in rebellion against Him,

I felt compelled to find out where the basis of this practice could have emerged from.

I believe the answer lies in one of the topics which was discussed in Rewriting History in chapter two, the topic of 'the Greek versus the Hebraic' basis of thinking and, hence, interpreting scriptures.

In summary, to the Greek mindset, obedience is intellectual (thinking and speaking-based), whereas to the Hebraic mindset, obedience is doing (action-based).

These are the traits of the Greek mindset when it comes to obedience.

Obedience = (equals) Intellectual assent, because Greek philosophy emphasised abstract reasoning, knowledge, and contemplation, with 'knowing' often separated from doing.

Plato, Aristotle, and later Hellenistic schools viewed the ideal life as a pursuit of correct understanding of forms, ideals, or truths and in this framework, belief or agreement in the intellect could be primary, and behaviour was often secondary. This is what influenced Western Christianity, where orthodoxy (right belief) often took priority over orthopraxy (right practice).

For example, "I know the word of God and so I will just speak it, and because I have spoken it, I have obeyed it, and so it shall come to pass".

The Greek mindset with regard to how it views obedience is likened to building on sand.

- o "Therefore whoever hears these sayings of Mine, and does them, I will liken him to a wise man who built his house on the rock: [25] and the rain descended, the floods came, and the winds blew and beat on that house; and it did not fall, for it was founded on the rock. [26] **"But everyone who hears these sayings of Mine, and does not do them, will be like a foolish man who built his house on the sand: [27] and the rain descended, the floods came, and the winds blew and beat on that house; and it fell. And great was its fall."** (Matthew 7:24-27 NKJV)

In turn, here are the traits of the Hebraic mindset when it comes to obedience.

Obedience = (equals) Action, because in Hebraic thinking, knowing and doing are inseparable. Shema, the famous word from Deuteronomy 6:4, means "hear," but it implies listening with the intention to act.

"Hear, O YASHARA'AL... You shall love YAHUAH your Aluah..."

In Hebrew, there is often no separate word for "obey", as "to hear" and "to do" are understood together and to be the same thing.

For example, in Exodus 24:7, after the Book of the Covenant was read to the children of YASHARA'AL, they responded with these words, *"We will do, and we will hear"*. The order of the words in their response shows the commitment to act came before fully understanding, because when YAHUAH had said it, then there was no need to intellectually think it through before responding to Him. Righteousness and faithfulness are demonstrated in practice, not just belief. Even the concept of AMUNAH (which is the word for faith) implies steadfastness and loyalty in 'doing obedience' and not just mental assent.

The Hebraic mindset with regard to how it views obedience is likened to building on the rock.

> o *"Therefore whoever hears these sayings of Mine, and does them, I will liken him to a wise man who built his house on the rock: [25] and the rain descended, the floods came, and the winds blew and beat on that house; and it did not fall, for it was founded on the rock.* [26] "But everyone who hears these sayings of Mine, and does not do them, will be like a foolish man who built his house on the sand: [27] and the rain descended, the floods came, and the winds blew and beat on that house; and it fell. And great was its fall." (Matthew 7:24-27 NKJV)

Interestingly, in most Bantu languages, there is also no separation between the words used for 'to hear', 'to obey', and 'to do'. For example, in my mother tongue of Shona, the word 'TEERERA' can mean 'listen to what I am saying' and equally mean 'do what I am saying', and the measurement of whether one has heard is based on whether one has performed the required action or not. This again illustrates the YASHARA'ALITE culture and language, ingrained and inseparable from what we would call African culture and language construction.

With this background, I come back to the issue of the prevalent practice taught in charismatic Christianity of making things happen by "just speak words of faith, just decree the word, just speak and release the power of agreement of God's word". I take a position to categorically state this does not work because it is not Hebraically biblical, nor is it part of how YAHUAH has designed His Kingdom to work. It is a practice that has been established through a Greek mindset that does not appreciate that obedience is doing what YAHUAH has said, which is simply obeying 'the Law, the Prophets, the Psalms and the Testimony of YAHUSHA'. The Greek mindset rather seeks to believe intellectually and hence speak out what it believes and thinks, convinced that is where the power to make things happen comes from. It is actually quite pagan.

🍂 **Tribes of Africa,** naming and claiming what we want and desire, independently of submission to YAHUAH's laws and commandments is not of YAHUAH and is praying amiss.

> o ***Ye ask, and receive not, because ye ask amiss****, that ye may consume it upon your lusts. (James 4:3 KJV)*

YAHUAH moves based on what He has given in His constitution (which are the words He spoke through The Law, the Prophets, the Psalms and The Testimony), and the terms of the agreement (the Covenant) He holds Himself accountable to. Anything else I believe is false doctrine. Please discern.

I fear and tremble that these power of words doctrines border very close to man (the created being), elevating himself above YAHUAH (the creator) and commanding YAHUAH to serve and fulfil the desires of the 'created being', while 'the created being' is in rebellion to YAHUAH. It seems too close to what Lucifer attempted to do as it is written:

> o *"How you are fallen from heaven, O Lucifer, son of the morning! How you are cut down to the ground, you who weakened the nations! [13] For you have said in your heart: 'I will ascend into heaven,* **I will exalt my throne above the stars of YAHUAH; I will also sit on the mount of the congregation** *on the farthest sides of the north; [14] I will ascend above the heights of the clouds,* **I will be like the Most High.'** *(Isaiah 14:12-14 NKJV)*

🍂 No man can command YAHUAH. Let us be very careful, for we might be fighting against YAHUAH.

CHAPTER TWENTY-TWO

Confronting And Resisting The White Horse That Came Conquering And To Conquer Africa

As it is written:

- *And I looked, and behold, a white horse. He who sat on it had a bow; and a crown was given to him, and he went out conquering and to conquer. (Revelation 6:2)*

During the period referred to as the 'dark ages', roughly spanning from the fifth to the fifteenth centuries (approximately 500 – 1500 AD), the Roman Catholic Church took sole control of the Holy Bible, making it inaccessible to the people. It was during this period that the original Hebrew, Aramaic and Greek texts were translated and transliterated into Latin. It was during this period of 'controlling the Bible' that textual variations occurred, influenced by theological and doctrinal biases to fit the Roman Empire and its agenda to bring unity in the empire by merging multiple beliefs into a single religion for the empire. This mixed religion is what became the foundation of modern Christianity under the authority of the Universal (Catholic) Church. This brought about Christian syncretism, which was the mixture of certain portions of the Truth, blended together with portions of other pagan beliefs.

The removal of the original names of YAHUAH and YAHUSHA is one of the primary and most destructive changes which were made.

Examples of other potential changes include:

- The Comma Johanneum (1 John 5:7-8): A disputed passage that some scholars argue was added to support the doctrine of the Trinity, as major pagan religions had this concept.
- The Vulgate's rendering of Matthew 16:18: Jerome's (one of the so-called church fathers) translation used 'petra' (rock) instead of "Petros" (Peter), which was influenced by Catholic teaching on the papacy, and to give the papacy a position that is not biblical.
- The addition of the Filioque clause: A phrase added to the Nicene Creed, which was influenced by the Catholic theology on the Holy Spirit.
- Further grammatical changes, interpretations and translations were influenced by prevailing doctrines such as the veneration of saints, purgatory and sacraments, the right to grant forgiveness, the position of Mary, etc.

All of this and many others, which are outside of the scope of this book, effectively took the purity and Holiness of the Word of YAHUAH and The Way of YAHUSHA and contaminated it to further the interests of empire building, control and power.

The rest of this section is a confrontation against what was birthed by the 'white horse' at the first ecumenical council of the religion of Christianity. The First Council of Nicaea was the first ecumenical council of the Christian church from the 20th of May to the end of July 325, called by Roman Emperor Constantine I. It was the platform which effectively placed global Christianity, at the time, under the authority of Roman Catholicism and the Roman Empire and continues to influence global Christianity today.

🐎 Tribes of Africa, we must pray for our Deliverance from lawlessness

What follows is a prayer to YAHUAH asking for the deliverance of Africa from the spiritual blanket that Roman Catholicism spread over the continent. A blanket that has drawn us into accepting a religion of lawlessness, which keeps us away from what YAHUAH requires of us. A blanket that is a stumbling block, preventing us from restoring the covenant relationship with our Father YAHUAH and entering into His Kingdom under His everlasting constitution.

PLEASE NOTE: *Again, this is not any form of condemnation for the millions of people who love the Father and yet have not fully understood for themselves what the agreement (the covenant) YAHUAH made with them, and the path that YAHUSHA established to give us The Way to return to the agreement (covenant), and the Spirit of YAHUAH (Holy Spirit) who empowers us to walk in The Way. The Apostle Paul had such a love for YAHUAH that as he persecuted and killed people of "The Way", he sincerely believed he was doing the right thing, until YAHUSHA appeared to him on the road to Damascus. YAHUSHA showed him the truth and poured out His amazing grace upon Paul to such an extent that he became one of the most powerful instruments for the truth. I pray that YAHUSHA will do the same for many who deeply love Him and yet are deceived by the institutions they have pledged allegiance to.*

- o *Then Saul, still breathing threats and murder against the disciples of YAHUSHA, went to the high priest [2] and asked letters from him to the synagogues of Damascus, so that if he found any who were of the Way, whether men or women, he might bring them bound to Jerusalem. [3] As he journeyed he came near Damascus, and suddenly a light shone around him from heaven. [4] Then he fell to the ground, and heard a voice saying to him, "Saul, Saul, why are you persecuting Me?" [5] And he said, "Who are You, Master?" Then YAHUSHA said, "I am YAHUSHA, whom you are persecuting. It is hard for you to kick against the goads." [6] So he, trembling and astonished, said, "Master, what do You want me to do?" Then YAHUSHA said to him, "Arise and go into the city, and you will be told what you must do." (Acts 9:1-6 NKJV)*

Intercession at the 1700-year anniversary of the First Council of Nicaea

We proclaim that:

* *The usage of the title God or Lord in all scripture references is replaced with the given name of YAHUAH (YHUH), the Alahym of Abraham, the Alahym of Isaac and the Alahym of Jacob (as per original biblical texts before changed by Greco-Roman power).*

* *Similarly, the usage of the name Jesus in all scripture references is replaced by His given name YAHUSHA (which means 'YAHUAH (YHUH) is our salvation' or 'YAHUAH (YHUH) saves') (as per original biblical texts before changed by Greco-Roman power).*

As it is written:

- *And Alahym said to Moses, "I AM WHO I AM." And He said, "Thus you shall say to the children of YASHARA'AL, 'I AM has sent me to you.'"* **15** *Moreover Alahym said to Moses, "Thus you shall say to the children of YASHARA'AL: 'YAHUAH (YHUH) Alahym of your fathers, the Alahym of Abraham, the Alahym of Isaac, and the Alahym of Jacob, has sent me to you. This is My name forever, and this is My memorial to all generations.' (Exodus 3:14-15)*

- *Alahym spoke further to Moses and said to him, "I am YAHUAH. **3** I appeared to Abraham, to Isaac and to Jacob, as El Shaddai. Yet by My Name, YAHUAH, did I not make Myself known to them. (Exodus 6:3 NKJV)*

- *And she will bring forth a Son, and you shall call His name YAHUSHA (YAHUAH saves/YAHUAH my salvation), for He will save His people from their sins." (Matthew 1:21 NKJV)*

- *For even if there are so-called gods, whether in heaven or on earth (as there are many gods and many lords), **6** yet for us there is one YAHUAH, the Father, of whom are all things, and we for Him; and one Master YAHUSHA MASHYACH, through whom are all things, and through whom we live. (1 Corinthians 8:5-6 NKJV)*

Acknowledgement of our history of covenant/agreement with YAHUAH, I AM, the ALAHYM of Abraham, Isaac and Jacob

YAHUAH, I AM WHO I AM, the ALAHYM of Abraham, Isaac and Jacob; You created Adam and placed him in the Garden of Eden. By Your Voice, You established Your first covenant with man as You gave Him the instructions (Your first command and law).

As it is written:

- *And YAHUAH Aluah took the man, and put him into the garden of Eden to dress it and to keep it. **16** And YAHUAH Aluah commanded the man, saying, of every tree of the garden* *thou mayest freely eat:* **17** *But of the tree of the knowledge of good and evil, thou shalt not eat of it: for in the day that thou eatest thereof thou shalt surely die. (Genesis 2:15-17 NKJV)*

YAHUAH, I AM WHO I AM, the ALAHYM of Abraham, Isaac and Jacob; You delivered Your people out of the land of Egypt, out of the house of bondage through Your servant Moses and established a covenant with us once again.

As it is written:

- *And Moses went up unto Aluah, and YAHUAH called unto him out of the mountain, saying, thus shalt thou say to the house of Jacob, and tell the children of YASHARA'AL;* **4** *Ye have seen what I did unto the Egyptians, and how I bare you on eagles' wings, and brought you unto myself.* **5** *Now therefore, if ye will obey my voice indeed, and keep my covenant, then ye shall be a peculiar treasure unto me above all people: for all the earth is mine:* **6** *And ye shall be unto me a kingdom of priests, and a holy nation. These are the words which thou shalt speak unto the children of YASHARA'AL. (Exodus 19:3-6 NKJV)*

YAHUAH, I AM WHO I AM, the ALAHYM of Abraham, Isaac and Jacob, we accepted the Words that You spoke. We accepted and committed to do them through the 70 elders who stood before You as representatives of the tribes and of those of the nations who would be grafted into the tribes.

As it is written:

- *And all the people answered together, and said, All that YAHUAH hath spoken we will do. And Moses returned the words of the people unto YAHUAH. (Exodus 19:8 NKJV)*
- *And he said unto Moses, Come up unto YAHUAH, thou,*

> and Aaron, Nadab, and Abihu, and seventy of the elders of YASHARA'AL; and worship ye afar off. **2** And Moses alone shall come near YAHUAH: but they shall not come nigh; neither shall the people go up with him. **3** And Moses came and told the people all the words of YAHUAH, and all the judgments: and all the people answered with one voice, and said, All the words which YAHUAH hath said will we do. **4** And Moses wrote all the words of YAHUAH, and rose up early in the morning, and builded an altar under the hill, and twelve pillars, according to the twelve tribes of YASHARA'AL. **5** And he sent young men of the children of YASHARA'AL, which offered burnt offerings, and sacrificed peace offerings of oxen unto YAHUAH. **6** And Moses took half of the blood, and put it in basons; and half of the blood he sprinkled on the altar. **7** And he took the book of the covenant, and read in the audience of the people: and they said, all that YAHUAH hath said will we do, and be obedient. **8** And Moses took the blood, and sprinkled it on the people, and said, Behold the blood of the covenant, which YAHUAH hath made with you concerning all these words. (Exodus 24: 1-8 NKJV)

- *And as they were eating, YAHUSHA took bread, and blessed it, and brake it, and gave it to the disciples, and said, Take, eat; this is my body.* **27 And he took the cup, and gave thanks, and gave it to them, saying, Drink ye all of it; 28** *For this is my blood of the new testament, which is shed for many for the remission of sins. (Matthew 26:26-28 NKJV)*

YAHUAH, I AM WHO I AM, the ALAHYM of Abraham, Isaac and Jacob, we therefore acknowledge that we committed ourselves to an agreement – a covenant with You which was sealed with blood that we would –

- Obey Your voice

- Keep Your covenant

- Obey Your laws and commandments

YAHUAH, I AM WHO I AM, the ALAHYM of Abraham, Isaac and Jacob, we understand the choices You gave us and the consequences thereof concerning the agreement, the covenant You made with us – that our obedience would be a choice for life and the blessing and that our disobedience would be a choice for death and the curse.

As it is written:

- *And it shall come to pass, if thou shalt hearken diligently unto the voice of YAHUAH thy Aluah, to observe and to do all his commandments which I command thee this day, that YAHUAH thy Aluah will set thee on high above all nations of the earth: 2 And all these blessings shall come on thee, and overtake thee, if thou shalt hearken unto the voice of YAHUAH thy Aluah. (Deuteronomy 28:1-2 NKJV)*
- *But it shall come to pass, if thou wilt not hearken unto the voice of YAHUAH thy Aluah, to observe to do all his commandments and his statutes which I command thee this day; that all these curses shall come upon thee, and overtake thee: (Deuteronomy 28:15 NKJV)*
- *For this commandment which I command thee this day, it is not hidden from thee, neither is it far off. 12 It is not in heaven, that thou shouldest say, who shall go up for us to heaven, and bring it unto us, that we may hear it, and do it? 13 Neither is it beyond the sea, that thou shouldest say, who shall go over the sea for us, and bring it unto us, that we may hear it, and do it? 14 But the word is very nigh unto thee, in thy mouth, and in thy heart, that thou mayest do*

> it. ***15 See, I have set before thee this day life and good, and death and evil; 16** In that I command thee this day to love YAHUAH thy Aluah, to walk in his ways, and to keep his commandments and his statutes and his judgments, that thou mayest live and multiply: and YAHUAH thy Aluah shall bless thee in the land whither thou goest to possess it. **17** But if thine heart turn away, so that thou wilt not hear, but shalt be drawn away, and worship other gods, and serve them; **18** I denounce unto you this day, that ye shall surely perish, and that ye shall not prolong your days upon the land, whither thou passest over Jordan to go to possess it. **19** I call heaven and earth to record this day against you, that I have set before you life and death, blessing and cursing: therefore choose life, that both thou and thy seed may live: **20** That thou mayest love YAHUAH thy Aluah, and that thou mayest obey his voice, and that thou mayest cleave unto him: for he is thy life, and the length of thy days: that thou mayest dwell in the land which YAHUAH sware unto thy fathers, to Abraham, to Isaac, and to Jacob, to give them. (Deuteronomy 30:11-20 KJV)*

YAHUAH, I AM WHO I AM, the ALAHYM of Abraham, Isaac and Jacob, we acknowledge that You have further told us 'What you require of Us.

As it is written:

- o "And now, YASHARA'AL, what does YAHUAH your Aluah require of you, but to fear YAHUAH your Aluah, to walk in all His ways and to love Him, to serve YAHUAH your Aluah with all your heart and with all your soul, **13** and to keep the commandments of YAHUAH and His statutes which I command you today for your good? **14** Indeed

- *heaven and the highest heavens belong to YAHUAH your Aluah, also the earth with all that is in it. (Deuteronomy 10:12 NKJV)*
  - *He hath shewed thee, O man, what is good; and what doth YAHUAH require of thee, but to do justly, and to love mercy, and to walk humbly with thy Aluah? (Micah 6:8 KJV)*
  - *Let us hear the conclusion of the whole matter: Fear YAHUAH, and keep his commandments: for this is the whole duty of man. (Ecclesiastes 12:13 NKJV)*

Acknowledgement of our transgression of the agreement – covenant and how the Council of Nicaea birthed lawlessness

YAHUAH, I AM WHO I AM, the ALAHYM of Abraham, Isaac and Jacob, today we come before Your throne knowing that You are our Judge, our Lawgiver and our King, our Salvation; to present our case as we recognize how we have transgressed the agreement You made with us through our ancestors and have departed from Your ways and burdened You with our sins and wearied You with our iniquities. We now take up the offer You have made to us to state our case before You, that we may be acquitted by Your righteous judgement.

As it is written:

- *For YAHUAH is our Judge, YAHUAH is our Lawgiver, YAHUAH is our King; He will save us; (Isaiah 33:22 NKJV)*
- *"But you have not called upon Me, O Jacob; And you have been weary of Me, O YASHARA'AL. **23** You have not brought Me the sheep for your burnt offerings, nor have you honored Me with your sacrifices. I have not caused you to serve with grain offerings, nor wearied you with incense. **24** You have bought Me no sweet cane with*

> *money, nor have you satisfied Me with the fat of your sacrifices; But you have burdened Me with your sins, You have wearied Me with your iniquities.* **25** *"I, even I, am He who blots out your transgressions for My own sake; And I will not remember your sins.* **26** *Put Me in remembrance; Let us contend together; State your case, that you may be acquitted.* **27** *Your first father sinned, and your mediators have transgressed against Me.* **28** *Therefore I will profane the princes of the sanctuary; I will give Jacob to the curse, And YASHARA'AL to reproaches. (Isaiah 43:22-28 NKJV)*

YAHUAH, I AM WHO I AM, the ALAHYM of Abraham, Isaac and Jacob, we recognise we have entered the 1700th cycle of time since the Roman Emperor Constantine brought the global Christian church to the First Council of Nicaea from the 20th May to the end of July 325CE to place them under the authority of Roman Catholicism and the Roman Empire.

It is at this First Council of Nicaea that many doctrines of demons and traditions of men derived from paganism were mixed into 'The Way', and likewise much truth of 'The Way' was removed to create a religion which was controlled from Rome through the Roman Catholic church.

The doctrines of demons and traditions of men, which were introduced and the truths of 'The Way', which were removed at this First Council of Nicaea, have filtered into most of the modern-day Christian faith.

YAHUAH, I AM WHO I AM, the ALAHYM of Abraham, Isaac and Jacob, we recognise the First Council of Nicaea was used as a platform to:

- Mix the worship of Sol Invictus (sun worship) and the

pagan deities of the nations into the original faith, which was called 'The Way' and later named Christianity. Even as it is recognised in scripture that the original followers of YAHUSHA HA MASHYACH were named and called themselves as 'the people of The Way'.

- Birth a new religion (through syncretism) which came from a seed and spirit of lawlessness because of the father of lies, the deceiver, the adversary Satan's deep hatred for The Most High Alahym of Abraham, Isaac and Jacob and likewise Satan's deep hatred for the chosen people of YAHUAH, YASHARA'AL (the true bloodline descendants of Jacob). It is the seed and spirit of lawlessness which rejected The Most High, His Ways, His Covenant with YASHARA'AL, His Commandments and Laws and the people through whom He designated to shine His light to the nations. A religious syncretism which rejected the plan of YAHUAH to bring His salvation to all nations through His firstborn people of YASHARA'AL. It is a religious system that removed the original name YAHUAH (YHUH) of the Aluah of Abraham, Isaac and Jacob from the Bible and also that of The Son YAHUSHA (YAHUAH saves) in violation of the 3rd Commandment, replacing them with Lord, God and Iesous (later to Jesus when the letter J was introduced in the alphabet in 1524).
- Appointed a man to carry the title 'Father/Pope' in direct disobedience to Your instruction that *'Do not call anyone on earth your father; for One is your Father, He who is in heaven'.* *(Matthew 23:9 NKJV)*
- Changed the times and laws as per the words of Daniel 7:25 *'He shall speak pompous words against the Most High, shall persecute the saints of the Most High, and shall intend to change*

times and law. Then the saints shall be given into his hand for a time and times and half a time,'

It is a religious syncretism which –

- Changed the Sabbath and removed the Holy Feasts of YAHUAH (Passover, Unleavened Bread, First Fruits, Shavuot/Pentecost, Trumpets, Day of Atonement and Tabernacles) and replaced them with pagan derived holidays of Easter, Christmas and others; thereby taking Your people away from obedience to the eternal laws and appointed times. Even as they changed the calendar to establish the Pope Gregory solar calendar, which is followed today and is in violation of Your eternal calendar.
- Venerated Mary, the mother of YAHUSHA (YAHUAH saves), making her the way to You and an object of worship in violation of the First and Second Commandments.

    o Venerated men as saints to be worshipped and bowed down to in violation of the First and Second Commandments.

    o Established the worship of the pagan trinity of Nimrod, Semiramis and Tammuz within the syncretism.

    o Established the worship of graven images, pictures, items made of wood and stone to bow and serve them in violation of the First and Second commandments.

    o Changed scriptures in the Bible including the 10 commandments and removed biblical books from the Bible in violation of *Deuteronomy 4:2 - You shall not add to the word which I command you, nor take from it, that you may keep the commandments of YAHUAH your Aluah which I command you*, and *Revelation 22:18-19 For I testify to everyone who hears the words of the prophecy of this book: If anyone adds to these things, YAHUAH will add to him the plagues that are written in this book; and if anyone takes away from the words of the book of this prophecy, YAHUAH shall take away his part from the Book of Life, from the holy city, and from the things which are written in this book.*

- o Established an altar of formal pagan worship within the temple of the Most High, the weeping for Tammuz (Ezekiel 8:14) and the worship of the Sun (Ezekiel 8:16) and make offerings to the queen of heaven (Ishtar) and other gods (Jeremiah 7:18 NKJV).

As it is written:

- *And it came to pass in the sixth year, in the sixth month, on the fifth day of the month, as I sat in my house with the elders of Judah sitting before me, that the hand of YAHUAH Aluah fell upon me there. 2 Then I looked, and there was a likeness, like the appearance of fire—from the appearance of His waist and downward, fire; and from His waist and upward, like the appearance of brightness, like the color of amber. 3 He stretched out the form of a hand, and took me by a lock of my hair; and the Spirit lifted me up between earth and heaven, and brought me in visions of YAHUAH to Yarushalayim (Jerusalem), to the door of the north gate of the inner court, where the seat of the image of jealousy was, which provokes to jealousy. 4 And behold, the glory of YAHUAH of YASHARA'AL was there, like the vision that I saw in the plain. 5 Then He said to me, "Son of man, lift your eyes now toward the north." So I lifted my eyes toward the north, and there, north of the altar gate, was* *this image of jealousy in the entrance. **6** Furthermore He said to me, "Son of man, do you see what they are doing, the great abominations that the house of YASHARA'AL commits here, to make Me go far away from My sanctuary? Now turn again, you will see greater abominations." **7** So He brought me to the door of the court; and when I looked, there was a hole in the wall. **8** Then He said to me, "Son of man, dig into the wall"; and when I dug into the wall, there was a door. **9** And He said to me, "Go in, and see the wicked abominations which they are doing there." **10** So I went in and saw, and there—every sort of creeping thing, abominable beasts, and all the idols of the house of YASHARA'AL, portrayed all around on the walls. **11** And there stood before them seventy men of the elders of the house of YASHARA'AL, and in their midst stood Jaazaniah the son of Shaphan. Each man had a censer in his hand, and a thick cloud of incense went up. **12** Then He said to me, "Son of man, have you seen what the elders of the house of YASHARA'AL do in the dark, every man in the room of his idols? For they say, 'YAHUAH does not see us, YAHUAH has forsaken the land.'" **13** And He said to me, "Turn again, and you will see greater abominations that they are doing." **14** So He brought me to the door of the north gate of YAHUAH's house; and to my dismay, women were sitting there weeping for Tammuz. **15** Then He said to me, "Have you seen this, O son of man? Turn again, you will see greater abominations than these." **16** So He brought me into the inner court of YAHUAH's house; and there, at the door of the temple of YAHUAH, between the porch and the altar, were about twenty-five men with their backs toward the temple of YAHUAH and their faces toward the east, and they were worshiping the sun toward the east. **17** And He said to me, "Have you seen this, O son of man? Is it a trivial thing to the*

> *house of Judah to commit the abominations which they commit here? For they have filled the land with violence; then they have returned to provoke Me to anger. Indeed, they put the branch to their nose.* **18** *Therefore I also will act in fury. My eye will not spare, nor will I have pity; and though they cry in My ears with a loud voice, I will not hear them." (Ezekiel 8:1-18 NKJV)*
> - *The children gather wood, the fathers kindle the fire, and the women knead dough, to make cakes for the queen of heaven; and they pour out drink offerings to other gods, that they may provoke Me to anger. (Jeremiah 7:18 NKJV)*

YAHUAH, I AM WHO I AM, the ALAHYM of Abraham, Isaac and Jacob, we recognise that at the First Council of Nicaea a 'false way' was formed and established – a false way which takes people away from The Way as given by the law, prophets and testimony of YAHUSHA (The full book of the Bible). A false way which takes people away from the only ancient path. A false way that creates a wide road which deceives people into thinking they are walking with You when in fact, they are being led to destruction. A false way which is an abomination to You and has provoked You to anger that You will not hear our cries in Your ears.

As it is written:

- *"Enter by the narrow gate; for wide is the gate and broad is the way that leads to destruction, and there are many who go in by it.* **14** *Because narrow is the gate and difficult is the way which leads to life, and there are few who find it. (Matthew 7:13-14 NKJV)*
- *Thus says YAHUAH: "Stand in the ways and see, and ask for the old ancient paths, where the good way is, and walk in it; Then you will find rest for your souls. But they said, 'We will not walk in it.'* **17** *Also, I set watchmen over you, saying, 'Listen*

to the sound of the trumpet!' But they said, 'We will not listen.' (Jeremiah 6:16 NKJV)

YAHUAH, I AM WHO I AM, the ALAHYM of Abraham, Isaac and Jacob, it is this false way which has and continues to draw people to the false father (the father of lies), through a false saviour (anti-Christ) who is operating in the world through an unclean spirit (the counterfeit Holy Spirit). It is this false way which will lead many to be rejected unless they repent from it, for it is the way of lawlessness that leads to death.

As it is written:

- *"Not everyone who says to Me, 'Lord, Lord (Master, Master),' shall enter the kingdom of heaven, but he who does the will of My Father in heaven. **22** Many will say to Me in that day, 'Lord, Lord (Master, Master), have we not prophesied in Your name, cast out demons in Your name, and done many wonders in Your name?' **23** And then I will declare to them, 'I never knew you; depart from Me, you who practice lawlessness!' (Matthew 7:21-23 NKJV)*

YAHUAH, I AM WHO I AM, the ALAHYM of Abraham, Isaac and Jacob, through this Council of Nicaea, lawlessness was released into Christianity as one of the primary mechanisms which Satan uses to continue his attempt to fulfil his mission revealed through the word You gave the prophet Isaiah (Yashayahu).

As it is written:

- *"How you are fallen from heaven, O Lucifer, son of the morning! How you are cut down to the ground, you who weakened the nations! **13** For you have said in your heart: 'I will ascend into heaven, I will exalt my throne above the stars of YAHUAH; I will* *also sit on the mount of the congregation On the farthest sides of the north; **14** I will ascend above the heights of the clouds, I will be like the Most High.' **15** Yet you shall be brought down to Sheol, To the lowest depths of the Pit. **16** "Those who see you will gaze at you, And consider you, saying: 'Is this the man who made the earth tremble, Who shook kingdoms, **17** Who made the world as a wilderness And destroyed its cities, Who did not open the house of his prisoners?' **18** "All the kings of the nations, All of them, sleep in glory, Everyone in his own house; **19** But you are cast out of your grave Like an abominable branch, Like the garment of those who are slain, Thrust through with a sword, Who go down to the stones of the pit, Like a corpse trodden underfoot. **20** You will not be joined with them in burial, because you have destroyed your land and slain your people. The brood of evildoers shall never be named. **21** Prepare slaughter for his children Because of the iniquity of their fathers, lest they rise up and possess the land, and fill the face of the world with cities." (Isaiah 14:12-21 NKJV)*

YAHUAH, I AM WHO I AM, the ALAHYM of Abraham, Isaac and Jacob, this being a strategy by the great dragon, the serpent of old, called the Devil and Satan to deceive the whole world and lure peoples of every tongue, tribe and nation to worship him by breaking the everlasting covenant and agreement with You and hence bring the whole world into a perpetual cycle of the curse and death through disobedience to Your Voice.

As it is written:

- *And war broke out in heaven: Michael and his angels fought with the dragon; and the dragon and his angels fought, **8** but they did not prevail, nor was a place found for them in heaven any longer. **9** So the great dragon was cast out, that serpent of* *old, called the Devil and Satan, who deceives the whole world; he was cast to the earth, and his angels were cast out with him. (Revelation 12:7-9 NKJV)*

Many have bowed down to the 'false way' and are trapped in deception, which will cause them to be rejected. I never knew you as it is written:

- *And then I will declare to them, 'I never knew you; depart from Me, you who practice lawlessness!' (Matthew 7:23 NKJV)*

Satan has used the Roman Catholic institution to plant tares by sowing the seeds of the doctrines of demons and traditions of men. Many have eaten these seeds of the tares instead of the seeds of the wheat and have themselves become tares which will be pulled out and burnt with fire.

As it is written:

- *Another parable He put forth to them, saying: "The kingdom of heaven is like a man who sowed good seed in his field; **25** but while men slept, his enemy came and sowed tares among the wheat and went his way. **26** But when the grain had sprouted and produced a crop, then the tares also appeared. **27** So the servants of the owner came and said to him, 'Sir, did you not sow good seed in your field? How then does it have tares?' **28** He said to them, 'An enemy has done this.' The servants said to him, 'Do you want us then to go and gather them up?' **29** But he said, 'No, lest while you gather up the tares you also uproot the wheat with them. **30** Let both grow together until the harvest, and at the time of harvest I will say to the reapers, "First gather together the tares and bind them in bundles to burn them, but gather the wheat into my barn." (Mathew 13:24-30 NKJV)*

YAHUAH, I AM WHO I AM, the ALAHYM of Abraham, Isaac and Jacob, Satan has used the Roman Catholic institution to take people away from Your cycle of time and to walk contrary to You and the times that You have ordained in heaven and established over the earth.

As it is written:

- *And all the days of the commandment will be two and fifty weeks of days, and (these will make) the entire year complete. Thus, it is engraven and ordained on the heavenly tablets. [31] And there is no neglecting (this commandment) for a single year or from year to year. [32] And command thou the children of YASHARA'AL that they observe the years according to this reckoning- three hundred and sixty-four days, and (these) will constitute a complete year, and they will not disturb its time from its days and from its feasts; for everything will fall out in them according to their testimony, and they will not leave out any day nor disturb any feasts. [33] But if they do neglect and do not observe them according to His commandment, then they will disturb all their seasons and the years will be dislodged from this (order), [and they will disturb the seasons and the years will be dislodged] and they will neglect their ordinances. [34] And all the children of YASHARA'AL will forget and will not find the path of the years, and will forget the new moons, and seasons, and sabbaths and they will go wrong as to all the order of the years. (Jubilees 6:30-34 KJV)*

YAHUAH, I AM WHO I AM, the ALAHYM of Abraham, Isaac and Jacob, You told us through what is written in Revelation 6:2 that a white horse would go out conquering and to conquer.

- *And I saw when the Lamb opened one of the seals, and I heard, as*

> *it were the noise of thunder, one of the four beasts saying, Come and see. 2 and I saw, and behold a white horse: and he that sat on him had a bow; and a crown was given unto him: and he went forth conquering, and to conquer. (Revelation 6:1-2 NKJV)*

YAHUAH, I AM WHO I AM, the ALAHYM of Abraham, Isaac and Jacob, we Your people have indeed been conquered by the white horse because of our sins, iniquities and transgressions against You, our Father, our Creator, our Husband, and so we cry out to You that You may deliver us Your people from the captivity we are currently in.

Admission of guilt for our sins, which have piled up before You

YAHUAH, I AM WHO I AM, the ALAHYM of Abraham, Isaac and Jacob, because we have listened to and followed the voice of lawlessness; our sins, iniquities and transgressions are piled up before You as we admit that we, and our ancestors across peoples of all tongues, tribes and nations have –

- Disobeyed Your voice and Your instructions.
- Broken the everlasting covenant You made with us.
- Rebelled against Your law and the commandments which You commanded us to obey (Your Torah)
- Rejected the righteousness which You have given us through Your SON, YAHUSHA (YAHUAH is our salvation), whom You sent as Your servant to fulfil Your promise to save us.
- Rejected the leadership of Your Set Apart (Holy Spirit) Ruach Ha Qadash.
- Rejected the fullness of what You have given us through 'The Law, the Prophets and the Testimony of the SON, YAHUSHA.'

Just like the voice of the serpent, which our ancestors Adam and

Eve listened to in the Garden of Eden, and obeyed to break covenant with You, so we have listened to the voice of the serpent speaking through the white horse of Rome to perpetually break covenant with You, disobey Your laws and commandments and depart from Your ways.

YAHUAH, I AM WHO I AM, the ALAHYM of Abraham, Isaac and Jacob, it is because of our great sin that today we arise as priests upon Your altar of righteousness to confess our sins, iniquities and transgressions against You, and to ask for forgiveness as we repent. We not only come for ourselves and our families but for people of all tongues, tribes and nations who have been deceived and hence captured into the system of lawlessness which leads to eternal death.

- We confess that we have been led astray from the WAY, the TRUTH and the LIFE, and we have followed the 'false way' of lawlessness as we have obeyed the voice of another – the false shepherd, the wolf in sheep's clothing.
- We confess that we have broken the eternal covenant which You, YAHUAH, I AM WHO I AM, the ALAHYM of Abraham, Isaac and Jacob, established with us at Sinai for –
    - We have 'Placed other gods before you' in violation of your commandment, which says: *"You shall have no other gods before Me".*
    - We have 'Created graven images which we have bowed down to and served them' in violation to your commandment that says: *"You shall not make for yourself a carved image—any likeness of anything that is in heaven above, or that is in the earth beneath, or that is in the water under the earth; you shall not bow down to them nor serve them. For I, YAHUAH your Aluah, am a jealous Aluah, visiting the iniquity of the fathers upon the*

children to the third and fourth generations of those who hate Me, but showing mercy to thousands, to those who love Me and keep My commandments".

- We have 'taken your name in vain', brought it to nought even as Your Holy Name, YAHUAH, has been removed from most Bibles and replaced with 'the title Lord or God' in violation of Your commandment, which says: *"You shall not take the name of YAHUAH your Aluah in vain, for YAHUAH will not hold him guiltless who takes His name in vain".*

- We have 'Ignored the Sabbath and have not kept it Holy to You' in violation of your commandment, which says: *"Observe the Sabbath day, to keep it holy, as YAHUAH Aluah commanded you. Six days you shall labor and do all your work, but the seventh day is the Sabbath of YAHUAH your Aluah. In it you shall do no work: you, nor your son, nor your daughter, nor your male servant, nor your female servant, nor your ox, nor your donkey, nor any of your cattle, nor your stranger who is within your gates, that your male servant and your female servant may rest as well as you. And remember that you were a slave in the land of Egypt, and YAHUAH your Aluah brought you out from there by a mighty hand and by an outstretched arm; therefore YAHUAH your Aluah commanded you to keep the Sabbath day."*

- We have 'not honoured our fathers and mothers' in violation of Your commandment, which says: *"Honor your father and your mother, as YAHUAH your Aluah has commanded you, that your days may be long, and that it may be well with you in the land which YAHUAH your Aluah is giving you".*

- We have 'murdered and shed much innocent blood on the land, even sacrificing our children upon the altar of Molech,' in violation of Your commandment which says: *"You shall not murder.'*
- We have 'committed adultery and defiled our bodies, which You have chosen as a temple for Yourself' in violation of Your commandment, which says: *"You shall not commit adultery".*
- We have 'stolen' in violation of Your commandment, which says: *"You shall not steal."*
- We have 'sworn and borne falsely against our neighbour' in violation of Your commandment, which says: *"You shall not bear false witness against your neighbor."*
- We have 'coveted what belongs to our neighbours' in violation of Your commandment, which says: *"You shall not covet your neighbor's wife; and you shall not desire your neighbor's house, his field, his male servant, his female servant, his ox, his donkey, or anything that is your neighbor's."*

We confess that we have disregarded and broken the everlasting covenant with You, YAHUAH, I AM WHO I AM, the ALAHYM of Abraham, Isaac and Jacob, and we have hence broken the greatest commandment that You gave us, and was repeated by YAHUSHA as it is written:

- *"Hear, O YASHARA'AL: YAHUAH our Aluah, YAHUAH is one! 5 You shall love YAHUAH your Aluah with all your heart, with all your soul, and with all your strength. (Deuteronomy 6:4-5 NKJV)*
- YAHUSHA said to him, "'You shall love YAHUAH your Aluah with all your heart, with all your soul, and with all your mind.'

> *38 This is the first and great commandment. 39 And the second is like it: 'You shall love your neighbor as yourself.' 40 On these two commandments hang all the Law and the Prophets."* (Matthew 22:37-40 NKJV)

We confess we have disregarded and disobeyed the very instructions given by YAHUSHA concerning Your Law and the Prophets and the Psalms.

As it is written:

- *"Do not think that I came to destroy the Law or the Prophets. I did not come to destroy but to fulfill. 18 For assuredly, I say to you, till heaven and earth pass away, one jot or one tittle will by no means pass from the law till all is fulfilled. 19 Whoever therefore breaks one of the least of these commandments, and teaches men so, shall be called least in the kingdom of heaven; but whoever does and teaches them, he shall be called great in the kingdom of heaven.* (Matthew 5:17-19 NKJV)
- *"The law and the prophets were until John. Since that time the kingdom of YAHUAH has been preached, and everyone is pressing into it. 17 And it is easier for heaven and earth to pass away than for one tittle of the law to fail.* (Luke 16:16-17 NKJV)

And as referenced in Romans 3:31 by the Apostle Paul, **as it is written:** *Do we then make void the law through faith? Certainly not! On the contrary, we establish the law.*

Because of all these sins, iniquities and transgressions that we have committed against You, YAHUAH, I AM WHO I AM, the ALAHYM of Abraham, Isaac and Jacob, the earth has been consumed by the curse:

As it is written:

- *Behold, YAHUAH makes the earth empty and makes it waste, Distorts its surface and scatters abroad its inhabitants. 2 And it shall be: As with the people, so with the priest; As with the servant, so with his master; As with the maid, so with her mistress; As with the buyer, so with the seller; As with the lender, so with the borrower; As with the creditor, so with the debtor. 3 The land shall be entirely emptied and utterly plundered, For YAHUAH has spoken this word. 4 The earth mourns and fades away, the world languishes and fades away; The haughty people of the earth languish. 5 The earth is also defiled under its inhabitants, because they have transgressed the laws, Changed the ordinance, Broken the everlasting covenant. 6 Therefore the curse has devoured the earth, and those who dwell in it are desolate. Therefore the inhabitants of the earth are burned, and few men are left. (Isaiah 24:1-6 NKJV)*

YAHUAH, I AM WHO I AM, the ALAHYM of Abraham, Isaac and Jacob, we acknowledge that You gave us forewarning of how we would turn against You and sin, the consequences thereof, and Your promise to restore us when we returned to You to honour and obey what You have spoken to us. We confess we have sinned according to all the things You said we would do.

As it is written:

- *And do thou write for thyself all these words which I declare unto, thee this day, for I know their rebellion and their stiff neck, before I bring them into the land of which I sware to their fathers, to Abraham and to Isaac and to Jacob, saying: ' Unto your seed will I give a land flowing with milk and honey. [8] And they will eat and be satisfied, and they will turn to strange* gods, to (gods) which cannot deliver them from aught of their tribulation: and this witness shall be heard for a witness against them. For they will forget all My commandments, (even) all that I command them, and they will walk after the Gentiles, and after their uncleanness, and after their shame, and will serve their gods, and these will prove unto them an offence and a tribulation and an affliction and a snare. [9] And many will perish and they will be taken captive, and will fall into the hands of the enemy, because they have forsaken My ordinances and My commandments, and the festivals of My covenant, and My sabbaths, and My holy place which I have hallowed for Myself in their midst, and My tabernacle, and My sanctuary, which I have hallowed for Myself in the midst of the land, that I should set my name upon it, and that it should dwell (there). [10] And they will make to themselves high places and groves and graven images, and they will worship, each his own (graven image), so as to go astray, and they will sacrifice their children to demons, and to all the works of the error of their hearts. [11] And I will send witnesses unto them, that I may witness against them, but they will not hear, and will slay the witnesses also, and they will persecute those who seek the law, and they will abrogate and change everything so as to work evil before My eyes. [12] And I will hide My face from them, and I will deliver them into the hand of the Gentiles for captivity, and for a prey, and for devouring, and I will remove them from the midst of the land, and I will scatter them amongst the Gentiles. [13] And they will forget all My law and all My commandments and all My judgments, and will go astray as to new moons, and sabbaths, and festivals, and jubilees, and ordinances. [14] And after this they will turn to Me from amongst the Gentiles with all their heart and with all their soul and with all their strength, and I *will gather them from amongst all the Gentiles, and they will seek me, so that I shall be found of them, when they seek me with all their heart and with all their soul. [15] And I will disclose to them abounding peace with righteousness, and I will remove them the plant of uprightness, with all My heart and with all My soul, and they shall be for a blessing and not for a curse, and they shall be the head and not the tail. (Jubilees 1:7-15 KJV)*

YAHUAH, I AM WHO I AM, the ALAHYM of Abraham, Isaac and Jacob, we submit to You the prayer which Your servant Daniel prayed:

As it is written:

- *In the first year of Darius the son of Ahasuerus, of the seed of the Medes, which was made king over the realm of the Chaldeans; 2 In the first year of his reign I Daniel understood by books the number of the years, whereof the word of YAHUAH came to Jeremiah the prophet, that he would accomplish seventy years in the desolations of Yarushalayim (Jerusalem). 3 And I set my face unto YAHUAH Aluah, to seek by prayer and supplications, with fasting, and sackcloth, and ashes: 4 And I prayed unto YAHUAH my Aluah, and made my confession, and said, O YAHUAH, the great and dreadful El, keeping the covenant and mercy to them that love him, and to them that keep his commandments; 5 We have sinned, and have committed iniquity, and have done wickedly, and have rebelled, even by departing from thy precepts and from thy judgments: 6 Neither have we hearkened unto thy servants the prophets, which spake in thy name to our kings, our princes, and our fathers, and to all the people of the land. 7 O YAHUAH, righteousness belongeth unto thee, but unto us confusion of faces, as at this day; to the men of Judah, and to the inhabitants of Yarushalayim (Jerusalem),* and unto all YASHARA'AL, that are near, and that are far off, through all the countries whither thou hast driven them, because of their trespass that they have trespassed against thee. **8** O YAHUAH, to us belongeth confusion of face, to our kings, to our princes, and to our fathers, because we have sinned against thee. **9** To YAHUAH our Aluah belong mercies and forgivenesses, though we have rebelled against him; **10** Neither have we obeyed the voice of YAHUAH our Aluah, to walk in his laws, which he set before us by his servants the prophets. **11** Yea, all YASHARA'AL have transgressed thy law, even by departing, that they might not obey thy voice; therefore the curse is poured upon us, and the oath that is written in the law of Moses the servant of YAHUAH, because we have sinned against him. **12** And he hath confirmed his words, which he spake against us, and against our judges that judged us, by bringing upon us a great evil: for under the whole heaven hath not been done as hath been done upon Yarushalayim (Jerusalem). **13** As it is written in the law of Moses, all this evil is come upon us: yet made we not our prayer before YAHUAH our Aluah, that we might turn from our iniquities, and understand thy truth. **14** Therefore hath YAHUAH watched upon the evil, and brought it upon us: for YAHUAH our Aluah is righteous in all his works which he doeth: for we obeyed not his voice. **15** And now, O YAHUAH our Elohim, that hast brought thy people forth out of the land of Egypt with a mighty hand, and hast gotten thee renown, as at this day; we have sinned, we have done wickedly. **16** O YAHUAH, according to all thy righteousness, I beseech thee, let thine anger and thy fury be turned away from thy city Yarushalayim (Jerusalem), thy holy mountain: because for our sins, and for the iniquities of our fathers, Yarushalayim (Jerusalem) and thy people are become a reproach to all that *are about us. **17** Now therefore, O our Aluah, hear the prayer of thy servant, and his supplications, and cause thy face to shine upon thy sanctuary that is desolate, for YAHUAH's sake. **18** O my Aluah, incline thine ear, and hear; open thine eyes, and behold our desolations, and the city which is called by thy name: for we do not present our supplications before thee for our righteousnesses, but for thy great mercies. **19** O YAHUAH, hear; O YAHUAH, forgive; O YAHUAH, hearken and do; defer not, for thine own sake, O my Aluah: for thy city and thy people are called by thy name. (Daniel 9:1-19 KJV)*

YAHUAH, I AM WHO I AM, the ALAHYM of Abraham, Isaac and Jacob, we pray and ask for the blood of the Lamb, the sinless blood of YAHUSHA to be poured down upon the sins, iniquities and transgressions which we have confessed and placed before You, for we know there is no forgiveness of sin without the shedding of blood.

As it is written:

- *And according to the law almost all things are purified with blood, and without shedding of blood there is no remission. (Hebrews 13:9)*
- *And as they were eating, YAHUSHA took bread, and blessed it, and brake it, and gave it to the disciples, and said, Take, eat; this is my body. 27 And he took the cup, and gave thanks, and gave it to them, saying, Drink ye all of it; 28 For this is my blood of the new testament, which is shed for many for the remission of sins. (Matthew 26:26-28)*
- *Then I heard a loud voice saying in heaven, "Now salvation, and strength, and the kingdom of YAHUAH, and the power of His MASHYACH have come, for the accuser of our brethren, who accused them before our Aluah day and night, has been*

cast down. 11 And they overcame him by the blood of the Lamb and by the word of their testimony, and they did not love their lives to the death. (Revelation 12:10-11 KJV)

YAHUAH, I AM WHO I AM, the ALAHYM of Abraham, Isaac and Jacob, as You see the blood of Your only begotten SON YAHUSHA MASHYACH/Yeshua Messiah, have mercy and compassion upon us according to Your lovingkindness.

YAHUAH, I AM WHO I AM, the ALAHYM of Abraham, Isaac and Jacob, we declare You have removed the law of animal sacrifice, and therefore, we are no longer under the curse of the law of animal sacrifice. We have, therefore, laid down our labour and work in animal sacrifice and accepted the perfect sacrifice which has been made for us, which we receive by faith through Your grace, which is YAHUSHA MASHYACH.

As it is written:

- *For sin shall not have dominion over you, for you are not under law but under grace. 15 What then? Shall we sin because we are not under law but under grace? Certainly not! (Romans 6:14-15 NKJV)*
- *Whosoever committeth sin transgresseth also the law: for sin is the transgression of the law. (1 John 3:4 KJV)*

YAHUAH, I AM WHO I AM, the ALAHYM of Abraham, Isaac and Jacob, remember Your words to our ancestors –

As it is written:

- *'But if they confess their iniquity and the iniquity of their fathers, with their unfaithfulness in which they were unfaithful to Me, and that they also have walked contrary to Me, 41 and that I also have walked contrary to them and have brought them into the land of their enemies; if their uncircumcised hearts are humbled, and they accept their guilt—* **42** *then I will remember My covenant with Jacob, and My covenant with Isaac and My covenant with Abraham I will remember; I will remember the land.* **43** *The land also shall be left empty by them, and will enjoy its sabbaths while it lies desolate without them; they will accept their guilt, because they despised My judgments and because their soul abhorred My statutes.* **44** *Yet for all that, when they are in the land of their enemies, I will not cast them away, nor shall I abhor them, to utterly destroy them and break My covenant with them; for I am YAHUAH their Aluah.* **45** *But for their sake I will remember the covenant of their ancestors, whom I brought out of the land of Egypt in the sight of the nations, that I might be their Aluah: I am YAHUAH.' (Leviticus 26:40-45 NKJV)*

YAHUAH, I AM WHO I AM, the ALUAH of Abraham, Isaac and Jacob, remember Your words to us –

As it is written:

- *When I shut up heaven and there is no rain, or command the locusts to devour the land, or send pestilence among My people,* **14** *if My people who are called by My name will humble themselves, and pray and seek My face, and turn from their wicked ways, then I will hear from heaven, and will forgive their sin and heal their land.* **15** *Now My eyes will be open and My ears attentive to prayer made in this place. (2 Chronicles 7:13-15 NKJV)*

YAHUAH, I AM WHO I AM, the ALAHYM of Abraham, Isaac and Jacob, we are the people who are called by Your name, restore us, we pray according to Your lovingkindness.

Restore us, O YAHUAH, I AM WHO I AM, the ALAHYM of Abraham, Isaac and Jacob, for Your Name's sake, forgive, restore and heal our land.

YAHUAH, I AM WHO I AM, the ALAHYM of Abraham, Isaac and Jacob, we pray and ask that the eyes of millions of people of every tongue, tribe and nation who are held in captivity to the false way of lawlessness and covenant-breaking religion will be opened to see the deception, and they will heed Your Voice to come out of her.

As it is written:

- *After these things I saw another angel coming down from heaven, having great authority, and the earth was illuminated with his glory. 2 And he cried mightily with a loud voice, saying, "Babylon the great is fallen, is fallen, and has become a dwelling place of demons, a prison for every foul spirit, and a cage for every unclean and hated bird! 3 For all the nations have drunk of the wine of the wrath of her fornication, the kings of the earth have committed fornication with her, and the merchants of the earth have become rich through the abundance of her luxury." 4 And I heard another voice from heaven saying, "Come out of her, my people, lest you share in her sins, and lest you receive of her plagues. 5 For her sins have reached to heaven, and YAHUAH has remembered her iniquities. (Revelation 18:1-5 KJV)*

YAHUAH, I AM WHO I AM, the ALAHYM of Abraham, Isaac and Jacob, we pray and ask You for the fulfilment of Your promise to destroy the covering cast over all people and the veil which is spread over the nations to bring death to them.

- *And in this mountain YAHUAH of hosts will make for all people A feast of choice pieces, A feast of wines on the lees, Of fat things*

> *full of marrow, Of well-refined wines on the lees. 7 And He will destroy on this mountain The surface of the covering cast over all people, And the veil that is spread over all nations. 8 He will swallow up death forever, And YAHUAH Aluah will wipe away tears from all faces; The rebuke of His people He will take away from all the earth; For YAHUAH has spoken. 9 And it will be said in that day: "Behold, this is our Aluah; We have waited for Him, and He will save us. This is YAHUAH; We have waited for Him; We will be glad and rejoice in His salvation." (Isaiah 25:6-9KJV)*

YAHUAH, I AM WHO I AM, the ALAHYM of Abraham, Isaac and Jacob, we decree in Your Name and the name of YAHUSHA, to Vatican Rome and all Catholic and other Christian churches that are still drunk with the wine of Rome and have spread a veil of death over the people; the words You gave Moses to speak to Pharoah – *"LET MY PEOPLE GO, that they may serve me"*.

As it is written:

- *And YAHUAH spoke to Moses, "Go to Pharaoh and say to him, 'Thus says YAHUAH: "Let My people go, that they may serve Me. (Exodus 8:1 KJV)*

YAHUAH, I AM WHO I AM, the ALAHYM of Abraham, Isaac and Jacob, we pray and ask for the fulfilment of Your words that 'in the days coming/after those days, You will put Your laws in our minds and write them on our hearts'. Most High ALAHYM of Abraham, Isaac and Jacob, may You now put Your laws in our minds and may You now write them on our hearts and forgive us of our iniquity and remember our sin no more.'

As it is written:

- *"Behold, the days are coming, says YAHUAH, when I will make a new covenant with the house of YASHARA'AL and with the house of Judah— 32 not according to the covenant that I made with their fathers in the day that I took them by the hand to lead them out of the land of Egypt, My covenant which they broke, though I was a husband to them, says YAHUAH. 33 But this is the covenant that I will make with the house of YASHARA'AL after those days, says YAHUAH: I will put My law in their minds, and write it on their hearts; and I will be their Aluah, and they shall be My people. 34 No more shall every man teach his neighbor, and every man his brother, saying, 'Know YAHUAH' for they all shall know Me, from the least of them to the greatest of them, says YAHUAH. For I will forgive their iniquity, and their sin I will remember no more." (Jeremiah 31:31-34 NKJV)*
- *For this is the covenant that I will make with the house of YASHARA'AL after those days, says YAHUAH: I will put My laws in their mind and write them on their hearts; and I will be their Aluah, and they shall be My people. 11 None of them shall teach his neighbor, and none his brother, saying, 'Know YAHUAH,' for all shall know Me, from the least of them to the greatest of them. 12 For I will be merciful to their unrighteousness, and their sins and their lawless deeds I will remember no more." (Hebrews 8:10-12 KJV)*

We close our case with our petition on behalf of peoples of all tongues, tribes and nations of Africa – 'May You, YAHUAH, I AM WHO I AM, the ALAHYM of Abraham, Isaac and Jacob, our Judge, our Lawgiver, our King and Savior forgive our iniquity and remember our sin no more according to the precepts and judgements of Your Word.

As it is written:

- *And they sung a new song, saying, Thou art worthy to take the book, and to open the seals thereof: for thou wast slain, and hast redeemed us to YAHUAH by thy blood out of every kindred, and tongue, and people, and nation; 10 **And hast made us unto our Aluah kings and priests: and we shall reign on the earth.** 11 And I beheld, and I heard the voice of many angels round about the throne and the beasts and the elders: and the number of them was ten thousand times ten thousand, and thousands of thousands; 12 Saying with a loud voice, Worthy is the Lamb that was slain to receive power, and riches, and wisdom, and strength, and honour, and glory, and blessing. 13 And every creature which is in heaven, and on the earth, and under the earth, and such as are in the sea, and all that are in them, heard I saying, Blessing, and honour, and glory, and power, be unto him that sitteth upon the throne, and unto the Lamb for ever and ever. 14 And the four beasts said, Amen. And the four and twenty elders fell down and worshipped him that liveth for ever and ever. (Revelation 5:9-14 KJV)*

- **HalleluYaH (Praise YAH)**
- **Even so, come King YAHUSHA**

CHAPTER TWENTY-THREE

The Call To Come Out Of Her

We cannot afford to be caught on the wrong side of the spiritual equation of good and evil, as there is no middle ground. We are either walking with YAHUAH, or we are not. We are either yoked to YAHUSHA, or we are not.

As it is written:

- o ***He who is not with Me [definitely on My side] is against Me,*** *and he who does not [definitely] gather with Me and for My side scatters. (Matthew 12:30 AMPC)*
- o ***No one can serve two masters;*** *for either he will hate the one and love the other, or else he will be loyal to the one and despise the other.* ***You cannot serve YAHUAH and mammon.*** *(Matthew 6:24 AMPC)*
- o ***Do two walk together*** *except they make an appointment and have agreed? (Amos 3:3 AMPC)*
- o ***Take My yoke upon you*** *and learn of Me, for I am gentle (meek) and humble (lowly) in heart, and you will find rest*

(relief and ease and refreshment and recreation and blessed quiet) for your souls. [30] For My yoke is wholesome (useful, good—not harsh, hard, sharp, or pressing, but comfortable, gracious, and pleasant), and My burden is light and easy to be borne. (Matthew 11:28-30 AMPC)

🌿 **Tribes of Africa,** COME OUT of religion and take up your divine destiny as the keepers of the covenant with the ALAHYM of Abraham, Isaac and Jacob.

🌿 **Tribes of Africa**, if you are in a religion which does not guard obedience to the voice of the ALAHYM of Abraham, Isaac and Jacob, to keep His covenant and to obey His law and commandments; COME OUT OF HER.

🌿 **Tribes of Africa,** if you are in the religion which does not accept YAHUAH, the ALAHYM of Abraham, Isaac and Jacob sent His son YAHUSHA as the Messiah (MASHYACH), to become the everlasting and final sacrifice and offering through His laid down life and poured out blood, and through that opened the Way for us to return to the covenant with the Father, COME OUT OF HER.

🌿 **Tribes of Africa**, if you are in a religion which does not define sin as YAHUAH defines Sin, COME OUT OF HER.

🌿 **Tribes of Africa**, if you are in a religion which does not define loving the Father, as He has defined how He wants to be loved, COME OUT OF HER.

🌿 **Tribes of Africa**, if you are in a religion which does not define TRUTH as the precepts of the Word of YAHUAH define Truth, COME OUT OF HER.

🌿 **Tribes of Africa,** if you are in a religion that does not honour, follow and teach according to the everlasting design of YAHUAH and has come up with its own design, COME OUT OF HER.

As it is written in Revelation 18:4, **COME OUT OF HER, MY PEOPLE.**

- o *And I heard another voice from heaven saying, "**Come out of her, my people**, lest you share in her sins, and lest you receive of her plagues. [5] For her sins have reached to heaven, and YAHUAH has remembered her iniquities.*

🔥 **Tribes of Africa,** 'Come out of her' (religion) and return to the Covenant relationship with YAHUAH.

🔥 **Tribes of Africa,** 'Come out of her' (the Greek cultural mindset) and return to your ancient Hebraic DNA.

🔥 **Tribes of Africa,** any person, institution or religion, which says or teaches that the Father's commandments and laws are no longer relevant is calling YAHUSHA a liar and is least in the Kingdom, as it is written:

- o *"Do not think that I came to destroy the Law or the Prophets. I did not come to destroy but to fulfill. [18] For assuredly, I say to you, till heaven and earth pass away, one jot or one tittle will by no means pass from the law till all is fulfilled. [19] **Whoever therefore breaks one of the least of these commandments, and teaches men so, shall be called least in the kingdom of heaven**; but whoever does and teaches them, he shall be called great in the kingdom of heaven. [20] For I say to you, that unless your righteousness exceeds the righteousness of the scribes and Pharisees, **you will by no means enter the kingdom of heaven**. (Matthew 5:17-20 NKJV)*
- o *He who says, "I know Him," and does not keep His*

commandments, is a liar, and the truth is not in him. *[5] But whoever keeps His word, truly the love of YAHUAH is perfected in him. By this we know that we are in Him. [6] He who says he abides in Him ought himself also to walk just as He walked. (I John 2:4-6 NKJV)*

🔥 **Tribes of Africa**, any person, institution or religion which teaches that what YAHUAH and His SON YAHUSHA said is no longer valid or relevant, has come up with a different Gospel and established a wide road which will lead to destruction. For anyone who teaches another gospel is deemed by YAHUAH to be accursed, COME OUT OF HER.

As it is written:

- *I marvel that you are turning away so soon from Him who called you in the grace of MASHYACH, to a different gospel, [7] which is not another; but there are some who trouble you and **want to pervert the gospel of MASHYACH (Christ)**. [8] But even if we, or an angel from heaven, preach any other gospel to you than what we have preached to you, let him be accursed. [9] As we have said before, so now I say again, if anyone preaches any other gospel to you than what you have received, let him be accursed. (Galatians 1:6-9 NKJV)*
- *Oh, that you would bear with me in a little folly—and indeed you do bear with me. [2] For I am jealous for you with godly jealousy. **For I have betrothed you to one husband, that I may present you as a chaste virgin to MASHYACH**. [3] But I fear, lest somehow, as the serpent deceived Eve by his craftiness, so your minds may be corrupted from the simplicity that is in MASHYACH. [4] **For if he who comes preaches another YAHUSHA whom we have not preached, or if***

- *you receive a different spirit which you have not received, or a different gospel which you have not accepted—you may well put up with it! (II Corinthians 11:1-4 NKJV)*
  - **For such are false apostles, deceitful workers, transforming themselves into apostles of MASHYACH. [14] And no wonder! For Satan himself transforms himself into an angel of light. [15] Therefore it is no great thing if his ministers also transform themselves into ministers of righteousness, whose end will be according to their works.** *(II Corinthians 11:13-15 NKJV)*
  - Thus says YAHUAH: **"Stand in the ways and see, and ask for the old paths, where the good way is, and walk in it**; *Then you will find rest for your souls. But they said, 'We will not walk in it.' [17] Also, I set watchmen over you, saying, 'Listen to the sound of the trumpet!' But they said, 'We will not listen.' (Jeremiah 6:16-17 NKJV)*
  - **"Enter by the narrow gate; for wide is the gate and broad is the way that leads to destruction, and there are many who go in by it.** *[14] Because narrow is the gate and difficult is the way which leads to life, and there are few who find it. [15]* **"Beware of false prophets, who come to you in sheep's clothing, but inwardly they are ravenous wolves.** *(Matthew 7:13-15 NKJV)*

Tribes of Africa, YAHUAH is our Creator and our Husband, yet we have gone out as prostitutes (harlots), breaking the covenant (agreement) of marriage with Him. It is time for us to return to our marriage commitment to YAHUAH.

As it is written:

- *"Do not fear, for you will not be ashamed; Neither be disgraced, for you will not be put to shame; For you will forget the shame of your youth, and will not remember the reproach of your widowhood anymore. [5]* **For your Maker is your husband, YAHUAH of hosts is His name; And your Redeemer is the Holy One of YASHARA'AL;** *He is called the Alahym of the whole earth. [6]* **For YAHUAH has called you Like a woman forsaken and grieved in spirit, like a youthful wife when you were refused,"** *says your Aluah. [7] "For a mere moment I have forsaken you, but with great mercies I will gather you. [8] With a little wrath I hid My face from you for a moment; But with everlasting kindness I will have mercy on you," Says YAHUAH, your Redeemer. (Isaiah 54:4-8 NKJV)*

- *Again, the word of YAHUAH came to me, saying, [2]* **"Son of man, cause Yarushalayim (Jerusalem) to know her abominations, [3] and say, 'Thus says YAHUAH to Yarushalayim (Jerusalem): "Your birth and your nativity are from the land of Canaan; your father was an Amorite and your mother a Hittite.** *[4] As for your nativity, on the day you were born your navel cord was not cut, nor were you washed in water to cleanse you; you were not rubbed with salt nor wrapped in swaddling cloths. [5] No eye pitied you, to do any of these things for you, to have compassion on you; but you were thrown out into the open field, when you yourself were loathed on the day you were born. [6] "And when I passed by you and saw you struggling in your own blood, I said to you in your blood, 'Live!' Yes, I said to you in your blood, 'Live!' [7] I made you thrive like a plant in the field; and you grew, matured, and became very beautiful. Your breasts were formed, your hair grew, but you were naked and bare. [8] "When I passed by you again and looked upon you, indeed your time was the time* *of love; so I spread My wing over you and covered your nakedness.* **Yes, I swore an oath to you and entered into a covenant with you, and you became Mine,"** *says* **YAHUAH Aluah**. *[9] "Then I washed you in water; yes, I thoroughly washed off your blood, and I anointed you with oil. [10] I clothed you in embroidered cloth and gave you sandals of badger skin; I clothed you with fine linen and covered you with silk. [11] I adorned you with ornaments, put bracelets on your wrists, and a chain on your neck. [12] And I put a jewel in your nose, earrings in your ears, and a beautiful crown on your head. [13] Thus you were adorned with gold and silver, and your clothing was of fine linen, silk, and embroidered cloth. You ate pastry of fine flour, honey, and oil. You were exceedingly beautiful, and succeeded to royalty. [14] Your fame went out among the nations because of your beauty, for it was perfect through My splendor which I had bestowed on you," says YAHUAH. [15]* **"But you trusted in your own beauty, played the harlot because of your fame, and poured out your harlotry on everyone passing by who would have it.** *[16] You took some of your garments and adorned multicolored high places for yourself, and played the harlot on them. Such things should not happen, nor be. [17]* **You have also taken your beautiful jewelry from My gold and My silver, which I had given you, and made for yourself male images and played the harlot with them.** *[18] You took your embroidered garments and covered them, and you set My oil and My incense before them. [19] Also My food which I gave you—the pastry of fine flour, oil, and honey which I fed you—you set it before them as sweet incense; and so it was," says YAHUAH. [20] "Moreover you* *took your sons and your daughters, whom you bore to Me, and these you sacrificed to them to be devoured.* **Were your acts of harlotry a small matter,** *[21] that you have slain My children and offered them up to them by causing them to pass through the fire? [22]* **And in all your abominations and acts of harlotry you did not remember the days of your youth, when you were naked and bare, struggling in your blood.** *[23] "Then it was so, after all your wickedness—'Woe, woe to you!' says YAHUAH — [24] that you also built for yourself a shrine, and made a high place for yourself in every street. [25] You built your high places at the head of every road, and made your beauty to be abhorred.* **You offered yourself to everyone who passed by, and multiplied your acts of harlotry.** *[26]* **You also committed harlotry with the Egyptians, your very fleshly neighbors, and increased your acts of harlotry to provoke Me to anger.** *[27] "Behold, therefore, I stretched out My hand against you, diminished your allotment, and gave you up to the will of those who hate you, the daughters of the Philistines, who were ashamed of your lewd behavior. [28]* **You also played the harlot with the Assyrians,** *because you were insatiable; indeed you played the harlot with them and still were not satisfied. [29]* **Moreover you multiplied your acts of harlotry as far as the land of the trader,** *Chaldea; and even then you were not satisfied. [30] "How degenerate is your heart!" says YAHUAH, "seeing you do all these things,* **the deeds of a brazen harlot.** *[31] "You erected your shrine at the head of every road, and built your high place in every street. Yet you were not like a harlot, because you scorned payment. [32]* **You are an adulterous wife, who takes strangers instead of**

***her husband**. [33] Men make payment to all harlots, but you made your payments to all your lovers, and hired them to come to you from all around for your harlotry. [34] You are the opposite of other women in your harlotry, because no one solicited you to be a harlot. In that you gave payment but no payment was given you, therefore you are the opposite." [35]* **'Now then, O harlot, hear the word of YAHUAH!** *[36] Thus says YAHUAH: "Because your filthiness was poured out and your nakedness uncovered in your harlotry with your lovers, and with all your abominable idols, and because of the blood of your children which you gave to them, [37] surely, therefore, I will gather all your lovers with whom you took pleasure, all those you loved, and all those you hated; I will gather them from all around against you and will uncover your nakedness to them, that they may see all your nakedness. [38]* **And I will judge you as women who break wedlock or shed blood are judged**; *I will bring blood upon you in fury and jealousy. [39] I will also give you into their hand, and they shall throw down your shrines and break down your high places. They shall also strip you of your clothes, take your beautiful jewelry, and leave you naked and bare. [40] "They shall also bring up an assembly against you, and they shall stone you with stones and thrust you through with their swords. [41] They shall burn your houses with fire, and execute judgments on you in the sight of many women; and* **I will make you cease playing the harlot, and you shall no longer hire lovers**. *[42] So I will lay to rest My fury toward you, and My jealousy shall depart from you. I will be quiet, and be angry no more. [43] Because you did not remember the days of your youth, but agitated Me with all these things, surely*

I will also recompense your deeds on your own head," says YAHUAH. "And you shall not commit lewdness in addition to all your abominations. [44] "Indeed everyone who quotes proverbs will use this proverb against you: 'Like mother, like daughter!' [45] You are your mother's daughter, loathing husband and children; and you are the sister of your sisters, who loathed their husbands and children; your mother was a Hittite and your father an Amorite. [46] "Your elder sister is Samaria, who dwells with her daughters to the north of you; and your younger sister, who dwells to the south of you, is Sodom and her daughters. [47] You did not walk in their ways nor act according to their abominations; but, as if that were too little, you became more corrupt than they in all your ways. [48] "As I live," says YAHUAH, "neither your sister Sodom nor her daughters have done as you and your daughters have done. [49] Look, this was the iniquity of your sister Sodom: She and her daughter had pride, fullness of food, and abundance of idleness; neither did she strengthen the hand of the poor and needy. [50] And they were haughty and committed abomination before Me; therefore I took them away as I saw fit. [51] "Samaria did not commit half of your sins; but you have multiplied your abominations more than they, and have justified your sisters by all the abominations which you have done. [52] You who judged your sisters, bear your own shame also, because the sins which you committed were more abominable than theirs; they are more righteous than you. Yes, be disgraced also, and bear your own shame, because you justified your sisters. [53] "When I bring back their captives, the captives of Sodom and her daughters, and the captives of Samaria and her daughters, then I will also bring back the captives of your captivity among them, [54] that you may bear your own shame and be disgraced by all that you did when you comforted them. [55] When your sisters, Sodom and her daughters, return to their former state, and Samaria and her daughters return to their former state, then you and your daughters will return to your former state. [56] For your sister Sodom was not a byword in your mouth in the days of your pride, [57] before your wickedness was uncovered. It was like the time of the reproach of the daughters of Syria and all those around her, and of the daughters of the Philistines, who despise you everywhere. [58] You have paid for your lewdness and your abominations," says YAHUAH. [59] For thus says YAHUAH: **"I will deal with you as you have done, who despised the oath by breaking the covenant.** *[60]* **"Nevertheless I will remember My covenant with you in the days of your youth, and I will establish an everlasting covenant with you.** *[61] Then you will remember your ways and be ashamed, when you receive your older and your younger sisters; for I will give them to you for daughters, but not because of My covenant with you. [62]* **And I will establish My covenant with you. Then you shall know that I am YAHUAH,** *[63] that you may remember and be ashamed, and never open your mouth anymore because of your shame, when I provide you an atonement for all you have done," says YAHUAH' (Ezekiel 16:1-63 NKJV)*

Tribes of Africa, YAHUAH, our Husband, has foretold the destruction that is coming upon the Mother of Harlots, Babylon the Great. The destruction will happen swiftly, in one day, for He

YAHUAH will judge and destroy her. But YAHUAH, our Husband, calls us to COME OUT OF HER, MY PEOPLE, so that we will not be destroyed with the prostitute, and the kingdom that she has established to cover and control the whole earth **religiously, economically and militarily**. It is the kingdom that is using all 12 'domains of control' to try to establish what Lucifer has been trying to achieve since he was in the presence of the Most High and chose to challenge YAHUAH's position on the Most High Throne.

> o *"How you are fallen from heaven, O Lucifer, son of the morning! How you are cut down to the ground, you who weakened the nations! 13 For you have said in your heart: 'I will ascend into heaven, I will exalt my throne above the stars of YAHUAH; I will also sit on the mount of the congregation On the farthest sides of the north; 14 I will ascend above the heights of the clouds, I will be like the Most High.' 15 Yet you shall be brought down to Sheol, To the lowest depths of the Pit. 16 "Those who see you will gaze at you, and consider you, saying: 'Is this the man who made the earth tremble, who shook kingdoms, 17 Who made the world as a wilderness and destroyed its cities, who did not open the house of his prisoners?' (Isaiah 14:12-17)*

Tribes of Africa, 'Babylon the Great is fallen, is fallen.'

> o *After these things I saw another angel coming down from heaven, having great authority, and the earth was illuminated with his glory. [2]* ***And he cried mightily with a loud voice, saying, "Babylon the great is fallen, is fallen, and has become a dwelling place of demons, a prison for every foul spirit, and a cage for every unclean and hated bird! [3] For all the nations have drunk of the wine of the wrath of her fornication, the***

kings of the earth have committed fornication with her, and the merchants of the earth have become rich through the abundance of her luxury." [4] And I heard another voice from heaven saying, "Come out of her, my people, lest you share in her sins, and lest you receive of her plagues. [5] For her sins have reached to heaven, and YAHUAH has remembered her iniquities.

[6] Render to her just as she rendered to you, and repay her double according to her works; in the cup which she has mixed, mix double for her. [7] In the measure that she glorified herself and lived luxuriously, in the same measure give her torment and sorrow; for she says in her heart, 'I sit as queen, and am no widow, and will not see sorrow.' [8] Therefore her plagues will come in one day—death and mourning and famine. And she will be utterly burned with fire, for strong is YAHUAH who judges her. [9] "The kings of the earth who committed fornication and lived luxuriously with her will weep and lament for her, when they see the smoke of her burning, [10] standing at a distance for fear of her torment, saying, 'Alas, alas, that great city Babylon, that mighty city! For in one hour your judgment has come.' [11] "And the merchants of the earth will weep and mourn over her, for no one buys their merchandise anymore: [12] merchandise of gold and silver, precious stones and pearls, fine linen and purple, silk and scarlet, every kind of citron wood, every kind of object of ivory, every kind of object of most precious wood, bronze, iron, and marble; [13] and cinnamon and incense, fragrant oil and frankincense, wine and oil, fine flour and wheat, cattle and sheep, horses and chariots, and bodies and souls of men. [14] The fruit that your soul longed for has gone from you, and all the things

which are rich and splendid have gone from you, and you shall find them no more at all. [15] The merchants of these things, who became rich by her, will stand at a distance for fear of her torment, weeping and wailing, [16] and saying, 'Alas, alas, that great city that was clothed in fine linen, purple, and scarlet, and adorned with gold and precious stones and pearls! [17] For in one hour such great riches came to nothing.' Every shipmaster, all who travel by ship, sailors, and as many as trade on the sea, stood at a distance [18] and cried out when they saw the smoke of her burning, saying, 'What is like this great city?' [19] "They threw dust on their heads and cried out, weeping and wailing, and saying, 'Alas, alas, that great city, in which all who had ships on the sea became rich by her wealth! For in one hour she is made desolate.' [20] "Rejoice over her, O heaven, and you holy apostles and prophets, for YAHUAH has avenged you on her!" [21] Then a mighty angel took up a stone like a great millstone and threw it into the sea, saying, "Thus with violence the great city Babylon shall be thrown down, and shall not be found anymore. [22] The sound of harpists, musicians, flutists, and trumpeters shall not be heard in you anymore. No craftsman of any craft shall be found in you anymore, and the sound of a millstone shall not be heard in you anymore. [23] The light of a lamp shall not shine in you anymore, and the voice of bridegroom and bride shall not be heard in you anymore. For your merchants were the great men of the earth, for by your sorcery all the nations were deceived. [24] And in her was found the blood of prophets and saints, and of all who were slain on the earth." (Revelation 18:1-24 NKJV)

"The solutions for the domains"

Section 7

Contents

Chapter 24.   The biblical antidote for the curse of Africa

Chapter 25.   Back to the 12 domains of control

Beloved, let us love one another, for love is of YAHUAH; and everyone who loves is born of YAHUAH and knows YAHUAH. [8] He who does not love does not know YAHUAH, for YAHUAH is love. (I John 4:7-8 NKJV)

CHAPTER TWENTY-FOUR

The Biblical Antidote For The Curse Of Africa

There are many 'practical' things across the 12 'domains of control' (which were mentioned in Section 2) that need to be done to overturn the position which Africa finds itself in, but all the solutions we come up with will fail if we are walking contrary to YAHUAH, the ALAHYM of Abraham, Isaac and Jacob who we have an everlasting agreement (covenant) with. An agreement that specifies the blessing which comes through our obedience and likewise the curses which come through our disobedience.

Tribes of Africa, everything that has happened, is happening and will happen to us is governed by the agreement.

- *'But if you do not obey Me, and do not observe all these commandments, [15] and if you despise My statutes, or if your soul abhors My judgments, so that you do not perform all My commandments, but break My covenant, [16] I also will do this to you: I will even appoint terror over you, wasting disease and fever which shall consume the eyes and cause sorrow of heart. And you*

> *shall sow your seed in vain, for your enemies shall eat it. [17]* ***I will*** *set My face against you, and you shall be defeated by your enemies. Those who hate you shall reign over you, and you shall flee when no one pursues you. [18]* ***'And after all this, if you do not obey Me, then I will punish you seven times more for your sins.*** *(Leviticus 26:14-18)*

If we go against this agreement (covenant), we will be fighting against our ALUAH (GOD).

The rebuilding of the walls of Africa needs to take place, but the success of that will be determined by the 'spiritual foundation' which must be first reestablished.

The prefix 'RE' always points to going back to something.

(RE)establish speaks about going back to what was originally established.

(RE)build speaks about building back to some original standard of specification. And so, we need to ask ourselves what we are building back to.

(RE)pent, (RE)turn speaks about turning back, going back to a destination or place that we have departed from.

(RE)store speaks about establishing things back to the way they were before.

🕯 **Tribes of Africa,** the restoration and reestablishment of the agreement with our Father, the ALUAH of Abraham, Isaac and Jacob, YAHUAH, is the most urgent and critical action. From there, all else that needs to be rebuilt will become seamless.

This is and will always be the biblical formula for those who are committed to rebuild according to the guidelines of the covenantal agreement they have with YAHUAH, the ALUAH of Abraham, Isaac and Jacob.

After the YASHARA'ALITES had completed the 'assigned' 70 years of Babylonian captivity, YAHUAH raised up a group of leaders led by Nehemiah and Ezra to start the process of rebuilding Yarushalayim (Jerusalem). Nehemiah tells us the process of rebuilding the walls of Yarushalayim (Jerusalem) miraculously took 52 days, as it is written:

- ***So the wall was finished on the twenty-fifth day of the month Elul, in fifty-two days.*** *[16] And when all our enemies heard of it, all the nations around us were afraid and fell greatly in their own esteem,* ***for they perceived that this work had been accomplished with the help of our Aluah (YAHUAH).*** *(Nehemiah 6:15-16 ESV)*

Despite many different forms of resistance, the rebuilding process was miraculously completed in a short time because YAHUAH was building with and for them Himself because of the commitment they had made to (RE)turn to Him and to (RE)establish the terms of the everlasting agreement (covenant) with Him. This was the key to their success because YAHUAH then fulfilled His end of the agreement, which is to fight for and restore His people (when they return to the terms of the agreement).

Tribes of Africa, the nations of the world will be astounded when they see how quickly Africa is built up, and they will perceive that the work was done by our ALUAH, YAHUAH. This is how YAHUAH will get the glory and the fame of His name into the nations.

Here are some passages which speak of the approach Nehemiah and Ezra took, as it is written:

o *The words of Nehemiah the son of Hachaliah. It came to pass in the month of Chislev, in the twentieth year, as I was in Shushan the citadel, [2] that Hanani one of my brethren came with men from Judah; and I asked them concerning the Jews who had escaped, who had survived the captivity, and concerning Yarushalayim (Jerusalem). [3] And they said to me,* **"The survivors who are left from the captivity in the province are there in great distress and reproach. The wall of Yarushalayim (Jerusalem) is also broken down, and its gates are burned with fire."** *[4] So it was, when I heard these words, that I sat down and wept, and mourned for many days; I was fasting and praying before the Aluah of heaven. [5] And I said: "I pray, YAHUAH Aluah of heaven, O great and awesome Aluah,* **You who keep Your covenant and mercy with those who love You and observe Your commandments***, [6] please let Your ear be attentive and Your eyes open, that You may hear the prayer of Your servant which I pray before You now, day and night, for the children of YASHARA'AL Your servants, and confess the sins of the children of YASHARA'AL which we have sinned against You. Both my father's house and I have sinned. [7] We have acted very corruptly against You, and have not kept the commandments, the statutes, nor the ordinances which You commanded Your servant Moses. [8] Remember, I pray, the word that You commanded Your servant Moses, saying, 'If you are unfaithful, I will scatter you among the nations; [9] but if you return to Me, and keep My commandments and do them, though some of you were cast out to the farthest part of the heavens, yet I will gather them from there, and bring them to the place which I have chosen as a dwelling for My name.' [10] Now these are Your* servants and Your people, whom You have redeemed by Your great power, and by Your strong hand. [11] O YAHUAH, I pray, please let Your ear be attentive to the prayer of Your servant, and to the prayer of Your servants who desire to fear Your name; and let Your servant prosper this day, I pray, and grant him mercy in the sight of this man." For I was the king's cupbearer. (Nehemiah 1:1-11 NKJV)

- In the month of Nisan, in the twentieth year of King Artaxerxes, when wine was before him, I took up the wine and gave it to the king. Now I had not been sad in his presence. [2] And the king said to me, "Why is your face sad, seeing you are not sick? This is nothing but sadness of the heart." Then I was very much afraid. [3] I said to the king, **"Let the king live forever! Why should not my face be sad, when the city, the place of my fathers' graves, lies in ruins, and its gates have been destroyed by fire?"** [4] Then the king said to me, "What are you requesting?" So I prayed to the Alahym of heaven. [5] And I said to the king, **"If it pleases the king, and if your servant has found favor in your sight, that you send me to Judah, to the city of my fathers' graves, that I may rebuild it."** (Nehemiah 2:1-5 ESV)

- So I came to Yarushalayim (Jerusalem) and was there three days. [12] Then I arose in the night, I and a few men with me; I told no one what YAHUAH had put in my heart to do at Yarushalayim (Jerusalem); nor was there any animal with me, except the one on which I rode. [13] And I went out by night through the Valley Gate to the Serpent Well and the Refuse Gate, and viewed the walls of Yarushalayim

(Jerusalem) which were broken down and its gates which were burned with fire. [14] Then I went on to the Fountain Gate and to the King's Pool, but there was no room for the animal under me to pass. [15] So I went up in the night by the valley, and viewed the wall; then I turned back and entered by the Valley Gate, and so returned. [16] And the officials did not know where I had gone or what I had done; I had not yet told the Jews, the priests, the nobles, the officials, or the others who did the work. [17] Then I said to them, **"You see the distress that we are in, how Yarushalayim (Jerusalem) lies waste, and its gates are burned with fire. Come and let us build the wall of Yarushalayim (Jerusalem), that we may no longer be a reproach."** *[18] And I told them of the hand of my Alahym which had been good upon me, and also of the king's words that he had spoken to me.* **So they said, "Let us rise up and build." Then they set their hands to this good work.** *(Nehemiah 2:11-18 NKJV)*

- *Then Eliashib the high priest rose up with his brethren the priests and* **built the Sheep Gate;** *they consecrated it and hung its doors. They built as far as the Tower of the Hundred, and consecrated it, then as far as the Tower of Hananel. [2] Next to Eliashib* **the men of Jericho built.** *And next to them Zaccur* **the son of Imri built.** *[3] Also* **the sons of Hassenaah built the Fish Gate;** *they laid its beams and hung its doors with its bolts and bars. [4] And next to them Meremoth the son of Urijah, the son of Koz,* **made repairs.** *Next to them Meshullam the son of Berechiah, the son of Meshezabel,* **made repairs.** *Next to them Zadok the son of Baana* **made repairs.** *[5] Next* to them the Tekoites **made repairs**; but their nobles did not put their shoulders to the work of their Lord. [6] Moreover Jehoiada the son of Paseah and Meshullam the son of Besodeiah **repaired the Old Gate**; they laid its beams and hung its doors, with its bolts and bars. [7] And next to them Melatiah the Gibeonite, Jadon the Meronothite, the men of Gibeon and Mizpah, **repaired the residence of the governor** of the region beyond the River. [8] Next to him Uzziel the son of Harhaiah, **one of the goldsmiths, made repairs**. Also next to him Hananiah, **one of the perfumers, made repairs; and they fortified Yarushalayim (Jerusalem)** as far as the Broad Wall. [9] And next to them Rephaiah the son of Hur, leader of half the district of Yarushalayim (Jerusalem), **made repairs**. [10] Next to them Jedaiah the son of Harumaph **made repairs in front of his house**. And next to him Hattush the son of Hashabniah **made repairs**. [11] Malchijah the son of Harim and Hashub the son of Pahath-Moab **repaired another section, as well as the Tower of the Ovens**. [12] And next to him was Shallum the son of Hallohesh, leader of half the district of Yarushalayim (Jerusalem); **he and his daughters made repairs**. [13] Hanun and the inhabitants of Zanoah **repaired the Valley Gate. They built it**, hung its doors with its bolts and bars, and repaired a thousand cubits of the wall as far as the Refuse Gate. [14] Malchijah the son of Rechab, leader of the district of Beth Haccerem, **repaired the Refuse Gate; he built it** and hung its doors with its bolts and bars. [15] Shallun the son of Col-Hozeh, leader of the district of Mizpah, **repaired the Fountain Gate; he built it**, covered it, hung its doors with its bolts and bars, **and repaired the wall of the Pool of Shelah** by the King's Garden, as far as the stairs that go down from the City of David. [16] After him Nehemiah the son of Azbuk, leader of half the district of Beth Zur, **made repairs** as far as the place in front of the tombs of David, to the man-made pool, and as far as the House of the Mighty. [17] After him the Levites, under Rehum the son of Bani, **made repairs**. Next to him Hashabiah, leader of half the district of Keilah, **made repairs for his district**. [18] After him their brethren, under Bavai the son of Henadad, leader of the other half of the district of Keilah, **made repairs**. [19] And next to him Ezer the son of Jeshua, the leader of Mizpah, **repaired another section in front of the Ascent to the Armory at the buttress**. [20] After him Baruch the son of Zabbai **carefully repaired the other section**, from the buttress to the door of the house of Eliashib the high priest. [21] After him Meremoth the son of Urijah, the son of Koz, **repaired another section**, from the door of the house of Eliashib to the end of the house of Eliashib. [22] And after him the priests, the men of the plain, **made repairs**. [23] After him Benjamin and Hasshub **made repairs opposite their house**. After them Azariah the son of Maaseiah, the son of Ananiah, **made repairs by his house**. [24] After him Binnui the son of Henadad **repaired another section**, from the house of Azariah to the buttress, even as far as the corner. [25] Palal the son of Uzai **made repairs** opposite the buttress, and on the tower which projects from the king's upper house that was by the court of the prison. After him Pedaiah the son of Parosh **made repairs**. [26] Moreover the Nethinim who dwelt in Ophel **made repairs** as far as the place in front of the Water Gate toward the east, and on the projecting tower. [27] After them the Tekoites **repaired**

> ***another section***, *next to the great projecting tower, and as far as the wall of Ophel. [28] Beyond the Horse Gate **the priests made repairs, each in front of his own house**. [29] After them Zadok the son of Immer made **repairs in front of his own house**. After him Shemaiah the son of Shechaniah, the keeper of the East Gate, **made repairs**. [30] After him Hananiah the son of Shelemiah, and Hanun, the sixth son of Zalaph, **repaired another section**. After him Meshullam the son of Berechiah **made repairs in front of his dwelling**. [31] After him Malchijah, one of the goldsmiths, **made repairs** as far as the house of the Nethinim and of the merchants, in front of the Miphkad Gate, and as far as the upper room at the corner. [32] And between the upper room at the corner, as far as the Sheep Gate, the goldsmiths and the merchants **made repairs**. (Nehemiah 3:1-32 NKJV)*

The whole team working under Nehemiah and Ezra were involved, and each took up their responsibility to build and repair so that the city was (RE)stored according to the original design which YAHUAH had given them for the city of Yarushalayim.

It is worthwhile to read the whole book of Nehemiah, as it serves as a biblical blueprint for the (RE)building.

Likewise, it is worthwhile to read the book of Ezra as it even outlines the strategy which YAHUAH invoked to get the (RE)building project funded, and all resources made available. When YAHUAH commissions the (RE)building of anything, He also commissions the strategy for the availing of the resources required. I believe this remains the case. Therefore, the funding and resources that YAHUAH has allocated to Africa for His rebuilding project are awaiting.

The primary principle that Nehemiah and Ezra understood was that if the curse of YASHARA'AL was because of a broken agreement (covenant), then that was the first thing they needed to correct before embarking on the mobilisation of the expertise that would do the physical work.

The same primary principle applies to Africa.

If indeed we are under the curse because we have violated the agreement (covenant) YAHUAH made with us, then the antidote is quite clear from everything we have covered throughout this book.

🌿 **Tribes of Africa**, we must acknowledge we have broken the agreement (covenant) with YAHUAH, our Aluah.

🌿 **Tribes of Africa**, we must confess our breaking of the agreement (covenant) with YAHUAH, our Aluah.

🌿 **Tribes of Africa**, we must ask YAHUAH, our Aluah, for forgiveness for breaking the agreement (covenant).

🌿 **Tribes of Africa**, we must (RE)pent, which is committing to (RE)turn to the agreement (covenant) and obey the terms of the agreement (covenant).

This is the only antidote YAHUAH has given for His people when they come into the realisation that they are under a curse.

Trying to solve the curse in any other way will always be futile, as YAHUAH will continue to fight against us until we do what He has said, which is:

1. Acknowledge our iniquity (constant transgression of YAHUAH's law and the breaking of His covenant) and that of our forefathers/ancestors.
2. Confess our iniquity, admit we are where we are now as a

result of our own iniquity (the choices we and our forefathers made in violation of the agreement with YAHUAH).
3. Ask YAHUAH our ALUAH for forgiveness.
4. (RE)pent, (RE)turn to the terms of the agreement (covenant).
5. Obey the terms of the covenant as we ask the Spirit of YAHUAH to help us do so.
6. Acknowledge, confess, ask for forgiveness and repent every time we transgress the agreement (sin), with the understanding that the atonement for our transgressions has been made by the everlasting sacrifice of the life of YAHUSHA and the debt is paid by YAHUSHA's Blood.

Continuing in this cycle is what will cleanse Africa from all unrighteousness before YAHUAH and cause Him to take up the fight for His people.

- o ***'But if they confess their iniquity and the iniquity of their fathers, with their unfaithfulness in which they were unfaithful to Me, and that they also have walked contrary to Me, [41] and that I also have walked contrary to them and have brought them into the land of their enemies; if their uncircumcised hearts are humbled, and they accept their guilt— [42] then I will remember My covenant with Jacob, and My covenant with Isaac and My covenant with Abraham I will remember; I will remember the land.*** [43] *The land also shall be left empty by them, and will enjoy its sabbaths while it lies desolate without them; they will accept their guilt, because they despised My judgments and because their soul abhorred My statutes.* [44] *Yet for all that, when they are in the land of their enemies, I will not cast them away, nor shall I abhor them, to utterly destroy them and break My* *covenant with them; for I am YAHUAH their ALUAH. [45]* **But for their sake I will remember the covenant of their ancestors, whom I brought out of the land of Egypt in the sight of the nations, that I might be their ALUAH: I am YAHUAH.'** *(Leviticus 26:40-45 NKJV)*

Tribes of Africa, when righteousness in the eyes of YAHUAH is established, YAHUAH will always fight for the cause of His people.

The Strong's Concordance reference for righteousness is H6662 and is the Hebrew word 'tsaddiq', and is described as follows -

The term "tsaddiq" is used in the Hebrew Bible to describe someone who is righteous or just, in the context of moral and ethical behaviour which aligns with YAHUAH's standards. It denotes a person who is in right standing with YAHUAH, living in accordance with His laws and commandments. The word is frequently used to contrast the righteous with the wicked, highlighting the moral and spiritual integrity of the former.

In ancient Israelite society, righteousness was not merely a personal attribute but a communal expectation. The concept of "tsaddiq" was deeply embedded in the covenantal relationship between YAHUAH and His people. Righteousness was seen as adherence to the Torah, the law given by God, and was often associated with justice, mercy, and faithfulness.

YAHUAH has many promises He has made to those He considers righteous, those He deems to be good in His sight.

- *A good man leaves an inheritance to his children's children,* **but the sinner's wealth is laid up for the righteous.** *(Proverbs 13:22 ESV)*
- **The righteous shall inherit the land** and dwell upon it

> *forever. [30]* ***The mouth of the righteous utters wisdom,*** *and his tongue speaks justice. [31]* ***The law of his Alahym is in his heart;*** *his steps do not slip. (Psalm 37:29-31 ESV)*
> - **For to the one who pleases him YAHUAH** has given wisdom and knowledge and joy, but to the sinner he has given the business of gathering and collecting, **only to give to one who pleases YAHUAH.** This also is vanity and a striving after wind. (Ecclesiastes 2:26 ESV)

Proverbs chapters 10, 11, 12, 13 and others are great references to see what YAHUAH says and promises to those who meet His criteria for righteousness and are deemed to be good in His sight.

Is the root cause not the curse?

If the condition Africa finds itself in today—and the struggles it has faced in the past—cannot be traced to a curse, then it becomes necessary to search deeper for the true root cause. Only by uncovering and understanding this foundation can meaningful and lasting solutions be found. Without clarity on the root, the problem will remain unsolved.

The summary of our story

A note on terminology – the description for Africa and its people will be interchanged with the use of the term 'the tribes' in this summary below.

The reason 'the conqueror' overcame 'the tribes' is because 'the tribes' forsook their ancestral agreement with YAHUAH, The Most High Alahym, The ALAHYM of Abraham, Isaac and Jacob; so, the curse had to come upon 'the tribes' to fulfil what is written in the terms of agreement according to the unchangeable design

YAHUAH has established for His Kingdom.

The tribes were left exposed—stripped of their covering and protection—when they turned away from their everlasting covenant with YAHUAH, their Aluah. In this vulnerable state, they became open to enslavement, colonisation, and oppression, in fulfilment of the warnings written in Deuteronomy 28:15-68, which outline the consequences of forsaking that covenant. Slavery, colonialism, apartheid, and other forms of oppression came upon the tribes not simply because of the oppressor's strength, but because of our own lawlessness and rebellion against the covenant established by our Maker, YAHUAH.

It is therefore vital to recognise that the oppressor's power to rule and afflict continues only so long as the tribes themselves break and dishonour their everlasting agreement with the Most High, the Aluah of Abraham, Isaac, and Jacob. Indeed, the greatest purpose of the oppressor's religion has been to ensnare the tribes into a lawless, covenant-breaking path—one that keeps them estranged from YAHUAH and walking contrary to His way, bound under the curse instead of the blessing of life

It is a plan which started through the 'white horse of Catholicism' that was unleashed upon the descendants of Jacob to conquer them by forcing them into a religion that is based on the removal of the foundation of the covenant, the law and the prophets and from the true faith of 'The Way', so that the consequences of breaking the covenant (terms of agreement with YAHUAH) would come upon 'the tribes' as per the conditions given in the covenant. It was and remains a plan that seeks to cut 'the tribes' off from being a nation and for their name to be remembered no more.

If the covenantal agreement between 'the tribes' and YAHUAH, the Most High Aluah, the Aluah of Abraham, Isaac and Jacob is restored, The Most High, the Ancient of Days, the Commander of heaven's armies will fight for the restoration of 'the tribes' irrespective of what the oppressor does or does not do, because He commits to do so according to the terms of agreement with His people.

The restoration of the Book of the Covenant, the Book of the Law, and the Book of the Testimony of YAHUSHA into the culture and traditions of 'the tribes' is key. It is 'The Key' that opens the door to the pathway which will bring 'the tribes' back into 'the blessings' that Deuteronomy 28:1-14 describes.

- *"Now it shall come to pass, if you diligently obey the voice of YAHUAH your Aluah, to observe carefully all His commandments which I command you today, that YAHUAH your Aluah will set you high above all nations of the earth. [2] And all these blessings shall come upon you and overtake you, because you obey the voice of YAHUAH your Aluah: [3] "Blessed shall you be in the city, and blessed shall you be in the country. [4] "Blessed shall be the fruit of your body, the produce of your ground and the increase of your herds, the increase of your cattle and the offspring of your flocks. [5] "Blessed shall be your basket and your kneading bowl. [6] "Blessed shall you be when you come in, and blessed shall you be when you go out. [7] "YAHUAH will cause your enemies who rise against you to be defeated before your face; they shall come out against you one way and flee before you seven ways. [8] "YAHUAH will command the blessing on you in your storehouses and in all to which you set your hand, and He will bless you in the land which YAHUAH your*

> *Aluah is giving you. [9] "YAHUAH will establish you as a holy people to Himself, just as He has sworn to you, if you keep the commandments of YAHUAH your Aluah and walk in His ways. [10] Then all peoples of the earth shall see that you are called by the name of YAHUAH, and they shall be afraid of you. [11] And YAHUAH will grant you plenty of goods, in the fruit of your body, in the increase of your livestock, and in the produce of your ground, in the land of which YAHUAH swore to your fathers to give you. [12] YAHUAH will open to you His good treasure, the heavens, to give the rain to your land in its season, and to bless all the work of your hand. You shall lend to many nations, but you shall not borrow. [13] And YAHUAH will make you the head and not the tail; you shall be above only, and not be beneath, if you heed the commandments of YAHUAH your Aluah, which I command you today, and are careful to observe them. [14] So you shall not turn aside from any of the words which I command you this day, to the right or the left, to go after other gods to serve them. (Deuteronomy 28:1-14 NKJV)*

These blessings are what YAHUAH has always wanted for 'the tribes', but He holds Himself accountable to only take 'the tribes' into these blessings based on the conditions that are set in the agreement (covenant). If He did otherwise, YAHUAH would be unrighteous and a liar if He were to do it in violation of what He has said in His own Word and agreement (covenant).

For 'the tribes' will remain defeated and oppressed if they remain in rebellion to the instructions (Torah) of The Most High Aluah, the Aluah of Abraham, Isaac and Jacob and reject His Covenant,

Laws and Commandments. This has always been the strategy of the 'man of lawlessness', 'the god of this world', 'the ruler of this age' who oversees 'the conquering white horse' and is worshipped by the 'lawless covenant-breaking religion'. It is the only strategy he (Satan) can use to overcome 'the tribes' because he can defeat 'the tribes' only when they (the tribes) are in rebellion to YAHUAH their ALUAH.

This is what YAHUSHA HA MASHYACH was sent by YAHUAH to address; 'to destroy the works of Satan' and bring 'the tribes' back into covenantal agreement through His absolute obedience to the instructions of YAHUAH, and through the offering and sacrifice of His own life and the shedding of His blood (and not of the animal sacrifices which foreshadowed Him). This is what YAHUSHA refers to as it written - *"For this is my blood of the covenant, which is poured out for many for the forgiveness of sins."* (Matthew 26:28 NKJV). It is the blood of YAHUSHA that has been poured out for the forgiveness of sins (the breaking of the agreement with YAHUAH and 'the tribes'' rebellion against His instructions), making a way for 'the tribes' to come out of the consequences of their rebellion (the curse) and (RE)enter into the fruit that comes from obedience to YAHUAH (which is the blessing).

 Tribes of Africa, this is our story, and this is the GOOD NEWS.

The curse

The conclusions in this book are based on the premise that Africa is under a curse because we are 'the people' who directly agreed to the covenant with YAHUAH through our ancestors, and we have been and are in violation of that agreement. We are of the House of YASHARA'AL, the scattered and 'lost tribes', and so our ALUAH, YAHUAH, has judged us according to the agreement as He said He would.

But now, YAHUAH is calling us to come up, for it is time for His promises of (RE)unification of all 12 tribes of the House of Jacob to take place as events in the world accelerate to the climax of what YAHUAH has foretold in the book of Revelation. The millennial reign of the King of kings, YAHUSHA, is nigh, and the process of (RE)storing the fallen tabernacle of the House of David is being undertaken.

CHAPTER TWENTY-FIVE

Back To The 12 Domains Of Control

There is real physical work which needs to take place, and it requires the best of what Africa has produced across industries, from farmers to miners, from engineers to AI specialists, from academics to housewives, from businesspeople to investment specialists, traditional kings and chiefs to government officials, and the list goes on. The key, though, will be for the best that Africa has to offer to be united and focused on the purpose of breaking the continent free from the chains of control it has been bound by for many generations. A task that will not be easy and can only be achieved by huge sacrifices. There needs to be both the breaking of the chains of bondage and the building of what the new should be across all the 12 'domains of control' and the governance ecosystem that will evolve from that.

A Rebuilt Africa

The big question that requires an answer is "What does a rebuilt Africa look like?".

If the premise is that the (RE)building of Africa is being led by YAHUAH to (RE)store Africa to the position He wants it to be in, then one should consider what this looks like.

I doubt YAHUAH would want to see an Africa that is driven by socioeconomic growth that fuels materialism, greed, pride, the worship of money and other vices of life, which drive His people away from Him. I doubt that it is an Africa that looks like a flashy Dubai or New York, which boasts hundreds of self-made millionaires driving fancy cars for the purposes of showing them off. I doubt it will be an Africa that is exploiting its workers to make money for the elite. I doubt it is an Africa driven by the principles of the Greco-Roman thinking of seeking the interests of the individual above the collective (the tribe and the village). Nor will it be based on the exploitation of others that "the conqueror" has used and taught as the strategy for achieving prosperity.

> o **One who increases his possessions by usury and extortion** *gathers it for him who will pity the poor. [9]* **One who turns away his ear from hearing the law, even his prayer is an abomination.** *(Proverbs 28:8-9 NKJV)*

Tribes of Africa, we certainly do not want our prayers to be an abomination before YAHUAH, by using the methods that 'the conqueror' has used to acquire his wealth and riches.

I believe YAHUAH wants an Africa that is restored to function according to the DNA He has created us with, which is foremost to seek the well-being and prosperity of all in the tribe. It is an Africa that is harnessing the abundant riches of natural resources for the purpose of ensuring that every African benefits from them, as every African is given the opportunity to contribute their labour towards adding value. An Africa where the lust of the flesh, the lust of the eyes and the pride of life are no longer what drives people's behaviour in the society.

> o *Do not love the world or the things in the world. If anyone loves the world, the love of the Father is not in him. [16]* **For all that is in the world—the lust of the flesh, the lust of the eyes, and the pride of life—is not of the Father but is of the world.** *[17] And the world is passing away, and the lust of it; but he who does the will of YAHUAH abides forever. (I John 2:15-17 NKJV)*

But rather an Africa that is built to ensure that,

- The voice of weeping shall no longer be heard in her, nor the voice of crying, as no person goes to bed hungry and receives all the social services, they should receive to live life in dignity.
- There is long life for all, people living the fullness of life.
- There is housing for all, every person and family in decent housing with all the amenities for dignified living.
- There shall be economic activity for all, every person and family eating off the land and contributing their labour to value-adding activities, as wealth is multiplied for all and widows, orphans, the elderly and the helpless (those who cannot work for themselves) are provided for adequately.
- Where children are raised to value and take pride in their identity, culture, heritage and inheritance.
- There is security for all, a society where people are protected and those who offend are rehabilitated.
- There is the everlasting commitment to living under the terms of the agreement (covenant) with YAHUAH.

> o *"For behold, I create new heavens and a new earth; And the*

former shall not be remembered or come to mind. [18] But be glad and rejoice forever in what I create; For behold, I create Yarushalayim (Jerusalem) as a rejoicing, And her people a joy. [19] I will rejoice in Yarushalayim (Jerusalem), And joy in My people; **The voice of weeping shall no longer be heard in her, nor the voice of crying. [20]** *"No more shall an infant from there live but a few days, nor an old man who has not fulfilled his days; For the child shall die one hundred years old, But the sinner being one hundred years old shall be accursed. [21]* **They shall build houses and inhabit them; They shall plant vineyards and eat their fruit.** *[22] They shall not build and another inhabit; They shall not plant and another eat; For as the days of a tree, so shall be the days of My people,* **and My elect shall long enjoy the work of their hands. [23] They shall not labour in vain, nor bring forth children for trouble; For they shall be the descendants of the blessed of YAHUAH, And their offspring with them.** *[24] "It shall come to pass That before they call, I will answer; and while they are still speaking, I will hear. [25] The wolf and the lamb shall feed together, the lion shall eat straw like the ox, and dust shall be the serpent's food.* **They shall not hurt nor destroy in all My holy mountain," Says YAHUAH.** *(Isaiah 65:17-25 NKJV)*

If these can form the foundational objectives of what the (RE)built Africa looks like, the strategy of what the building of the other 11 'domains of control' can be established and executed upon.

The greater plan

But perhaps the plan for Africa goes further than what we can think of logically, into an Africa that is rebuilt for greater purposes within the plan of YAHUAH for His people.

An African economy that will function outside of what the Bible refers to as the 'beast system' that is arising and will control all trade such that no one will be able to buy and sell without the mark, name or number of the beast, as is written in Revelation 13:16-17:

- *Then I saw another beast coming up out of the earth, and he had two horns like a lamb and spoke like a dragon. [12] And he exercises all the authority of the first beast in his presence, and causes the earth and those who dwell in it to worship the first beast, whose deadly wound was healed. [13] He performs great signs, so that he even makes fire come down from heaven on the earth in the sight of men. [14] And he deceives those who dwell on the earth by those signs which he was granted to do in the sight of the beast, telling those who dwell on the earth to make an image to the beast who was wounded by the sword and lived. [15] He was granted power to give breath to the image of the beast, that the image of the beast should both speak and cause as many as would not worship the image of the beast to be killed. [16]* **He causes all, both small and great, rich and poor, free and slave, to receive a mark on their right hand or on their foreheads, [17] and that no one may buy or sell except one who has the mark or the name of the beast, or the number of his name.** *[18] Here is wisdom. Let him who has understanding calculate the number of the beast, for it is the number of a man: His number is 666. (Revelation 13:11-18 NKJV)*

An African economic and social framework that YAHUAH will use to preserve His people and empower them to thrive, without having to take the mark of the beast as a pledge of allegiance to Satan, and so will be able to produce, manufacture and trade within the continent without any reliance on the systems of the Western world. This would make Africa a refuge of blessing for His people, just as He did when He established Goshen for His people before the first exodus when He was releasing the plagues of judgement upon Egypt. An Africa that becomes a set-apart place that is preserved from the judgements that come to the rest of the world. The scriptures have already revealed to us that the same is soon to happen again as YAHUAH releases His judgement upon 'the Babylon of today', of which the global economic system that is referenced in Revelation chapter 18 is a part. This is why He is calling His people out of her. I believe this is the Africa YAHUAH is seeking to be built.

- **You shall dwell in the land of Goshen,** and you shall be near to me, you and your children, your children's children, your flocks and your herds, and all that you have. (Genesis 45:10 NKJV)
- **And in that day I will set apart the land of Goshen, in which My people dwell, that no swarms of flies shall be there, in order that you may know that I am YAHUAH in the midst of the land. [23] I will make a difference between My people and your people.** Tomorrow this sign shall be." (Exodus 8:22-23 NKJV)
- [8] **Therefore her plagues will come in one day—death and mourning and famine. And she will be utterly burned with fire, for strong is YAHUAH Aluah who judges her.** [9] "The kings of the earth who committed fornication and lived luxuriously with her will weep and lament for her, when they see the smoke of her burning, [10] standing at a distance for fear of her torment, saying,

> *'Alas, alas, that great city Babylon, that mighty city! For in one hour your judgment has come.'* [11] *"And the merchants of the earth will weep and mourn over her, for no one buys their merchandise anymore:*
>
> *[15] The merchants of these things, who became rich by her, will stand at a distance for fear of her torment, weeping and wailing,*
>
> *[17]* ***For in one hour such great riches came to nothing.*** *' Every shipmaster, all who travel by ship, sailors, and as many as trade on the sea, stood at a distance [18] and cried out when they saw the smoke of her burning, saying, 'What is like this great city?' [19] "They threw dust on their heads and cried out, weeping and wailing, and saying, 'Alas, alas, that great city, in which all who had ships on the sea became rich by her wealth!* ***For in one hour she is made desolate.*** *'(Revelation 18:8-11, 15, 17-19 NKJV)*

As mentioned in Chapter 3, Africa has the potential to become an economic powerhouse in the world, but not in the way the Western world would define it. YAHUAH's plan is for Africa to be an economic powerhouse that demonstrates what the economy of His Kingdom looks like for the rest of the world to see, and one that will be the platform for Him to preserve His people in times of judgement upon the earth.

As was already indicated earlier, the primary purpose of this book is to address the first 'domain of control', which is the spiritual domain, and not to get into details of what should be done in the other 11 domains, as that would be outside of the scope.

Nonetheless, here are some summarised thoughts -

1. **Reclaim identity, cultural and spiritual sovereignty** (rooted in the truth of biblical identity, heritage and values).

2. **Build self-sustaining economies** (value adding, beneficiation, processing raw materials, establishing new value chains and growing intra-African trade).

3. **Strengthening political and judicial independence against foreign manipulation.**

4. **Educate with purpose** (with a focus on restoring history and driving technology and critical thinking, which contributes to a vision for 'the Africa we want' (because YAHUAH wants it for us)).

5. **Use technology to leapfrog old systems** (harness innovation and access to technology from the expertise of Africans to build systems in a new way).

6. **Negotiate new global relationships** (based on a new paradigm of value-adding driven economies and the strength Africa has in numbers and the value of the natural resources it has that the rest of the world needs to survive).

To do this, we must focus on some strategically linked priorities.

Priority	Strategy
Redeem the truth of our Spirituality	Return to the covenantal and constitutional requirements of our God (the Aluah of Abraham, Isaac and Jacob, I AM, YAHUAH)
Redeem our identity as given in the Bible	Restore biblical truth and reject religious doctrine that has been delivered through institutional religion.
Build Economic Sovereignty	Local value-add industries, intra-African trade

Priority	Strategy
Reform Institutions	Strengthening self-governing legal and political systems
Empower Youth	Invest in purpose-driven, African-centred education
Reassert Control	Over media, resources, infrastructure, banking and financial flows

It is worthwhile repeating a statement made earlier –

'If the covenantal agreement between the tribes and The Most High , The Aluah (God) of our forefathers Abraham, Isaac and Jacob is restored, The Most High, the Ancient of Days, the Commander of heaven's armies will fight for the restoration of 'the tribes' irrespective of what the oppressor does or does not do. This is because YAHUAH has obligated Himself to do so in His design as part of His commitment to keep His side of the covenantal agreement."

> o *Behold, I will bring it health and healing; I will heal them and reveal to them the abundance of peace and truth. [7] And I will cause the captives of Judah and the captives of YASHARA'AL to return, and will rebuild those places as at the first. [8] I will cleanse them from all their iniquity by which they have sinned against Me, and I will pardon all their iniquities by which they have sinned and by which they have transgressed against Me. [9]* **Then it shall be to Me a name of joy, a praise, and an honor before all nations of the earth, who shall hear all the good that I do to them; they shall fear and tremble for all the goodness and all the prosperity that I provide for it.**' *(Jeremiah 33:6-9 NKJV)*

The Covenant Economy

A big question which always arises when thinking of the magnitude of YAHUAH's plan for Africa is, "But how is this possible"? How can Africa establish and thrive in an economic and social framework that is outside the systems controlled by the Western world? Where will Africa get the funding and resources to build what needs to be built?

One of the most exhilarating discoveries for me was beginning to understand aspects of the covenant economy, which is the framework for how the economy and flow of resources are designed in the Kingdom of YAHUAH. It is a framework which is intertwined with the Constitution (the Laws and Commandments of YAHUAH) and is part of the terms of the agreement (Covenant) with YAHUAH, where He obligates Himself to do certain things based on our compliance with all the components of the framework.

The word economy comes from the Greek word Oikonomia, which means 'management of the household', and in this case, refers to YAHUAH's House, in which His people are the residents (or, in other words, the citizens of His Kingdom). This citizenship in YAHUAH's Kingdom is based on agreement and submission to the terms of agreement and the constitution. YAHUAH has a predesigned economic system which governs and determines the economic flow within His House/Kingdom. The rules of His Kingdom are very different to how the kingdom of the world operates.

It is based on obedience to the Commandments and Laws, is linked to the appointed times, the Sabbath, the Feasts, the 7-year, 49-year and 50-year cycles (Jubilee) and to the plan YAHUAH wants executed to fulfil outcomes He has spoken into existence. In a nutshell, YAHUAH works all things so that everything He has scripted in His ultimate plan for the nations is fulfilled.

If all the components of YAHUAH's framework are fitted together through our obedience, they produce a flow from YAHUAH as He takes up the position as the provider (the investor) into the system to ensure every resource requirement (capital) is fed into the multiplication algorithms, which drive the covenant economy.

It is not a capitalist system, it is not a socialist system, but it is based on the agreement (Covenant) YAHUAH has established with His people.

YAHUAH already owns all things, and so He will release the resources He needs to release when we (His people) meet the conditions for Him to do so, according to the terms of the agreement (the Covenant), because YAHUAH is righteous and He holds Himself accountable to release based on His own Word. He will not go against His own Word (terms of agreement).

- *'The silver is Mine, and the gold is Mine,' says YAHUAH of hosts. (Haggai 2:8 NKJV)*
- *The earth is YAHUAH's, and all its fullness, The world and those who dwell therein. (Psalms 24:1 NKJV)*
- *For YAHUAH gives wisdom and knowledge and joy to a man who is good in His sight;* **but to the sinner He gives the work of gathering and collecting, that he may give to him who is good before YAHUAH.** *This also is vanity and grasping for the wind. (Ecclesiastes 2:26 NKJV)*
- *A good man leaves an inheritance to his children's children,* **But the wealth of the sinner is stored up for the righteous.** *(Proverbs 13:22 NKJV)*

All the wealth and resources on earth belong to YAHUAH, even those which are in the hands of the wicked (those who are in rebellion against Him), and He can shift anything around at any time, but it will always be according to the everlasting terms of agreement He established with His people. If His people are not meeting the terms of the agreement, the shift does not happen until they do. It is all dependent on the choices we (His people) make.

YAHUAH gives the power to His people to attain wealth when they are living according to the terms of the agreement (the Covenant).

> o **"And you shall remember YAHUAH your Aluah, for it is He who gives you power to get wealth, that He may establish His covenant which He swore to your fathers, as it is this day.** *[19] Then it shall be, if you by any means forget YAHUAH your Aluah, and follow other gods, and serve them and worship them, I testify against you this day that you shall surely perish. [20] As the nations which YAHUAH destroys before you, so you shall perish, because you would not be obedient to the voice of YAHUAH your Aluah . (Deuteronomy 8:18-20 NKJV)*

YAHUAH swore to our ancestors/forefathers what He would do to fulfil His side of the agreement, if we fulfil ours. Likewise, YAHUAH swore to our ancestors/forefathers what He would do if we do not fulfil our side of the agreement.

The flow of wealth and resources in the Kingdom is directly linked to obedience and the keeping of the covenant.

YAHUAH gives a bit more insight into this, as is written in this famous scripture:

> o *"Therefore do not worry, saying, 'What shall we eat?' or 'What shall we drink?' or 'What shall we wear?' [32]* **For after all these things the Gentiles seek.** *For your heavenly*

> *Father knows that you need all these things. [33]* ***But seek first the kingdom of YAHUAH and His righteousness, and all these things shall be added to you.*** *(Matthew 6:31-33 NKJV)*

Why does the scripture say the Gentiles have to seek after these things? It is because they don't have a covenant and are not operating under the terms of agreement with YAHUAH, and so they must go and seek out wealth for themselves. This is largely what the systems of capitalism and socialism are designed to do; they are systems for Gentiles to go and seek out things. When "the conquerors" came and took over the lands of the indigenous people (the conquered), they were seeking after things (the resources and wealth) that belonged to others.

For those who are in Covenant and living according to the terms of agreement with YAHUAH, it says the things will be added because that is what YAHUAH commits to do when His people are seeking first to live under His rule and reign, and to live and abide by the constitution of His Kingdom. The responsibility for 'things' getting to His people rests on Him.

- The Gentiles (those without the covenant) will seek after the things.
- YAHUAH's people will seek the covenant, and things will come as a result of their obedience to it because YAHUAH has obligated Himself to create the flow that releases the things to His people.

YAHUAH calls us to seek the covenant and the constitution, for those are the preconditions for us to enter His system, which operates with different rules than the Gentile systems, which focus on seeking after "things". The system YAHUAH is inviting us into is one where seeking Him, His Covenant, and His constitution are the priority and doing so is what releases the flow of 'all things' to us. This is the Covenant economy.

One cannot operate in the covenant economy if they are not in a Covenant (agreement), just like one cannot operate in the covenant economy of the House of YAHUAH (His Kingdom) if one is not a citizen in the Kingdom, abiding by the rules and constitution of that Kingdom. Rejection of the Covenant and the constitution disqualifies us from participating in the Covenant economy.

This is one of the key reasons why I believe we have seen very little flow of resources that line up with the magnitude of what YAHUAH has promised in His Word. He is still waiting for His people to meet the terms of the agreement before He releases.

There is much which could be shared about this topic, but it is a subject for a separate book.

Do I claim to fully understand Covenant economics? Not yet. Am I seeing the fruit of it? I believe we are starting to see glimpses of the flow. The more aligned with the terms of the agreement (Covenant) and the constitution of the Kingdom of YAHUAH, the more the pipes in the system will continue to connect so that we can see greater manifestations of the 'Covenant economic' flow trickling through. I believe the pipes are still connecting, and the trickles will soon increase to become large waves as YAHUAH releases what is required for His Covenant plan for Africa and the nations to be fulfilled.

Tribes of Africa, resources are not the constraint to the rebuilding Africa project, Obedience to YAHUAH is.

YAHUAH will provide the flow of resources for His rebuilding project.

- *Then He (YAHUSHA) said to His disciples, "Therefore I say to you, do not worry about your life, what you will eat; nor about the body, what you will put on. [23] Life is more than food, and the body is more than clothing. [24] Consider the ravens, for they neither sow nor reap, which have neither storehouse nor barn; and YAHUAH feeds them. Of how much more value are you than the birds? [25] And which of you by worrying can add one cubit to his stature? [26] If you then are not able to do the least, why are you anxious for the rest? [27] Consider the lilies, how they grow: they neither toil nor spin; and yet I say to you, even Solomon in all his glory was not arrayed like one of these. [28] If then YAHUAH so clothes the grass, which today is in the field and tomorrow is thrown into the oven, how much more will He clothe you, O you of little faith? [29] "And do not seek what you should eat or what you should drink, nor have an anxious mind. [30] For all these things the nations of the world seek after, and your Father knows that you need these things. [31] But seek the kingdom of YAHUAH, and all these things shall be added to you. [32] "Do not fear, little flock, for it is your Father's good pleasure to give you the kingdom. [33] Sell what you have and give alms; provide yourselves money bags which do not grow old, a treasure in the heavens that does not fail, where no thief approaches nor moth destroys. [34] For where your treasure is, there your heart will be also. (Luke 12:22-34 NKJV)*

"Tribes of Africa awaken to your God"

Section 8

Contents

Chapter 26.   What does The Most High Require of Africa?

Chapter 27.   African Leaders arise and shine

Chapter 28.   Personal parting words

CHAPTER TWENTY-SIX

What Does The Most High Require Of Africa?

There are many things that compete for our attention, and each puts a requirement on us.

Men might have what they require of us, so might religion, likewise Christianity or maybe the church.

But all that matters is what YAHUAH requires of us, for if we place what man, religion, Christianity or church requires of us above what YAHUAH requires of us, we fall into idolatry and prostitution when we place something else above what He requires.

Several times in scripture, YAHUAH reveals what He requires of His people.

In one passage of scripture, He says:

1. To reverentially fear Him.
2. To walk in all His ways.
3. To Love Him (remembering the biblical equation that **love = obedience**).
4. To Serve Him.
5. To guard His Commandments and Statutes.

> And now, YASHARA'AL, **what doth YAHUAH thy Aluah require of thee,** but to fear YAHUAH thy Aluah, to walk in all His ways, and to love Him, and to serve YAHUAH thy Aluah with all thy heart and with all thy soul, [13] to keep the commandments of YAHUAH, and His statutes, which I command thee this day for thy good? (Deuteronomy 10:12-13 KJV)

In another passage of scripture, He says:

1. To do right (make the right choices based on the instructions He has given us).
2. To love kindness.
3. To walk humbly with Him (remembering the biblical precept (equation) – can two walk together unless they are in agreement?).

> He hath shewed thee, O man, what is good; and **what doth YAHUAH require of thee,** but to do justly, and to love mercy, and to walk humbly with thy Aluah? (Micah 6:8 KJV)

In a third passage of scripture, He says:

1. To reverentially fear Him.
2. To keep His commandments.

> **Let us hear the conclusion of the whole matter: Fear YAHUAH, and keep His commandments: for this is the whole duty of man.** [14] For YAHUAH shall bring every work into judgment, with every secret thing, whether it be good, or whether it be evil. (Ecclesiastes 12:13-14 KJV)

Many people spend a lifetime seeking the answer to the question,

"What is YAHUAH's will?"

YAHUAH's primary will is for us to do what He said He requires of all mankind, which is to obey all that He instructs.

- *And He was withdrawn from them about a stone's cast, and kneeled down, and prayed, [42] saying, Father, if thou be willing, remove this cup from Me: **nevertheless not My will, but thine, be done.** [43] And there appeared an angel unto Him from heaven, strengthening Him. [44] And being in an agony He prayed more earnestly: and His sweat was as it were great drops of blood falling down to the ground. (Luke 22:41-44 KJV)*
- ***I delight to do thy will**, O my Aluah: Yea, thy law is within my heart. (Psalm 40:8 KJV)*
- *YAHUSHA saith unto them, **My meat is to do the will of Him that sent Me**, and to finish His work. (John 4:34 KJV)*
- *I can of mine own self do nothing: as I hear, I judge: and my judgment is just; **because I seek not mine own will, but the will of the Father which hath sent me.** (John 5:30 KJV)*
- *For I came down from heaven, **not to do mine own will, but the will of Him that sent Me.** (John 6:38 KJV)*
- *Then said I, Lo, I come (In the volume of the book it is written of Me,) **To do thy will, O YAHUAH**. (Hebrews 10:7 KJV)*

YAHUSHA's first word when He started His ministry (the assignment that YAHUAH sent Him to fulfil on earth) was REPENT (which means return).

(RE)TURN to what?

Return to the terms of the agreement (the covenant) with the FATHER, return to His instructions, return to obeying His Commandments, His Law, His Statutes, His Precepts and His Judgements. Return to your first love, to love the FATHER by doing all the FATHER has said.

> o *From that time **YAHUSHA** began to preach, and to say, **Repent**: for the kingdom of heaven is at hand. (Matthew 4:17 KJV)*

I believe this call to repent is fulfilled by the following -

1. **"Honouring YAHUAH's Voice and obedience to all that He says"**: a greater focus on understanding and obeying what He has said in the past through 'the Law, the Prophets and the Psalms', and connecting everything we do back to that foundation. Refrain from falling into the trap of seeking prophetic words today that point to so-called 'new revelations, new secrets, new things' and yet do not draw us back to the foundational script that YAHUAH has already given His people.

2. **"Keeping the Covenant YAHUAH has made with and for His people"**: honouring the agreement He has established with us. A relational agreement that sets the standard of how He wants us to relate to Him. A relational agreement linked to obedience, which is the fear of YAHUAH and a demonstration of our love for YAHUAH.

3. **"Obeying His Commandments and Law"**: embracing and committing to obey His instructions. To honour, respect, embrace and commit to obey the constitution YAHUAH has established to govern His Kingdom, which is the basis for His rulership and reign as King and the foundation of His judgments as Judge. Even more importantly, it is the basis for

our submission to His Kingship and hence our submission to be 'citizens' in His Kingdom and to be governed by how He has designed things to work based on the choices we make that can either lead to curse/death or to blessing/life.

4. **"Receiving the fullness of the Righteousness we can attain only through the finished work of YAHUSHA"**: understanding that as much as we are to submit ourselves to His Voice, Covenant and Torah (Instructions and constitution) and commit to obey them; our efforts (works) will never be counted to us as righteousness because that is imputed unto us only through the sacrifice and offering of YAHUSHA's sinless life and blood. But this should not give us the license to be lawless people.

5. **"Being led by the HOLY SPIRIT"**: as we deny ourselves, choose to die to self and allow the Spirit of YAHUAH to flow through us to make us channels that bring His thoughts, plans, and purposes to pass on the earth just as YAHUSHA did.

CHAPTER TWENTY-SEVEN

African Leaders Arise And Shine

Tribes of Africa, the final trumpet call in this book is for leadership.

Africa needs its leaders to come into order and alignment according to YAHUAH's requirement for leadership.

- Leaders who will first and foremost recognise the story and journey that Africa has gone through, seeing it through the eyes of YAHUAH and not through the logic and understanding of man or the narrative that 'the conqueror' has scripted over Africa.
- Leaders who will understand that taking Africa forward will require doing so according to the methods which YAHUAH has already outlined.
- Leaders who will execute the plan already given by YAHUAH to restore the covenant with Him first before the (RE) building project can commence in earnest.
- Leaders who will then mobilise the people to a vision as per 'the Africa that YAHUAH wants' for His people.

- Leaders who will empower the people to do their part in contributing to the fulfilment of the vision (as demonstrated by Nehemiah), with each person and family doing their part, whether big or small, to build and to repair sections they can contribute towards based on their skills, abilities and resources.

It requires Kings who will bring (RE)FORM to Africa, and this entails bringing back the form that YAHUAH established in and for Africa before that form was destroyed by "the conquerors".

The 3-strand cord of governance

Throughout the scriptures, one can see a three-strand cord of governance offices through which YAHUAH's nation of YASHARA'AL operates under. The 3 offices are (1) the King with executive authority, (2) the Prophet with advisory authority, and (3) the Priest with the authority to represent the people before YAHUAH and guard YAHUAH's instructions to the people. The 3 positions would honour and respect each other and would be accountable to each other as they were accountable to YAHUAH.

The Priests took the responsibility of guarding YAHUAH's covenant, laws and commandments by ensuring that the people, including the King, would always know them and comply with them. We see an example of this with Ezra, as it is written:

- *For Ezra had prepared his heart to seek the law of YAHUAH, and to do it, and to teach in YASHARA'AL statutes and judgments. (Ezra 7:10 KJV)*

The Prophets would convey the word of YAHUAH to the people, the King and to the Priest when YAHUAH had something to say about what was taking place in and around the nation that needed attention and action. If the nation was deviating from the instructions of YAHUAH, the prophets would indicate that, and give a warning of the consequences if the King, Priest and the people did not take action to rectify it.

The King held the executive office to ensure all of YAHUAH's terms of agreement (covenant) were complied with by the entire population, and violations were dealt with according to the guidelines given in the constitution (the laws, commandments, and judgements given by YAHUAH). He would ensure all the requirements of the constitution, such as the Feasts of YAHUAH, the requirement for Sabbath, the economic principles of Jubilee, and others, were always adhered to so that the nation functions in alignment with the agreement with YAHUAH, as this would be the guarantee for prosperity

- o **When the righteous are in authority, the people rejoice:** But when the wicked beareth rule, the people mourn. (Proverbs 29:2 KJV)

 So, Tribes of Africa, there is a model available to replicate.

Kings of Africa Arise and Shine

Africa has King Josiahs and King Davids on the continent who now need to awaken to the call for Africa's (RE)formation. To lead Africa in the return to the original formation YAHUAH established for Africa, with its spirituality based on the covenant (agreement) with Him. It's an Africa whose identity, culture, heritage, language, and inheritance are found in YAHUAH and the plan that has long been established for the continent and its people.

King David was a man after YAHUAH's own heart and was

committed to do all the will of YAHUAH. We need such Kings to "arise and shine" in Africa.

- o *And when He had removed him, He raised up unto them David to be their king; to whom also He gave testimony, and said,* **I have found David the son of Jesse, a man after mine Own heart, which shall fulfil all My will.** *(Acts 13:22 KJV)*

King Josiah is a perfect example of a leader who drove and executed a (RE)formation plan to bring the nation of YASHARA'AL back into alignment with YAHUAH.

- o **Josiah was eight years old when he became king**, *and he reigned thirty-one years in Yarushalayim (Jerusalem). His mother's name was Jedidah the daughter of Adaiah of Bozkath. [2]* **And he did what was right in the sight of YAHUAH, and walked in all the ways of his father David; he did not turn aside to the right hand or to the left.** *[3] Now it came to pass, in the eighteenth year of King Josiah, that the king sent Shaphan the scribe, the son of Azaliah, the son of Meshullam, to the house of YAHUAH, saying: [4] "Go up to Hilkiah the high priest, that he may count the money which has been brought into the house of YAHUAH, which the doorkeepers have gathered from the people. [5] And let them deliver it into the hand of those doing the work, who are the overseers in the house of YAHUAH; let them give it to those who are in the house of YAHUAH doing the work, to repair the damages of the house— [6] to carpenters and builders and masons—and to buy timber and hewn stone to repair the house. [7] However there need be no accounting made with them of the money delivered into their hand, because they deal faithfully." [8]*

Then Hilkiah the high priest said to Shaphan the scribe, **"I have found the BOOK OF THE LAW in the house of YAHUAH."** *And Hilkiah gave the book to Shaphan, and he read it. [9] So Shaphan the scribe went to the king, bringing the king word, saying, "Your servants have gathered the money that was found in the house, and have delivered it into the hand of those who do the work, who oversee the house of YAHUAH." [10] Then Shaphan the scribe showed the king, saying, "Hilkiah the priest has given me A BOOK." And Shaphan read it before the king. [11]* **Now it happened, when the king heard the words of the BOOK OF THE LAW, that he tore his clothes. [12] Then the king commanded Hilkiah the priest, Ahikam the son of Shaphan, Achbor the son of Michaiah, Shaphan the scribe, and Asaiah a servant of the king, saying, [13] "Go, inquire of YAHUAH for me, for the people and for all Judah, concerning the words of this BOOK that has been found; for great is the wrath of YAHUAH that is aroused against us, because our fathers have not obeyed the words of this BOOK, to do according to all that is written concerning us."** *[14] So Hilkiah the priest, Ahikam, Achbor, Shaphan, and Asaiah went to Huldah the prophetess, the wife of Shallum the son of Tikvah, the son of Harhas, keeper of the wardrobe. (She dwelt in Yarushalayim (Jerusalem) in the Second Quarter.) And they spoke with her. [15] Then she said to them, "Thus says YAHUAH ALAHYM of YASHARA'AL, 'Tell the man who sent you to Me, [16] "Thus says YAHUAH: 'Behold, I will bring calamity on this place and on its inhabitants—all the words of the BOOK which the king of Judah has read— [17] because they have forsaken Me and burned incense to* other gods, that they might provoke Me to anger with all the works of their hands. Therefore My wrath shall be aroused against this place and shall not be quenched." [18] But as for the king of Judah, who sent you to inquire of YAHUAH, in this manner you shall speak to him, **'Thus says YAHUAH ALAHYM of YASHARA'AL: "Concerning the words which you have heard— [19] because your heart was tender, and you humbled yourself before YAHUAH when you heard what I spoke against this place and against its inhabitants, that they would become a desolation and a curse, and you tore your clothes and wept before Me, I also have heard you," says YAHUAH.** [20] "Surely, therefore, I will gather you to your fathers, and you shall be gathered to your grave in peace; and your eyes shall not see all the calamity which I will bring on this place." So they brought back word to the king. (II Kings 22:1-20 NKJV)

- **Now the king sent them to gather all the elders of Judah and Yarushalayim (Jerusalem) to him. [2] The king went up to the house of YAHUAH with all the men of Judah, and with him all the inhabitants of Yarushalayim (Jerusalem)—the priests and the prophets and all the people, both small and great. And he read in their hearing all the words of the BOOK OF THE COVENANT which had been found in the house of YAHUAH. [3] Then the king stood by a pillar and made a covenant before YAHUAH, to follow YAHUAH and to keep His commandments and His testimonies and His statutes, with all his heart and all his soul, to perform the words of this covenant that were written in this BOOK. And all the people took a stand for the** covenant. *[4] And the king commanded Hilkiah the high priest, the priests of the second order, and the doorkeepers, to bring out of the temple of YAHUAH all the articles that were made for Baal, for Asherah, and for all the host of heaven; and he burned them outside Yarushalayim (Jerusalem) in the fields of Kidron, and carried their ashes to Bethel. [5] Then he removed the idolatrous priests whom the kings of Judah had ordained to burn incense on the high places in the cities of Judah and in the places all around Yarushalayim (Jerusalem), and those who burned incense to Baal, to the sun, to the moon, to the constellations, and to all the host of heaven. [6] And he brought out the wooden image from the house of YAHUAH, to the Brook Kidron outside Yarushalayim (Jerusalem), burned it at the Brook Kidron and ground it to ashes, and threw its ashes on the graves of the common people. [7] Then he tore down the ritual booths of the perverted persons that were in the house of YAHUAH, where the women wove hangings for the wooden image. [8] And he brought all the priests from the cities of Judah, and defiled the high places where the priests had burned incense, from Geba to Beersheba; also he broke down the high places at the gates which were at the entrance of the Gate of Joshua the governor of the city, which were to the left of the city gate.* [9] Nevertheless the priests of the high places did not come up to the altar of YAHUAH in Yarushalayim (Jerusalem), but they ate unleavened bread among their brethren. [10] And he defiled Topheth, which is in the Valley of the Son of Hinnom, that no man might make his son or his daughter pass through *the fire to Molech. [11] Then he removed the horses that the kings of Judah had dedicated to the sun, at the entrance to the house of YAHUAH, by the chamber of Nathan-Melech, the officer who was in the court; and he burned the chariots of the sun with fire. [12] The altars that were on the roof, the upper chamber of Ahaz, which the kings of Judah had made, and the altars which Manasseh had made in the two courts of the house of YAHUAH, the king broke down and pulverized there, and threw their dust into the Brook Kidron. [13] Then the king defiled the high places that were east of Yarushalayim (Jerusalem), which were on the south of the Mount of Corruption, which Solomon king of YASHARA'AL had built for Ashtoreth the abomination of the Sidonians, for Chemosh the abomination of the Moabites, and for Milcom the abomination of the people of Ammon. [14] And he broke in pieces the sacred pillars and cut down the wooden images, and filled their places with the bones of men. [15] Moreover the altar that was at Bethel, and the high place which Jeroboam the son of Nebat, who made YASHRAEL sin, had made, both that altar and the high place he broke down; and he burned the high place and crushed it to powder, and burned the wooden image. [16] As Josiah turned, he saw the tombs that were there on the mountain. And he sent and took the bones out of the tombs and burned them on the altar, and defiled it according to the word of YAHUAH which the man of YAHUAH proclaimed, who proclaimed these words. [17] Then he said, "What gravestone is this that I see?" So the men of the city told him, "It is the tomb of the man of YAHUAH who came from Judah and proclaimed these things which you have done against the altar of*

Bethel." [18] And he said, "Let him alone; let no one move his bones." So they let his bones alone, with the bones of the prophet who came from Samaria. [19] Now Josiah also took away all the shrines of the high places that were in the cities of Samaria, which the kings of YASHRAEL had made to provoke YAHUAH to anger; and he did to them according to all the deeds he had done in Bethel. [20] He executed all the priests of the high places who were there, on the altars, and burned men's bones on them; and he returned to Yarushalayim (Jerusalem). [21] **Then the king commanded all the people, saying, "Keep the Passover to YAHUAH your Aluah, as it is written in this BOOK OF THE COVENANT."** *[22] Such a Passover surely had never been held since the days of the judges who judged YASHRAEL, nor in all the days of the kings of YASHRAEL and the kings of Judah. [23] But in the eighteenth year of King Josiah this Passover was held before YAHUAH in Yarushalayim (Jerusalem). [24] Moreover Josiah put away those who consulted mediums and spiritists, the household gods and idols, all the abominations that were seen in the land of Judah and in Yarushalayim (Jerusalem), that he might perform the words of the law which were written in THE BOOK that Hilkiah the priest found in the house of YAHUAH. [25]* **Now before him there was no king like him, who turned to YAHUAH with all his heart, with all his soul, and with all his might, according to all THE LAW of Moses; nor after him did any arise like him.** *(II Kings 23:1-25 NKJV)*

Priests of Africa Arise and Shine

Africa has Priest Ezras on the continent who now need to awaken to the call for Africa's (RE)turn to the covenant with YAHUAH. Those who will take a position of boldness to uncompromisingly (1) seek the Law of YAHUAH, (2) to do it, and (3) to teach statutes and ordinances in Africa.

- *this Ezra went up from Babylon; and **he was a ready scribe in the law of Moses, which YAHUAH Aluah of YASHARA'AL had given**: and the king granted him all his request, according to the hand of YAHUAH his Aluah upon him. (Ezra 7:6 KJV)*
- ***For Ezra had prepared his heart to seek the law of YAHUAH, and to do it, and to teach in YASHARA'AL statutes and judgments**. (Ezra 7:10 KJV)*

As the scriptures say, *'and it shall be like people, like priests'* as it is written in Hosea 4:9. When the appointed guardians of YAHUAH's law and covenant in a nation fall by committing harlotry (forsaking absolute allegiance to YAHUAH alone) and have ceased to obey YAHUAH by transgressing His Law and Commandments, the whole nation gets polluted and drawn into rebellion.

- *"Now let no man contend, or rebuke another; For your people are like those who contend with the priest. [5] Therefore you shall stumble in the day; The prophet also shall stumble with you in the night; And I will destroy your mother. [6] My people are destroyed for lack of knowledge. Because you have rejected knowledge, **I also will reject you from being priest for Me; Because you have forgotten the law of your Aluah, I also will forget your children.** [7] "The more they increased, the more they sinned against*

> *Me; I will change their glory into shame. [8] They eat up the sin of My people; They set their heart on their iniquity. [9]* ***And it shall be: like people, like priest.*** *So I will punish them for their ways, and reward them for their deeds. [10]* ***For they shall eat, but not have enough; They shall commit harlotry, but not increase; Because they have ceased obeying YAHUAH.*** *(Hosea 4:4-10 NKJV)*

There are too many false priests and shepherds in Africa who are leading the flock into rebellion, lawlessness and breaking covenant with YAHUAH. The state of Africa today is a result of the state of the priesthood on the continent.

Prophets of Africa Arise and Shine

Africa has Prophet Isaiahs (YASHAYAHUs), Jeremiahs (YARAMAYAHs), Ezekiels (YACHAZQELs) on the continent who now need to awaken to the call of YAHUAH for Africa to (RE) pent from breaking the everlasting covenant with YAHUAH and for being in rebellion and disobedience to Him. The true prophets and shepherds of the people who will only speak what YAHUAH gives them to speak and will boldly and fearlessly warn the people (including the kings and priests) when they violate the agreement with YAHUAH. Those who will, without fear or favour, pronounce judgement when YAHUAH warns of it and calls the continent and its nations to repentance. True prophets, whose foreheads will be hardened, are prepared to be persecuted and lose their lives for standing up for the Word of YAHUAH and never back down from it.

> o *Then He said to me: "Son of man, go to the house of YASHARA'AL and speak with My words to them. [5] For you are not sent to a people of unfamiliar speech and of*

hard language, but to the house of YASHARA'AL, [6] not to many people of unfamiliar speech and of hard language, whose words you cannot understand. Surely, had I sent you to them, they would have listened to you. [7] But the house of YASHARA'AL will not listen to you, because they will not listen to Me; for all the house of YASHARA'AL are impudent and hard-hearted. [8] **Behold, I have made your face strong against their faces, and your forehead strong against their foreheads. [9] Like adamant stone, harder than flint, I have made your forehead; do not be afraid of them, nor be dismayed at their looks**, *though they are a rebellious house." (Ezekiel 3:4-9 NKJV)*

When we have the 3-strand cord comprised of the true Kings, Priests and Prophets standing together, in submission to each other for the benefit of the people, and in absolute obedience to YAHUAH, change will come very quickly to Africa.

Kings of Africa arise and shine, Priests of Africa arise and shine, Prophets of Africa arise and shine.

- *Arise, shine; for thy light is come, and the glory of YAHUAH is risen upon thee. [2] For, behold, the darkness shall cover the earth, and gross darkness the people: but YAHUAH shall arise upon thee, and His glory shall be seen upon thee. [3]* **And the Gentiles shall come to thy light, and kings to the brightness of thy rising.** *(Isaiah 60:1-3 KJV)*

YAHUAH has established His people as kings and priests to serve His purposes on the earth. This function must be performed by those YAHUAH has appointed to serve Him in this way.

- *Now therefore, if ye will obey My voice indeed, and keep*

> *My covenant, then ye shall be a peculiar treasure unto Me above all people: for all the earth is Mine: [6]* **and ye shall be unto Me a kingdom of priests, and an holy nation.** *These are the words which thou shalt speak unto the children of YASHARA'AL. (Exodus 19:5-6 KJV)*
> - **But ye are a chosen generation, a royal priesthood, an holy nation, a peculiar people; that ye should shew forth the praises of Him who hath called you out of darkness into His marvellous light:** *[10] which in time past were not a people, but are now the people of YAHUAH: which had not obtained mercy, but now have obtained mercy. (1 Peter 2:9-10 KJV)*
> - *and from YAHUSHA MASHYACH, who is the faithful witness, and the first begotten of the dead, and the prince of the kings of the earth. Unto Him that loved us, and washed us from our sins in His own blood, [6]* **and hath made us kings and priests unto YAHUAH and His Father;** *to Him be glory and dominion for ever and ever. Amen. (Revelation 1:5-6 KJV)*

The African Renaissance

From the time Ghana gained political independence from colonial rule on the 6th of March 1957, the dream has been to see the fruit of an African renaissance in which Africans overcome the systemic challenges confronting the continent and achieve a renewal in identity, culture and prosperity. It is the basic premise of the desire for a strong and flourishing Africa that led to the creation of organisations such as the Organisation of African Unity (OAU) and later the African Union (AU).

It seems, though, the efforts of these organisations have produced very limited fruit, perhaps because the missing link is the return to the blueprint of the continent, which is inextricably linked to an agreement with the ALAHYM of Abraham, Isaac and Jacob.

There is no doubt Africa requires a (RE)naissance.

"Naissance" is French for (1) birth, (2) origin and (3) beginning.

It can refer to (1) the act of being born, (2) the origin or starting point of something, or (3) the beginning of a new idea, project, or era.

 Africa requires a (RE)birth, a (RE)origination and a (3) (RE)beginning. Going back to what YAHUAH birthed Africa to be.

The most widely accepted scientific evidence points to Africa as the 'cradle of humankind,' the place where human life first began. It follows, then, that this is also the continent where YAHUAH established His very first covenant with mankind—beginning with Adam, the first man He created, in the garden of Eden, a place described as rich in gold.

Africa is the place of birth.

> o *And YAHUAH said, Let us make man in our image, after our likeness: and let them have dominion over the fish of the sea, and over the fowl of the air, and over the cattle, and over all the earth, and over every creeping thing that creepeth upon the earth. [27]* **So YAHUAH created man in His own image, in the image of YAHUAH created he him; male and female created he them.** *[28] And YAHUAH blessed them, and YAHUAH said unto them, be fruitful, and multiply, and replenish the earth, and subdue it: and have dominion over the fish of the sea, and over the fowl of the air, and over every living thing that moveth upon the earth. (Genesis 1:26-28*

KJV)

- And YAHUAH Aluah planted a garden eastward in Eden; and there he put the man whom He had formed. [9] And out of the ground made YAHUAUH Aluah to grow every tree that is pleasant to the sight, and good for food; the tree of life also in the midst of the garden, and the tree of knowledge of good and evil. [10] And a river went out of Eden to water the garden; and from thence it was parted, and became into four heads. [11] The name of the first is Pison: that is it which compasseth the whole land of Havilah, where there is gold; [12] and the gold of that land is good: there is bdellium and the onyx stone. [13] And the name of the second river is Gihon: the same is it that compasseth the whole land of Ethiopia. [14] And the name of the third river is Hiddekel: that is it which goeth toward the east of Assyria. And the fourth river is Euphrates. [15] And YAHUAH Aluah took the man, and put him into the garden of Eden to dress it and to keep it. [16] And **YAHUAH Aluah commanded the man, saying, Of every tree of the garden thou mayest freely eat: [17] but of the tree of the knowledge of good and evil, thou shalt not eat of it: for in the day that thou eatest thereof thou shalt surely die.** (Genesis 2:8-17 KJV)

Interestingly, the Book of Jubilees (which was not made part of the current biblical canon) gives a very descriptive overview of the Garden of Eden, its geography and layout. All of which seems to provide much evidence of Africa being the location.

The African Renaissance, which will take Africa and the world back to the place of origin for a (RE)birth.

❡ **Tribes of Africa**, arise and shine, those of you called to lead Africa into its destiny to be a light and blessing to all the nations as per the original design of YAHUAH.

What the world has called the dark continent for many centuries is in fact YAHUAH's continent of Light from where His Light will be released to the nations of the world to point them to His Covenant, which is a key of entry into the "New Yarushalayim (Jerusalem)".

HalleluYAH

- *And in that day thou shalt say, O YAHUAH, I will praise thee: though thou wast angry with me, thine anger is turned away, and thou comfortedst me. [2] Behold, YAHUAH is my salvation; I will trust, and not be afraid: for YAHUAH JEHOVAH is my strength and my song; He also is become my salvation. [3] Therefore with joy shall ye draw water out of the wells of salvation. [4] And in that day shall ye say, Praise YAHUAH, call upon His name, declare His doings among the people, make mention that His name is exalted. [5] Sing unto YAHUAH; for He hath done excellent things: this is known in all the earth. [6] Cry out and shout, thou inhabitant of Zion: for great is the Holy One of YASHARA'AL in the midst of thee. (Isaiah 12:1-6 KJV)*

CHAPTER TWENTY-EIGHT

Personal Parting Words

Until recently, I had lived most of my life within the religion of institutionalised Christianity, professing Jesus, having a zeal for the Most High, and proclaiming the Kingdom of God on many platforms. All the while not knowing that, according to the truth of 𐤉𐤄𐤅𐤄 YAHUAH's word, I was in rebellion against Him, living in lawlessness and breaking the everlasting covenant with Him. I knew all the right 'kingdom buzz words' yet I was so far from knowing who the FATHER is and understanding that there is an active covenant (agreement and terms of agreement) that is in place between Him and me and His people. I did not appreciate that the whole reason the FATHER sent His SON, 𐤉𐤄𐤅𐤔𐤏 YAHUSHA, was to restore me to this covenant (agreement) with Him.

"The lamp of the body is the eye. If therefore your eye is good, your whole body will be full of light. But if your eye is bad, your whole body will be full of darkness. If therefore the light that is in you is darkness, how great is that darkness! (Matthew 6:22-23 NKJV)

I thought I had been found, yet I was lost and did not even realise it.

I thought I was walking in truth, yet I was deeply deceived, living a lie and did not even realise it.

I thought I was in the light, yet I was in the dark and did not even realise it.

I thought I could see, yet I was blind and did not even realise it.

I thought I knew the Bible and the word of 𐤄𐤅𐤄𐤉 YAHUAH, yet I was semi-illiterate, only knowing it through the lens of the doctrines and the theological interpretations that form the foundation of the religion of Christianity.

The worst form of slavery is when one thinks they are free when, in actual fact, they are bound in captivity and don't realise it. When one thinks they know the FATHER 𐤄𐤅𐤄𐤉 YAHUAH and the SON 𐤏𐤔𐤅𐤄𐤉 YAHUSHA and the SPIRIT of 𐤄𐤅𐤄𐤉 YAHUAH, but don't.

I have a sense there are many others like me out there in the 'tribes of Africa' who are searching for 'the truth'.

My prayer for every reader is that this book is a catalyst to take you on your own journey of discovery, to ask the questions that need to be asked, to challenge the status quo of what institutional religion has taught, and more importantly encourage you to read the Bible yourself from beginning to end and search the scriptures to get the true Good News outside of the controlled narratives of religion. To find for yourself the relational connection 𐤄𐤅𐤄𐤉 YAHUAH has always desired to have with His people, with you, and the terms He has given for that to take place.

The height of human arrogance and pride is thinking we can set the terms of the relationship with the FATHER and override the terms He has given and commanded, and then expect Him to bow down and conform to what we want. This makes man the 'most high' and relegates 𐤉𐤄𐤅𐤄 YAHUAH to be the servant of man. This is the same thing Lucifer tried to do.

𐤉𐤄𐤅𐤄 YAHUAH will only do what He has obligated Himself to do based on the terms of the Covenant (agreement) He has established with His people. He holds Himself responsible and accountable for what He does to and for His people by the terms of the Covenant (agreement). That is how He has designed it to be. He is 𐤉𐤄𐤅𐤄 YAHUAH and He changes not.

This brings me back to the four questions I posed at the onset, in Chapter One.

1. "Why do I live in a country where people who supposedly profess Christianity are the majority and yet there is very little evidence of the culture that the Bible speaks of prevailing in the society?"
2. "How is it possible that Africa is now considered to be the most Christian evangelised continent (with 'crusades' where millions of people seemingly pledge allegiance to Christianity daily) and yet there is no manifestation of 'the blessing' that the Bible speaks of that should flow upon a people who are walking in agreement with God?"
3. "Why has God blessed us with such abundance in the riches and wealth of natural resources, which is more than any other people on earth and yet we continue to be the begging bowl of the world?" Why does everyone else in the world prosper from what we as Africa have been given and yet we are the poorest people on earth, failing to convert our God given wealth from the land into prosperity for all on the continent?
4. "Are we as dark-skinned people cursed by God, and does He

really love us in the same way as He loves Caucasians (white skinned people)? Because when I look at systemic poverty, depravity, the scourge of sickness and disease, it always seems to be the dark-skinned people in the world who are affected the most."

When the people ask, "Why does YAHUAH do all these things to us?"

"Nevertheless, in those days," says YAHUAH, "I will not make a complete end of you. And it will be when you say, **'Why does YAHUAH our ALUAH do all these things to us?'** *then you shall answer them, 'Just as you have forsaken Me and served foreign gods in your land, so you shall serve aliens in a land that is not yours.' (Jeremiah 5:18-19 NKJV)*

Who gave Jacob for plunder, and YASHARA'AL to the robbers? *Was it not YAHUAH, He against whom we have sinned? For they would not walk in His ways, nor were they obedient to His law. (Isaiah 42:24 NKJV)*

After reading the last 27 chapters, I hope that you have garnered some definitive answers to these questions.

Tribes of Africa, the most urgent thing for us to do is to:

- **Repent:** turn away from lawlessness and rebellion against YAHUAH's Laws and Commandments and turn to honour and commit to obey the Laws and Commandments of YAHUAH.
- **Be baptised** in the name of YAHUSHA.
- **Learn all the commandments and instructions** of YAHUAH and embrace and receive all that YAHUSHA came to fulfil as He was sent by the FATHER.

- **Commit to obey** everything that the FATHER, YAHUAH, has instructed as we endure in faith to the end.
- **Return and keep the everlasting covenant** (terms of agreement) with YAHUAH.
- **Forgive** 'the conqueror' and all who have oppressed us as we love our enemies and bless them according to what YAHUAH has instructed.
- **Wait for YAHUAH** to move as He has committed to do according to the terms of the agreement (the everlasting Covenant) He established with us (His people).

If we do, our deliverance will come very quickly.

If we don't, the curses of Deuteronomy 28 will remain upon us for another generation until a generation arises that will do what YAHUAH has instructed to be done. I pray we will be the generation that responds to the trumpet of YAHUAH over Africa. YAHUAH is waiting for our response.

> - *Now may the Alahym of peace who brought up our (Master) Adun* OWꓘAY *YAHUSHA from the dead, that great Shepherd of the sheep, through the blood of the everlasting covenant, make you complete in every good work to do His will, working in you what is well pleasing in His sight, through* OWꓘAY *YAHUSHA MASHYACH, to whom be glory forever and ever. Amen. (Hebrews 13:20-21 NKJV)*
> - *Now to Him who is able to keep you from stumbling, and to present you faultless Before the presence of His glory with exceeding joy, to* ꓱYꓱꓕ *YAHUAH our Savior, Who alone is wise, Be glory and majesty, Dominion and power, Both now and forever. Amen. (Jude 1:24-25 NKJV)*

🔥 **Tribes of Africa, this is your time to arise and shine in love, for YAHUAH is love.**

🔥 **Tribes of Africa,** because YAHUAH is love, He exhorts us to love. The task that lies ahead cannot be accomplished without YAHUAH, and therefore, it cannot be accomplished without love.

Beloved, let us love one another, for love is of YAHUAH; and everyone who loves is born of YAHUAH and knows YAHUAH. [8] He who does not love does not know YAHUAH, ***for YAHUAH is love****. (I John 4:7-8 NKJV*

And 𐤉𐤅𐤄𐤆 YAHUAH spoke to Moses, saying: "Speak to Aaron and his sons, saying, 'This is the way you shall bless the children of YASHARA'AL. Say to them: "𐤉𐤅𐤄𐤆 YAHUAH bless you and keep you; 𐤉𐤅𐤄𐤆 YAHUAH make His face shine upon you and be gracious to you; 𐤉𐤅𐤄𐤆 YAHUAH lift up His countenance upon you and give you peace." "So, they shall put My name 𐤉𐤅𐤄𐤆 on the children of YASHARA'AL, and I will bless them." (Numbers 6:22-27 NKJV)

www.ingramcontent.com/pod-product-compliance
Lightning Source LLC
Chambersburg PA
CBHW030235240426
43663CB00037B/465